John R. Graham
University of British Columbia

Micheal L. Shier
University of Toronto

Roger Delaney
Lakehead University

CANADIAN
SOCIAL POLICY

A New I

FIFTH E

D0732112

 Pearson

EDITORIAL DIRECTOR: Claudine O'Donnell
ACQUISITIONS EDITOR: Kimberley Veevers
MARKETING MANAGER: Michelle Bish
PROGRAM MANAGER: John Polanszky
PROJECT MANAGER: Susan Johnson
MANAGER OF CONTENT DEVELOPMENT: Suzanne Schaan
DEVELOPMENTAL EDITOR: Lila Campbell
PRODUCTION SERVICES: Cenveo® Publisher Services

PERMISSIONS PROJECT MANAGER: Shruti Jamadagni
PHOTO PERMISSIONS RESEARCH: Phyllis J. Padula
TEXT PERMISSIONS RESEARCH: Sohail Akhter
INTERIOR DESIGNER: Anthony Leung
COVER IMAGE: SergeyIT/Shutterstock
VICE-PRESIDENT, CROSS MEDIA AND PUBLISHING SERVICES: Gary Bennett

Pearson Canada Inc., 26 Prince Andrew Place, Don Mills, Ontario M3C 2T8.

ISBN 978-0-13-416498-4

1 16

Library and Archives Canada Cataloguing in Publication

Graham, John R. (John Russell), 1964–, author
    Canadian social policy : a new introduction / John R. Graham,
Micheal L. Shier, Roger Delaney. — Fifth edition.

Includes bibliographical references and index.
ISBN 978-0-13-416498-4 (paperback)

    1. Canada—Social policy—Textbooks. I. Shier, Micheal L.,
author II. Delaney, Roger, author III. Title.

HV108.G735 2016   361.6'10971   C2016-903376-7

For my parents, Elaine and Ed; and to Susan Graham and Tatyanna Morgan

Brief Table of Contents

Detailed Contents

Preface

There are numerous books on social policy in the United Kingdom and the United States. *Canadian Social Policy: A New Introduction* is a response to the need for a Canadian perspective. It is a single-volume introduction to a highly diversified field, one that provides a framework for analyzing social policies and understanding the social welfare context. Our thinking owes much to recent forces in social policy practice and scholarship, particularly as they relate to feminist, postmodern, social diversity, and civil society writings, widely construed, and to the concerns of social justice raised by this scholarship.

Social policy is a fundamental component of social work practice and should never be seen as an ethereal or aloof add-on to the curriculum. It is important in other ways, perhaps more so than at any other time either in our country's history or in the history of the social work profession. The now prolonged assault on universal programs, the ever more limited scope of policies, the ascendancy of neo-conservative ideology, the growth of globalization, the imperative of diversity, the increasing reliance on citizen participation and nonprofits, and new social financing initiatives to fund services—these issues, among other phenomena, will greatly influence social work practice and social policy analysis in future years. It is essential, therefore, that students introduced to Canadian social policy understand these dynamics and have at their disposal an analytical frame of reference that will make them sensitive to the nuances of policy work and to the diverse needs of society's most marginalized people.

Canadian Social Policy: A New Introduction examines major social policy considerations in Canada. It is intended for an audience of graduate, senior undergraduate, and senior community college students in social work, and for professionals who want to update their knowledge of current policy contexts. It is also intended to offer insights to students and practitioners of other disciplines, such as anthropology, business administration, Canadian studies, clinical psychology, development studies, divinity, economics, education, geography, history, nursing, occupational therapy, political science, public administration, rehabilitation studies, and sociology.

This textbook is now in its fifth edition and has a history extending back to the late 1990s. The first edition started out as a proposal submitted by Roger Delaney. Once a publishing contract was received and the work begun, Roger invited John Graham and Karen Swift to be co-authors. The textbook's initial focus then expanded to place greater emphasis on the historical origins of Canadian social policies and on the impact of social diversity on all aspects of policy formation and analysis. This fifth edition sees the addition of a fourth author, Micheal Shier, with the continuation of Roger Delaney, now – like a previous coauthor, Karen Swift - retired. The addition of Micheal Shier to the text has resulted in a significant rewrite of several chapters in the book, all of which is intended to provide an up-to-date account of contemporary realities in social welfare development and social policy practice in Canada. The writing process has been truly collaborative, with Graham and Shier contributing to the others' sentences, paragraphs, references, and ideas, and acting as a sounding board for all matters related to authorship. Micheal took the lead in Chapters 1, 7, 8, and 9, with updates to the whole of Chapter 6 and the latter part of Chapter 5; John in Chapters 2, 3, 4, and the first part of Chapter 5. We are, of course, grateful for the longstanding influence that Karen and Roger continue to have on the book and on our thinking.

The authors are grateful for so many things, including the kind encouragement of readers and our press; and for the resulting opportunity of these influences and broader social and intellectual forces that have shaped the progress of the book over a nearly 20-year period. The second edition, released in 2003, expanded beyond the first edition to include greater discussion of Canada's welfare-state institutions, social welfare theory, socio-economic class, social policy practice, globalization, the physical ecology, and social movements. The third edition considerably updated and provided further analysis of social policy practice and social policy development in a market-state era of less government and ascendant liberal capitalist ideology. The fourth edition expanded the scope of analysis used in the third edition. It was updated with new secondary literature on Canadian social policy and social policy writ large, and with new social policy theories that emphasized the increasing importance of globalization, the escalation of income inequality, neo-liberalism, and the changing patterns of international relations.

The fifth edition has seen a most significant amendment to our thinking, largely in the expansion of writing on third sector/civil society influences upon social policy, and the organizational and community contexts of social policy practice. The entire book has been updated with new secondary literature on Canadian social policy and social policy writ large (written for Canadian and non-Canadian audiences). It has likewise been updated with new social policy theories that emphasize the increasing importance of globalization, the escalation of income inequality, neo-liberalism, third-sector and participatory models of governance, the nonprofit and voluntary sector, the social economy, and social innovation. Chapter 1 has been rewritten to provide greater conceptual clarity to the terms *social policy* and *social welfare* used throughout the text, and to provide an overview of contemporary theories of social welfare, in particular the emergence of the nonprofit and voluntary sector in shaping social policy and social welfare development. Chapters 2–5 have been updated to draw attention to the role of the nonprofit and voluntary sector in both historic and contemporary periods of Canadian social welfare, and highlight existing realities affecting the focus of social policy efforts. Chapter 6 has been updated with new statistics and secondary literatures. Chapters 7 through 9 have been rewritten to focus primarily on the application of social policy in direct practice—whether through engagement in socially innovative efforts at an organizational level of practice or through efforts of assessing the impact of social policy on the lived experiences of service users. Together, this revised edition provides opportunity for discussion and development of a broader perspective of the Canadian social welfare system and the role of social work in shaping social policy.

Chapter 1 outlines some conceptual ideas that form a foundation for social policy practice, analysis, and application. Chapter 2 considers historical influences on Canadian social policies; Chapter 3, some of the country's major social welfare programs; and Chapter 4, significant policy-related ideological, social, and economic facets. Chapter 5 covers globalization, the environment, social inclusion, and citizen participation. Chapter 6 introduces the key notion of diversity to social policy formation; Chapter 7 presents how social policies are applied to social work practice and to social service delivery in general, with emphasis on the mezzo-level (i.e., organizational) of practice in influencing social policy and social welfare development. Chapter 8 provides an overview of social policy analysis and the theoretical context of social policy development, with clear examples of application throughout. The final chapter provides a summation of the book and highlights four intersecting areas of future social policy and social welfare development in Canada: social rights, socio-economic equality, Canada's social economy, and citizen participation.

Acknowledgments

Many people, too numerous to mention, have been extremely influential in the completion of this text throughout its five editions. Special thanks are extended to Tanjeem Azad, Helen Boukos, Andreas Breuer, Cathryn Bradshaw, Xiaobei Chen, Stefanie Kaiser, Patricia Bianchini, Susan Graham, Sarah Meagher, Nikoo Najand, Louise Querido, Andrea Newberry, David Sandoz, Josée Couture, Heath McLeod, and Elena Esina, to whom we extend sincere thanks. Likewise, thank you to Leslie Stirritt for his contribution to the HST case study. John Graham's father, Russell Graham, read the entire first-edition manuscript and provided, as always, exceptionally valuable editorial advice. Staff at Pearson Education Canada remain unendingly cooperative and encouraging.

In the early 1970s, the late Albert Rose of the Faculty of Social Work, University of Toronto, conceived a social policy chart for teaching purposes. In light of substantial policy changes since then, part of the conceptualization in Chapter 3 is loosely based on Dr. Rose's original chart and is dedicated to his memory. A major contributor to the development of Figure 4.2 is Raika Abdulahad, a Ph.D. student at the University of Calgary. Keith Brownlee, Issam Dawood, Paul DeBakker, M.D., Gayle Gilchrist-James, Jacqueline Ismael, Margaret McKee, and Bob Luker were among colleagues who provided much-appreciated support and advice. Funding from the University of Calgary Starter Grant for newly recruited faculty provided money for research assistanceship for the first edition; particular thanks are extended to the University of Calgary and the Alberta government for this critical support. Grateful acknowledgment is extended for grant support from SSHRC to the Caring Labour Network and the project on "Risk and risk assessment in child welfare," influencing a previous edition. A Senate Research Grant from Lakehead University was likewise instrumental in moving the first edition toward completion. Finally, thanks are extended to the Caledon Institute of Social Policy, the Canadian Council on Social Development, Human Resources and Skills Development Canada, the National Council of Welfare, Statistics Canada, and those publishing companies that allowed us to cite various research.

The editors and authors would like to thank the following reviewers for their helpful commentary on previous editions: Robert Marino of King's College, University of Western Ontario; Francis Turner of Wilfrid Laurier University; Brian Wharf of the University of Victoria; Sheila Neysmith of the University of Toronto; Douglas Durst of the University of Regina; Michael J. Holosko of the University of Windsor; Lynda E. Turner of Kwantlen University College; Thérèse Jennissen of Carleton University; Horatio Sam-Aggrey of Carleton University; Bruce Northey of the College of New Caledonia; Mojgan Rahbari of the University of Ontario Institute of Technology; and Kimberley Wilson of the University of Guelph.

Chapter 1
Introduction to Canadian Social Policy

Social policies have a range of implications for all members of a society. They define the mechanisms for the provision of social services and their emphasis. For instance, provincial government frameworks on the provision of service for developmentally delayed adults concentrate on efforts that support independence and inclusion in employment and social life for this group of people. Social policies establish the guidelines and regulations for which individuals, families, groups, and communities can meet their basic needs. This can become manifested in eligibility requirements to receive income support—such as age requirements for pension benefits or income eligibility for social assistance. Social policies also establish standards and thresholds of entitlement and expectation among citizens. For example, the *Canada Health Act* guarantees a standard of health care that is accessible in every provincial and territorial jurisdiction in the country. Similarly, social policies establish the way people should be treated by other individuals, groups, and even the government. For instance, the enactment of the *Canadian Charter of Rights and Freedoms* established a foundation for the rights and freedoms of all Canadians.

Social policies have implications for the day to day life of individuals and, in particular, the focus of efforts for social service delivery and intervention. As subsequent chapters will explain, every social work intervention—be it with an individual, a family, a group, an organization, or within the wider community—is somehow related to multiple social policies. For example, assisting a family to seek adequate housing invariably relates to social housing and income security policies; assisting an individual to re-enter the community after a prolonged period of incarceration may relate to employment support policies; or supporting an individual with serious mental health issues will relate to policies associated with health and mental health care. These considerations therefore influence the nature of Canadian social work practice and education. From a curriculum perspective, the Educational Policy Statements of *The Manual of Standards and Procedures for the Accreditation of Canadian Programs of Social Work Education* (1996), approved by the Canadian Association of Schools of Social Work (CASSW), state that the social work curriculum at the first university level (HBSW) shall ensure that social work students learn "critical analysis of social work and social welfare history, and social policy as socially constructed institutions and their implications for social work practice" (CASSW, 1996, 3). Developing a foundation of knowledge on social policy, and more generally social welfare, is required in the professional training of social workers. And this is certainly one of the purposes of this book. However, we also want students to gain an appreciation of how macro-level discussions of social policy and social welfare shape the overarching identity of the profession of social work and a social worker's professional sense of self.

Social policies are a source of constant debate and reframing. These considerations are typically rooted in cultural traditions, ideological beliefs and stereotypes, a range of international (such as the global capitalist economy) and domestic (such as the changing demographic base of the population) conditions, available resources and changing priorities, and research investigating the conditions of groups of people that are meant to benefit from a particular policy. Moreover, it is quite likely that there will be differing perspectives among your social work colleagues and even instructors about what is the best approach or method to address a negative social situation for a group in society. However, it is widely perceived that the ideal approach is to support greater citizen engagement and advocacy to promote advancements in government services and mandates for the provision of social services. Therefore, ongoing efforts to promote equity within Canadian society are fundamental to the discipline of social work. As a student of social policy and social work, it is necessary that you maintain a firm understanding of how this network of social policies impacts the lives of Canadians within our current context, and subsequently constrains and supports efforts to create social change through direct practice efforts at individual and organizational levels of practice.

We will discuss the meaning of social policy shortly. But first, it is imperative to take a step backwards and understand the context of how and why social policies emerge. This more general context is widely referred to as *social welfare*.

CONTEMPORARY SOCIAL WELFARE THEORY

Social welfare is an abstract concept. It refers to something that cannot be seen or held. However, there are several proxies that can help illuminate what social welfare might be. It can occur at multiple levels—among individuals and families; within communities; and via such formal instruments as non-governmental institutions, as well as through governmental policies. At its most basic level, social welfare can be seen in acts of kindness (or reciprocal exchanges) within families or between neighbours. This is a common form of exchange, and we do this regularly without even realizing it is happening. For example, you might shovel your neighbour's driveway after a snowfall, or you will help your brother and his family move into their new house. I am sure if you thought about it, you will find you have engaged in several acts of reciprocal exchange during the past week. In more formalized ways, micro-level forms of social welfare are carried out by individuals who donate money or volunteer their time. For example, you might donate winter jackets to a local homeless shelter, organize a fundraising function for your church, or provide a large endowment to the local library.

There are also more structured ways in which social welfare is manifested. For example, service delivery organizations (like shelters or daycares) and income security programs (like the Guaranteed Income Supplement and provincial social assistance programs), both of which demonstrate the existence of redistributive exchanges between governments and groups of individuals that meet some set of eligibility criteria. Those eligibility criteria can be defined by a maximum annual income, citizenship status, age, health status, and many other ways that the population is divided into groups.

Together, these examples highlight that social welfare can be economic in nature; where reciprocal and redistributive forms of exchange are simply just mechanisms that support the economic integration of individuals in society (Hettne, 1995). While it might be hard to relate to, given the current hegemonic position of capitalism in contemporary society, reciprocal and redistributive economic integration mechanisms came into existence long before the presence of the capitalist marketplace. However, as argued by Karl Polanyi (1944) in his book *The Great Transformation*, both reciprocity and redistribution had been undermined in some way by the emergence of market exchange (i.e., the commodification of land, capital, and labour). Summarizing Polanyi's thesis, Hettne notes:

> "As the market principle penetrated all spheres of human activity, thereby eroding social structures, redistribution had to be reinvented in order to provide people with the necessary social protection. Polanyi called this type of reaction on the part of society the second part of a 'double movement', the first part being the expansion and deepening of market exchange. This was the origin of the modern welfare state, as well as of other types of interventionist economy. Thus, modern industrial societies were typically distinguished by a market-redistribution mix. Depending on the nature of this mix, we called some 'capitalist' and others 'socialist'. In neither system does reciprocity play a role in economic transactions outside the family and kinship groups." (p. 5)

The welfare state refers to those governments that commit themselves to the development of social policies for the collective well-being of all. One of the welfare state's objectives has been to redistribute wealth; some refer to that activity as traditional social welfarism (Evers, 2009). In most social policy textbooks in Canada (including previous editions of this book), the notion of social welfare has focused predominantly on these redistributive efforts (which are discussed in detail in Chapter 3). The present edition continues to emphasize the extreme importance of governmental intervention, as well as of social workers' professional responsibilities to advocate for the sorts of policies at any level of government that would maximize social justice across a range of issues covered throughout this book. But this edition emphasizes a further range of analysis beyond this: the historical and contemporary role of local community-based efforts in shaping the social policy efforts and focus in our country. This revised approach, in our view, is with good reason. Writing more than two decades ago about the transition in contemporary social welfare, Hettne (1995, p. 5) points out:

> "After the present phase of neo-liberal hegemony and social marginalization, reciprocity—or what in other theoretical frameworks is called 'community' or 'civil society'—is bound to become more important again, simply as a mode of survival when the protective redistributive political structures break up."

Increasingly, non-profit organizations, volunteerism, and philanthropy have taken growing roles in Canada's social welfare tapestry, and their influences deserve sufficient attention. Canada's approach to social welfare has changed. Beginning with retrenchment efforts in the mid-1970s, the scope and activities of governmental policies were systematically—and in our view, most problematically—eroded. And at the same time, there has been a growing appreciation of the importance of social inclusion of minority groups on the basis of ethnicity, gender identity, geography, race, range of ability, sexual orientation, socioeconomic class, and other identifiers—each of which intersects with the others to help create a distinct sense of identity (Rice & Prince, 2013). Social, economic, and political advocacy for social justice generally, and the rights of minority groups in particular, have been a part of this phenomenon. Grassroots organizations and civil society or non-profit institutions, as well as private sector entities, have been actors in shaping and providing social welfare, sometimes in collaboration with governmental efforts.

Some go so far as to claim that contemporary social welfare in Canada is emerging as a shared effort between government, the for-profit sector, and the nonprofit and voluntary sector (or civil society). Each has a partnership role to play in the social welfare development of Canada's contemporary *welfare regime* (Evans & Wellstead, 2014; Jenson & Saint-Martin, 2003; Jetté & Vaillancourt, 2011; Phillips, 2012; Vaillancourt & Tremblay, 2002). Unlike a welfare state, a welfare regime refers to the intersecting roles and responsibilities played by dominant societal sectors that produce social welfare in a country. Canada's contemporary welfare regime, like most industrialized and developing nations, can be envisioned through a metaphor of a diamond. This has been referred to as a *welfare diamond* (Evers, Pilj, & Ungerson, 1994).

Picture a diamond in your mind. It has four points—one on the top, the bottom and one on each of the two remaining sides. Each of the four points is covered by one of the following groups:

1. Government
2. Nonprofit and Voluntary Sector (also referred to as civil society, community, or the "Third Sector")
3. Private Sector or Market
4. Individuals and Families

In this sense, Canada's contemporary system of social welfare has participation of all four sectors, each of which potentially influences the others. As well, there could be varying rates of participation of any of these four sectors in social welfare across a given time period. Some scholars see third or voluntary sector actors taking on increasing importance as governments in Canada have contracted their scopes of social welfare involvement (Rice & Prince, 2013).

A few further comments on the above-mentioned social welfare "diamond" of four points. We do not, in describing it, intend to leave the impression that we are advocates for this four-sided approach, or that we in some way or another celebrate the rise of any one of the four sides against the very real decline in governmental ranges of social welfare responsibility that Canada has experienced since the mid-1970s and as discussed in greater detail in Chapter 2. The first edition of this book, published in 2000, greatly lamented governments' decreasing responsibility in scope and coverage across virtually all domains of social welfare. As scholars and citizens of the country, we lament it, and in pursuing just social policies, we encourage activists to hold governments accountable for their social welfare responsibilities, generally. We are not stating that private or market-sector activities are desirable in the human services; there are aspects, indeed, in which private-sector involvement in prisons—to cite just one example—could have enormously worrisome impacts on social justice practices. But a growing conceptual and empirical literature has shown the importance of all four domains in social welfare in advanced industrialized societies such as, and extended beyond, Canada (Anheier, 2009; Holosko, Holosko, & Spencer, 2009; Powell, 2007; Prince, 2014; Ryser & Halseth, 2014; Salamon, 1993, 2002; Shier & Graham, 2013). And to this precise extent, it is important for the reader to have some knowledge of each domain.

There are many examples of each of these four sectors having a fundamental role in the development of Canada's social welfare regime in contemporary times. For example, the government maintains income security programs and establishes frameworks for the provision of specific types of social services. These are examples of redistributive social welfare efforts. The nonprofit and voluntary sector has grown considerably over the last two decades (which is discussed further in Chapter 2 and 6). With 170000 nonprofit organizations, Canada has the second largest per capita nonprofit sector in the world (Imagine Canada, 2015). Nonprofits are responsible for developing programs and initiatives to support improved outcomes among service user groups, for meeting the needs of vulnerable populations, addressing negative perceptions among service user populations, and advocating for service users (Shier & Handy, 2015). The efforts of these organizations are examples of reciprocal social welfare efforts. The private sector or market has also begun to take on an increasing role. We have seen a steady increase in the level of involvement in philanthropic activities from wealthy Canadian families and corporations through the establishment of foundations. During the period from 2002 to 2012, there was nearly a 100 percent increase, to $23.7 billion, in assets among all grant-making foundations that provide funding to social, cultural, economic, and environmental causes in Canada (Philanthropic Foundations Canada, 2014). Furthermore, nonprofits have been engaging in market-based activities—such as social enterprise. Together, these act as examples of market-based social welfare efforts.

And finally, families take on social welfare responsibilities: for example, in caring for sick or aged relatives or in sponsoring migrating family members from other countries. Likewise, there has been greater emphasis in the child welfare system to keep children with family members. Yet there are worrisome aspects to family responsibility as a last resort, particularly when governments do not provide sufficient ranges of social support or social care for individuals whose only other resort is the family—should there even be family members who are known to the individual and who are able to help. Governments have responded to social pressures to support individual and family care structures in certain instances, such as the inclusion of compassionate care benefits in the Employment Insurance program to support individuals to care for terminally ill family members. As you read this book, it is important to think critically about these emerging dynamics in Canadian social welfare. Similarly with other dominant eras of Canadian social welfare (discussed in greater detail in Chapter 2), our contemporary social welfare system is far from perfect. For instance, with cutbacks to government income security programs, reductions in resources to build affordable housing, and shifts in eligibility criteria, many social groups have become more vulnerable than they previously were. And, it is presently unclear, if not doubtful whether, other dominant sectors—such as the for-profit and the nonprofit and voluntary sectors—will be able to make up the difference.

This emerging model of contemporary social welfare fits into a wider theoretical discussion of contemporary governance. As social workers, it is important to understand these theoretical debates, as they provide the impetus for understanding your fundamental occupational role in providing support to service user groups. Distinct from government, governance is "the actions of government, but also the role of citizens, both individually and organized in various forms of association, and the way groups and communities within society organize to make and implement decisions of general concern" (Brinkerhoff & Brinkerhoff, 2002, p. 5). Governance refers to the range of actors that have an influence on the way decisions are made. Historically, we have seen the role of social work in governance through political advocacy efforts to change or create legislation to provide improved social welfare outcomes for vulnerable groups in society. However, due to changing relationship dynamics between government and civil society actors (such as direct social service nonprofits), the role of social workers has expanded to also include social welfare leader, social entrepreneur, and social innovator. The roles of social work in relation to social welfare development and social policy are discussed in greater detail in Chapter 7.

This model of governance has emerged in response to a number of theoretical advancements pertaining to the social and economic failure of governments and the market to address the persistent and emerging challenges experienced by citizens (Anheier, 2004; Brinkerhoff & Brinkerhoff, 2002; Hansmann, 1980; Muukonen, 2009; Nichols, 2006; Smith, 2011; Weisbrod, 1975). For instance, the role of nonprofits in traditional welfare state countries has continued to grow as a result of the enactment of neo-liberal economic policies (which has reduced government influence on the social and economic well-being of citizens), and a transition from a welfare state predicated on income redistribution, to one that emphasizes community-based support (Anheier, 2009; Smith, 2011). This book's authors do not celebrate this transition, but we recognize its occurrence, and we cite scholarship that refers to it.

While the manner in which social welfare is achieved has changed throughout Canada's history, the purpose of social welfare has not. *Social welfare* is the promotion of, and provision for, improved societal level well-being. These improvements might be efforts to address the experiences of a single group of service users, such as improvements to the average number of days of housing loss experienced by the episodically homeless. They may also be efforts that address the needs of a single individual, such as a crowd-sourcing campaign for a person diagnosed with a disabling illness. This latter example improves societal level well-being by promoting citizen engagement and participation. Moreover, these improvements can be made to the overall population in a country, such as the creation of a minimum wage. Taken together, the United Nations uses measures of societal level well-being to make statements about the social health of nations on the basis of data collected on a variety of quality-of-life indicators. These include:

- physical and mental health;
- education and occupational achievements;
- development in the arts and sciences;
- production and consumption;
- wealth and income (including child poverty);

- conditions of the natural environment;
- patterns of recreation;
- patterns of social participation;
- patterns of social morality; and
- social deviance and alienation.

Quality-of-life indicators allow social workers to compare their country's social welfare programs internationally (a focus of social policy analysis discussed in Chapter 8). These quality of life indicators can fit into four broad categories of well-being:

1. Socio-economic well-being. Includes efforts to mitigate increasing income inequality, to redistribute resources, to alleviate poverty, and to increase the social inclusion and upward social mobility of lower income populations.

2. Socio-political well-being. Includes efforts to create equal political representation, to improve human rights, and to create shared power relationships between members of society.

3. Socio-cultural well-being. Includes efforts that promote respect for diversity, the prevention of discrimination and racism, and efforts to promote social cohesion among diverse groups

4. Psycho-social wellbeing. Includes efforts that address the mental and emotional health needs of the population and improvements to individual level functioning.

Each of these aspects of societal well-being is discussed in further detail in Chapters 4, 5, and 6. For example, socio-economic well-being has traditionally been wrapped up in discussions about income inequality and poverty. Socio-political well-being is achieved in part by social movements and the work of advocacy groups to create political change. Socio-cultural well-being is addressed through efforts to prevent discrimination, such as public awareness campaigns or efforts to better address the needs of diverse cultural groups. You may be able to begin to see the relationship between social policy and social welfare. In Canada, there are many examples of policies at the various levels of government and within service delivery organizations that aim to address these areas of well-being. The extent to which these efforts achieve outcomes is the subject of social policy analysis (Chapter 8).

It is important to note too, while these areas of well-being might be presented here as distinct categories, you should recognize that they overlap. For example, in social work we might be concerned with the psycho-social well-being of a group of service users experiencing symptoms of psychological distress, and we might implement an intervention that focuses on aspects of individual level coping or resilience to address the mental and emotional health needs of this group of people. However, the source of the mental health condition might be a result of individual experiences with discrimination. For example, in the case of sexual minority or transgendered youth who have had negative experiences with bullying in the secondary school system, the discrimination they have experienced can be directly related to their mental health. As a result, to adequately address the psycho-social well-being needs of this group, you would have to also address elements affecting individuals related to their socio-cultural well-being.

Together, these four areas of well-being have been the focus of a substantial body of interdisciplinary social science research and literature, globally. While this book focuses on the social policy and social welfare context in Canada, with content related to training and education of social work students specifically, it is important to recognize that the study of social welfare and social policies is of interest across the social sciences and humanities disciplines. Understanding and determining the optimum conditions for human well-being has been the focus of scholarship and action for centuries. How it has become manifested in our historical context in Canada is described in detail in Chapter 2.

WHAT ARE SOCIAL POLICIES?

Social policy is a dominant mechanism (although not the only mechanism) through which societal well-being can be improved. Unlike social welfare, social policy is less abstract. For example, legislation exists that provides income security to individuals and families; frameworks define how services are provided to specific service user groups; and regulations are in place that constrain the way people are supported. In Canadian academics, there have been several definitions of social policy that provide meaning to what social policy is and what it is not. Many of these define social policy in relation to competing choices or opportunities to improve the social well-being of the population (or specific segments of the population based on some eligibility criteria).

Considering the structure and nature of contemporary social welfare described in the previous section, social policy must encompass a wide range of government, nonprofit, and private-sector decisions that seek to improve some aspect of societal well-being. Historically, it would be common to refer to social policies only as those which were legislated by a level of government (such as a municipal, provincial, or federal government). However, social policy is being created by nonprofits, and other formal voluntary sector forms of association, through the development of service delivery frameworks and models of practice. Across all domains, social policies are influenced by social activists and other committed individuals and groups who play an important role in advocating just and inclusive policies and societal responsibility for responding to needs. Social policy is being created in the private sector through policies that shape investments in Canada's social economy and in the creation of employee assistance programs. These are all discussed in further detail in Chapters 7 and 9. The following section describes the range of social policy definitions that exist, or have existed. Some are more abstract then others. However, more recent discussions begin to provide a description of social policy in relation to the multiple actors (for-profit, non-profit, and government) that influence or shape the social well-being of Canada's citizens.

Definitions of Social Policy

Richard Titmuss—Models of Social Policy Richard Titmuss (1974) argued that social policy is basically about "choices between conflicting political objectives and goals and how they are formulated" (p. 49). These choices are influenced by views of what constitutes a good society, based on that which "culturally distinguishes between the needs and aspirations of social man [sic] in contradiction to the needs and aspirations of economic man [sic]" (p. 49).

Titmuss argues that social policy can best be understood in terms of the following three models or functions:

1. *The Residual Welfare Model of Social Policy:* This model argues that the private market and the family are responsible for meeting an individual's needs. Only when these options break down should social welfare institutions intervene. As discussed in Chapter 3, proponents of neo-conservative and liberal ideologies favour this model.

2. *The Industrial Achievement-Performance Model of Social Policy:* This model argues that social needs should be met on the basis of merit, work performance, and productivity. Known as the *Handmaiden Model*, it is favoured by positivists (Federico, 1983) and other economic and psychological theorists who advocate incentives, effort, and reward.

3. *The Institutional Redistributive Model of Social Policy:* This model argues that social welfare should be a major, integrated institution in society, providing universal services outside the market, based on the principle of need.

Policy can emerge from these approaches only in areas of life where choices exist. Without choices, there is no policy; rather, there is a law, either natural or legislated. For example, since people cannot control the weather, societies have no policies concerning weather control. However, should science ever learn how to control weather, then societies would have to make choices about how to control the weather. Tension might arise between people who want warm sunshine and farmers who want rain (*preferential choices*). Further, controlling the weather might cause well-known ecological effects, such as sterilizing some insects or wildlife (*anticipated consequences*). Finally, controlling the weather might have detrimental effects that are not even known (*unanticipated consequences*). In this example, the choice to control weather would result in an anticipated consequence for insects and wildlife, some potential unanticipated consequences, and a decision about whether the farmer gets rain or the public gets sunshine.

Martin Rein—Value-Driven Policy The weather example shows that values and beliefs are important to decisions in social policy. The American scholar Martin Rein (1974) suggested that "social policy is, above all, concerned with choice among competing values" (p. 298). From Rein's perspective, society consists of people holding diverse values (world views), and these people compete with one another and one another's values in an effort to achieve maximum power. So ingrained are values in every aspect of social, economic, and public policies that many social policy theorists—such as Rein (1983), Gil (1998), and Wharf and McKenzie (2010)—warn that a major role of policy-makers is to learn how to control their own values and prejudices.

Rein suggests that values influence social policy in five major ways:

1. Values influence the definition of the purpose of the policy, especially policies dealing with "moral" decisions. An example would be a policy addressing abortion.

2. Values influence priorities by assigning greater "value" to some courses of action than to others. An economic example would be the decision to reduce the rate of inflation by increasing interest rates. This decision assigns higher value to the protection of business interests and lower value to the maintenance of employment levels.

3. Values demand change when they are formally and legally articulated. Once a position is articulated and the means to bring it about are put in place, people will assign

its importance (which is value-derived) simply because it exists (has form). As a result, society may have to change in order to allow that form to exist. For example, the North American Free Trade Agreement has caused significant changes to the Canadian economy, leading to the closure of some industries, the increase in some markets, the decrease in others, and so on.

4. Values focus on usefulness and feasibility. Policymakers can become preoccupied with usefulness and political feasibility rather than with societal need. An example is the federal government's Axworthy social policy reform document of 1994, which many people think has done little to change social policies, since few of the proposals were ever implemented.

5. Values influence the interpretation and evaluation of outcomes. One example is the claim that certain poverty lines do not really describe poverty. As discussed in Chapter 4, Canada has many different poverty lines, each with its own threshold below which a person's annual income is declared "in poverty"; ultimately, the threshold level is determined by some value of what is seen to be fair (adapted from Rein, 1974, p. 298).

Since social policy is often articulated as public policy, public policy documents reflect values that gain dominance. Public policies are legislated acts, regulations, and bylaws (including all associated policies in the ministerial, agency, and public arenas) at the federal, provincial, and municipal levels of government (Doern & Aucoin, 1971). As such, public policies are *social statements* reflecting the values and ideology of the political party or parties sponsoring them. Because public policies are encased in law, they have three distinct attributes:

1. Public policies are *legitimate*. Although an issue may be heavily debated—gun control, for example—once a policy is legislated, it is the law and is right or legitimate. Those who opposed the issue must now accept it as law, even if they are working to change it.

2. Public policies are *universal*—that is, they apply to everyone.

3. Because government *controls* (much, but not all) *coercion* in society, public policies can be enforced. Governments control enforcement agencies, such as the police, government investigators (e.g., income tax and welfare fraud investigators), and, in the case of the federal government, the army. These enforcement agencies ensure that the government can enforce the law.

Public policies provide boundaries and controls to regulate citizen behaviour, either directly (e.g., game and fishing policy, housing policy, taxation policy) or indirectly (e.g., foreign policy). As such, public policies play an instrumental part in all aspects of societal life.

David Gil—Social Justice David Gil (1970) suggested that social policies are concerned not only with the life-sustaining activities that ensure minimum basic needs, but also with those that stimulate our human potential. But the range of possibilities for these activities is as great as the range of world views that influence them. From a *polycentric perspective*, variation in views allows a more complete world view to emerge. A polycentric perspective, first articulated by McPherson and Rabb (1994), argues that radically different world views not only reveal something about culture and language, but about reality itself and the ways different people have come to know it. Therefore, each world view reveals something about the total picture, which can never be fully known. An accurate picture of reality is only possible by attempting to accommodate and reconcile as many world views as possible (Delaney, 1995, 13).

Moreover, Gil (1998) saw a need for social transformation. Systemic inequalities based on world views supporting "inequality, individualism, selfishness, domination, competition, and disregard for community (from local to global)" (p. 35) need to be replaced by world views "affirming equality, individuality, liberty, cooperation, community and global solidarity" (p. 35). Fundamental to this perspective is the view that human beings have physical, emotional, and spiritual dimensions and that human social functioning is impeded without the resources that meet these physical, emotional, and spiritual dimensions. The result would be humans whose potential is limited or constrained. Should one group of people attempt to ensure that their physical, emotional, and spiritual dimensions are satisfied at the expense of another group, then this action would be one of oppression.

Other approaches to social policy tend to reflect the comprehensive–incremental continuum.

Braybrooke and Lindblom—Incrementalism Braybrooke and Lindblom (1963) identified *incrementalism* as a key feature of social policy. They suggested that the world is just too complex and organic to allow for comprehensive policy and planning. For one thing, comprehensive policymakers themselves have to fill in variables about society and people about which they do not have valid and reliable information, thus allowing their own values to influence the design of social policies. Instead, these authors suggested that throughout history, people have simply corrected problems as they arose, and, over time, made substantive changes.

This incrementalist approach to social policy analysis is limited to considerations of alternative policies that are only incrementally different from the status quo. Because incrementalist theory has no major framework, the overall policy approach tends to be disjointed. Because different people are preparing policies for different problems independently, the term *disjointed incrementalism* is often applied to examples of this approach, which displays the following characteristics:

1. Analysis is limited to a few familiar alternatives.
2. Analysis of policy goals is intertwined with empirical aspects of the problem.
3. Analysis is concerned with remedying ills rather than with seeking positive goals.
4. Policies undergo a sequence of trials, errors, and revised trials.
5. Analysis of only some of the important consequences of those alternatives is considered.
6. Analytical work is fragmented among many partisan participants in policymaking (Hogwood & Gunn, 1984).

Some observers argue that incrementalism closely approximates *functionalism*. Functionalism suggests that every social system must meet four functional prerequisites in order to persist. These four prerequisites apply to all social systems:

1. *Adaptation:* The policy is adapted to the external environment;

2. *Goal attainment:* The policy coordinates collective activities to reach certain goals;

3. *Integration:* The policy integrates members of society to maintain solidarity and harmony; and

4. *Pattern maintenance (or latency):* The policy ensures that the activities required by members are performed with optimum compliance.

Functionalists view social welfare activities as a means of helping to create harmony among social institutions and individuals and hence to maintain communal solidarity. The essential framework of functionalism is to value stability and continuity above social change. In other words, society as it currently exists is considered to be good; therefore, only when something goes wrong should it be changed.

Critics of functionalism, such as Mishra (1981), suggest that the increase in poverty, privilege, and exploitation in the United States and the universal problems of racism and sexism have served to undermine the validity of the functionalist model. Mishra and other scholars argue that the dominant metaphor for social organization is conflict between groups in society, rather than social stability, as functionalist theory implies.

But more important than incrementalist and functionalist approaches is the question of who determines the priorities, the structure, and the method of implementation of social welfare programs.

Turner and Yelaja—Group Goals and Objectives Canadian scholar Francis Turner views social policy as statements of the social goals and objectives to which various groups—professional, governmental, or private—are committed. "They are the mission statements of various groups, and . . . vary widely in a country such as ours. . . . [A]s responsible citizens in a democratic country, we have a responsibility to understand this important component of our lives. This responsibility exists whether our goal is to become a social worker, a member of other related professions, a better-informed recipient of services, an advocate for social change, or a fully participating member of society" (1995, p. 10).

While reflecting the competition among values held by various groups for domination, Turner's view also states that social policy is culturally relevant—that is, Canadian social policies are not the same as those of other countries.

Another rather comprehensive definition of social policy comes from Canadian scholars Shankar Yelaja (1987), Ann Westhues (2003), and Rosalie Chappell (2006), whose definitions of social welfare reflect a social administration approach. For Yelaja, social policy is concerned with

> the public administration of welfare services, that is, the formulation, development and management of specific services of government at all levels, such as health, education, income maintenance, and welfare services. Social policy is formulated not only by government, but also by institutions such as voluntary organizations, business, labour, industry, professional groups, public interest groups, and churches. Furthermore, social policy is to be understood within the framework of societal ends and means, which are interdependent. (1987, p. 2)

Westhues (2003) furthers Yelaja's position by viewing social policies as courses of "action or inaction chosen by public authorities to address a given problem or interrelated set of problems" (p. 8). Public authorities include decision makers in government, social service organizations, and collective agreements. Moreover, Westhues (2006) cautions that not only can the social policy process be very slow and resource (time, energy, and financial) intensive, but also its outcomes may not be congruent with social justice principles, let alone gain political approval. Chappell (2006) views social policies as sets of guidelines that provide structure and direction to Canada's social welfare programs. According to this perspective, social policy reflects social reality within a cultural context.

Gilbert and Specht; Marshall, Rice, and Prince; Mishra, Finkel, and Lightman—Social Action
American scholars Gilbert and Specht (1974) tried to teach social workers how policies affect the populations they work with. They define the institution of social welfare as "that patterning of relationships which develops in society to carry out mutual support functions" (p. 5). A British social policy theorist with a similar social administration orientation is T.H. Marshall (1965), who notes that *social policy* is not a technical term with an exact meaning; instead, it refers to

> the policy of governments with regard to action having a direct impact on the welfare of the citizens by providing them with service or income. The central core consists, therefore, of social insurance, public (or national) assistance, the health and welfare services, [and] housing policy. (p. 7)

Marshall argues that the best way to ensure the welfare of citizens is to cultivate a sense of the right (or entitlement) to the following three things:

1. Civil rights, which guarantee individual liberty and equality before the law;
2. Political rights, which ensure the right to vote and seek political office; and
3. Social rights, which ensure equal access and opportunities to all social institutions.

To ensure these rights, social policy advocates rely on the legal system to monitor and correct any abuses of these rights. However, Drover (2000) warns that globalization requires a redefinition of Marshall's notion of social citizenship, because nations now have restricted ability to respond to the rights of their citizens.

Rice and Prince (2000) envision a cooperative union between the forces driving economic policies and social policies, where social policy is treated as a partner of economic policy rather than as a drain of national and international economies.

Mishra (1981) defines social policy as referring "to the aims and objectives of social action concerning needs as well as to the structural patterns or arrangements through which needs are met" (p. x). For Mishra, social policy is concerned with deliberately and rationally matching ends and means through social institutions designed for that purpose.

Finkel (2006) views social policy as "the set of non-market decisions, public or private, that determine the distribution of wealth to individuals and families and the degree of availability of human services to all members of society" (p. 3). Clearly, Finkel's view calls for an analysis of those who hold power and how their decisions influence those without power.

Lightman (2003) views Canadian social policy as a spectrum. At one end is a set of values, programs, and practices designed to (theoretically) bring Canadians together as a community by relating to shared experiences and mutual interdependence. At the other end of the spectrum, social policies are sets of programs designed for Canada's poor and vulnerable populations. Lightman views social policies as the choices made with respect to a group, community, or collective, and these choices have real consequences and costs for people and society.

In a similar argument, Lafitte (1962) claimed that social policy is "an attempt to steer the life of society along lines it would not follow if left to itself" (p. 9).

Freeman and Sherwood (1970) view social policy as consisting of "conclusions reached by persons concerned with the betterment of community conditions and social life, and with the amelioration of deviance and social disorganization" (p. 13).

Together, these definitions of social policy provide a robust understanding of what social policy is. Many of these definitions combine notions of social welfare with social policy. Here, we have differentiated them. Where social welfare is the overarching vision for the social well-being of the citizens of a country, and social policy is a mechanism through which this vision can be achieved. Below (Figure 1.1) is an example of how social policy might impact the social well-being of an individual service user. In this example, we have used the case of a single person experiencing housing loss and accessing shelter services. For specificity purposes, this individual resides in Toronto, Ontario. The various policies impacting this service user would be different depending on the local context in which they were accessing services.

In this model it is apparent that there are several levels of social policy that have an impact on this person's experiences. Likewise, there are a wide range of policies that have an impact on efforts to improve the well-being of individuals who are experiencing housing loss. We have also differentiated between direct and indirect policies. Some social

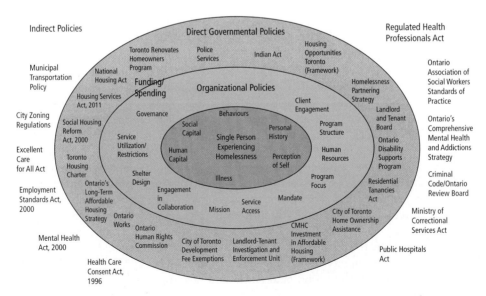

Figure 1.1 Levels of Policy Impact on Service User Social Welfare: A Case Example of Single Person Experiencing Homelessness

policies indirectly impact the social well-being of this individual, or might only impact certain people with certain characteristics. For example, the *Mental Health Act (2000)* in Ontario would have implications for this individual if he or she was experiencing serious mental health issues.

At the centre of the model is the single person experiencing housing loss, who is surrounded by a number of individual characteristics and qualities that have a direct influence on their current situation. We have identified six: personal history (e.g., experiences with trauma); perception of self (e.g., low self-esteem); illness (e.g., chronic disease or mental health issues); human capital (e.g., labour market integration); social capital (e.g., loss of a spouse); and behaviours (e.g., addictions). As social workers, these might be the things that we would address in a one-on-one intervention with this service user. However, the extent that we are able to address these issues is directly influenced by the surrounding policy environment. This is inclusive of organizational level policies and both direct and indirect government policies, along with the regulations controlling funding and spending.

From the model there are several obvious examples of social policies that can impact the well-being of people experiencing housing loss. For instance, one example is the income security programs of Ontario Works or the Ontario Disability Supports Program (ODSP). There are several other government level policies and frameworks – such as the Ontario Government's *Social Housing Reform Act* or the Toronto Housing Charter – that are related directly to the housing needs of individuals and that set standards of access and eligibility. At the organizational level, there are several policies that can have an impact on the social well-being of this service user population. For instance, policies related to service access can have a negative effect on clients working in paid employment situations during the hours in which services can be accessed. Or, for example, organizational policies on engaging in collaborations that might better address the intersecting needs (such as employment support or addictions treatment) of their service user population.

The model also shows a comprehensive social policy framework that can have an impact on groups of service users. It is important for social workers to be able to recognize the specific policies that are having a negative impact on achieving social outcomes. By identifying the policy areas that are having a negative impact, efforts can be made to change those policies, whether that is through political advocacy efforts directed towards government level policies, or through socially innovative efforts at the organizational level. This relationship between social policy and social work practice is discussed briefly in the following section, but elaborated further in Chapter 7.

SOCIAL WORK AND SOCIAL POLICY

The study of social policy can increase our sensitivity to the people we serve. Because we know the circumstances under which many of our clients live, we can become proponents for policies that will enhance their well-being and social welfare leaders that aim to change policies that negatively affect them.

The study of social policy also allows you to learn how social inequalities, disempowerment, marginalization, and oppression can seep into political agendas and affect those least able to fight against them. Bishop (1994) sees these elements as part of a "power-over" agenda. A power-over agenda seeks to create a world of systems designed to keep people unequal. It uses four types of power over people. The first type, *political power*, concentrates power in the hands of fewer and fewer people because those making decisions build up the power of their own group. The second type, *economic power*, occurs when one group has more access to economic resources than others have. The third type, *physical force*, uses the army and the police to back up economic and political power. The fourth type, *ideological power*, allows one group to influence thought and shape popular ideas of what is possible, desirable, and valuable (pp. 36–37). Power can be carried out by government political parties, social activists, for-profit actors, nonprofit organizations, committed individuals, and groups of professionals like social workers.

Understanding how groups gain social, economic, and political power through social policy is important for social workers. Wharf (1990) suggests that social work that is insufficiently oriented to social change fails in four ways. First, it makes the assumption that once a problem is identified, change will occur and the problem will be solved. This situation is rarely the case in real practice. Second, it ignores power and its distribution in Canada. Third, because society does not assign social workers responsibility for bringing about change, some agencies may become the problem and not the solution. Fourth, the issue of auspices is not addressed: because social workers are employed in agencies that receive their mandates from those holding political power, each agency's political and social agendas limit the social workers' efforts to change the system (Wharf, 1990, pp. 23–25).

By understanding the policymaking process, social workers can learn to advocate for social changes that benefit those in society least able to advocate for themselves. Many current beliefs about leadership, privilege, hierarchy, power, and wealth have developed over long periods of history and have created patterned inequalities of status and rights (Gil, 1970, 1992). By exposing these historical inequalities and confronting the metaphors that support social inequality, social workers can participate in the policy debate. In fact, both the Canadian and American Social Work Codes of Ethics make the study of social justice a practice requirement.

It is important for social workers to understand and be sensitive to the different life experiences of Canadians. Moreover, understanding social policies' impact on issues of human diversity is critical for social workers who live in a pluralist society (and is the focus of Chapter 6). Social workers are asked to play a variety of practice roles—leader, manager, teacher, enabler, facilitator, mediator, organizer, advocate, resource broker, and administrator, among others. Social policy gives an added contextual dimension to these roles because it places the client situation within the social arena—an arena that too often has little or no regard for the client or the client's situation.

Finally, social policy provides a wealth of information on such issues as how our current social structures came to be; who is benefiting from these structures; who has the real power to make social changes; what the most effective approaches to citizen participation are; who is being oppressed, isolated, or ignored in society; and what array of ideological powers exists to maintain the current social agenda regarding the distribution of wealth, powers, and privilege.

CONCLUSION

Theories about social welfare, and the manifestation of that social welfare through social policies, help social workers to better understand people. It does this by describing both the social context in which people live and the forces that created this context. It allows us to appreciate that the world in which we live did not just happen. Rather, it was created on the basis of decisions people made about what this society would look like and what values and beliefs would drive its development. In contemporary times, social welfare has shifted from what has become known as traditional social welfare (or the modern welfare state). While always having an influence on Canada's welfare regime, the nonprofit and for-profit sectors are taking on an increasing role in addressing the social well-being needs of the population. The result is an evolution towards a more partnership-based form of social welfare. The extent to which this model has been, and possibly can be, successful in improving the societal well-being of Canadians is still unknown. As social welfare continues to transition, the extent of influence of these nongovernmental actors (both for-profit and nonprofit) will become clearer. The next chapter discusses how understanding the historic origins of social policies means appreciating how social policies evolved, what the major factors in this evolution were, and what might be a reasonable basis for thinking about their present and future development.

Chapter 2
Historical Influences

Social policies are in a constant state of change, but their roots may be traced back to the earliest stages of human evolution. Familiarity with history therefore provides you with tools for thinking about how social policies could be constructed for today and tomorrow. Rather than being constrained by the present-day circumstances of time or place, your imagination can be free to consider possibilities. You can readily challenge prevailing assumptions, rather than benignly accepting them. You can also use creative approaches, rather than overlooking them or assuming that they are untenable.

This chapter examines several areas of primarily English Canadian social welfare history; further elaboration of the experiences of Aboriginal people and of French-speaking Canada appear later in the book. Although this chapter also presents data in chronological order, the following 12 themes are evident throughout:

1. Policies are in a constant state of evolution—they have taken on different forms during different periods of history.

2. Social policies are "cultural constructs"—they are profoundly influenced by myriad cultures, values, and ideologies in a society.

3. Social policies sometimes represent the highest aspects of being human. At their very best, they reflect a basic concern for other people, a recognition of our interdependence, and an impulse to act upon this recognition.

4. Social policies have a contradictory nature. Among recipients, some aspects have been beneficial, while others, as will be seen, have not. Motivations among proponents of social policies, whether conscious or not, have been just as variable. As a result, social policies may reflect motivations and/or have consequences that are troubling: the drive to contain social unrest, to maintain social control, or to reproduce social inequalities with respect to gender, ethnicity, race, range of mental or physical ability, sexual orientation, or other areas of diversity.

5. Social policies have different impacts on different groups in society. Recipients of a particular policy, for instance, may have an experience disparate from that of the person who is paid to carry out the policy.

6. Various concepts in the history of policy development remain with us to the present day, such as the distinction between deserving and undeserving poor, or the local responsibility for social welfare.

7. In contemporary times, social policies have mirrored the growing social and economic complexities of modern life: the increasing mobility of people, the spread of urbanization, the deep impact of industrial capitalist development, and the gradual appreciation of human diversity. Corresponding also with industrial capitalist development has been the increasingly atomized and stratified nature of society, and the rise of bureaucratic structures, of which social work has been an important part.

8. The arrangements of capitalism during the past several decades have eroded the range of social policies and their comprehensiveness. Across the globe, more flexible forms of capital accumulation, labour market organization, and consumption patterns have prevailed. These, in turn, are seen by many observers to have compromised the range of social policy choices available to political leaders. International industrial capitalism and its multinational corporations have been increasingly freed from earlier notions of national responsibility. Environmental policy, workplace conditions, job security, wages, and social policies may well be determined less by national policy and more by the market-driven, lowest-bidder ethos of an increasingly international and competitive industrializing world.

9. The state has increasingly relinquished social service delivery to the private realm, a process often called the *privatization of social services*. This development reflects current national and international trends that emphasize the private marketplace over the direct role of government.

10. More and more, the economy requires a flexible workforce made up of part-time jobs, underemployment, and limited employment in the form of contract jobs of short duration. Social workers, like their clients, will be expected to respond to this new workplace environment, where, among other things, lifelong learning and vocational flexibility prevail.

11. Reflecting the inherently political nature of social policies, the Constitution of Canada is significant in determining which level of government has a particular administrative or financing authority. At the beginning of the twentieth century, local or municipal governments funded and administered most social services. But over the course of the century social welfare responsibilities gradually emerged among provincial and, in particular, federal jurisdictions.

12. The conceptualization of social welfare has transformed from a "residual" to an "institutional" perspective (Wilensky & Lebeaux, 1958) and then finally to a "market-state" perspective (Bobbitt, 2002).

It is this final theme that provides a framework for exploring the preceding ones, as these terms—*residual, institutional,* and *market state*—describe approaches that represent the three major periods in which Canadian social welfare history unfolded from European contact to the present time.

Further comments on this final theme are now warranted. The interpretation of history changes over time. Previous editions of this book emphasized a particular teleology, or pattern of historical change. In the residual stage of social welfare, prior to the twentieth century, community, voluntary, neighbour, and family structures were vitally important. These gave way, the theory had it, to greater levels of government involvement—gradually at first over the latter half of the nineteenth century (but with some important precedents in the centuries before that). The twentieth century, particularly from the mid-1940s to the mid-1970s, was the great period of state involvement. With its decline, after the mid-1970s, the state, and therefore the collective caring actions of our society, withdrew its formerly robust scope of activities.

While that pattern of history is on one level true, on another level it is insufficient. For it wrongly infers a transformation: all sorts of civil society actors—voluntary, charitable organizations, and other nongovernmental organizations and structures—giving way to greater government involvement. In fact, the civil society, or non-governmental components, never particularly disappeared. Fundraising is a vitally important component to social policies. In the nineteenth century, various charities held public events, encouraged private subscriptions, and pursued other incentivized ways of raising money for the work that was carried out. In the late nineteenth century, as with greater consolidation in the early twentieth century, these ad hoc approaches were unified, as charities banded together under united appeals through community chests, red feather campaigns, and later the United Way. Indeed as Graham (1992) and later Tillotson (2008) infer, the fundraising activities for much of the nongovernmental sector of social welfare, circa 1900 to 1950, precipitated several important developments.

The first was the rise of professional, scientific approaches to social work intervention prior to the 1930s (Graham, 1992). Those charities that pursued these ideals were incentivized with United Way money; those that did not, were at risk of not receiving funds. The second facet was ideological. As Tillotson notes, "the ideological work of [charitable] fundraisers during the interwar years had helped to make the progressive income tax model [that governments adopted] politically acceptable" (2008, p. 4). And the fundraisers "generated a particular kind of awareness of welfare needs" that ultimately made a universal, government administered and funded welfare state possible (2008, p. 5). A further component bears emphasis: socio-economic class. Emerging social planning councils at the municipal level, which conducted important social research to which charities responded, were extremely business friendly and business oriented—and indeed the people on the boards of these organizations frequently represented mainstream, business opinion (Wills, 1995). Charities themselves increasingly came to be dominated by these same business principles of fiscal prudence, scientific management—ultimately giving way, in the post-institutional period, to corporate philanthropy, in which companies' public relations are inextricably linked to the very public nature of the social causes they support (Liverant, 2009).

Having stated this, the remainder of this chapter will focus, albeit not exclusively, on the rise, and decrease, of government involvement in Canadian social welfare. We begin first with the earliest period. And in doing so, we refer to traditions that precede the origins of our country.

THE RESIDUAL APPROACH

In Canada, the residual concept of social welfare predominated until the twentieth century. During times of sickness, unemployment, or interrupted or insufficient income, the family and the economic marketplace were considered the "normal" channels of help. For example, if sickness made it impossible for a family member to go to work, alternative sources of income—credit, a loan, or a different family member taking on additional employment—were sought. Alternatively, the family could turn to relatives for temporary assistance. Only after these sources were exhausted would other parties intervene, including members of the immediate community, religious institutions, or, later, charities (Emery & Emery, 1999). This residual model of social welfare contrasts with the institutional approach. The institutional model emphasizes the role of government in responding to social needs, and is elaborated later in this chapter.

Classical Civilizations

The impulse to come to another's assistance is a fundamental part of what it is to be human. Indeed, anthropologists have observed that sharing is an essential characteristic of some of the earliest forms of human organization (Berman, 2000). Among early hunting-gathering societies, when food became scarce and hunger acute, generosity and sharing prevailed over hoarding. This tendency was more than a simple matter of etiquette, because the maintenance of social bonds was essential to determining a group's fertility and rate of survival (Dolgoff & Feldstein, 1984, pp. 16, 26). Given the threat of raids from other tribes or species, and the hazards of eking out an existence amid a harsh physical climate, an individual could not survive without belonging to the collective. In the real life and death context, people were aware of the symbiotic benefits of doing good unto their neighbours.

The present discussion of hunting–gathering societies indicates how the responses we make to those in our identified group differ from those we make to people who are considered outsiders. Traditional societies often differentiate their treatment of members inside their own group from those outside it. In the same manner, contemporary social policies provide benefits for members of Canadian society, yet not to members of other societies. Social welfare assistance is an example of a program that applies only to Canadians living in Canada. Canadian social policies have other subtle ways of distinguishing between insiders and outsiders. As will be seen, particularly in Chapter 6, various areas of diversity—such as race, ethnicity, gender, range of ability, sexual orientation, and others—influence social policies.

Many ancient cultures throughout the world expressed social responsibilities in religious terms. As early as 2000 BCE, Sumerian society placed a divine value on the protection of widows, orphans, and the poor. In fourth-century–BCE China, Confucian ideals of humane and righteous leadership compelled rulers to target public funds toward the care of the aged, the poor, orphans, or those affected by natural disasters, as well as toward the creation of public lands for the gathering of wood and herbs (Dolgoff & Feldstein, 1984, pp. 28–30). Aboriginal societies in present-day North America continue to use such symbols as the medicine wheel to express the sacred bond between humanity and the physical and spiritual planes of existence (Bopp, Bopp, Brown, & Lane, 1985; Feehan & Hannis, 1993). In the Judeo-Christian tradition, several Old Testament injunctions compel part of an annual harvest to be donated to the poor (Leviticus 19: 9–10) and to the widowed and strangers (Deuteronomy 24: 19–22). The New Testament instructs Christians to care for the disadvantaged (Matthew 25: 31–46) and to forsake the love of material possessions (Luke 6: 20–38). Muslims also have a strong tradition of concern for the poor. In fact, one of the Five Pillars of Islam, alms-giving, is described not as a tax or a charity, but as a religious duty (Sura 9: 60).

Such widespread religious ideals were manifest in tangible forms. Ancient Grecian temples served as medical centres and care stations for the poor. In Roman society, a system of public charity was so advanced that, during the second century AD, as much as half of Rome's population relied on some form of public assistance. In the Byzantine East, a complex system of maternity hospitals, medical facilities, and food rationing was provided from the revenues of the Orthodox Christian patriarchs (Dolgoff & Feldstein, 1984, pp. 31–40). In our own time, social legislation has been the bedrock of the welfare state and is far from a historical aberration or a peculiarity of our own time. Indeed, one of the earliest explicit social policies, the 1349 Statute of Labourers, occurred in medieval England. In the aftermath of the Black Plague, this statute froze workers' wages to pre-Plague levels and limited the mobility of labour outside of one's home parish (de Schweinitz, 1943, pp. 1–2).

The Medieval and Elizabethan European Heritage

Many of the direct roots of Canadian social policy are derived from a European heritage. Three non-governmental forms of European institutionalized charity gradually developed and were particularly significant. The first of these were the medieval guilds, representing various merchant classes and artisans. Acting as mutual aid societies and charitable organizations for their members, the guilds built and maintained hospitals, distributed food to the needy, provided lodgings for the travelling poor, and gave other forms of incidental help. The second form of charity, the private foundations, were established by affluent benefactors and devoted to the construction and maintenance of hospitals, almshouses, and other such institutions. By the early sixteenth century, there were 460 such foundations in England alone. The third source of charity was the Church, providing assistance through various monastic orders among the thousands of local parishes across the continent. In Western Europe, among other parts of Christendom, tithing to the Church was compulsory, and one-third of all collections went to the poor (Dolgoff & Feldstein, 1984, pp. 39–44). The tithe may be seen as an early precursor to the contemporary income tax system, which helps to finance the modern welfare state.

This elaborate system of medieval charity was turned upside down by the sixteenth-century Protestant Reformation. In England, as in other parts of Europe, Protestant sects emerged, and Roman Catholic monasteries were dissolved. A new system of English social welfare was established and enshrined in the Elizabethan Poor Laws of 1601. Earlier voluntary modes of charity now fell to the local (Parish) governments on a national scale, with accompanying punishments for non-compliance. Each parish was required to appoint an overseer of the poor, who, in consultation with church wardens, dispensed relief to the poor. The significance to the present day is twofold. First, the overseer was an obvious precursor to the modern-day social worker. The role of overseer also had an obvious social control function. Indeed, the fact of Elizabethan overseers provides an excellent reminder that not all of social work's roots have been altruistic. Secondly, these changes meant that for the first time in history, social welfare responsibility became, in practice and in legislation, a formalized, local arrangement. Voluntary forms of charity, including orphanages, hospitals, and almshouses for the old, remained alongside other local arrangements (Leiby, 1978, pp. 38–41). The establishment of a comprehensive state role, a concept that emerged in its complete form in the twentieth century, saw its beginnings, therefore, in the sixteenth century. Up to the present time, this strong presence of local jurisdictions in social service delivery has persisted.

Other aspects of the Elizabethan Poor Laws remain with us today. The principle of local residency was legislated, requiring that an individual receiving alms (or, in contemporary usage, welfare) within a particular parish had to be a resident of that parish. In our own time, local governments as well as provinces have legislated that recipients must live within a particular province or municipality for a certain length of time before being entitled to receive social assistance (Stedman Jones, 2004).

A final feature of Elizabethan welfare was the differentiation made between deserving and undeserving poor, an aspect that had been part of previous forms of charity but which was now outlined in legislation. While present-day terminology and practices may be different, this compulsion to distinguish between those who are worthy and those who are not has endured. In Elizabethan times, the classification was threefold: the impotent poor—that is, those who could not work (pregnant women, extremely sick men or women, those over the age of 60)—were allowed to live in what became known as poorhouses; any able-bodied people who could not seek employment or were temporarily unemployed were consigned to workhouses; and "unregenerate idlers" were placed in houses of correction (Bruce, 1961, p. 26; Dolgoff & Feldstein, 1984, p. 46). Today, income security programs differentiate among classes of eligibility. Able-bodied individuals who temporarily cannot work because of work-related illness or injury may apply for Workers' Compensation. Able-bodied individuals who are capable of working but are between jobs may be eligible to receive Employment Insurance (EI), or if EI entitlements run out, provincially/locally administered social assistance programs under various names, including Ontario Works, may be granted. Those who cannot work because of physical or psychiatric incapacity may receive Workers' Compensation long-term disability, Canada Pension Plan long-term disability, or provincially administered income security programs. Those who cannot work because of the responsibilities of single parenthood may receive benefits from provincially administered income security programs (Graham, 2008).

The Elizabethan Poor Laws also distinguished between men and women. For example, women were classed in the impotent poor category. In our own time, as will be seen, social policies have continued to be constructed differentially for men and women.

In the 1600s, as in previous centuries, the plight of the poor was deplorable. Hospitals, poorhouses, workhouses, and other such institutions were invariably overcrowded, lacked public health standards familiar to the contemporary reader, and were the loci of such deadly diseases as cholera, tuberculosis, and typhoid (Desert, 1976; Gonthier, 1978). Marginalized members of society—vagrants and those who were sick or disabled, among others—were forced into poorhouses that were as wretched as—and were sometimes one and the same as—local jails. Levels of alms were deliberately minimal. To seek assistance beyond the residual bounds of one's immediate family or the economic marketplace could be the source of frequent and intense public derision. Idle men refusing work were whipped, sent to prison, or both. Others were permanently maimed in an effort to rid them of their idleness. For these and other reasons, people were known to turn to prostitution, theft, or other crimes to avoid the disgrace and hardships of receiving alms (de Schweinitz, 1943, pp. 20–22; Dolgoff & Feldstein, 1984, p. 49).

Before leaving the Elizabethan period in England, one final point should be emphasized: the Reformation Protestant theology of Calvin, Luther, and other thinkers influenced virtually all aspects of society, social welfare included. This thinking, moreover, continues to resonate in those twenty-first century countries, such as Canada, where the historical influence of a Protestant theology remains strong. In Calvinist terms, work was a divine vocation and therefore a religious activity; idleness and worldly temptations interfered with the glory of God. Personal responsibility, discipline, and intense individualism were all revered (Weber, 1930/1958). As for social welfare, a legacy of punitive and repressive approaches found new rationalization. In this Protestant world view, pauperism was thought to result from the character defects of an individual or the flaws of a family. For moral and religious reasons, indiscriminate alms-giving was condemned, and the poor were visited by Poor Law overseers or by other community representatives, such as clergy, to root out the drunk, the idle, and other undesirables (Dolgoff & Feldstein, 1984, pp. 46–47).

The 19th-Century European Heritage

For several centuries, the principles established during the Elizabethan era predominated, but in the early nineteenth century, changes came about because of two issues of public concern: the rising costs of British poor relief and the rising numbers of relief recipients. A three-year Royal Commission was struck, resulting in the Poor Law Reforms of 1834. These reforms established several new principles. The first was the "less eligibility" principle, which stated that the basic provisions one received while on relief were to be *less* than the lowest-paying available job. The rationale was to dissuade people from receiving relief and to encourage self-reliance via the economic marketplace. This "less eligibility" principle continues to dominate social welfare thinking in our own time. Throughout the 1990s, economists and other analysts referred to and supported the development of policies to encourage swift return to work rather than reliance on income security programs (Burns, Batavia, & DeJong, 1994; Lewin & Hasenfeld, 1995; Schansberg, 1996; Shah & Smith, 1995; Smith, 1993). Beginning in the mid-1990s, social assistance programs in Canada, as in the United States, increasingly tied benefit entitlement to job skill development, job search, and, in some jurisdictions, welfare for work. In the provinces of Alberta and Ontario, for example, social assistance programs have been renamed "Alberta Works" and "Ontario Works," respectively, to reflect this greater emphasis on job retention. Furthermore, over the last decade, some politicians and policy analysts have called for further reductions in social welfare entitlements, described in the next chapter.

The second 1834 principle was delineation between outdoor and indoor relief, the forerunner of the current Canadian system of provincially/municipally administered social assistance. Outdoor relief provided material assistance to a select category of recipients who were allowed to live at home: the sick, the aged, the orphaned, or the widowed. Indoor relief, in contrast, was limited to able-bodied men who were deemed employable. Indoor relief could not be received at home. Recipients were obliged to live in workhouses and to undertake hard, manual labour—for example, breaking piles of large stones—in compensation for work. The intention was to punish and to limit the appeal of relief so as to encourage the able-bodied to fend for themselves. This distinction in legislation between outdoor and indoor relief spelled out different categories of the poor and was reminiscent of comparable Elizabethan notions. Also present were various assumptions anchored to the Protestant Reformation: that those poor who had been responsible for their own poverty were morally at fault, but, at the same time, were capable of "uplift"—to use a term from the Victorian era—through discipline, thrift, hard work, and righteous living.

Three prominent thinkers of the nineteenth century also reinforced Poor Law thinking. The first was the Reverend Thomas Malthus, who in the late eighteenth century wrote that the human population was increasing at a greater rate than the food supply. This idea, to many, was a clarion call to limit the appeal of relief: if the dependent classes were "coddled," or so the thinking went, they would multiply too quickly and start to exert undue pressure on society's limited material wealth. The second individual was the economist Adam Smith, who saw a natural harmony between the self-seeking of an individual and the well-being of society. His view was typical of the strongly individualist outlook of the eighteenth and nineteenth centuries, which encouraged minimal standards of relief. The third thinker was philosopher Jeremy Bentham, who introduced the utilitarian notion that society should promote the greatest possible good for the greatest possible numbers (Bruce, 1961, pp. 46–47, 78): a form of collectivism, but one that tended to promote the views of the majority and to minimize the benefits for those who were poor or in other ways disempowered.

A final historical experience bears emphasis. The Speenhamland experiment of 1795 was a remarkable example of a social policy that challenged prevailing assumptions. Because of a short harvest and a severe winter, local justices of the peace of the Speenhamland area of England decided to pay subsidies to low-income employed individuals who had families to support—setting a minimum based on the price of bread and scaled according to family size. The Speenhamland experiment, as it later became known, spread to other parts of England. Following its implementation, familiar criticisms led to its abolition. Some argued that individual initiative would cease, the numbers of dependent people would grow, productivity would drop, and costs of relief would rise inordinately. Others argued, in hindsight, that its major problems were the maintenance of artificially low market wages, and the creation of artificial barriers to labour mobility (Bruce, 1961, pp. 41, 76–77; de Schweinitz, 1943, pp. 72–73; Dolgoff & Feldstein, 1984, p. 55). While historically brief, the Speenhamland experiment highlights the issue of wage supplementation for low-income citizens, which contemporary governments continue to debate. Some Canadian provinces have provisions in their welfare programs to defray additional expenses that recipients face when they start working, such as daycare, transportation, work clothing, and tools. Others have considered programs that ease the transition from welfare to work via a "top-up" income supplementation program during the initial re-entry into the workforce (National Council of Welfare, 2006b). The Speenhamland experiment demonstrates that wage supplementation has historical roots.

Canada Up to 1945

The European heritage blended with a North American context to create a distinctly Canadian approach to social welfare. One of the most significant and tragic aspects of North American history has been the colonization of Aboriginal peoples. Sporadic attempts by the Vikings to live along the northeast coast in the tenth century were followed by the permanent settlement of French *habitants* in the sixteenth century. The *habitants* lived largely along the St. Lawrence River, in a land they named Nouvelle

France. The French—and, after the 1759 conquest of Nouvelle France, the British—forever changed North America. The continent's Aboriginal peoples, decimated by disease and war, were forced onto reserves of land in the late nineteenth and early twentieth centuries, where they were further marginalized—economically, politically, and socially. As elaborated in Chapter 6, the resolutely Eurocentric orientation of Canadian social policies contributed much to the tragedy of the colonization of Aboriginal peoples.

Nouvelle France and, later, British North America possessed an isolating geography, tormenting physical elements, and numerous forms of social misfortune: poverty, vagrancy, alcoholism, illegitimate births, and debtor classes, among others. Long-standing models of European social organization, however, could be adapted only haphazardly to the patterns of sparse inhabitation of frontier settlement. In Nova Scotia and New Brunswick, locally financed overseers of the poor administered Poor Laws. Present-day Québec, like Newfoundland, relied on the Roman Catholic Church to administer and dispense a complex system of social welfare, in addition to public education and health services. In Ontario, the absence of either Poor Law legislation or a strong Roman Catholic influence meant that spontaneous forms of community concern had to prevail (Boychuk, 1998; Graham, 1995; Splane, 1965).

These machineries of social welfare carried on into the seventeenth, eighteenth, and early nineteenth centuries. But they were later transformed, mirroring the ferment of economic, social, and political changes of the day. Throughout this period, a series of primary economic staples dominated the economy. The cod fisheries of present-day Newfoundland became important in the sixteenth century, and were supplemented from the sixteenth through to the nineteenth century by the fur trade, corresponding with the slow but persistent westward pattern of human settlement. The fur trade gave way to a timber trade in the nineteenth century, and then to a wheat staple, first in present-day Central Canada, and then, after the 1880s, in Western Canada. Over the last quarter of the nineteenth and into the twentieth century, Canada experienced an industrial revolution, making Montréal and Toronto the leading urban centres of a growing network of national cities (Easterbrook & Aitken, 1956).

During this time, there were several waves of immigration, highlighted by Loyalist settlement from south of the border after the American Revolution, significant British immigration during the middle of the nineteenth century, followed by a more diverse European settlement, much of it westward bound, during and after the 1880s (Lower, 1958, p. 187). From a scattered population of 70 000 in 1759, there appeared significant demographic growth. In 1851, present-day Ontario, Québec, and the Maritime provinces had a combined population of 2.5 million people. In 1901, Canada's population had risen to 5.37 million, and in 1921, to 9 million (Easterbrook & Aitken, 1956, pp. 395, 400; Prentice et al., 1988, p. 108). Meanwhile, the percentage of Canadians living in urban centres steadily climbed from 13 percent in 1851, to 35 percent in 1901, to 47 percent in 1921, and to 52.5 percent by 1931 (Artibese & Stelter, 1985, p. 1887).

At the same time, a further—and tragic—demographic transformation was well under way. Aboriginal peoples had been decimated by colonialism. First Nations and Inuit peoples were once unknown to European peoples, and vice versa. Western Europe at the turn of the first millennium was, compared with the Muslim Middle East, Japan, or southern China, intellectually and materially inferior. But by the late 1400s, its countries gained increasing dominance such that by 1914 western European countries occupied

84 percent of the world and had colonies on every inhabited continent (Hoffman, 2015, pp. 2–4). The rise of European power has been variously explained. A recent, and to us convincing argument, lies in the European development of military technology—particularly the use of gunpowder (Hoffman, 2015).

In Canada, as with so much of the world, European contact with the new world forever changed indigenous peoples. At first, as a summary of the Report of the Royal Commission on Aboriginal Peoples puts it, "cautious cooperation, not conflict" described at least part of Aboriginal-European relations. "For the most part, Aboriginal and non-Aboriginal people saw each other as separate, distinct and independent. Each was in charge of its own affairs. Each could negotiate its own military alliances, its own trade agreements, its own best deals with the others" (Royal Commission on Aboriginal Peoples, 1996). But as European settlement was established and grew, ad hoc agreements with Aboriginal peoples were initiated, including the *Royal Proclamation of 1763*, which established a boundary, long since abandoned, along the Appalachian Mountains, delineating colonial and Aboriginal lands. The Royal Proclamation is frequently seen as an important document, recognizing Aboriginal rights. But Aboriginal peoples were decimated by European diseases (influenza, measles, and smallpox, to which they had no natural immunities) and war, and the taking of Aboriginal lands had an incalculable impact on all aspects of Aboriginal societies. As colonial settlement further unfolded, Aboriginal peoples were subjected to further land grabs, and to cultural and economic assimilation. Subsequent negotiated treaties between 1871 to 1921 enabled western colonial settlement across what became northern Ontario to British Columbia and the Yukon Territory. We return to this topic in subsequent paragraphs.

In 1867, the former colonies of British North America united to form Canada. Equally significant, the effects of industrialization, urbanization, and demographic growth transformed Canada from a small, resource-based mercantilist economy into an industrializing nation. As society became increasingly complex, social welfare had to adapt accordingly. Houses of Industry—in effect, workhouses for the poor—emerged in Canada in the 1830s, through the influence of the British Poor Law Reforms of that decade. These institutions tended to be administered on a local basis and alongside local and provincial hospitals, with the latter signaling governments' growing responsibility for social welfare. The voluntary sector at the same time remained vital, and a profusion of publicly and privately founded specialized charities were established over the next 80 years, among them: Houses of Providence, Boys' and Girls' Homes, city missions, Protestant and Roman Catholic orphanages, Jewish philanthropic organizations, hospitals for the sick, and refuges for the old. A distinct form of charity also came into being in the late nineteenth century—the settlement house, wherein the well-to-do, often university students, lived among and sought to help a city's poor. These settlement houses were often significant loci of community social change (Desroches, 2009; Irving, Parsons, & Bellamy, 1995). The voluntary sector and the government had a close relationship; neither worked in isolation, nor did the government ever replace the voluntary sector, despite the former's growing involvement in social welfare over the early nineteenth century through to the late twentieth century. As one sociologist points out, "At least since the 1830s, governments [in English-speaking Canada] have been in the business of regulating and funding charities. And the expansion of the voluntary sector historically, as in the contemporary context, has always hinged on substantial government involvement" (Maurutto, 2009, p. 159).

Likewise, nineteenth-century social welfare institutions and social movements were inextricably linked. For example, religious organizations provided tangible services and a moral rationale for expanded activities, and proved to be a political force compelling greater state intervention into the country's social milieu. The Social Gospel Movement, a loose coalition of Protestant denominations influenced by British and American counterparts, emerged in Canada in the 1890s, applying Christian principles to prevailing social and economic issues. Similar forces were evident in twentieth-century Québec, where, through the *Semaines sociales*, Roman Catholic clergy and laity discussed social issues. The Social Service Council of Canada, so named in 1913, was a public education and advocacy organization; originally created in 1907, it included representatives from the Anglican, Methodist, Presbyterian, and Baptist churches, as well as the Trades and Labour Congress of Canada (Guest, 1997, p. 34). Protestant clergy had been particularly important in the creation, leadership, and perpetuation of the Co-operative Commonwealth Federation (renamed the New Democratic Party in 1961), a social democratic political party elected to national and provincial legislatures and advocating a more comprehensive welfare state (Allen, 1971).

In the late 1880s, what became known as an *urban reform movement* emerged—a loose coalition of journalists, clergy, charity workers, government officials, and other interested parties. It pursued a broad array of public causes: public control of utilities, including public transit; better public health provisions, including the expansion of public health nursing services, improved sanitation, improved housing standards, and improved standards of meat processing and water quality; the establishment of more green spaces (parks and playgrounds) in urban areas; and improved standards of relief, child welfare, and other social programs (Stelter & Artibese, 1977). A leading proponent was Toronto *Globe* journalist J.J. Kelso, founder of the Toronto Humane Society in 1887, later renamed the Children's Aid Society (Fingard, 1989, p. 171; Jones & Rutman, 1981). Another was Herbert B. Ames, a well-to-do Montréal manufacturer who published an 1897 study titled *City on the Hill*, documenting the deplorable living conditions endured by Montréal's working class (Copp, 1974).

The working class itself did much to assist the working poor; nineteenth-century workers organized fraternal societies, with each member contributing a small regular amount to a fund from which they could draw if sickness or an accident interfered with work. Canadian trade unions helped to raise standards of living, protect workers' wages, and improve workplace conditions (Kealey, 1980; Palmer, 1979). Women were responsible for fundraising and service provision within many local charities. By the end of the nineteenth century, these women's activities had expanded to include a number of reform organizations, many now national in scope. The National Council of Women (established in 1893), the Woman's Christian Temperance Union (1874), and the Young Women's Christian Association (established nationally in 1895), to name three, sought numerous social improvements, including women's right to vote (obtained federally in 1918 and provincially shortly before and afterwards), and social policies that would assist women and children (Kealey, 1979; Strong-Boag, 1976).

One of the most important social effects of industrialization was the segregation of people according to gender. In earlier economies, a family's income would often focus on agricultural production and take place at home, relying on the work of men, women, and children within families. But in an industrial economy, a family's livelihood depended more and more on men's employment outside the home; some literature refers to this as the phenomenon of the *breadwinner male*. Increasingly in the industrial economy, women remained at home and focused their attention on such domestic work as raising children, cooking, laundering, and sewing, and less on producing goods for trade or barter; certain literature refers to this phenomenon as *women's domesticity*, or *the domestication of women*. In an industrial society, there emerged a gendered split between the public realm outside the home, dominated by men, and the domestic realm of women and children. However, women's social advocacy and charitable activities, it should be stressed, did take women outside the home, which were important precedents to the growing presence of women employed outside the home during the post-1960s period.

Patriarchy was and still is a major theme of social welfare history. The political franchise had been extended in the nineteenth century to include men who did not hold property. But only in the post-World War I period did women achieve the right to vote in federal elections—a right that was established in the West during the war and spread to other provinces until 1940, when Québec women got the right to vote. Another land-mark was the 1929 Famous Five court challenge, in which five Canadian women success-fully sought legal recognition as persons under the *British North America Act*.

The Industrial Revolution of the nineteenth century ushered in massive disparities in health and standards of living between those who worked in factories and those of greater means. It also created large concentrations of urban poverty (Ball & Gready, 2006). Unions were at the fore of the charge to change these inequalities, always against concerted opposition. After much effort, a nine-hour work day was successfully obtained in 1872, and the Canadian Labour Union was created but then abolished that same decade. The Royal Commission on the Relations of Labour and Capital (1887) ultimately recognized the social value of unions. By the 1890s, there were 240 unions nationwide, and with a growing urban reform and women's movement, positive change was occurring. By 1894, labour had become so respectable that the first Monday in September became a national holiday (now known as Labour Day). In 1900, the federal government established the Department of Labour to mediate disputes between workers and owners.

The nineteenth and twentieth centuries also covered the tragic story of oppression of Aboriginal peoples—first by the experience of European contact, disease, and eco-nomic exploitation; and then, during the development of Nouvelle France, British North America, and Canada, by the conquest of an entire continent by colonizers. A series of land treaties were negotiated between successive colonizing governments, and the 1876 *Indian Act* enshrined this colonial orientation—defining what was meant by *Indian*, extending power to the Canadian government to regulate Aboriginal peoples, provid-ing federal government guardianship over Aboriginal lands, and restricting the political franchise to those who assimilated. An infrastructure of assimilation emerged during the post-Confederation period, during which some Christian churches and government officials collaborated to provide residential schooling for Aboriginal children. The legacy of residential schooling has traumatized generations of Aboriginal peoples and continues to have massive negative repercussions to this day. Also during the post-Confederation period, Aboriginal peoples were relegated to reserves of land, many of which remain chronically underserviced for basic urban infrastructures and became places of high unem-ployment and high despair. Chapter 6 elaborates.

Chapter 6 also discusses the impact of racism on Canadian society— a major theme in the history of Canadian social policy, as in Canadian history in general. Prior to the early 1960s, Canadian immigration policy was overtly racist, stating preferences for immigration to certain preferred ethnic and racial backgrounds. The state promoted racist policies. It interned Ukrainian Canadians during World War I and Japanese Canadians during World War II; in 1885, it imposed a head tax on people of Chinese background to reduce immigration, and in 1923, it excluded Chinese immigration entirely (rescinded in 1947).

The Canadian social work profession in its early years therefore was largely white. It also had strong roots in national organizations that represented women, churches, and trade unions, as discussed above. It was likewise influenced by the Charity Organization movement, which was preceded by American and British counterparts and which sought to rationalize charity, to make it more efficient, more humane, and more proficient in its techniques. The world's oldest schools of social work opened in Great Britain in 1890 and the United States in 1903, and Canada's first school appeared soon afterwards, at the University of Toronto in 1914. It was followed by similar schools at McGill University (1918), the University of British Columbia (1928), the Université de Montréal (1939), and at an independent institution that ultimately became affiliated with Dalhousie University (1941) in Halifax. The Canadian Council on Child Welfare was founded in 1920 (renamed the Canadian Welfare Council in 1935 and the Canadian Council on Social Development in 1969). The Canadian Association of Social Workers was founded in 1926, and two years later, the First International Conference of Social Work was convened, spawning the International Association of Schools of Social Work. These were among the myriad organizations that sought more comprehensive social policies at the provincial, national, and international levels (Graham, 1996b).

All of the activities of social workers, and the growing institutional arrangements in which they operated, were funded by some combination of private, voluntary, and public means. They remained vitally important throughout the twentieth century, and into the twenty-first. Leaders in these sectors were vitally important advocates in ushering in an institutional stage of social welfare.

Social Policies

Among the most significant pieces of social policy legislation before World War II was the *Workmen's Compensation Act* of 1914, first established in Ontario but soon imitated by other provinces. It provided injured workers with regular cash income as a right, rather than as something that followed (often lengthy) litigation against an employer. As early as 1919, the federal government was pledging to create national systems of health insurance and unemployment insurance (UI, now named Employment Insurance or EI). But a national system of health insurance did not come into being until 1966. UI finally came into force in 1940, several decades after the establishment of comparable programs in Britain and other advanced industrialized nations. Its introduction had been delayed for decades because of the federal government's reluctance to amend the Canadian Constitution to allow the federal government jurisdiction in this area. Meanwhile, in 1916, Manitoba became the first province to introduce Mother's Pensions, a selective program providing a small, means-tested income to widows and divorced or deserted wives and their children (Guest, 1997). The next major piece of legislation—also selective—was the 1927 *Old Age Pensions Act*, the cost of which was shared on a 50–50 basis by the federal and provincial governments.

Under Section 92 of the Canadian Constitution (the *British North America Act, 1867*, renamed in 1982 as the *Constitution Act, 1867*), the areas of education, health, and welfare were (and remain to this day) provincial prerogatives. But by strength of precedent, local governments continued to take on funding and administrative responsibilities for many social programs. As creatures of the provinces with no constitutionally prescribed autonomy of their own, municipalities could be created and disbanded by provincial writ and tended to have a limited tax base (this remains the case today). But because of the unprecedented extent and duration of unemployment during the 1930s, local governments could not withstand the financial and administrative commitments of unemployment relief, among other social programs for which they had always been held responsible. Over the course of that decade, higher levels of government consequently took on greater financial responsibility (Graham, 1995). Likewise, the voluntary and charitable sectors were increasingly stressed by client need. The 1917 *Income War Tax and Charities Act*, had given tax deductions for donations to war-related charities such as the Red Cross. This was expanded in 1930 to cover a wider array of tax-exempt charities, which were then regulated (Elson, 2011, pp. 27, 30). Through these twin avenues– expanding the scope and revenues of the voluntary sector, and increasing the scope and mandate of provincial and federal levels of government, charity was transformed. With the twin impacts of these changes to the charitable sector, as well as growing higher-level responsibility for social affairs, social welfare was massively transformed.

THE INSTITUTIONAL APPROACH
Canada, 1945–1973

Canada changed dramatically after World War II. Immigration levels increased significantly. New immigration selection practices came into effect in 1962, intending to introduce principles that were universal and non-discriminatory; in 1967, further selection practice changes led to the introduction of what was intended to be a more objective points system. This is not to suggest, however, that Canadian immigration practices became entirely objective. Indeed, as several scholars point out, there remain discriminatory standards, sometimes less obvious and sometimes different from earlier practices. Excellent current examples relate to the rules and procedures that categorize immigrants in three main groups (family class, economic class, and refugee class), that limit the number of individuals who can be admitted in each of these categories, and that emphasize integration into Canadian society in relation to societal barriers for immigrants in each of these categories (Beach, Green, & Reitz, 2004).

The country's growing racial and ethnic diversity, discussed in Chapter 6, was further reinforced by the federal government's introduction of an official policy of multiculturalism in 1971, the *Charter of Rights and Freedoms* in 1982, and the *Canadian Multiculturalism Act* in 1987. In addition to being significantly more diverse, the country's population was also more numerous. In 1971, Canada consisted of 21.6 million people, nearly a twofold increase from 1941. In the same year, 1971, the percentage of Canadians living in urban centres had increased to 76.1 percent, and by 2011 it had grown to 81.1 percent (Statistics Canada, 2015, Canada Goes Urban).

Social work grew proportionately. In 1941, the census reported 1767 social workers in Canada. By 1981, there were more than 27 590 (Drover, 1988, p. 2034). An earlier reliance on a two-year, post-BA diploma (following a one-year, post-BA certificate) gave way, in the post-war era, to the dominance of the Bachelor of Social Work/Master of Social Work sequence.

The country's first Doctor of Social Work program was inaugurated at the University of Toronto in 1952. Moreover, by 1949, there were eight Canadian social work schools—nearly a threefold increase over a 10-year period—and by 1970, there were 12 (Graham, 1996a, 129). Numerous social workers forever changed the face of Canadian society. Harry Cassidy (1900–1951), an economist at the University of Toronto School of Social Work, wrote numerous studies on Canadian social security programs. Charlotte Whitton (1896–1975), director and driving force behind the Canadian Welfare Council (later named the Canadian Council on Social Development), was responsible for several aspects of the profession's history in Canada. Yet although she crusaded for improved standards of child welfare and for changes in social policies, she also advocated harsh welfare assistance eligibility requirements for single mothers, among other practices that might be considered less than progressive by today's standards (Rooke & Schnell, 1987). Bessie Touzel (1904–1997) was trained in the 1920s at the University of Toronto and held a succession of appointments of increasing responsibility, such as Chief of the Ottawa Public Welfare Department, Executive Secretary of the Toronto Welfare Council, and Executive Director of the Ontario Welfare Council. A staunch advocate of improved casework practices, she wrote numerous policy studies, was an adviser to the Marsh Commission (see below), and served with the United Nations in Tanzania (Obituaries, *The Globe and Mail*, April 26, 1997).

Social Policies

Everything changed after the 1943 *Report on Social Security for Canada* (the Marsh Report), written by economist Leonard Marsh, who taught social work at McGill University. The Marsh Report echoed the famous 1942 Beveridge Report in Great Britain. Both were blueprints for a comprehensive and largely universal welfare state in their respective countries, and both provided a rationale for what scholars describe as an institutional model of social policy. In contrast to the residual approach, the institutional approach saw the welfare services as normal, "first line" functions of modern industrial society, a proper, legitimate function of modern industrial society in helping individuals to achieve self-fulfillment (Wilensky & Lebeaux, 1958, p. 138). The tendency to construct stigmatizing programs was much reduced, and means testing, under a universal program, was no longer the primary requirement for eligibility. Under universal programs, a sense of entitlement, or right of citizenship, prevailed (Graham, 2008).

As noted in Figure 2.1, spending for social programs increased markedly over the following several decades. Following the introduction of UI, the next major Marsh Report proposal, a universal Family Allowances (FA) program, came into being in 1944:

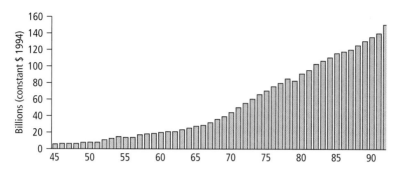

Figure 2.1 Total Social Spending in Canada, 1945–46 to 1992–93

Source: Caledon Institute of Social Policy (1995). *The comprehensive reform of social programs: Brief to the standing committee on human resources development*, Caledon Institute of Social Policy, 1995. Renouf Publishing. Reprinted with permission.

regardless of family income, *all* Canadian mothers of children under the age of 16 would receive a monthly allowance (Blake, 2009). The next major development after that was the 1951 conversion of the Old Age Security (OAS) program from a selective to a universal program. As of that year, all seniors over the age of 70 would receive a pension, regardless of their level of income.

A universal system of health insurance first appeared in Saskatchewan, under the political leadership of the first social democratic government elected in North America: the Co-operative Commonwealth Federation. In 1945, Premier Tommy Douglas set up a social assistance medical care plan covering old age pensioners, recipients of mothers' allowances, blind pensioners, and wards of the state. This selective program was supplemented in 1947 by the introduction of universal, state-administered hospital insurance, and in 1959, by universal, province-wide medical insurance. Meanwhile, in 1956, the federal government initiated the *Hospital Insurance and Diagnostic Services Act*, a negotiated cost-sharing agreement between Ottawa and the provinces, covering a basic range of in-patient hospital services. Again, following the lead of Saskatchewan, the federal government installed a universal healthcare system in 1966; and by 1972, each province and territory was administering its own health services. The story of social policy has been one of intense competition between groups in society, and healthcare was no exception. Companies that had provided private health insurance resisted what some perceived to be the intrusion of the state. So, too, did many physicians acting individually and through professional associations, claiming that physicians' autonomy would be compromised, and that access to comprehensive healthcare services would be reduced (Naylor, 1986).

As the legislation described it, "programs for the provision of assistance and welfare services to and in respect of persons in need" were cost-shared equally, on a 50-50 basis, by the federal government and each province under the Canada Assistance Plan (CAP). The *Medical Care Act* (1966) was another cost-sharing plan. Under the CAP, provinces also set up and administered such social services as child welfare protection, rehabilitation, home support for the elderly and people who were disabled, employment programs, child care, and social assistance. The federal government, with massive revenue sources from the income tax system, corporate taxes, and tariffs, was expected to provide otherwise vulnerable programs with a solid basis of funding.

As early as 1966, the federal government had introduced the Canada Pension Plan (CPP), providing social insurance protection for retirement and disability, as well as survivors' benefits. A national program (with the exception of Québec, which legislated an equivalent in the Québec Pension Plan), the CPP was a compulsory plan tied to workplace earnings and was portable if the individual moved or took on a different job within Canada. The CPP and OAS were supplemented in 1966 by an income-tested pension plan for low-income earners, the Guaranteed Income Supplement.

But as Andrew Jackson and Matthew Sanger (2003) point out, "from the 1950s through to the mid-1970s, even as state provision of direct care expanded, the voluntary social services sector" increased in like proportion (p. 30). In Canada, voluntary sectors were not automatically replaced by an increasingly robust government responsibility for social well-being: "It is wrong to see a process of one-dimensional evolution from voluntaristic charity provision" of the residual era to the formal, state structures of institutionalism. "As the welfare state grew, so did the non-profit sector" (2003, p. 30).

On the international scene, the seeds of an emerging globalization of the market-state era had already been sown. Post–World War II economic arrangements were concluded by the Bretton Woods Agreements (1944), which culminated in the development of the International Monetary Fund (IMF), the International Bank for Reconstruction and Development (later renamed the World Bank, or WB), and a proposal for an international trading organization (developed in 1947 as the General Agreement on Tariffs and Trade—GATT—later, in 1994, becoming the World Trade Organization, or WTO). These new international economic institutions were driven by American economic and foreign policy (Hobsbawm, 1995) and coincided with the emergence of more powerful transnational corporations (Ellwood, 2006). Europe in the post–World War II period experienced the Marshall Plan (1947), in which billions of dollars of aid and technical assistance poured into those European countries that had joined the Organisation for Economic Co-operation and Development (OECD, established 1948). In the 1960s, a comparable Marshall Plan was proposed for an emerging, post-colonial Africa but was rejected by Global North policy elites—a move that development economist Jeffrey Sachs has labelled racist.

Several important international institutions had emerged after World War I, including the precursor to the United Nations: the League of Nations (1919); its member agency, the International Labour Organization (1919), which intended to promote the rights of labour worldwide; and the International Council on Social Welfare (1928). In the aftermath of World War II, the United Nations was established in 1945, and with it came the emergence of a battery of social welfare institutions at the international level, including the World Health Organization (1948), the United Nations Children's Fund (UNICEF) (1946), and the United Nations Development Programme (1965). The 1948 *Universal Declaration of Human Rights* is an exemplary international covenant adopted by the United Nations, and a succession of other policies followed: the *International Covenant on Economic, Social, and Cultural Rights* (1966); the *International Covenant on Civil and Political Rights* (1966); and the *Convention on the Rights of the Child* (1984), among others (Ball & Gready, 2006).

THE MARKET-STATE APPROACH

By the late 1960s and early 1970s, it seemed as though a comprehensive base of government sponsored social welfare programs had been established, and continued policy initiatives would simply fill in the gaps that had been overlooked or had not yet been developed. The UI program was considerably expanded in 1971 by increasing benefit rates, widening the program's compulsory coverage to include nearly all employees and easing qualifying conditions. During the same decade, the CPP benefit rates were also elevated, and OAS benefits were extended to recipients' widows (Guest, 1997, pp. 173, 188). A growing awareness of female poverty led to the 1975 introduction of the Spouse's Allowance, a means-tested supplement paid to old age pensioners' spouses. Several studies in the late 1960s and 1970s, including a Senate Committee report, *Poverty in Canada* (1971), revealed as many as one in five Canadians were living in poverty (Guest, 1997, p. 156). The report called for a Guaranteed Annual Income (GAI), which would have provided, had it been adopted, a minimum threshold of income below which no individual would fall. There also emerged a gradual recognition of poverty and inequality as a reflection of such social diversities as gender, ethnicity, race, Aboriginal status, range of ability, and geography. These, given their critical significance, are examined in greater depth in Chapter 6.

Historian Philip Bobbitt considers the rise of the twentieth-century welfare-state period in a broad historical context, from the mid-fifteenth-century emergence of the European princely state (which was founded when people rallied around a prince for mutual protection) through to the late nineteenth-century nation-state, when the twentieth-century welfare state began to unfold (Bobbitt, 2002). The post-welfare-state period of the mid-1970s to the present is manifestly different, a cataclysmic shift from the nation-state structure to a market-state structure (Bobbitt, 2002).

Just as many countries of the previous period, Canada included, could be described as nation-states, so too are many countries in addition to Canada now market-states. The market-state is characterized by a number of factors, including computer technology and communication on a global scale, the decentralization of governments, the reduced scope and sanction of government, the increased significance of liberal ideology (as elaborated in the next chapter), and the increasing importance of the private sector. The "market" has become a defining metaphor, the benchmark by which government and non-government sectors operate. In a market-state, the growing role of the private and voluntary sectors has occurred. The state's primary purpose, although limited in scope, is to support private-sector goals and the economic growth and accumulation that represent them. As Bobbitt (2002) points out, governments within the market-state are no longer mandated to provide for the welfare of the nation. The extent of the social welfare responsibilities of government are entirely reduced from that which Marsh and Beveridge envisioned in the mid-1940s. In the institutional period, Canadians were citizens; in the market-state era, Canadians are consumers.

Social Policies

As the market-state emerged in the mid-1970s, several factors conspired to gradually erode Canadian social policies, and this erosion marks the underlying difference between the institutional and market-state models of social policy. Eight aspects relating to the market-state period are of particular significance. The first is that overall, the amount

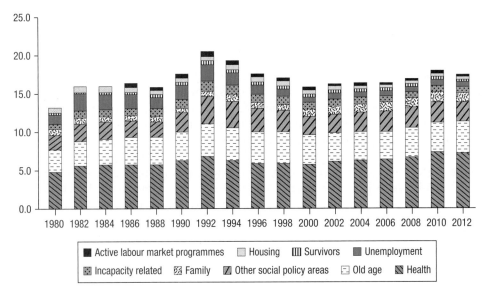

Figure 2.2 Public Social Spending in Canada by Program Area (% of GDP) 1980–2012

Source: Data from OECD.Stat, https://stats.oecd.org/Index.aspx?DataSetCode=SOCX_AGG#

of social spending compared with the percentage of Gross Domestic Product (GDP, the value of goods and services produced in the economy based on earnings inside the country) has dropped several points since the mid-1990s, essentially demonstrating the reduced spending in this budgetary sector (see Figures 2.2 and 2.3). The turning point in the history of social spending in Canada occurred in the early 1990s. These figures show income security expenditures and demonstrate increases into the mid-1990s.

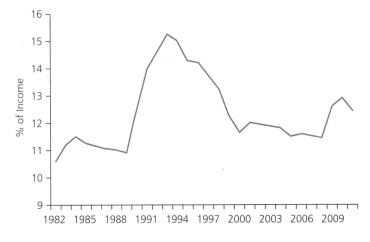

Figure 2.3 Government Transfers as a Share of Canadian Household Income

Source: Statistics Canada, Special Report: The case for leaning against income inequality in Canada. Copyright © 2015. Reproduced and distributed on an "as is" basis with the permission of Statistics Canada.

Several factors have influenced the erosion of these traditional social policies. A primary factor is the decline of federal government transfer payments to provinces, which began under the CAP in the 1970s and accelerated up to 1992–93, when the federal share of CAP transfers to the country's three wealthiest provinces was down to 28 percent in Ontario and 36 percent in British Columbia and Alberta (National Council of Welfare, 1995, p. 7). The CAP itself was replaced in 1996 by the Canada Health and Social Transfer (CHST), which reduced federal government contributions to education, health-care, and social welfare by another 15 percent during the first two years of its implementation (Graham, 2008). The CHST also reduced the federal government's ability to enforce standards as to how the money would be spent and to which of the three major block areas money would be allocated (National Council of Welfare, 1995). Following the CHST, in 2004, two separate transfer programs were created: the Canada Health Transfer and the Canada Social Transfer. Changes in the 2007–08 federal budget sought to improve the transparency of how transfer money is spent. Provincial governments, meanwhile, have tended to reduce transfers to local governments for the delivery of programs administered and partially financed by municipalities. These programs vary from province to province but, depending on the province, may include child welfare, general welfare assistance, homemaking, rehabilitation services, and other forms.

At the same time, the contributions of individuals and their employers to various programs such as UI/EI (see below) and CPP have increased steadily. Funding reductions of the CAP and of social programs not associated with the CAP (e.g., UI, FA, CPP, OAS) have helped to create a second feature of the market-state era: the persistent and definite shrinkage in the comprehensiveness and extent of social programs. For example, after 50 years of funding the UI program, the federal government removed its financial support in 1990, making the program fully funded by employer and worker contributions. In the same year, more restrictive eligibility criteria were introduced, alongside shortened benefit periods, higher premiums, and more severe penalties to claimants quitting their jobs without "just cause" (Human Resources and Social Development Canada, 2007; Chappell, 2006, p. 49). In 1996, UI was changed to Employment Insurance (EI), and various reforms, intended to produce further savings of $1.9 billion, sought to reduce the maximum stay on insurance, penalize repeat users, and take back a proportion of payments from wealthier recipients (Battle, 2001).

A second factor bearing emphasis is healthcare, particularly in relation to other expenditures at the provincial level. In the healthcare domain, there has been consider-able push-back to the idea of reducing government involvement, and health expenditures have been a growing portion of provincial government spending. The federal government released an important 1984 policy document, the *Canada Health Act* (CHA), which was widely viewed as an instrument to maintain federal standards. The document reaffirms five principles of our universal healthcare system: universality, comprehensiveness, accessibility (minimal barriers to services), portability (transferability of services from province to province), and public administration. Compared to other advanced industrialized countries, Canada ranks in the top quartiles of Organization for Economic Development (OECD), "with per person spending on health care in 2012 at US$4602, below that of the United States (US$8745) and comparable with figures for Denmark (US$4698) and Luxembourg (US$4578)" (CIHR, 2014, p. 13). Figure 2.4 shows the growth of expenditures in healthcare since 1975, while Figure 2.5 shows total health expenditures according

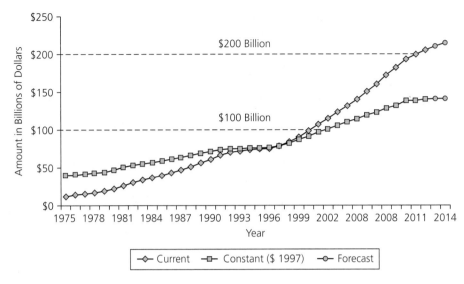

Figure 2.4 Total Health Expenditure, Canada, 1975 to 2014

Source: "Total Health Expenditure, Canada, 1975 to 2014", in National Health Expenditure Trends, 1975 to 2014, at p.21; Reproduced by permission of Canadian Institute for Health Information.

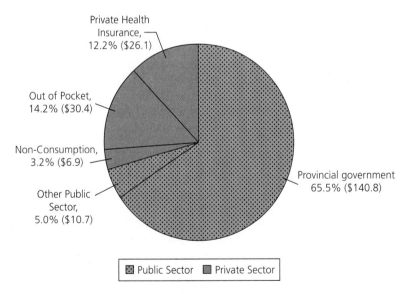

Figure 2.5 Total Health Expenditure by Source of Finance, 2014 (Percentage Share and Billions of Dollars)

Source: "Total Health Expenditure by source of finance, 2014 (Percentage Share and Billions of Dollars)", in National Health Expenditure Trends, 1975 to 2014, at p.31; Reproduced by permission of Canadian Institute for Health Information.

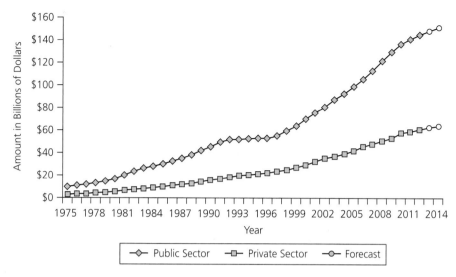

Figure 2.6 Health Expenditure by Source of Finance, Canada, 1975 to 2014

Source: "Health Expenditure by source of Finance, Canada, 1975 to 2014", in National Health Expenditure Trends, 1975 to 2014, at p.32; Reproduced by permission of Canadian Institute for Health Information.

to public and private sources. As Figure 2.6 shows, the proportion of non-governmental expenditures has increased markedly since 1975. And Figure 2.7 shows the gradual reduction since 1975 of hospital costs as a portion of overall healthcare expenditures, and the rise of pharmaceutical expenditures.

Overall, the country's commitment to our universal healthcare system remains strong, notwithstanding the significant growth of non-governmental expenditures (primarily private sector health insurance, and out-of-pocket expenditures) as noted in Figure 2.6. Perhaps the most important point to note is the growing portion of provincial government expenditures constituting healthcare. Governments must make choices in spending limited funds. As healthcare has consumed more and more of those funds, provincial government expenditures in other areas such as post-secondary education and social welfare have decreased, as a proportion of overall provincial expenditures (Di Matteo, 2011). Figure 2.8 elaborates.

A third factor typifying the market era in which we live is the replacement of universal programs with selective programs. An excellent example is the 1992 replacement of the universal Family Allowances (FA) with the Child Tax Benefit, which combines the former FA and child tax credits into one refundable, income-tested child tax credit. In addition, the 1989 introduction of a clawback on OAS payments to upper-income Canadians essentially abolished the universal basis of this program. As one policy document observed, the de-indexing against inflation of the threshold beyond which the OAS is taxed back meant that an increasing number of Canadians receive partial or no benefits (Battle & Torjman, 1993, p. 4). Increasingly, user fees rather than universal access are common for parks, museums, and other community services; some have advocated user fees for access to health services, in an effort to reduce costs (MacKinnon, 2013).

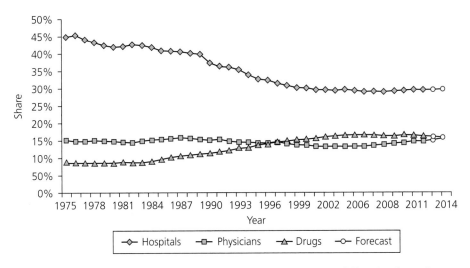

Figure 2.7 Total Health Expenditure, Share of Selected Use of Funds, Canada, 1975 to 2014

Source: "Total Health Expenditure, Share of Selected Use of Funds, Canada, 1975 to 2014", in National Health Expenditure Trends, 1975 to 2014, at p.44; Reproduced by permission of Canadian Institute for Health Information.

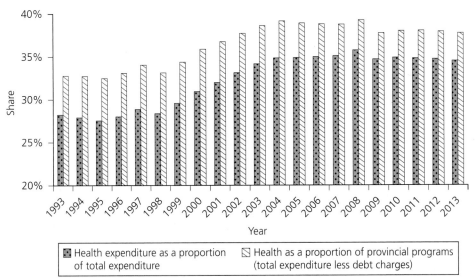

Figure 2.8 Provincial Government Health Spending as a Share of Program Spending: 1975–2010

Source: "Provincial Government Health Spending as a Share of Program Spending: 1975-2010", in National Health Expenditure Trends, 1975 to 2014 at p.44, Reproduced by permission of Canadian Institute for Health Information.

A fourth aspect underlying many of the above changes is the growth of government debt. The debt is a cumulative, multiyear calculation based on the total amount of money that the government owes. It is different from a deficit, which is a yearly calculation of annual operating costs where spending exceeds revenues. While all levels of government experience debts and deficits, the present analysis, for sake of illustration, considers only the federal scene. In 2014, the federal government's total debt was $611.8 billion, or $17 406 for every Canadian (RBC, May 1, 2015). Between 1965 and 1975, the federal government's deficits were still below 2 percent of GDP, and the debt was a low 18 percent. A combination of circumstances—a recession, accelerated borrowing, and an inability to match revenues with expenses—increased the debt to 48 percent of GDP by 1982, and by 1994 it was 71 percent ("Fair Taxes", 1995). During the following decade, reduced interest rates on the debt and drastic trimming of program expenditures helped to spur an economic climate of recovery in the country. In 2001, the debt ratio fell to 53 percent (Little, 2001), and by 2006 it decreased to 35 percent (Department of Finance Canada, 2006). Despite lengthy and costly military involvement in Afghanistan and a recent recession, the current net debt-to-GDP ratio is estimated at 31.2 percent (RBC, May 1, 2015). The Canadian government aspires to reduce it to 25.3 percent by 2019–20. Its $616 billion pricetag is expected to reach $605.2 billion by 2019–20. It is not debt in itself that matters, however, but rather how policy analysts, politicians, and others interpret the causes and significance of debt. When social programs are considered the cause of debt, then these programs get cut.

A fifth theme is the gradual recognition—through federal and provincial human rights legislation, the 1982 *Charter of Rights and Freedoms*, and other policy initiatives—of the rights of historically disempowered peoples, such as Aboriginal peoples, members of ethnoracial and religious minority communities, women, gays and lesbians, and people with disabilities, among others. Yet some of the institutions that had sought these rights in the past are disappearing. In 2013, 31.5 percent of Canadian workers belonged to a union, continuing a steady downward trend from 38 percent in 1981 (Government of Canada: Labour Program, June 11, 2014). In addition, as Chapter 6 points out, new conceptions of community and individual rights are developing. This development is a sea change in social policy: moving from an institutional era of justice as distribution and redistribution, to a market era of justice as the politics of recognition and individual rights (Bakan, 1997; Fraser, 1995).

Likewise, a sixth theme, as elaborated in Chapter 6, is the rise of a neo-liberal ideology. This includes the primacy of financial markets and private sector participation in all parts of social life. Individuals are increasingly encouraged to provide for themselves, rather than relying on the state to cover the costs. As university tuition fees have risen markedly across much of Canada, Registered Educational Savings Plans (RESP) have been increasingly emphasized by the federal government as a tax-friendly means for post-secondary savings. Similar thinking prevails with the growing contribution room encouraged in the Registered Retirement Savings Plan (RRSP), the 2008 introduction of the Tax Free Savings Accounts (TFSA), or the federal government's 2014 policy of Pooled Registered Pension Plans (PRPP). Not surprisingly, people of greater means are able to contribute to these programs more so than those of lesser means. Also noteworthy is the presence of private sector dental and prescription drug insurance, the financial sector's growing involvement in retirement provisions, given the decreasing proportion of

Canadians having defined benefit pensions provided by their employers. These developments are elaborated in Chapter 3.

We now turn to a seventh and final theme. Whether it is one of the factors associated with the erosion of government responsibility for social policy is unclear. But it is an important historic theme all the same. The third sector, civil society, or voluntary sector has also been transformed in this period—taking on, arguably, an increasing presence (Rice & Prince, 2000). Between 1900 and 1940, as Bettina Liverant points out, philanthropic structures "came to be structured along corporate/professional models, with a new insistence that charities be well managed, fiscally responsible, and scientific in approach" (p. 191). After World War II, philanthropy and corporate capitalism were increasingly intertwined. "Donations programs were brought into the management structure with formal applications processes, administrative mechanisms, selection criteria, and a set funding cycle. Methods of giving broadened to include donations, sponsorships, gifts-in-kind, cause-related marketing, and organized employee volunteerism" (p. 193). Moreover, the private sector gradually saw its role grow in the social milieu. "The logic of investment became increasingly explicit, with programs strategically developed to contribute to company profits or offset public relations problems. Corporate philanthropy evolved from a discretionary to an expected practice, offering visible testimony of business commitment to social responsibility" (Liverant, 2009, p. 193). Social giving, and corporate public relations, are in this sense closely—and obviously—intertwined.

By the 1970s, as one observer notes, "representative voluntary organizations were being accepted as important vehicles to help citizens advocate for social rights and to enhance the fairness of the democratic process" (Elson, 2011, p. 60). Whether it was the National Action Committee on the Status of Women (established 1971 and largely funded by the federal government until the 1980s), through to the Pembina Institute (established 1985): organizations were increasingly involved in the social and political facets of Canadian life. The National Advisory Committee on Voluntary Action (established 1974) and the Coalition of National Voluntary Organizations (formed the same year), provided an increasing degree of coherence across the third sector (Elson, 2011, p. 61). Various reports were increasingly critical of government bureaucracy, and the People in Action Report (1977), the Broadbent Report (1999) and the Canadian Centre for Philanthropy (2002) each called for changes in the definition of charities, many calling for tax-exempt status for those third sector organizations that advocated politically (Elson, 2011, p. 49). While the above organizations have longevity, many civil society organizations come and go. A process of "deliberate relations" has been established by some, in which joint meetings are held with third sector and provincial/territorial representatives. At the second such national meeting, occurring in 2009, most of the third sector organizations were less than 10 years old (Elson, 2011, p. 157). Fluidity, dynamism, and change are the obvious norms.

According to Statistics Canada, "in 2013, 44% of Canadians volunteered their time and almost twice as many (82%) gave money to a charitable or non-profit organization—rates that have been relatively consistent for the past several years. Moreover, the overall impact of community volunteering is quite high." "In 2013, volunteers devoted almost 2 billion hours to their volunteer activities, or the equivalent of about 1 million full-time jobs." "The average annual amount" of charitable donations "per donor in 2013 was $531," and "Canadians gave $12.8 billion to charitable or non-profit organizations in 2013, 41% of which going to religious organizations, 13% to the health sector, and 12% to social service institutions" (Statistics Canada, 2015a). Another important source of funding for the third sector is foundations. Among Canada's foundations—not unlike contemporary capitalism itself—there are enormous concentrations of wealth. A recent survey found that the country's 150 largest foundations had assets of $18.7 billion, and that the largest six of these constituted nearly 50% of that total (Imagine Canada, 2014, p. 2). All told, however, there have been considerable governmental cutbacks in supporting certain third sector roles, particularly involving what a given government might deem overly political (i.e., with an agenda contrary to the government's intentions). The National Action Committee on the Status of Women, established in 1971, experienced considerable cuts during the Conservative government of Brian Mulroney, and still further cuts during the Liberal regime of Jean Chrétien that followed.

As for volunteers, an increasing proportion, 28% in 2013, was 55 or older. As Statistics Canada notes, "the typical donor is also getting older. In 2013, 35% of all donors were aged 55 and over, up from 29% in 2004." Not surprisingly, given the concentration of wealth among older cohorts, older donors give more than other age categories, on average. It is estimated that there are more than 170 000 charities and non-profit organizations in Canada (Imagine Canada, 2015). "With over 170 000 charitable and nonprofit organizations in Canada (85 000 of these are registered charities), the charitable and nonprofit sector contributes an average of 8.1% of total Canadian GDP". The scope of impact overall is considerable. "That's more than the retail trade industry and close to the value of the mining, oil and gas extraction industry." The sector generates $176 billion in income, employs two million people and accounts for more than 8% of Canada's GDP (Imagine Canada, 2015).

The non-profit sector depends on receiving income from a variety of sources. The total income for the charitable and nonprofit sectors in 2012 amounted to $176 billion. In the most current breakdown of income sources, Statistics Canada found that in 2008 sales of goods and services accounted for 45.1 percent of total income while government transfers were also significant at 20.9 percent; membership fees accounted for 17.1 percent, and donations from households accounted for 11.2 percent (Imagine Canada, 2014b). Statistics Canada reported that businesses contributed a mere 2.1 percent of the total income received by the non-profit sector in 2008 and that investment income comprised only 3.6 percent (Imagine Canada, 2014). But between 1994 and 2014, the number of public foundations has grown by 76% (to 5300), and private foundations by 69% (to 5100) (Imagine Canada 2014, p. 1).

CONCLUSION

As this chapter demonstrates, the historical experience is profoundly important in shaping the current nature of social policies. To best understand the present, social work students need to learn about the past and to have some commensurate appreciation of the future prospects of social policies. The next chapter, which emphasizes ideological, political, social, and economic aspects of Canadian social policies, will help you to better appreciate the contexts in which social policies are conceived, carried out, and changed.

Chapter 3
Contemporary Social Policy Structures

This chapter examines some major social policy structures in Canada. As discussed in Chapter 2, between the mid-1940s and the mid-1970s, Canada could have been considered a welfare state. But up to and after the early 1990s, so much retrenchment has occurred that some would describe Canada today as a post-welfare or (as described in Chapter 2, market-) state. The welfare state refers to those governments that commit themselves to the development of social policies for the collective well-being of all. This commitment occurs via social policy structures, and the following pages outline several directions these commitments can take. Despite the welfare state's decline, governments remain important to the funding and delivery of social policies. Albeit, local community-based organizations (such as nonprofits and other forms of collective association) have taken on an increasing role in the interpretation and application of these social policies. Armitage (2003) outlines seven types of programs and services; some are offered through government structures and others by non-government structures—including the non-profit and voluntary sector and the private sector:

1. cash programs, such as Old Age Security, Canada Child Tax Benefit, Canada Pension Plan, and postsecondary student loans;

2. fiscal measures, including tuition-fee deductions, child-care expense deductions, and RRSP exemptions;

3. goods and services measures, such as hospital insurance, legal aid, and education;

4. measures related to employment, including minimum-wage legislation and employment equity programs;

5. occupational welfare measures, such as pension and insurance plans, and sports and recreational facilities;

6. family care and dependency programs, such as home-care provisions; and

7. voluntary/charitable programs, such as shelters, soup kitchens, and food banks.

Governments, we stress, do not use revenues solely to help individuals and families. We hasten to add that there are innumerable governmental programs that are at the behest of the private sector: various monetary, tax, and other forms of incentives that governments provide to the private sector.

This chapter and the next touch on many of the governmental components, particularly income security. The chapter first introduces the political and fiscal arrangements in Canada that make contemporary welfare-state institutions possible. It then focuses on income security programs and concludes by discussing several related, emerging social policy issues in Canada.

But we need to stress, too, the enduring importance of what is called the "third sector," or "civil society": those voluntary civic and social organizations and institutions that fall between the private sector of companies and the public sector. These include advocacy groups and networks, interest associations, local organizations, membership organizations, non-profit or not-for-profit organizations (either with or without charitable status), people's organizations, quasi–non-governmental organizations, self-help organizations, and volunteer organizations (Lewis & Kanji, 2009, p. 9). Civil society can include things that occur both seemingly without traditional institutional structures and through the social media via Twitter, Facebook, blogs, and the Internet (Shirky, 2008). Social media activists can be responsible for many significant political phenomena, including, for example, the 2010 election in Calgary of Canada's first Muslim mayor. Major social and economic trends are likewise influenced by social media. In all instances, civil society is responsible for a vast array of social change through the development and implementation of socially innovative initiatives (Shier & Handy, 2015a).

Also noteworthy is the rise of social entrepreneurship: a response to a social problem by using the principles of entrepreneurship to organize, fund, and administer an institution, which can be either for-profit or not-for-profit (Bornstein & Davis, 2010). Its advocates can be extraordinarily confident of its impacts and derisive of what might be deemed "traditional," including governmental, means of responding to social need. "For social entrepreneurs, the bottom line is to maximize some form of social impact, usually by addressing an urgent need that is being mishandled, overlooked, or ignored by other institutions. . . . Unlike governmental efforts, it flows from the bottom up" (Bornstein & Davis, 2010, p. 30). Social entrepreneurs "can recruit talented executives more easily than government . . . because nobody has to worry about being attacked in the press for joining a citizen organization. (Many executives cringe at the thought of putting themselves forward for high-level governmental posts)" (Bornstein & Davis, 2010, pp. 34, 36). Such things as charter schools, microfinance, and independent living centres can be attributed to the efforts of social entrepreneurs. Through notions of social innovation and social entrepreneurship, citizens (including social work professionals) become active participants in shaping social policy structures at the local level.

Over the past several decades, a further development has been consolidated, that of "corporate social responsibility," wherein the private sector sponsors activities in the social services through either cash donations or employee volunteerism, and often with the explicit understanding that the corporation will be widely acknowledged as a sponsor (thus deriving recognition for its work). Internet and social media-based breakthroughs are now prevalent: for example, innovative idea generation and publicity through crowdsourcing; fundraising, advocacy, community organization or all three through the Internet and other social media. These tactics have massively transformed the scope and impact of civil society activities on social policy in Canada. These topics (i.e., social innovation, social entrepreneurship, and corporate social responsibility) and their relationship to contemporary social welfare and social policy in Canada and social work practice will be discussed in further detail in Chapters 5 and 7.

FISCAL AND POLITICAL ARRANGEMENTS IN THE CANADIAN STATE

The Context

Most of the world's countries are unitary; that is, political power is centralized in one central or national level of government. Canada is among the world's approximately 26 countries that are federal states; political power in Canada is divided between a central or national level of government and several provincial levels of government. Canada has 10 provinces, as well as three territories: the Northwest Territories, Yukon Territory, and Nunavut. The provinces have clearly defined jurisdiction areas and tend to have large governments. The territories do not have the constitutionally prescribed autonomy that provinces have; each is governed by the federal government and by territorial governments that have been delegated authority. Since the 1970s, the federal government, through the Minister of Indian and Northern Affairs Canada, has increasingly devolved responsibilities to territorial legislatures. Similarly, Aboriginal peoples have assumed either delegated or inherent powers to raise revenues and deliver services to people living on reserves.

The Canadian Constitution defines the framework for working out social policy within the federal political system by giving both the national and the provincial governments' sovereign yet interdependent jurisdictions. As a pre–welfare-state document, the Constitution (known as the *British North America Act* in 1867) was not entirely clear whether the federal or provincial governments were responsible for social welfare. Sections 91 through 95 of the Constitution outline the main division of powers and responsibilities; powers not expressly given to the provinces were to remain the domain of the federal government (Irving, 1987). Only a few social issues are mentioned at all. Under section 91, the federal government has jurisdiction over quarantine and marine hospitals, penitentiaries, and Aboriginal peoples; section 92 makes provincial governments responsible for building and maintaining hospitals, asylums, charities, and public or reformatory prisons (Chappell, 1997, p. 80).

Over several decades, major legal decisions tended to place social welfare under provincial rather than federal jurisdiction (Irving, 1987; Thomlison & Bradshaw, 1999). Irving (1987) suggests two reasons for these decisions. First, the Great Depression highlighted the imbalance between community-based social welfare initiatives and the ability of local communities to pay for these; for this reason, responsibility for social welfare moved to the provinces. Second, the courts began to interpret the provinces' property and civil rights responsibilities as a mandate to deal with social problems; and the federal government, in contrast, was mandated responsibility for those issues not directly associated with social problems, namely "peace, order, and good government." Thus, responsibility for social welfare, healthcare, and employment services came to be principally under provincial control.

Many social policies, such as Unemployment Relief in the 1930s, were historically delivered at the municipal or local level of government. In some regions, local governments continue to be responsible or co-responsible for the funding and delivery of social assistance, supported housing, home care, daycare, and other services. Types of Canadian local governments include cities, towns, villages, and municipalities (which range from rural municipalities to regional and metropolitan governments that serve major urban areas). Under the Constitution, local governments are creations of the provinces;

provincial governments can create or disband them, as recent amalgamations of such major urban centres as Toronto, Ottawa, and Montreal illustrate. Municipal powers are set out by provincial legislation often known as the Municipal Act, the Local Government Act, the Cities and Towns Act, or a similar name. Local governments, like their provincial and federal counterparts, are democratically accountable; legislation determines cycles of municipal elections of mayors, councillors, or their equivalents. Local councils make and carry out policies and receive revenue, principally through municipal taxes on real property and grants from provincial governments.

In addition to receiving transfers from provincial governments, local governments also receive specific-purpose transfers from the federal government, usually for infrastructure and transportation services. In both cases, the higher level of government tends simply to impose specific rates and amounts, rather than negotiating, in the way that federal and provincial governments negotiate federal–provincial transfers. Just as the federal government has been criticized for off-loading responsibilities for funding major social programs to provincial governments, provincial and federal governments—particularly provincial governments—have been criticized for off-loading to local governments, without commensurate increases in cash transfers (Graham, 1995). Municipal budgets for social services have become constrained.

In 1988, transfers from federal, provincial, and territorial governments accounted for 23 percent of the total revenue collected by municipal governments (Statistics Canada, 2006a). Much of the 1990s was punctuated by drastic transfer cuts, as the federal, provincial, and territorial governments strove to eliminate their deficits. A recent study shows "overall poverty reduction effectiveness of the provinces declined during a decade of devolution" between 1995 and 2006 (Weaver, Habibov, & Fan, 2010, p. 80). Other analysts call for greater fiscal and administrative autonomy among local governments, to encourage situation-specific policy needs (Kwok & Tam, 2010). Local governments do not have the status or autonomy comparable to that of their higher level counterparts. And so municipalities rely heavily on provincial and federal transfers. Federal investment in Canadian cities increased markedly between 2003 and 2010. But, as the Federation of Canadian Municipalities notes, local governments' strong reliance on transfers from higher levels of government, and our current fiscal system in which local governments only collect eight cents of every tax dollar, "is not sustainable" (FCM, 2012, p. 1). Local governments are responsible for an array of services—from sewers, roads, transit, public libraries, parks and other infrastructures through to police and fire services, and the management of some social assistance, arts, and cultural services. Yet their principal form of revenue, the property tax, becomes less robust during economic downturns—as property values plummet.

Higher levels of government became involved more extensively in the Canadian welfare state over the course of the early twentieth century, with accelerated presence in the aftermath of the Great Depression of the 1930s: a decade in which municipal authorities were cash strapped, with growing social need and reduced fiscal room due to the perilous reliance on the property tax. As the need for health and welfare services increased across Canada during that calamitous decade, the financial burden became too heavy for the provinces and their municipal counterparts to carry (Graham, 1995). Most taxation powers resided with the federal government. A constitutional dilemma ensued: how to develop strategies for securing federal monies without violating the provincial jurisdictions of social welfare delivery. After World War II, in particular, with the rise of a more comprehensive welfare state, the federal government developed cost-sharing programs as a means of providing financial assistance for the delivery of social programs by the provinces and the territories. These arrangements facilitated the development of our current social policies. Federal powers, such as the responsibility for public debt and property and the ability to raise monies by taxation, were important for supporting social policies. Through the spending power of the federal parliament, social welfare transfer monies became available to the provinces and the territories without changing much of the original constitutional jurisdiction.

Note that not all social programs are cost-shared and provincially delivered, as the following pages will show. Several, such as Employment Insurance, are federally administered and employer–employee funded.

The Fiscal Context

Intergovernmental finance refers to the web of financial flows that link governments in a federal system. Since the federal government has especially comprehensive tax-raising capacities, a considerable portion of intergovernmental finance involves federal-to-provincial transfers; provincial-to-municipal transfers and federal-to-municipal transfers also occur.

The literature often refers to seven types of transfers (also noted in the glossary at the end of this book). Some intergovernmental grants are *block grants* (or general-purpose grants), while others are *specific-purpose grants*. A block grant is a cash transfer provided by one level of government to another, the amount of the transfer being fixed independently of the purpose to which the funds are put. Its opposite is a specific-purpose grant, the amount of which is tied to its intended purpose. An example would be a matched or shared-cost program.

Thirdly, there are unconditional grants, or *equalization payments*, which require no particular commitment by the recipient government to tie the grant to an expected type of expenditure. Equalization payments are intended to address two types of imbalances. The first is a *horizontal imbalance* between provinces—differences in fiscal capacity between "richer" and "poorer" provinces. The second is a *vertical imbalance*—differences in fiscal capacity between the federal government and a particular province. *Fiscal capacity* refers to a particular level of government's ability to change the total or composition of its revenues (e.g., taxes) or expenditures (e.g., social programs). The final type of transfer is a *conditional grant*, which is tied directly to an expected type of service delivery. An example of a conditional grant is the Canada Assistance Plan (1966–1996), which provided federal transfers to provincial governments to cover the provincial delivery of health, education, and social services.

Horizontal imbalances between provinces can be addressed in two ways. First, the federal government can take over a particular responsibility. For example, Unemployment Insurance was inaugurated in 1941 as a federal, rather than a provincial, social program. A second way of addressing a horizontal imbalance is the direct transfer of federal monies to a province, via either an unconditional grant (equalization payment) or a conditional grant. Vertical imbalances are usually addressed through equalization payments from the federal government to "poorer" provinces.

As indicated in Figure 3.1, in the 2015–16 fiscal year, the federal government transferred roughly $68 billion to provincial and territorial governments, which included

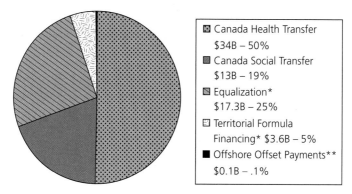

Figure 3.1 Total Federal Transfers, 2015–16 $63.8 Billion to Provinces and Territories

Notes:

* Includes payments, additional amounts and data revisions.

** Offshore Offset Payments include cash amounts from the 1985 and 1986 Accords and cash and national amounts from the 2005 Arrangements. Include $37 million in 2015-16 in 2005 Arrangements.

Source: Department of Finance Canada. *Federal support to provinces and territories.* Copyright © 2015 by Department of Finance Canada. Used by permission of Department of Finance Canada.

$34 billion for the Canada Health Transfer (CHT), $13 billion for the Canada Social Transfer (CST), $17.3 billion for equalization payments, and a further $0.1 billion for the funding of various other programs (Department of Finance Canada, 2015). This is an increase of $3 billion from the previous year. For 2014–15, the major transfers accounted for about 19 percent of aggregate provincial and territorial estimated revenues. Precise values vary by province and are more significant for less financially wealthy provinces than more prosperous provinces. For example, according to the 2014–15 provincial budgetary figures, federal support payments represented 33 percent of revenue in Nova Scotia, compared to just 12 percent in Alberta (Department of Finance Canada, 2015).

EQUALIZATION PAYMENTS

Initial arrangements for Canada's system of intergovernmental finance were set out in the Canadian Constitution and have been revised periodically as federal–provincial relations and governmental services have become more complex. The first formal equalization program was introduced in 1957 as a cost-shared program, in order to ensure that per capita revenues of all provinces—personal income taxes, corporate taxes, and succession duties—matched those of the country's wealthiest provinces, which were British Columbia and Ontario at the time. In the first of the required five-year revisions to these arrangements, the level to which these transfers were equalized became the all-province average, rather than that of the wealthiest two provinces. Also in this first revision, recipient provinces were guaranteed revenues equal to 50 percent of the all-province per-capita resource revenues. The system evolved during the 1960s until the present time, with changes to actuarial formulas for determining how to measure a fair transfer of revenue.

Such changes were generally determined via conferences of federal and provincial first ministers. But a 2005 critique describes it as a program with "reasonable origins" that has become "a self-propelling monster based on obscure calculations" and that discriminates against certain provinces (Naylor & Martin, 2005).

One of the more contentious equalization issues is a perceived disincentive for equalization-receiving provinces to develop revenue capacities. For example, the federal government would "claw back" in equalization payments the amount that a province such as Newfoundland and Labrador or Nova Scotia collected in offshore oil or onshore mineral production projects. Transfer arrangements were further adjusted in late 2013, infuriating provincial government leaders in Ontario, who anticipated a 3.24 percent reduction in the following year's transfer payments (Torjman, 2014). Yet the Constitution is clear that the federal government is responsible for ensuring delivery of reasonably comparable levels of public services at reasonably comparable levels of taxation to all Canadians, regardless of where they live. Depending mostly on population and natural resources, the capacity of generating revenue is vastly disparate across the country (Makarenko, 2008). This reason, to many, is the rationale for continuing equalization, in the face of calls for its modification.

Equalization has received further criticism. Alberta, at one time a "have" province, consistently did not obtain money through equalization (in fact, Alberta citizens have contributed greatly to the federal government to support equalization efforts), while other provinces such as Québec have gained considerably: in 2015–16, it was $9.52 billion—nearly double the 2004–05 amounts of a decade earlier (Department of Finance Canada, Federal Support to Provinces and Territories, 2015). Québec revenues in 2014–15 relied on federal transfers (equalization, CST, and CHT as we discuss below) for 27% of its budget, as compared to Alberta relying on federal monies for a mere 12% (Department of Finance Canada, Federal Support to Provinces and Territories, 2015). Some, in Alberta, might look to Québec's generous daycare policies, or its low tuition policies for students resident of, or born in, Québec and think that the "have" provinces such as Alberta are in effect underwriting Québec's largesse. Such are the political, and regional, dynamics of this one program. (And in fairness to Québec, other provinces such as New Brunswick rely on a still greater proportion of their budget from federal funds, and the territories are among the highest proportionate recipients of federal funding. The 2014–15 Yukon Territory budget, for instance, has 74% of federal funds as its revenue source; in Nunavut it is 85%.)

Other critics point out that provinces that receive federal equalization payments tend to have better health and education services. In effect, the argument goes, equalization arrangements disadvantage the "have" provinces. The Ontario Chamber of Commerce, for example, commissioned a report, which indicated that children in Ontario (then a "have" province that did not receive equalization transfers) had less access to regulated childcare spaces than did children in Manitoba, Québec, Nova Scotia and Newfoundland and Labrador. Its young adults paid more for undergraduate education than their counterparts in all equalization-receiving provinces except Nova Scotia. The province's senior citizens had access to fewer residential care beds per capita than recipient provinces did. And Ontarians with illnesses had fewer nurses per capita than all other provinces except British Columbia and "fewer physicians" per capita than "most recipient provinces" (MacKinnon, 2011, pp. 4–6).

The Canada Health Transfer (CHT) and the Canada Social Transfer (CST), 2004

Perhaps the apex of the creation of a universal welfare state in Canada occurred after the 1966 introduction of the Canada Assistance Plan (CAP, 1966–1996). The CAP was a funding agreement that enabled the federal government to cost-share with the provinces for the delivery of education, health, and social service commitments. The CAP was a landmark social policy, allowing the federal government to ensure minimum standards of service delivery and relatively equal standards of services across the provinces.

The CAP started to unravel in the mid-1970s, as reductions in cost-sharing arrangements eroded the amount of money transferred to provinces. By 1992–93, the federal share of CAP transfers to the country's three wealthiest provinces was down to 28 percent in Ontario and 36 percent in British Columbia and Alberta (National Council of Welfare, 1995, p. 7). The CAP had ceased to be a 50–50 cost-shared relationship. Many provinces, in turn, downloaded significant financial responsibility to local governments, such as social assistance, supported housing, home care, daycare, and other services.

The Canada Health and Social Transfer (CHST) replaced the CAP in 1996 and resulted in a 15 percent decrease in federal transfers intended for health, postsecondary education, and social services over the following two years (Scott, 1998, p. xv). In response, provinces reduced benefit rates for social assistance and other programs. The CHST therefore eroded enforceable federal government standards, leaving provinces free to allocate the funds however they wished—even if this meant substantial reductions in program entitlements and restrictions on eligibility and access. One of the country's foremost social policy think tanks, the Caledon Institute of Social Policy (CISP), contended that this change in enforceability "constitute[d] one of the worst mistakes in the history of our social security system." In fact, the CISP continued, it turns back "the social policy clock" to a period of minimal standards and far greater risks for society's most vulnerable (Torjman & Battle, 1995a, p. 5). A second CISP document warns, "There will be no guarantee of a safety net in the country" (Torjman & Battle, 1995b, p. 2).

This one piece of legislation—passed in the federal House of Commons in 1995—highlighted the extent to which social policy directs social work practice and affects the lives of many social work clients. For example, the federal government's CHST cutbacks to provincial governments for the cost-shared funding of health services, social services, and education had an impact on provincial government delivery of services, as well as on the relative role of each level of government (federal, provincial, and municipal) in social policy. One observer insists that the "relative power of the provinces over social policy" increased as a result of these cutbacks, as well as the devolution of labour market social programs, such as employment training, to the provinces (Battle, 2001, p. 16). Yet the federal government "dominates income security policy" and the provinces deliver "most welfare, social service, and health care" policies, depending on cost-sharing arrangements with the federal government (p. 16). As a result of new imbalances, federal–provincial fiscal and administrative relations were in "full evolutionary flight" (p. 16). But the funding of health and social programs continued to evolve. In 2004, the CHST was divided into two separate block transfer programs: the Canada Health Transfer (CHT, 2004) and the Canada Social Transfer (CST, 2004).

The CHT governs the main transfer of federal money to the provinces in support of healthcare, and the CST governs the funding arrangements in support of education, social services and social assistance, and child development programs. One goal of these two transfer programs is to provide greater spending accountability. First, the creation of two separate block transfer programs clarifies how much federal transfer money was spent specifically on each program area. Second, and of greater significance, the block transfer nature of these grants makes clear what proportions of the transfers are to be spent on each program area. While the new funding arrangements do not replace the restrictions and levels of accountability on provincial spending and program delivery that were present during the time of the CAP, they provide a greater check on government spending and program funding than was present during the period of the CHST.

In 2015–16, provinces and territories will receive $68 billion through major transfers from the federal government. These consist of the CHT and the CST, already discussed, and a system of "equalization," which is intended to even out fiscal disparities between richer and poorer provinces/territories in Canada (Department of Finance, 2011). These transfer payments account for a percentage of each province and territory's yearly revenue. For 2014–15, the total aggregate of all federal transfer amounts ranged from a low of nine percent of total provincial budget for Newfoundland and Labrador, 12 percent for each of Alberta and Saskatchewan, and 27 percent for Québec; to a high of 85 percent for the Territory of Nunavut (Department of Finance, 2015). The relative balance of participation of the provincial and federal governments, and the dynamics that create these ever-shifting arrangements, are examined in greater detail in the next section.

FEDERAL–PROVINCIAL RELATIONS

Canadian federalism has never been static. With the increased scope of the post–World War II Canadian welfare state, and with federal and provincial responsibilities for social welfare becoming more complex, federal–provincial relationships have become increasingly important to government and to the country's policy-making processes. Indeed, most of the important areas of contemporary social policy cut across loosely defined boundaries of federal and provincial jurisdiction. National policies can often be carried out only with some degree of provincial cooperation; and most provincial responsibilities rely on some degree of federal cooperation—in social policy, this "cooperation" often means the transfer of federal monies to provinces.

The Political Context

Federal–provincial relations take place in many arenas. They range from informal, sometimes daily, contact between federal and provincial civil servants, to formal contact that includes large-scale conferences of provincial and federal first ministers (i.e., the Prime Minister and provincial Premiers). Contact itself covers the widest gamut of jurisdictions—from international trade to fiscal arrangements to economic development. Each year, formal contacts usually number in the hundreds, while less formal contacts are far more numerous. Joint federal–provincial agreements are essential to many types of social policies, particularly in relation to joint funding arrangements.

The tone and nature of federal–provincial relations have changed significantly through history. Some scholars argue that the end of World War II until the early 1960s was an era of "cooperative federalism," in which federal–provincial relations were relatively cordial. During the late 1960s and 1970s, an era of "executive federalism"—as one scholar describes it—emerged: federal–provincial relations became more acrimonious (Smiley, 1976, p. 54). Several factors may have precipitated this changing dynamic. Provincial responsibilities had grown in scope and magnitude since the cooperative federalism era. In addition, during the 1960s, a Quiet Revolution was occurring in Québec: a renewed sense of nationality was propelling the Québec government to assert its right to withdraw from certain federal social welfare programs, such as the CPP (and to create its Québec counterpart, the QPP), and its right to modernize Québec's social and political affairs (Trofimenkoff, 1983). During the 1970s and afterward, Western provinces were likewise increasingly asserting their rights (Inwood, 2000). Moreover, federal–provincial constitutional struggles became increasingly visible, with more elaborate and formal federal–provincial "diplomacy": institutionalized first ministers' conferences and the creation of entire specialist bureaucracies to support these exchanges (Inwood, 2000, p. 129).

Several major attempts at re-establishing a Canadian constitutional framework over the past 30 years have had a significant, incremental impact on federal–provincial relations. In 1976, the Parti Québécois was elected in Québec; and in 1980, it held a provincial referendum on sovereignty association with Canada. Sovereignty association referred to the political sovereignty of Québec, with economic and other types of ties with Canada, including a common currency, a free-trade zone, a common tariff, and a court of justice composed of equal numbers of Canadians and Québécois to oversee this associative arrangement. The referendum was defeated by a 60 percent *No* to 40 percent *Yes* return. While campaigning for the *No* side during the referendum campaign, Prime Minister Pierre Trudeau promised to repatriate Canada's Constitution—then called the *British North America Act*, which was still held in London, England. In 1982, the federal government repatriated the Canadian Constitution and added to it the *Charter of Rights and Freedoms*. However, the government of Québec had never agreed to the repatriation process and refused to sign the new constitution. Québec's Premier, René Lévesque (whose government had lost the 1980 referendum), publicly expressed a feeling of betrayal of Québec by the other premiers and Prime Minister Trudeau.

In 1987, a new federal government under Prime Minister Brian Mulroney sought to induce the government of Québec to officially accept repatriation of the Constitution through the Meech Lake Accord, a set of new constitutional reforms. The Accord's five basic points, proposed by Québec Premier Robert Bourassa, included a guarantee of Québec's special status as a "distinct society" and a commitment to Canada's linguistic duality; increased provincial powers over immigration; provincial input in appointing Supreme Court judges; restricted federal spending power; and restoration of the provincial right to constitutional veto. Prime Minister Mulroney and all the provincial premiers agreed to the Accord on April 30, 1987, although the premiers of Ontario and Manitoba, several women's groups, and Native groups expressed strong objections. The Accord died on June 22, 1990, when the legislatures of Newfoundland and Labrador and Manitoba failed to approve it before the deadline. This led to a national referendum in 1992 over a proposed constitutional renewal (the Charlottetown Accord), which contained several provisions, including Québec's special status within the Canadian federation. The Charlottetown national referendum of 1992 was defeated nationally by 54 percent of votes cast. It did, however, receive approval in New Brunswick, Newfoundland and Labrador, Prince Edward Island, the Northwest Territories, and, by the narrowest of margins, Ontario. Three years later, in 1995, the sovereigntist government in Québec held a referendum on whether or not Québec should become sovereign, after having made a formal offer to Canada for a new economic and political partnership. This referendum narrowly lost by a vote of 50.6 percent against and 49.4 percent for.

Since then, federal–provincial relations have been relatively cordial, but Québec has remained on the periphery of some federal–provincial agreements. One example is the 1999 social union agreement struck between the federal government and all the provinces except Québec. Its goal was to improve transparency, accountability, and mutual collaboration in social policy, and it remains an important benchmark for current federal–provincial relations in this area (Inwood, 2000, p. 128; Federal/Provincial/Territorial Ministerial Council on Social Policy Renewal, 2003).

An excellent example of the spirit of intergovernmental cooperation is the Canada Child Tax Benefit (CCTB) program. The CCTB consists of the Canada Child Tax Benefit, which provides federal income support to all low- and middle-income families with children; the Child Disability Benefit, a benefit provided to families caring for a child with a mental and/or physical disability; and the National Child Benefit (NCB) supplement for low-income families (National Council of Welfare, 2001, p. 43). The CCTB is the culmination of a much-simplified federal approach to child poverty, blending several older programs (Family Allowances, children's tax exemption, and the refundable child tax credit) into one federal benefit. Moreover, it introduced new provincial income-tested child benefits to be administered on behalf of the provinces by the federal government through the income tax system (Battle, 2001, p. 40). Because of the joint nature of the CCTB, federal and provincial governments shared administrative data in these areas.

Some analysts assert that at the best of times, Canada's federal system creates a form of "institutional fragmentation" that limits the state's capacity to create social policies (Banting, 1985, p. 49). This drawback is precisely what the CCTB attempted to overcome. But there is a long historical legacy of fragmentation, as the following section on income security illustrates. Take just one example: child care. In provinces such as Alberta, the markets determine child care costs. In Québec, the provincial government funds a program that charges "$7.30 per day for families with incomes under $50 000, $8 per day on incomes of $50 000 or more. And on incomes of $75 000 or more, the daily rate will gradually increase to reach $20 per day on incomes of roughly $155 000" (Government of Québec, 2015). A survey of the percentage of income going to child care costs across 22 Canadian cities shows tremendous variance: Gatineau, 4%, Laval 5%, Montreal 6%, Winnipeg 15%, Calgary 26%, Halifax 28%, St. John's 32%, London 34%, and Toronto 34% (Macdonald & Friendly, 2014, p. 22).

The federal government is responsible for such programs as Employment Insurance, Old Age Security, and the Canada Pension Plan. Provinces have jurisdiction over social assistance and Workers' Compensation. These different federal and provincial roles, as pointed out in Chapter 2, evolved for historically specific reasons. We turn to these now, and conclude with some private sector programs.

INCOME SECURITY PROGRAMS

Canadian social policies cover a wide range of health, education, and income security measures. The present chapter, for purposes of brevity, concentrates on income security programs—that is, those social programs that provide cash payments to recipients. As

Chapter 2 emphasizes, prior to the development of a comprehensive welfare state in the 1940s and 1950s, Canadians living in poverty had few avenues of assistance. They were expected to be self-reliant. If, however, they had no options but to seek help from others, they would ordinarily go first to family, then to friends, and then to such community sources as a church or a charity (Graham, 1992; Splane, 1965). When these were exhausted, "unemployment relief"—the precursor to contemporary social assistance—was accessed (Graham, 1996c; Struthers, 1983).

In today's world, a far more elaborate system of income security exists, encompassing all three levels of government (and hence different offices with which a social worker might be in contact) and falling under a wide spectrum of categories. Different income security programs have been designed for the following, among other categories:

- lone-parent families (income support programs—the exact name varies by province);
- families with children (Canada Child Tax Benefit; Universal Child Care Benefit);
- individuals experiencing lengthy periods of unemployment (income support programs—the exact name varies by province);
- individuals experiencing a short period of unemployment (Employment Insurance);
- youth without guardian support (income support programs—the exact name varies by province);
- individuals who are injured at work (Workers' Compensation);
- people with a disability (income and health benefits programs, the exact name varies by province; or Canada Pension Plan; or Workers' Compensation);
- senior citizens (Canada Pension Plan, International Benefits, and Old Age Security—which includes the Guaranteed Income Supplement and Spousal Allowance programs; some provinces have top-up programs for the elderly poor);
- refugees new to Canada receiving Government of Canada assistance (Resettlement Assistance Program); and
- veterans of wars (War Veterans' Allowance).

Social workers need to be fully familiar with this system in order to help clients to identify the programs for which they are eligible and to ensure prompt and full access to these programs. The social worker's success may be of crucial significance to the client. It may make the difference, for example, between a client going hungry or having food, being homeless or being able to secure accommodations, being in despair or feeling hopeful, being trapped in poverty or having the means to better their standard of living.

SOME KEY TERMS AND CONCEPTS

There are two major forms of income security programs in Canada: selective and universal. Each has its own assumptions. We will discuss additional income security program terms at the end of this section, which includes comments about demogrants, social assistance, and social insurance.

Selective Programs

Selective programs have a long history, extending to Elizabethan poor relief in England, and were brought to Canada with European colonization. Unemployment Relief was a selective program, as is its contemporary successor, general welfare assistance, also called *social assistance, social allowance,* or, more recently, *income support* or *social benefit.* The usual form of a selective payment involves a transfer of money from a level of government to an individual. Eligibility for selective programs is based on a means test. Means tests are carried out to evaluate, first, a person's financial resources—such as income, assets, debts, and other obligations—and second, other criteria, such as number of dependents or health status of the applicant.

Selective programs are subject to several criticisms. One criticism is that they personalize problems of poverty, rather than focusing attention on broader societal structures that create the conditions for poverty. The economy is one example of a societal structure. Say, for instance, that a weak economy leads to the closure of a pulp and paper mill in a one-industry town. This external condition would cause job losses, leading individuals to apply for assistance.

Moreover, selective programs, critics contend, may stigmatize people who, through factors outside their immediate control, experience temporary or permanent loss of income. Selective programs devote considerable administrative resources to monitoring the lives of individual clients, rather than focusing on broader community and societal changes that might improve the opportunities of a client. Proponents, on the other hand, believe that selective programs are the most efficient means of targeting money to those in need. As well, some believe means tests may motivate recipients to return to the workforce.

Universal Programs

Universal programs provide cash benefits to *all* individuals in a society who fall into a certain category. They differ from selective programs in that eligibility is a right of citizenship, rather than an entitlement that has to be proven through a means test. The implications are several-fold. A recipient's level of specific needs, or economic status, is not taken into account when determining eligibility. Where selective programs focus attention on an individual claimant's worthiness to receive benefits, universal programs operate under manifestly different assumptions. The state expresses responsibility to provide income security for all citizens, and society implicitly recognizes the presence of conditions beyond an individual's control that may impede economic well-being. Stigma has little place in a universal program, since all people, regardless of level of need, may have access to benefits as long as they fulfill eligibility conditions (such as age for Old Age Security).

While universal programs may target money to a greater number of people, including the well-to-do, many argue that the income tax system can be used to counterbalance payments to the rich—and not the social program itself. In a progressive income tax system, the proportion of taxes paid increases with earnings; those with a greater ability to pay end up paying more taxes. In contrast, in a regressive tax system, taxes are not collected on an ability-to-pay basis. The most extreme instance of a regressive tax—such as a sales tax—is one that is levied across the board, regardless of wealth or income. How so? Whether a person paying a sales tax is below the poverty line or the president of a major bank, the sales tax charged remains the same, even though the poor person has much less ability to pay this tax. Canada's tax system is somewhat—although far from completely—progressive. Thus, higher income earners pay a greater proportion of their money on income tax than do those in lower income categories. Governments try to offset the regressive nature of sales taxes through refund cheques to people who qualify. Some people might argue that universal programs do *not* wrongfully direct money to the better off, given the existence (or potential existence) of a progressive income tax system and refund programs (Muszynski, 1987). But some argue that with everyone receiving benefits from a universal program, the middle and upper classes are politically co-opted into supporting the program. This means that benefits are less likely to be reduced in scope or eligibility than in a selective program that is geared only toward the less politically powerful poor (Titmuss, 1958, 1970).

Universal programs came to the fore during the World War II period. But they have eroded over the past 35 years, as selective programs have found new favour, with greater prominence of Conservative governments and neoliberal ideology. The reasons for these changes were elaborated in Chapter 2.

Demogrants, Social Assistance, and Social Insurance

Several other terms are used to describe income security programs. Familiarity with them is essential to social work practice. A *demogrant* is a cash payment to an individual or family based on a demographic characteristic (usually age), as opposed to need; an example is Old Age Security. *Social assistance* refers to selective income security programs that use a means or needs test to determine eligibility; these are often administered at the provincial or local governmental level, depending on the province. *Social insurance* refers to income security programs in which eligibility for benefits is determined by a previous record of contribution and on the occurrence of a particular contingency, such as unemployment, retirement, injury, or widowhood; examples include the Canada Pension Plan and Employment Insurance (Armitage, 1996, pp. 190–195).

MAJOR INCOME SECURITY PROGRAMS IN CANADA

Several levels of government deliver income security programs. These programs constitute part of, but not the entirety of, transfers to persons and transfers to governments. The following programmatic descriptions are deliberately succinct and simplified, covering major aspects of eligibility and benefits but omitting minor details that are too numerous to discuss. Many programs are not discussed because of the need for brevity.

Federal Government Programs

Employment Insurance (EI, 1996–) Employment Insurance was previously known as Unemployment Insurance (1940–1996). There are three ways to obtain EI: loss of job because of termination, temporary disruption of work because of illness, and application for maternity/parental benefits. EI is based on hours worked, rather than weeks worked—which is a fairer practice for part-time and multiple–job-holding workers. The entrance requirements have become more stringent over the past 15 years but continue to vary depending on job type and rate of unemployment in the region where the claimant lives. For example, in areas with high unemployment (above 13 percent), a minimum of 420 hours is needed, whereas in places of low unemployment (below 6 percent), 700 hours are needed (Government of Canada, 2015b). Furthermore, if a worker happened to be unemployed for a period greater than two years or was entering the labour market for the first time, they would have to prove 910 worked hours prior to qualifying for Employment Insurance benefits (Government of Canada, 2015b).

These restrictions have important implications. The first is the obvious disincentive for labour mobility embedded in the legislation. Where entrance requirements are lower in higher unemployment regions, individuals are less incentivized to move to areas of the country with lower levels of unemployment. Others counter that income security programs like EI are part of a community's social fabric, and that encouraging people to stay in high unemployment regions is often necessary in economic sectors that have, for example, seasonal work.

A further implication is the large percentage of jobless people not qualifying for benefits. In 2009, 49 percent of jobless individuals in Canada did not qualify for Employment Insurance benefits (Jackson & Schetagne, 2010, p. 2). Various people, such as the precariously employed (poorly paid, insecure, frequently without benefits), are particularly hit hard by ineligibility for EI in the first place. Urban Aboriginals are among the hardest hit (Fernandez & Smirl, 2013).

As of June 2015, the maximum EI benefits payment was $524 per week (Service Canada, 2015b). The program used to be funded by the federal government and employer–employee contributions but is now funded only by employer–employee contributions. Furthermore, the length of time an individual can receive Employment Insurance benefits is restricted, based on where an individual resides. The maximum time for receipt of EI benefits ranges from 14 to 45 weeks, depending on the unemployment rate in the region and on the number of hours of insurable employment accumulated by the claimant (Service Canada, 2015b).

Canada Pension Plan/Québec Pension Plan (CPP/QPP, 1966–) The Canada and Québec Pension Plans are insurance plans to which people must contribute during their working years. Both were created the same year and are similar in design; the QPP is administered by the Québec provincial government and is solely for people working in that province; the CPP is administered by the federal government and is for those in all other provinces and territories. CPP and QPP also comprise survivor's pensions for the spouses of deceased pensioners, disability pensions, children's benefits, and death benefits. Eligibility is based on past contributions to the plan; however, CPP retirement pension does not start automatically. It must be applied for. In instances of retirement (as distinct from disability or spousal death), it is paid to contributing claimants over the age of 65 (or 60 at a reduced rate) and is intended to replace about 25 percent of the income the claimant was earning while paying into the plan. As of June 1, 2015, the maximum benefits are $1,065 per month for retirement payments, $1264.59 for disability payments, $639 for spousal survivors' payments (age 65 or over), and $234.87 for children's survivor payments

(Service Canada, 2015a). The program is funded by employer and employee contributions at a combined rate of 9.9% of the employee's annual pensionable earnings. For 2015, the maximum annual pensionable earnings is $53,600 (Canada Revenue Agency, 2015c). The program is considered social insurance. "Workers in economic regions that had a higher unemployment rate were expected to retire two years earlier, on average, than workers in economic regions with a lower unemployment rate. . . . In 2007, for example, workers in the economic regions with higher unemployment rates, 9.7% on average, were expected to retire at 62.7 years of age. Conversely, workers in economic regions with lower unemployment rates, 3.9% on average, were expected to retire at 64.2 years of age" (Statistics Canada, 2015a).

Old Age Security (OAS, 1952–) The Old Age Security pension is a monthly benefit for people 65 years of age or over. It originated in 1927 as a selective, means-tested program but was transformed into a universal program in 1951. Because it is a universal program, employment history does not play a part in eligibility, and a claimant need not be retired. Those on an OAS pension pay both federal and provincial income tax on the money they receive. Those with higher incomes repay part or all of their benefit through the tax system. As such, some argue that OAS ceases to be a universal program, because of this clawback of benefits from higher–income-earning Canadians. As a result, it excludes many people from full entitlement and a substantial number from ever receiving any compensation. Moreover, clawback amounts have systematically increased since the late 1980s. As of June 30, 2015, the maximum benefits were $563.74 per month. As of July 2013, OAS can be deferred for up to 60 months in exchange for a higher monthly amount (Service Canada, 2015c). The program is financed from federal government general tax revenues and is considered a demogrant.

Guaranteed Income Supplement (GIS, 1966–) The Guaranteed Income Supplement was established to supplement the earnings of low-income OAS recipients and is administered under the OAS program. Eligibility is determined by need and may increase or decrease according to a claimant's overall yearly income. As of June 30, 2015, the maximum benefits are $764.40 per month for a single applicant and $506.86 for individual applicants who are married or living common-law (Service Canada, 2015c). The program is funded through federal government general tax revenues and is considered social insurance.

Spouse's Allowance (SPA, 1976–) The Spouse's Allowance was established to provide income to the spouse of an OAS pensioner or to a widow or widower. Like the GIS, eligibility is based on need, and the SPA is provided only to those within certain income limits. The SPA stops when the recipient turns 65 and becomes eligible for the OAS, or if the recipient leaves the country or dies. As of June 30, 2015, the maximum benefits were $1070.60 per month for a beneficiary married to an OAS pensioner, and $1,198.58 for a widow or widower of a former OAS pensioner (Service Canada, 2015c). The program is funded from federal government general tax revenues and is considered social insurance.

Veterans' Pensions (VP, 1919–) Those members of the armed forces who incur a disability during wartime (Active Force), peacetime (Special Duty Area), or other military service are eligible for the Veterans' Pension. The amount of pension is determined by degree of disability and varies accordingly; maximum rates for 2015 are $2,663.76 for the pensioner and $665.94 for spousal recipients (Veterans Affairs Canada, 2015). The program is funded from federal government general tax revenues and is considered a demogrant.

War Veterans Allowances (WVA, 1930–) This income-related program ensures a minimum annual income for wartime/peacetime service veterans who served in World Wars I or II or the Korean War. Eligibility is based on need and a minimum qualifying age of 60 for a man and 55 for a woman. Survivors' allowances are also available. As of June 1, 2015, the maximum benefits were $1,441.98 per month for single claimants and $2,186.99 for those living with a spouse (Veterans Affairs Canada, 2015). This program is funded from federal government general tax revenues and is considered a form of social assistance.

Resettlement Assistance Program (RAP, 1998–) Administered by Citizenship and Immigration Canada (CIC), the Resettlement Assistance Program provides financial assistance for up to one year after arrival to government-assisted refugees arriving to Canada (it may be extended up to two years under special circumstances). In many instances, funding may also be provided via cost-sharing sponsorship agreements between CIC and sponsorship agreement holders at the local, regional, and national levels. For instance, since 2007, more than 6000 Bhutanese and 20 000 Iraqi refugees have arrived in Canada (Government of Canada, 2015a).

Almost all newcomers to Canada are independent-class immigrants or are sponsored by others, such as Canadian family members. A small proportion of immigrants are refugees, defined as having "a well-founded fear of persecution in his or her country of origin because of race, religion, nationality, membership in a social group, or political opinion" (Government of Canada, 2007). RAP is only for refugee-class immigrants. Benefit levels are consistent with provincial social assistance programs and are intended to provide the necessary financial resources for food, shelter, and clothing. Various programs and services are available including: loans to help come to Canada, counselling and cultural orientation, and translation and interpretation. The program also seeks to provide opportunities for new Canadians to enroll in English or French language classes and to develop the means to secure employment (Government of Canada, 2015a). RAP is parallel to the Immigrant Loans Program, which is also intended to assist the resettlement process. Local, regional, and national immigration-service organizations provide hands-on transition assistance to help a refugee to secure housing, education, employment, and other services, and RAP is delivered in collaboration with these organizations. The program is funded through federal government general tax revenues and is considered a form of social assistance.

Canada Child Tax Benefit (CCTB, 1998–) The Canada Child Tax Benefit (formerly the Child Tax Benefit, 1993–1998) replaced the following three benefits: the Family Allowance (1944–1992) and refundable and non-refundable tax credits. Under the CCTB, the federal government provides payments to parents or guardians on behalf of children under the age of 18. Payments are usually made to the mother of the child if the child lives with her. The amount differs according to the family income, the number of children, and the children's ages. This program also coincides with comparable programs at the provincial and territorial levels; eligibility for those programs is determined by information provided for the CCTB application. The three main components of the CCTB are the base benefit, the National Child Benefit (NCB) supplement, and the Child Disability Benefit. The CCTB is tax free; and as of June 1, 2015, in all provinces except Alberta (which has a sliding scale based on the age of the child), the basic benefit can be as much as $120.50 per child per month for the first two children and only $8.41 a month for each additional child (Canada Revenue Agency, 2015a). The NCB supplement, an important component of the system, is a federal, provincial, and territorial initiative designed to tackle child poverty and is available to low-income families. In June 2015, the supplement provides $186.75 per month for the first child and $165.16 for the second child in families with an annual income of less than $25,584 (Canada Revenue Agency, 2015a). The Child Disability Benefit program provides a maximum of $224.58 per month for dependents with a severe and prolonged impairment in physical or mental function (Canada Revenue Agency, 2015b). The CCTB is an example of a formerly universal program (the Family Allowance) that has been replaced by a selective/income-tested program (the CCTB). Some commentators have been critical of tax benefits to the poor, claiming that money is not well spent. Recent research challenges this assumption. Compared to higher income families, low income families receiving child benefits spend more on education, including tuition and computers; on food, child care, transportation, and recreation. Moreover, there are decreases in expenditures on alcohol and tobacco—a finding confirmed in American research on income benefit receipts among expectant mothers (Jones, Milligan, & Stabile, 2015).

Registered Retirement Savings Plans (RRSP, 1957–) Introduced by the federal government in 1957, RRSPs are tax deferral instruments intended to encourage retirement savings. Contributions reduce a contributor's annual taxes. By the age of 71, individuals are required to convert their RRSPs to Registered Retirement Income Funds (RRIFs) and to begin withdrawing money from the fund (which is then taxed). Individuals may contribute money to their RRSPs up to the age of 71, and annual contributory room is determined as a proportion of annual income minus the remaining limit after a company-sponsored contribution. Contribution rooms from a previous year may be carried over into the next. Higher income Canadians are more likely to contribute than those with lower incomes. Moreover, many Canadians invest poorly within RRSPs (Mackenzie, 2014)—investing in mutual funds or other instruments that have high fees, profiting the financial and investment sectors greatly.

Pooled Registered Pension Plans (PRPP, 2013–) Introduced by the federal government, PRPP is similar to the RRSP. It is a portable, individual contribution plan intended to supplement the RRSP, and designed for the self-employed and for the increasing number of workers whose employers do not provide a workplace pension scheme. A recent policy report is critical of the PRPP:

- "Participation will not be mandatory;
- Contributions from employers will not be required;
- They will offer no relief from exorbitant investment management fees and unacceptably low returns; and
- They will not offer participants the option of converting their accumulated retirement savings into a lifetime pension" (Mackenzie, 2014, p. 7).

There is an intensely political nature to all social policies, income security included, and the tax system especially. The tax system is best understood as a mechanism that collects, and distributes/redistributes money and resources. The RRSP lowers taxable income, and has higher participation rates among higher over lower income Canadians. The program can be critiqued for not benefiting modest income Canadians and therefore for being a tax transfer from poor to rich people. There are other examples beyond this: further discussion of various tax credits (which reduce the amount of taxes one pays) and tax deductions (which reduce taxable income) will be discussed in Chapter 4.

Provincial Programs

Workers' Compensation (WC, 1914–) Workers' Compensation is designed to make payments to and cover rehabilitation and medical costs for workers who have been injured on the job. In the case of workplace death, it also provides payments to an employee's survivors. It was first introduced in Ontario and subsequently spread to other provinces. Assistance levels vary from province to province. Eligibility criteria are stricter now than in the past, and benefits have been reduced in scope. In Alberta, for example, benefits as of 2015 are 90 percent of net taxable income up to $95,300 (The Workers' Compensation Board-Alberta, 2015). In Ontario, 85 percent of net taxable income is covered up to $85,200 (Workplace Safety and Insurance Board of Ontario, 2015). The program is funded by worker and employer contributions and is considered a form of social insurance.

Social Assistance (SA, various years) Social assistance, often called welfare or public assistance, helps people in need who are not eligible for other benefits and is one of the most important income security programs with which a social worker should be familiar. It is typically delivered to three broad categories of people: families with dependent children in need (often this is long-term need), individuals with disabilities (often this is long-term need), and individuals or families in short-term need. These three categories may have different names and may be administered out of different offices. The last category—short-term assistance—is seen as an income program of last resort. Benefit payments help to pay for food, shelter, fuel, clothing, prescription drugs, and other health services.

Eligibility rules and amounts of payment differ from province to province and from municipality to municipality in provinces where municipalities administer and/or partially fund programs. Especially for short-term need assistance, means tests are common. Applicants must be of a certain age, usually between 18 and 65, but some provinces have provisions for minors under the age of 18 not living with a legal parent or guardian. Under certain circumstances, full-time students in postsecondary education may be eligible for assistance in some provinces but not in others. Single parents seeking assistance must have already tried to secure court-ordered maintenance and child support from the other spouse if they were entitled to it. Workers on strike are usually not eligible for assistance, nor are sponsored refugees or sponsored family-class immigrants during their period of sponsorship. In general, social assistance is granted if a household's net assets are less than the cost of regularly recurring basic needs for food, shelter, and other necessities.

Fixed and liquid assets are usually assessed in the application process. Most provinces exempt the value of a car, a principal residence, furniture, clothing, Retirement Savings

Plans that are locked in, and Registered Education Savings Plans. Other allowable assets—cash, bonds, securities that are readily convertible to cash, the value of life insurance—are limited by household size and employability. Applicants are usually required to convert non-exempt fixed assets into liquid assets and to deplete those assets before qualifying for welfare (National Council of Welfare, 2006b).

Benefit rates fall well below low-income cut-off (LICO) poverty lines, as indicated in Table 3.1. (The calculation of poverty lines is elaborated in Chapter 4.)

Table 3.1 Social Assistance Nationwide, 2013

	Total Welfare Income	Poverty Line* (LICO)	Poverty Gap	Welfare Income as % of LICO
Newfoundland and Labrador				
Single, employable	$10 876	$16 723	−$ 5 847	65.0%
Person with disability	$10 881	$16 723	−$ 5 842	65.1%
Lone parent, one child	$20 986	$20 353	$ 633	103.1%
Couple, two children	$24 307	$31 618	−$ 7 311	76.9%
Prince Edward Island				
Single, employable	$ 7 233	$16 514	−$ 9 282	43.8%
Person with disability	$ 9 501	$16 514	−$ 7 013	57.5%
Lone parent, one child	$18 172	$20 100	−$ 1 928	90.4%
Couple, two children	$26 690	$31 225	−$ 4 535	85.5%
Nova Scotia				
Single, employable	$ 7 076	$16 723	−$ 9 648	42.3%
Person with disability	$ 9 908	$16 723	−$ 6 815	59.2%
Lone parent, one child	$16 219	$20 353	−$ 4 134	79.7%
Couple, two children	$23 114	$31 618	−$ 8 504	73.1%
New Brunswick				
Single, employable	$ 6 807	$16 723	−$ 9 917	40.7%
Person with disability	$ 8 967	$16 723	−$ 7 756	53.6%
Lone parent, one child	$16 769	$20 353	−$ 3 584	82.4%
Couple, two children	$20 724	$31 618	−$10 894	65.5%
Québec				
Single, employable	$ 8 441	$19 774	−$11 333	42.7%
Person with disability	$12 250	$19 774	−$ 7 524	61.9%
Lone parent, one child	$19 413	$24 066	−$ 4 653	80.7%
Couple, two children	$25 166	$37 387	−$12 221	67.3%

(continued)

Table 3.1 (continued)

	Total Welfare Income	Poverty Line* (LICO)	Poverty Gap	Welfare Income as % of LICO
Ontario				
Single, employable	$ 8 224	$19 774	–$11 550	41.6%
Person with disability	$13 934	$19 774	–$ 5 840	70.5%
Lone parent, one child	$18 854	$24 066	–$ 5 212	78.3%
Couple, two children	$25 437	$37 387	–$11 950	68.0%
Manitoba				
Single, employable	$ 7 143	$19 774	–$12 632	36.1%
Person with disability	$ 9 742	$19 774	–$10 032	49.3%
Lone parent, one child	$15 117	$24 066	–$ 8 949	62.8%
Couple, two children	$22 000	$37 387	–$15 387	58.8%
Saskatchewan				
Single, employable	$ 8 901	$16 723	–$ 7 822	53.2%
Person with disability	$11 364	$16 723	–$ 5 359	68.0%
Person with disability - SAID	$13 978	$16 723	–$ 2 745	83.6%
Lone parent, one child	$18 976	$20 353	–$ 1 377	93.2%
Couple, two children	$25 171	$31 618	–$ 6 447	79.6%
Alberta				
Single, employable	$ 7 787	$19 774	–$11 988	39.4%
Person with disability	$ 9 988	$19 774	–$ 9 786	50.5%
Person with disability - AISH	$19 446	$19 774	–$ 328	98.3%
Lone parent, one child	$16 564	$24 066	–$ 7 502	68.8%
Couple, two children	$23 175	$37 387	–$14 212	62.0%
British Columbia				
Single, employable	$ 7 866	$19 774	–$11 909	39.8%
Person with disability	$11 470	$19 774	–$ 8 304	58.0%
Lone parent, one child	$ 7 329	$24 066	–$ 6 737	72.0%
Couple, two children	$ 22 041	$37 387	–$15 346	59.0%

* The poverty line used in the table comes from Canada's after-tax low-income cut-off (LICO), as reported in the Caledon Institute of Social Policy's publication *Welfare in Canada 2013*.

Sources: Caledon Institute of Social Policy's publication Welfare in Canada. Copyright © 2014 by Caledon Institute of Social Policy. Reproduced with the permission of The Caledon Institute of Social Policy

Provincial Top-Ups for Senior Citizens (various years) The combined OAS and GIS supplements are low enough to qualify most elderly couples in most provinces for social assistance. To avoid having senior citizens as SA recipients, some provinces have introduced seniors' income supplemental programs. Benefit rates vary from province to province and are intended to raise incomes of recipients to roughly the income levels of public assistance recipients. Not all provinces have these particular benefits programs. An example of a provincial top-up for senior citizens is the Seniors Income Plan (SIP), which, as of June, 2015, provided a maximum of $260 per month to single claimants and $225 each to married claimants (Government of Saskatchewan, 2015). Another program, the Ontario Guaranteed Annual Income System (GAINS), provides a maximum of $83 per month for a single claimant, an amount that has remained unchanged since before May 1, 2007 (Government of Ontario, 2015). Provincial top-ups for senior citizens are selective social assistance programs, funded jointly by federal and provincial monies under the CST.

Private Sector: Pensions, Health Care

Employee pensions, or employment-based Registered Pension Plans (RPP), grew significantly over the twentieth century. In the late nineteenth century, RPPs tended to be restricted to some employees in the federal civil service, railways, and some private banks. By the late 1940s, one in five workers had an RPP, and by the late 1970s more than half of male employees benefitted from the RPP. This proportion fell below 50% in 1986 and by 2003 it had dropped to 40%. Today's rate, 37%, has been fairly consistent over several years.

According to Statistics Canada, nearly three quarters of this decrease can be attributed to men's diminishing employment in high RPP sectors that are either unionized, in the manufacturing sector, or both. Meanwhile, women's RPP participation has grown, as noted in Figure 3.2. Part of this increase is due to the higher proportion of RPP-friendly jobs that women have held. In 1986, 36% of female paid workers aged 35 to 54 were in the category of professionals, managers, or holding positions in natural or social sciences; by 1997 that had increased to 42%. Likewise, in 2014 accountancy and financial auditing for this same age category of women rose to 56%, from 42% in 1987 (Statistics Canada, 2015, Pensions: The ups and downs of coverage).

All of this is big money. In 2014, the market valuation of all Canadian RPPs was $1.4 trillion. It is also big business. Of the 6.2 million Canadian workers who held RPPs, 83.6 percent are managed by trusteed funds, and the remainder are by insurance company contracts (Statistics Canada, 2014. Employer pension plans (trusted funds)).

The unlucky majority who do not have RPPs need to rely on a combination of other income sources, particularly the CPP, OAS, PRPP, RRSPs, TFSAs – as discussed and defined previously in this chapter and in Chapter 2. The latter three—PRPPs, RRSPs, and TFSAs—involve user decision making on private investments in either a bank account (with low interest returns), mutual funds, stocks, investment certificates, or other instruments (all of which involve the private sector and operate via a profit motive). Annual participation rates are not high. In 2011, 24 percent of tax filers contributed to an RRSP, and nearly 40 percent more people have TFSAs. RRSP contributions for 2011 were a little over $30 billion, which is just over four percent of the total

Figure 3.2 Percentage of Male and Female Employees with a Registered Pension Plan, 1947 to 2011

Source: Statistics Canada, Pensions: The ups and downs of pension coverage in Canada, 1947-2011. Reproduced and distributed on an "as is" basis with the permission of Statistics Canada.

available contribution room across all tax filers. Total RRSP holdings are $775 billion (Canadian Broadcasting Corporation, 2015)—which is 55% of the aggregate RPP market valuation of $1.4 trillion. Meanwhile, the total value of TFSA holdings nation-wide is $73.9 billion—one tenth of the total RRSP holdings, and a little over five percent of the total market valuation of the RRPs (Canadian Broadcasting Corporation, 2015).

In 2005, 60 percent of Canadians had purchased an RRSP in at least one year; the median value of that cohort's RRSPs is $25 000. "A smaller proportion of younger families (major income recipient [MIR] aged 25 to 44) than those in the years before retirement (MIR 45 to 54) held RRSPs (56% and 68%, respectively)" (Statistics Canada, 2015. RRSP Investments). The economic inequities are striking. Over 90% of families with after-tax income of $85 000 or higher held RRSPS, compared to 35% of families at the level of $36 500 or less (Statistics Canada, 2015. RRSP Investments.)

The financial sector administers and obtains enormous fees and profits from the bank accounts, mutual funds, stocks, bonds, and other instruments generally holding RRSPs and TFSAs. It stands to make great profit from any increased contributions. It is not surprising, therefore, that some affiliated with this sector might prefer an expansion of PRPPs, RRSPs, TFSAs, or all three—over any expansion of the CPP (the latter is publicly administered). In contrast, the Canadian Union of Public Employees (CUPE), among other centre-left organizations, calls for an expansion of the CPP from its current replacement rate of 25 percent to 50 percent (Canadian Union of Public Employees, 2015). That same rationale motivated the Ontario government to pursue the ORPP in 2015. Indeed, as the Ontario government asserted: "Two thirds of Ontario workers do not have a workplace pension plan. Pension coverage for younger workers is even lower—in 2012, only about one quarter of workers aged 25 to 34 participated in workplace pension plans, compared to nearly half of workers aged 45 to 54. A number of studies show that many people are not saving enough to maintain a similar living standard in retirement" (Ontario Ministry of Finance, 2015).

Another area of enormous profitability is the insurance sector. Ontario Blue Cross, part of a national network of not-for-profit health and travel insurance providers, had net assets of over $728 million and revenues of $272 million in 2014 (Ontario Blue Cross, 2014, p. 14). A second major provider of health, prescription drug, and dental insurance in Canada is the for-profit Sun Life Assurance Company, whose net income from all activities (including other insurance products beyond the above) across the world was $1.92 billion (Sun Life Assurance Annual Report, p. 19). These insurance sectors have their sights set on further expansion. So do their intellectual backers (Ferguson, 2007). The debate is far ranging—covering all aspects of healthcare, some of which, to be sure, are not covered by any universal national plans (such as dentistry, the provision of eyeglasses, the administration of certain health providing organizations, and so on). One area of potential government growth is in universally covering costs for prescription medication for all Canadians. An argument could be made that such a scheme—sometimes referred to as "pharmacare"—could lower overall costs, given the economy of scale in which the federal government operates. Indeed, as one observer remarked, "implementing pharmacare for at least the 80 most commonly prescribed generic drugs would save governments almost a quarter of a billion dollars annually, while allowing everyone who needs those medicines to access them at little or no cost" (Dutt, 2014, p. 1).

CONCLUSION

Income security policies work best when they are integrated with other social and economic policies and when they successfully address categories of people who are most in need. The disgraceful incidences of poverty among Aboriginal peoples, children, people with disabilities, and women, among other social groups, ought to compel more comprehensive and successful policy responses.

One of the dynamics of Canadian labour market policy is the minimum wage—which is determined by provincial legislation. A 2015 study shows that the minimum wage has maintained constant value, in real dollar terms, between the late 1970s and 2013. The proportion, however, of those receiving the minimum wage increased from 5% to 6.7% from the late 1990s to 2013, much of the change occurring after 2010. The profile of those earning the minimum wage is fairly consistent over time, with particular presence among the young, less-educated, and those employed in the service sectors (Galarneau & Fecteau, 2014).

In light of the poverty issues we discuss in Chapter 4, as well as the overall combined inadequacies of the income security programs we describe in the present chapter, further comments are now made on a living wage, and on a guaranteed income or basic income. Living wage frameworks have been developed for communities across the country, capturing the regional variances of costs of living, unemployment, employment, and other important indicators. Rather than being at a minimum level, a living wage captures what are the realistic (or normative) costs of living adequately in a given place (LivingwageCanada, 2015). Living wage amounts for 2015 in Calgary were $17.29/hour, in Regina $16.46/hour, in Toronto $18.52/hour, and so on (LivingwageCanada, 2015).

The concept of a guaranteed annual income (GAI), sometimes referred to as a negative income tax (i.e., the government giving rather than taking), has been in mainstream policy circles since the 1960s. In 1970, the federal government issued a white paper cautiously exploring GAI, and a 1971 national poverty report confirmed commitment to the idea. (Hum & Simpson, 1993, pp. 169–70). A 1974 agreement with the province of Manitoba led to a GAI demonstration project in Dauphin, involving 300 families, dubbed "Mincome". The project lasted until 1979, but with little immediate follow through (Hum & Simpson, 1993, p. 271). A 2011 retrospective study was encouraging: "We found a significant reduction in hospitalization, especially for admissions related to mental health and to accidents and injuries, relative to the matched comparison group. Physician contacts for mental health diagnoses fell relative to the comparison group. A greater proportion of high school students continued on to Grade 12. We found no increase in fertility, no increase in family dissolution rates and no improvement in birth outcomes" (Forget, 2011, p. 1). A further point bears emphasis. The GAI is much less administratively cumbersome—and hence less administratively expensive—than typical SA programs. Provinces like Ontario reconcile their accounts and payments to all SA recipients on a monthly basis—rather than the yearly basis that would occur through the income tax system under most GAI schemes (Stapleton, 2015).

These issues are all related to poverty reduction, and are examined in further detail in Chapter 4. But before discussing them, the following two chapters also examine some social, economic, and political consequences of social welfare (Chapter 4), as well as some broader contextual issues, such as globalization, social movements, social inclusion, and social welfare retrenchment (Chapter 5).

Chapter 4
Ideological, Social, and Economic Influences

Chapter 1 points out that the various definitions of social policy influence how policies are conceived and carried out. Chapter 2 shows that history is important in determining how policies developed into their current state (Chapter 3) and in determining their future prospects. This chapter builds further on the preceding three chapters. It considers the ideological, social, and economic factors that influence social policy development. After reading the chapter, you will have a better understanding of how such dynamics influence social policies—and hence how they affect the lives of social work clients. In addition, this chapter will help you to appreciate why social workers who are genuinely concerned about the people they work with are interested in such forces; and why, as a result, social workers and their professional associations ought to be continuously engaged in social advocacy leading toward social change.

IDEOLOGY AND THE POLITICAL SPECTRUM

Ideology refers to a shared way of thinking based on a set of ideas that reflect the values, beliefs, attitudes, and experience of a particular person or group. Ideological beliefs focus on the nature of the ideal political system, the ideal economic order, and the ideal social goals. Political ideology places a special emphasis on the role government should play in economic and social matters.

Ideology provides a way of interpreting problems and designing appropriate solutions. Ideological considerations are not the only factors that influence political decisions about social policy and social problems; but political parties attempt to shape social policy decisions from their ideological base. Individuals such as social workers also embrace particular ideologies because all social policy decisions influence the work social workers perform. Social policy decisions affect the funding and delivery of social services, as well as who will receive what services.

This section very briefly explores different ideological approaches to social policy and then relates these approaches to the way the major Canadian political parties think about social policy. But before beginning either, we will cover a few core definitions for terms that are key to ideology: *communism, socialism, liberalism, Toryism, neo-conservatism,* and *fascism* (see Figure 4.1). Note that there is tremendous diversity of views within each term; as a result, consider the following to be a short and necessarily non-comprehensive paraphrase of major attributes within each.

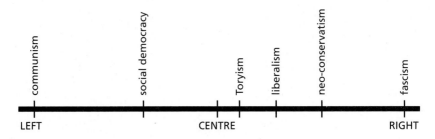

Figure 4.1 Major Political Ideologies: The Political Spectrum

The six political ideologies presented in Figure 4.1 are ordered along a continuum from communism on the extreme political left to fascism on the extreme political right. It is important to remember, as you read about these political ideologies, that they do not necessarily represent the Canadian political parties that may bear the same name. The Liberal Party of Canada, as an example, has some aspects that are liberal in ideology and others that are not. Though political parties may have their foundations in certain ideological positions, each party has been uniquely shaped by historical, economic, and social forces as much as by ideological values and beliefs. Those to the left of the spectrum have tended to emphasize an institutional perspective to social welfare, as discussed in Chapter 2. The neo-conservative ideology on the right end of the spectrum tends to emphasize the market state. Tory and liberal ideologies have emphasized both institutional and market-state perspectives, depending on the moment in history.

Because most political ideologies have something to say about the social unit of attention—the collective (society) or the individual—the following concepts, individualism and collectivism, and egalitarianism and elitism, are often used in ideological descriptions:

■ *Individualism* emphasizes the individual's freedom, worth, and self-determination in the political, social, and economic spheres.

■ *Collectivism*, by way of contrast, places the rights and welfare of the group or society above those of any and all individuals.

■ *Egalitarianism* is the belief that all people should have equal political, social, and economic rights.

■ *Elitism* is the organization of society around interrelated but unequal functional groups, usually with those in the political or economic leadership group referred to as the *elite*. Elitism is a hierarchical rather than an egalitarian organizational view.

The central organizing principles of each political ideology will be discussed according to its stance on such dimensions as liberty or regulation, equality or hierarchical organization, and individualism or collectivism.

Communism

Distinguishing between Marxist, radical, and communist perspectives is important; since each of these ideologies is based on particular assumptions, they should not be used interchangeably. As one author points out, "Whereas Marxist social work is certainly radical, the reverse is not necessarily true" (Webb, 1981, p. 145). *Radical social work* emerged from a variety of theoretical traditions that included labelling theory and new criminology (Webb, 1981, p. 145). Marxism, for the purposes of this chapter, represents a variety of approaches based on the writings of Karl Marx; as such, Marxism is one part of the broader rubric of communist political ideology.

Although the term *communism* has roots extending back centuries, as a contemporary ideology, it owes much to the contributions of such nineteenth- and early-twentieth-century thinkers as Karl Marx, Vladimir Ilyich Lenin, and Friedrich Engels. Communism often brings to mind the twentieth-century communist regimes of the Soviet Union, China, and Cuba (Krieger, 1993) and is a distinct version of socialism. Communism has become associated with a political movement directed by the working class to establish an alternative to capitalist societies and also with a societal ideal of egalitarianism.

The focus of communism is collectivism—that is, social ownership and control of lands as well as the *means of production* (the land, labour, and capital used by a society to produce material goods). State ownership and production is directed toward meeting human need rather than for profit, as in a capitalist state. Communism assumes that citizens will regard themselves as co-owners of the means of production, acknowledge their true needs and the needs of fellow citizens, and work diligently to produce what is necessary to accomplish these ends (Krieger, 1993; Marchak, 1988). According to some communists, these goals have to be organized under a dictatorship of the proletariat; for example, during the Russian Revolution, the Communist Party assumed political control in Russia without democratic elections and created a classless, communist society. In summary, the core ideological principles of communism are a highly communal and egalitarian social and economic order (Chappell, 2006).

The Communist Party of Canada was founded in 1921, preceded by various activities within trade unions, collectives, and former political organizations, such as the Socialist Party of Canada (British Columbia, founded 1904). Until 1937, the Communist Party was illegal under the Canadian Criminal Code, and its members were persecuted. Party members took leadership positions in some trade unions and were elected to the federal legislature (Fred Rose, 1943) and provincial legislature (W.A. Kardash & Manitoba, 1941; A.A. MacLeod & J.B. Salsberg, Ontario, 1943), as well as to many municipal councils. One of the party's founders, Jacob Penner, served on Winnipeg City Council between 1931 and 1960; his son Roland became the province's Attorney General in 1981. The Communist Party (Marxist-Leninist), founded in 1970, espouses similar ideology to the Communist Party of Canada (Penner, 1992).

Social Democracy

Contemporary social democracy finds its roots in nineteenth-century Europe, which was strongly associated with labour activism and criticism of both capitalism and an unbridled free-market economy (Krieger, 1993). Social democrats believe that free-market economies cannot ensure the efficient and effective allocation of economic resources to meet the needs of all citizens. Most support the market economy model, but with some important state interventions; the degree of support for either may vary from one social democrat to the next. Social democrats often focus on economic issues, such as the ownership and regulation of basic or key economic resources. From this perspective, the state is responsible for planning, directing, and regulating economic sectors as well as providing social welfare services for those in need. In the Western world, socialism has most often become associated with social democrats as opposed to communists. Social democrats advocate free elections and democracy.

Unlike communism, in which a dictatorship of the proletariat without recourse to democratic elections may exist, social democrats limit the extent of state control to that determined by a democratic election process, and temper capitalism with egalitarianism through government legislation and regulation (Chappell, 2006; Krieger, 1993). Texts often cite Sweden and other Scandinavian countries as quintessential examples of social democracy (although there have been shifts to the political right in these countries); to some extent, the province of Québec retains some social democratic traditions more obviously than other parts of Canada. In summary, social democracy seeks collective and egalitarian means to moderate the effects of capitalist, free-market economic forces.

It is important to reiterate that these definitions are "ideal types": conceptually precise terms that have divergent applications in real life. While the New Democratic Party (NDP) in Canada is seen as a major locus of our country's social democratic ideas, there are many social democrats who disagree with the NDP's approach to current social, political, and economic issues, perceiving them to be too right-wing. These same criticisms may be applied to social democratic parties in other industrialized countries, such as France, Germany, and Great Britain.

Toryism

In the eighteenth century, conservatism was a movement to counter the liberalization of traditional ideals and the advent of egalitarian ideologies that threatened the status quo (Hoover, 1992). A "Tory" conservative ideology contrasts with American brands of "liberal conservatism" because it retains its British roots (Horowitz, 1970; Mishra, 1995). The traditional Canadian attitude of deference to authority is seen as an expression of Tory elitism (Horowitz, 1970). Toryism also sees itself as collectivist in an organic sense of society, because the ideal of social and economic hierarchies contributes to economic security and social stability (Mishra, 1995). Toryism's social "law and order" orientation contrasts with liberalism's individual liberty and freedom perspective. Marchak (1988) places Toryism as slightly right of centre on the egalitarian–elitist and the individualist–collectivist spectrum, but left of the neo-conservative position on these dimensions. Historically, the term Tory has been used to describe members of the former Progressive Conservative Party of Canada. But, as we shall see, political parties change; and today very few contemporary Conservatives are Tory. Some conservative thinkers in social work, on the other hand, have a great deal in common with their Tory predecessors (Thyer, 2010).

Liberalism

The ideology of liberalism evolved in the eighteenth and nineteenth centuries as a change-oriented perspective that emphasized individual development in a social, political, and economic order unencumbered by government restraints (Krieger, 1993). Modern liberal doctrine for many liberals acknowledges the constraints of capitalism and the free-market economy in the unequal distribution of wealth and its attendant status and power (Chappell, 1997). This realization has led to a tempered liberal outlook with stronger humanistic values becoming more prominent. The liberal ideology is strongly individualistic, though its proponents claim it staves off the extremes of the left and the right by developing policies that reduce economic and social inequalities (see Krieger, 1993, for a more extensive historical review). Nineteenth-century liberalism in economic matters was often referred to as *laissez-faire*, which called for no government interference in the marketplace. But liberalism has since moved from a belief that individual differences accounted for economic and social inequalities to a recognition that some government intervention is needed to facilitate equality of opportunity (Marchak, 1988). The extent of this intervention would be less, as a rule, than what a social democrat might advocate. The Liberal Party of Canada should not be confused with the ideology of liberalism described here. The terms *Liberal*, with a capital letter and describing the Canadian political party, and *liberal*, with a lower-case letter and describing the ideology, are not the same. Only *some* Liberals are liberal in ideology; others have social democratic leanings, and others are neo-conservative.

Neo-Conservatism

Conservatism recognizes the inequalities among people but sees differences as more important than similarities (Hoover, 1992). Neo-conservatism refers to the "new right"— the rejection of collectivist values and the return to laissez-faire economics, which advocates less government and a more minimalist position toward social and economic affairs. Hoover (1992) identifies neo-conservatives as "individualist conservatives," sharing much in common with liberals. More traditional Tories and "red Tory" conservatives accept inequality less willingly, whereas neo-conservatives more strongly revere freedom and personal initiative. Many policy scholars use the terms *neo-liberal* and *neo-conservative* interchangeably in the popular media. We tend not to, largely because of some neoconservatives' social views on issues like opposition to abortion: social views which may not be shared with some neoliberals.

Fascism

Fascism refers to a government or political philosophy that is typically totalitarian, extreme right-wing, and nationalist. Twentieth-century fascist political parties rose to power between the two world wars in Mussolini's Italy and Hitler's Germany. Payne (1992) describes fascism as an ideology opposed to almost all other political ideologies of the time—communism, socialism, and liberalism. The strong, radical, nationalist stance of fascism arose out of several forces, among them an intense fear of communist and socialist ideology, and a racist assertion of nationality. Fascism gave rise to a one-party authoritarian state that maintained an active control of the economy, but without socialist ownership of the means of production. Like communism, fascism is inherently undemocratic. Once a fascist government comes to power, it tends to ban open elections.

In addition, fascists embrace a radical collectivist stance (i.e., a particular form of nationalism, often racially and/or ethnically based). They place the interest of the nation or groups within a nation ahead of any particular class or individual. They also reject the egalitarian perspective of communism and socialism and maintain an elitist or class structure in society, *but* with the belief that the class structure should be subordinate to the social cohesion of the nation.

MAINSTREAM CANADIAN POLITICAL PARTIES

There are numerous political parties in Canada, and many that do not have representatives in federal or provincial legislatures represent theoretical concerns of interest. But for purposes of brevity, this section examines four divergent political ideologies as represented in mainstream Canadian political parties: neo-conservatism, Toryism, liberalism, and social democracy. Common to all the major political parties of Canada are some basic values, such as the inherent right of citizens to self-determination, a belief in democracy, and a commitment to varyingly regulated forms of industrial capitalism—depending on the political ideology. But among our major political parties, and indeed within society, principles of egalitarianism appear to be weakening, as liberal tenets of individualism gain greater currency.

It is best, though, to appreciate the complex, sometimes contradictory and divergent ideological base within the same party. Holding each party together and determining its social policy stance is a complex set of interactions among ideological, historical, economic, political, and social forces. Some scholars used to characterize the Liberal and former Progressive Conservative parties as governing by "brokerage" politics since the 1960s: this means that their respective ideological tenets held only a marginal place in decision-making processes and outcomes (Carty, Cross, & Young, 2000; Turner, 1995). But to some, ideology has become increasingly prevalent to Canadian political parties, with appreciable differences between the centrism of the Liberal Party, versus the neo-conservative nature of the Conservative Party ideology. It is important, too, to appreciate that the parliamentary and economic (political, civil society, business, media, and others) mechanisms often cause non-incremental change to party policies, some of which are unpredictable and some of which vary from issue to issue (Gormley, 2007).

Liberal Party of Canada

The Liberals, or "Grits," were part of Canada's political structure at its founding in 1867. Christian and Campbell (1990) characterize the Liberals as comprising two ideological factions: business liberalism and welfare liberalism. These party factions are held together by the common traditional liberal values of liberty and individualism. Welfare liberalism, on the one hand, places human rights above the economic rights of individuals. This type of liberalism expresses itself in the policies that impose taxation and other forms of economic regulation, as well as those that facilitate the development of social welfare programs. Business liberalism, on the other hand, interprets taxes and regulation as economic restraints to individual freedom. The business faction of the Liberal Party prefers minimizing government law-making and regulation, especially in economic matters.

Any interpretation of Liberal social policy must begin by assessing which side of the business–welfare liberalism tension is in the ascendancy position within the party. When business liberalism dominates, social policy focuses on costs and thus limits access to and reduces emphasis on universal programs. In contrast, when welfare liberals speak for the party, they emphasize universal access and standards in social policies. At these times, emphasis on the costs of *not* providing these services overrides concerns about the financial costs of providing them.

Conservative Party of Canada

The country's conservative tradition originated with the original Conservative Party (1867–1942) and the Progressive Conservative Party (1942–2003). The Progressive Conservative Party always had a wide spectrum of proponents. Those in the "Tory" tradition of eighteenth- and nineteenth-century England were conscious of the interdependence of socio-economic classes and were more open to government involvement in the economy and society than many liberals. This group was once so powerful in the party that the Progressive Conservatives were known as *the Tories*. Others in this party were stauncher advocates of the free market and individualism. In 1987, the Reform Party of Canada arose in Western Canada as a populist right-wing protest party, rejecting the "Toryism" of the Progressive Conservatives. Its presence split the right-wing vote, assuring a succession of Liberal Party governments in the late 1980s and 1990s. The Reform Party (renamed the Alliance Party in 2000) amalgamated with the federal Progressive Conservative Party in 2003, creating a new Conservative Party that came to federal power in 2005. At the provincial level, Progressive Conservative Parties remain in most Canadian provinces. The new Conservative Party of Canada, like its provincial counterparts, has strong ideological anchors in neo-liberalism/neo-conservatism. As a result, social policy proposed by the Conservative Party of Canada tends to promote reduced government involvement in social policy and increased reliance on self, families, and the economic marketplace. This approach has a lot in common with the market-state stage of social policy discussed in Chapter 2. A final point bears emphasis. Keep in mind that this entire definition emphasizes general principles only. For example, while it is true, on balance, that the Conservative Party of Canada prefers selective programs, some Conservative policies retain certain universal programs, as occurred with the creation of the Universal Child Care Benefit (2006).

New Democratic Party

The New Democratic Party is a social-democratic–oriented party that originated as the Co-operative Commonwealth Federation (CCF) party, established during the Great Depression of the 1930s, among trade unions and farmer cooperatives. It was renamed the New Democratic Party (NDP) in 1961. The NDP has ideological roots in welfare liberalism and is a reaction to the Tory hierarchical view of society. Historically, a collectivist but egalitarian stance characterizes the Canadian socialism portrayed by the NDP. Legal equality and equality of opportunity have been major features of its view of Canadian social democracy. NDP social policy tends to support universal programming, with broad access and a uniformity of distribution across Canada. To many party faithful, part of the costs of sustaining these social programs should be borne more prominently by corporate Canada. The NDP, like its Labour Party counterpart in the United Kingdom, can veer to the center ideologically – as some claim the NDP did in the 2015 election, and as others felt occurred with the United Kingdom's Labour Party leader Tony Blair, who was Prime Minister of that country from 1997 to 2007.

Bloc Québécois Party

The Bloc Québécois, a federal political party that elected its first leader in 1991, has had as its principal mandate the promotion of Québec sovereignty. In 1993, the Bloc gained the second largest number of seats in the general election and therefore became the official opposition (McMenemy, 1995). Although the Bloc has a very clear and precise political agenda, it has had support from diverse parts of Québec society. For example, it is currently centrist but has also had trade union support and other social democratic influences. The Bloc, whose political fortunes declined in 2011, is also closely associated with the Parti Québécois, a provincial political party founded in 1968 and also devoted to the sovereignty of Québec.

A final point on these four political parties bears emphasis. Political parties are elected at the provincial and federal levels to govern for a maximum of five years. Governments can be elected with a majority of seats (half the seats plus one) or a minority of seats (less than half of the seats but with more seats than any other party). When acting as a majority, a governing party can pass legislation regardless of opposition if all members of that party vote. For minority governing parties, any legislation can be defeated if all members of the opposition vote against it. Thus, minority governments often need to negotiate with the other parties.

THEORIES OF SOCIAL WELFARE

Ideology is the foundation of social welfare theory and the extent of programs and services delivered through the welfare state. Figure 4.2 illustrates the interconnection of ideology and social welfare by demonstrating, in general terms, the relationship between ideology and social responsibility. For example, at the left end of the political spectrum, there is strong emphasis on societal responsibility, which results in an institutionalized approach to social welfare. Alternatively, at the other end of the spectrum, individuals are challenged to meet their own basic needs, with emphasis placed on the development of social or human capital. A current example is the use of welfare-to-work programs: these programs emphasize the development of individual skills to create greater social capital. Social capital is defined as the attitude, spirit, and willingness of people to engage in collective civic activities or networks of relationships with people in their community and family.

As with any continuum, the political spectrum contains a wide range of ideological beliefs, each with a distinct interpretation of social responsibility. This discussion is based on Mulvale's outline of theoretical approaches to social welfare (2001, 15–29)—practice frameworks used within the social work profession. Adapting Mulvale, we have eight perspectives.

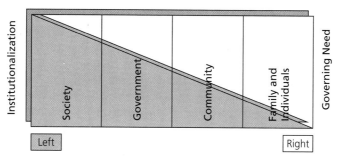

- Institutionalization of a particular set of social values
- Commitment to social justice
- Equality
- Universality
- Collective responsibility for individual welfare
- Support the principles of civil rights, political rights, social rights, and altruism

- Social capital creates value for the people who are connected (information flows, norms of reciprocity, "mutual aid", and solidarity that help translate an "I" into "we")
- Social capital emphasizes benefits that flow from the trust, reciprocity, information, and cooperation associated with social networks
- Undermining any necessary connection between government and the people
- Providing a confrontational and persuasive way of thinking about power
- Citizens must discipline themselves as theirs becomes a self-governing society
- Individuals become subject of government
- Earned access, possessive individualism, and utilitarianism
- Believe in "expectant giving" welfare policy: giving with a definite expectation or contribution from the person being assisted "hands up"

Figure 4.2 Model of Social Responsibility and Social Capital

The first, a social democratic perspective, assumes that the welfare state emerged out of democratic political pressures, be it via trade unions, political parties, or other social institutions. Often these pressures come from the left end of the political spectrum (Struthers, 1994).

The second perspective, premised on Marxist thought, deems the welfare state an instrument of social control; for instance, it forestalls class insurrection. Social welfare serves the needs of capital accumulation—ensuring, for example, economic growth and relative peace with labour. It also serves the needs of the state: post–World War II economic growth financed a burgeoning welfare state, which in turn kept unemployment relatively low; political parties were elected in part on their ability to help to facilitate these outcomes (Offe, 1984). Many Marxists believe the welfare state has contradictory purposes in meeting the needs of the state and of capital. Some, in fact, accept right-wing arguments that some welfare programs create disincentives for work and diminish profit margins (Offe, 1984). Most see the post–World War II universal welfare state as decidedly a thing of the past. As elaborated in Chapter 2, economic growth in the 1970s faltered and governments abandoned the principles of intervening in the economy. Consequently, "two legs (high levels of employment and consumer demand, both premised on strong economic growth)" of the welfare state became wobbly; the third, the government's commitment to social welfare programs, was weakened as a result (Mulvale, 2001, p. 19).

A third perspective, based on feminist thought, sees the welfare state as having profoundly reinforced dependency of women and children on the breadwinner male. Women are fundamental actors in social welfare: as the clients, reformers, and state employees of social welfare (Ursel, 1992). Yet the welfare state has been modest at best in meeting women's needs, and oppressive at worst in reproducing gender inequalities that arise within patriarchal structures. Income security programs, for instance, have been bifurcated into insurance-based entitlements for men and needs-tested, stigmatizing programs for women. Feminist theorists call for greater support for women in the workplace, the expansion of affordable daycare, and the transformation of income security programs to reflect women's needs, among many other measures. These concerns are elaborated in Chapter 6.

A fourth perspective is an anti-racist critique of social welfare. One writer describes the double process of disadvantage experienced by members of ethnoracial communities. Their less-advantaged positions on economic and social grounds make them more reliant on social welfare. Yet the welfare state treats them "on systematically less favourable terms than members of the majority community" (Pierson, 1991, as cited in Mulvale, 2001, p. 23). This perspective is also discussed in Chapter 6.

Fifth, a green critique sees the welfare state as "embedded in an industrial order"— meaning an economy based on growth that is no longer sustainable (Pierson, 1991, as cited in Mulvale, 2001, p. 23). Green critics assert that the welfare state is premised on an expanded economy that overproduces, depletes resources, and creates pollution (Payne, 2010). These concerns are elaborated in Chapter 5.

A sixth perspective calls for a shift in social welfare from compensation to empowerment. Rather than emphasizing individual deficits and providing an agreed-upon community standard, such as a poverty line, empowerment social welfare assumes that all people require help in order to develop (Drover & Kerans, 1993, as cited in Mulvale, 2001, 26–27). Central to this view is a critique of the way needs are interpreted and claims are made.

The market state, discussed in Chapter 2, challenges several of these perspectives— particularly the social democratic perspective and any others that do not adhere to individualist or liberal assumptions. The market state represents a seventh and important perspective unto itself. While many social workers do not adhere to it, some may; and many governments, particularly those of the right, do.

A penultimate perspective was honed in the late 1990s and the first decade of the twenty-first century by British Prime Minister Tony Blair. It emphasizes what sociologist Anthony Giddens (1998) coined a "Third Way" in that it attempts to combine market-state principles with social democratic principles. Giddens and a colleague at the London School of Economics, Julian Le Grand, advised Blair extensively, and Le Grand writes that the best solution for social services is to offer choice to users and encourage competition among providers (Le Grand, 2007). Others see choice as a Trojan Horse that could eventually lead to the privatization of social, health, and educational services by "piece-mealing it and starving it of funds" (Sadava, 2010, 29).

Finally, there is an approach to social welfare that emphasizes the third sector, or the voluntary sector, as increasingly important—and indeed historically the bedrock to state involvement in social welfare and the emergence of the welfare state. The third sector encompasses activities that are neither governmental, nor strictly private sector—and as this book argues, it is increasingly important to how social welfare is conceived, delivered, funded, and legitimated.

SOCIAL WELFARE AS A RESPONSE TO NEED

Social welfare programs may be categorized as functioning in one of the following three ways (Macarov, 1995a):

1. Intervention is made before a problem arises. This function of social welfare is perhaps the least addressed, given that scarce resources are most often used to address existing cases of economic hardship.

2. Maintenance is provided for at-risk individuals or groups, such as families with children, who receive various tax credits in the hope that they will not slip into the poverty ranks.

3. Social policy is directed at the amelioration of existing problems through such programs as social assistance. This category is the most commonly used. Governments and social agencies strive to develop clear indicators for identifying when personal economic troubles should fall within the realm of a social economic problem.

There is a great deal of debate about how to define the need worthy of social intervention, as well as how to respond to identified need. It is important to remember that there is a direct relationship between how a social problem is defined and its perceived solution. In this section, we will consider how poverty is defined and the solutions that these definitions imply. To do this, we will distinguish needs from wants, categorize types of economic need, and examine how benchmarks for measuring economic need that societal intervention will address are created.

Need versus Want

A four-part typology helps social workers to determine the exact nature of a particular human need. The types include felt needs, expressed needs, normative needs, and comparative needs (Chappell, 2006):

- *Felt needs* are defined on a personal or subjective level.
- *Expressed needs* are felt needs that are communicated to others.
- *Normative needs* are determined by someone other than the individual by applying a benchmark or standard to the individual case.
- *Comparative needs* are determined by comparing one individual or group to another.

Establishing the benchmarks for normative needs and the boundaries of specific social groups, such as those living in poverty, is of major concern for the creators and administrators of social policy.

Theoretical and/or ideological perspectives influence how social policy planners determine the nature of a human need. Psychologist Abraham Maslow's *hierarchy of needs*

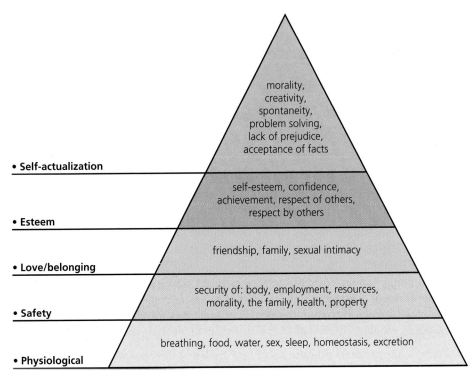

Figure 4.3 Maslow's Hierarchy of Needs

YAY Media AS/Alamy Stock Photo

theory (see Figure 4.3) is an excellent means of considering these distinctions (Maslow, 1954; Macarov, 1995b). Maslow's theory categorizes needs according to a hierarchy ranging from *having* (physiological needs) to *loving* (social needs) and finally to *being* (self-actualizing needs) (Macarov, 1995b). Maslow defined the basic physiological needs (i.e., food, shelter, and clothing) as essential survival needs. Social policy is most often directed at this "having" aspect of need. Maslow's theory is based on the principle of deficiency needs; that is, if a particular need is not being sufficiently met, then the person or group will seek to make up for this deficiency. This theory highlights a motivational element in meeting common human needs (adapted from Chappell, 2006).

Differential Human Needs

While Maslow's hierarchy distinguishes types of common needs, it does not address special conditions that create these specific needs. Macarov (1995b) identified five categories of people with special needs:

1. the *incapable*, such as children;

2. the *unprepared*, such as recent immigrants to a new country and those who cannot read;

3. *disaster victims*, such as victims of war or environmental situations;

4. the *unconforming*, or those who do not abide by societal norms; and

5. the *unmotivated*, or people who lack the motivation to meet their own needs.

All five categories are essential to social policies.

Besides common human needs and special needs, some needs are created by society (Macarov, 1995b). Institutionalized discrimination—along lines of race, gender, culture, or other areas of social diversity—may create obstacles to developing and implementing social policy. These include, but are not restricted to, lack of access to services, inadequate funding and representation in community-based programs, and ethnocentric values and practices in existing services and programs policy (Galabuzi, 2006). Discriminatory policies are examined in greater depth in Chapter 6.

Denying the impact of institutionalized discrimination affects the definition of the problems and, therefore, the anticipated solutions. This denial may lead to an interpretation of needs based on membership in the unconforming and/or the unmotivated categories mentioned earlier. As a result, social needs—for housing, income security, or other things—may be restricted or even denied to a particular person or group, because they are evaluated as deserving or undeserving.

As society changes, the social attention to needs may also change. Policy-makers decide how and when societal resources are directed at certain needs and when social norms dictate that social institutions other than social welfare (e.g., the individual, family, or informal social networks) should be directed at finding a solution.

Measurements of Well-Being

There are several ways to measure well-being. Measuring the strength of a country's economy by means of the Gross Domestic Product (GDP) and Gross National Product (GNP) is one. GDP is "a measure of the total flow of goods and services produced by the economy over a specified time period" (Bannock, Baxter, & Davis, 1998a). GNP is a more comprehensive measure, which includes "gross domestic product plus the income accruing to domestic residents arising from investment abroad less income earned in the domestic market accruing to foreigners abroad" (Bannock, Baxter, & Davis, 1998b). Unemployment levels are another measure; a full employment economy means that unemployment levels are 3 percent or less: anyone wanting a job could have one (albeit not necessarily a well-paying job). According to Vosko (2006), *precarious employment* refers to

> Forms of work involving limited social benefits and statutory entitlements, job insecurity, low wages, and high risks to health. It is shaped by employment status (i.e., self-employment or wage work), form of employment (i.e., temporary or permanent, part-time or full-time), and dimensions of labour market insecurity as well as social context (such as occupation, industry, and geography) and social location (the interaction between social relations, such as gender and race, and political and economic conditions. (3–4)

New immigrants and racialized groups are overrepresented among Canada's precariously employed (Galabuzi, 2006).

Table 4.1 Social Determinants of Improved Health

1. Don't be poor. If you can, stop. If you can't, try not to be poor for long.
2. Don't have poor parents.
3. Own a car.
4. Don't work in a stressful, low-paid, manual job.
5. Don't live in damp, low-quality housing.
6. Be able to afford to go on a foreign holiday and sunbathe.
7. Practise not losing your job, and don't become unemployed.
8. Take up all benefits you are entitled to, if you are unemployed, retired, sick, or disabled.
9. Don't live next to a busy major road or near a polluting factory.
10. Learn how to fill in the complex housing benefit/asylum application forms before you become homeless and destitute.

Source: Table from Social Determinants of Health: Canadian Perspectives. Copyright © 2004 by Canadian Scholars' Press Inc. Reprinted with permission from Canadian Scholars' Press Inc.

Several conditions related to precarious employment—such as job insecurity, excessive work hours, work–life conflict, effort–reward imbalance, and job strain—are also work-related determinants of health (Raphael, 2004, p. 97). The social determinants of health determine the conditions of a person's life. Table 4.1 lists other social determinants of health (Raphael, 2004, p. 13).

In 1990, the United Nations created a popular measure of human well-being called the Human Development Index (HDI). HDI is based on three indicators: longevity, education, and standard of living. These constructs are measured by analyzing the rates of life expectancy, adult literacy, enrolment in education facilities, purchasing power parity, and income. Canada often scores high; in 1992 and 1994 through to 2000, it had the world's highest HDI. In 2010, Canada ranked eighth out of 169 countries—following Norway, Australia, New Zealand, the United States, Ireland, Liechtenstein, and the Netherlands (United Nations Development Programme, 2014). At the same time, the HDI, like so many indicators, need to be looked at sceptically, since they capture aggregate population trends. Specific groups may have much lower rates of HDI: those who are preciously employed, unemployed, underemployed, and/or living in poverty, among others.

Another recent measure of well-being results from people evaluating the well-being within their own lives: subjective well-being (SWB). SWB is measured by personal perceptions of life satisfaction as they relate to, for example, one's moods and emotions and one's living and work situations (Graham, Trew, Schmidt, & Kline, 2007). Understanding well-being in this manner is largely individualistic, but it provides a picture of a wide range of conditions that influence a person's happiness. According to SWB, happiness is more than simply monetary gains—in contrast to the corporate message promulgated through the popular media (Graham, 2008). SWB has been used as an official indicator of well-being in such countries as France, and much empirical research is used via World Values Surveys to determine SWB levels within and between countries (Kingdon & Knight, 2007).

Conceptualizing and Defining Poverty

Perhaps the most important concept of well-being in social policy is the notion of poverty. The concept of poverty dates back to ancient times. *Poverty* is a state of deficiency in money or the means of subsistence. Welfare-state governments want to know how many citizens live in a state of poverty, and these governments are not content to rely on subjective assessment. To this end, governments and organizations set *poverty lines* that measure the necessary amount of money for living at a determined *standard of living*. A standard of living refers to the "necessities, luxuries, and comforts" needed to sustain oneself or one's family at a determined level (Barker, 1991).

Defining poverty with a poverty line means measuring the difference between *what is* and *what should be*. As indicators of an income level below which living would be seriously difficult, poverty lines may be set at absolute or relative levels. Absolute and relative definitions of poverty are based on destitution and disparity models, respectively. *Absolute need* definitions of poverty answer the question "What is the bare minimum (destitution) level in order for an individual or family to survive?" Writing for the Canadian Council on Social Development, policy analysts Ross, Scott, and Smith (2000) set an absolute poverty line at about $2000 per person per annum in Canada (6). Adjusting this figure for inflation, in 2015 the absolute poverty line would be approximately $2664 per person per annum. This amount is a mere survival rate that includes using all local resources such as basic provincial health care, community shelters, food banks, and thrift shop clothing. In contrast, *relative need* definitions are based on social values, rather than absolute needs, and start with a prevailing standard of living and then deduce the level below this standard that is intolerable to society. Relative poverty lines are concerned with what *should* be; they establish the norm against which an individual or family can be compared.

Normative Basis of the Poverty Line

How do Canadians define poverty? Table 4.2 summarizes major indexes for defining Canadian poverty lines, and shows that Canadians cannot agree on a definition of poverty. Statistics Canada's low-income cut-off (LICO) definition is the best known of these indicators. The LICO has been a standard since 1959 and is based on a 1959 survey of family spending patterns conducted by Statistics Canada. The survey showed that the average Canadian family spent 50 percent of its gross income on essentials: food, shelter, and clothing. It was estimated that any family spending more than 50 percent on these essentials was living in constrained circumstances, and any family spending more than 70 percent on essentials was designated as *low-income*. In essence, these definitions created a poverty line. In subsequent years, the poverty cut-off has been adjusted by using the same formula (i.e., spending on essentials for the average Canadian family,

Table 4.2 Measuring Poverty

Poverty Lines in 2012	Cut-Off Income for Household of Four*
Sarlo Basic Needs** (Canada)	$24 323
Montreal Diet Dispensary (minimum adequate standard)**	$25 212
Market-Based Measure***	Toronto: $39 084
	Québec community with population between 30 000–99 999: $31 821
After-Tax Low-Income Measure (Canada)***	$41 866
After-Tax Low-Income Cut-Off (community of 500 000+)***	$37 387
Before Tax Low-Income Measure (Canada)***	$47 208
Before Tax Low-Income Cut-Off (community of 500 000+)***	$44 340

Notes:

*A *household of four* refers to households with two adults and two children, or one adult and three children.

**Source: Sarlo, C. (November, 2013). Poverty: Where do we draw the line? Fraser Institute. Accessed August 14, 2015 from: http http:////ssrn.com ssrn.com//abstract abstract==2354442.Sarlo Basic Needs updated 2009: Montreal Diet Dispensary updated 2010.

***Source: Statistics Canada (2015). Income, pensions, spending and wealth.206 0091; 206 0992; 206 0093; Retrieved August 14, 2015 from: http://www5.statcan.gc.ca/subject-sujet/result-resultat?pid=3868&id=3874&lang=eng&type=ARRAY&pageNum=1&more=0

plus 20 percent). For example, in the *2013 Survey of Household Spending*, one-fifth of Canadian households with the lowest incomes spent almost 49.5 percent of their gross family spending budget on essential expenditures. Since 1973, Statistics Canada has also distinguished among five different sizes of urban and rural communities—the larger the community, the higher the LICO for any family (Statistics Canada, Income Statistics Division, 2010).

In 1991, Statistics Canada calculated a second poverty line, based on median after-tax incomes rather than the average gross income. This measurement became known as the *low income measure* (LIM). The LIM is based not on the proportion of income spent on food, clothing, and shelter, but rather on income itself. It is calculated on the basis of one-half of median net (i.e., after-tax) income, where median income is first adjusted for family size. Be careful not to confuse *median* with *average*: the median income represents the income that half of all income earners earn more than and half earn less than, while an average income represents the sum of all incomes divided by the number of income earners (Statistics Canada, Income Statistics Division, 2010). An after-tax index may be a truer standard than the commonly used gross or before-tax measures. Statistics Canada nonetheless continues to use its LICO measurement as the standard for assessing poverty. As Table 4.2 makes clear, the LIM approach and the LICO provide different measurements. The LIM tends to reduce the number of people in poverty by two or three percentage points.

Another measure of poverty is the market basket measure (MBM). The MBM is distinct from the other two measures discussed here because it creates a measure of poverty that is based on the actual calculated market costs of shelter, food, clothing and footwear, transportation, and other goods and services—such as hygiene products and furniture (Human Resources and Social Development Canada, 2006). The MBM includes a greater spectrum of necessary goods and services for living a decent life, and is also calculated to a specific community, rather than being calculated as an average applicable to all Canadians.

Defining the Problem, Defining the Solution In 1984, the Canadian Council on Social Development (CCSD) outlined the following four rationales for establishing poverty lines, all of which are still relevant today:

1. Poverty lines are needed to determine the number of people living in poverty. In Canada, the Statistics Canada LICO measurement is most frequently used to determine this figure.

2. Poverty indicators are used to inform and perhaps motivate those receiving and administering social service programs. This rationale explains why social assistance payments are set at a minimal level: to motivate people to view this financial program as temporary.

3. Poverty lines help to set the parameters of an accepted "market basket" (the amount of goods and services consumed by a family or individual over the course of a typical month). This market basket approach contributes to the development of only a few of the major poverty indicators, such as Social Planning Toronto's budget guides and the Montréal Diet Dispensary's budget guidelines of basic needs.

4. Poverty indexes inform future social policy planners, especially with respect to setting income security levels.

The various poverty lines described above can be pegged across the political spectrum. The conservative "right" of the political spectrum is represented by the Fraser Institute (also referred to as the *Sarlo measure*, named after Dr. Christopher Sarlo of the Fraser Institute) and Montreal Diet Dispensary definitions of poverty. This position asserts that poverty levels using other standards are grossly exaggerated. The Social Planning Toronto figures represent the "left" or social democratic end of the political spectrum, or a more social-justice or equality focus. Statistics Canada maintains poverty measures that are closer to the political centre.

It should be stressed that the agreed-upon definition of poverty is the one that Canadian society accepts. In the face of rising numbers of persons living in poverty, society ultimately has three options, none of which are mutually exclusive. Society can:

1. decide to leave more and more people behind;

2. find ways to distribute wealth more efficiently and equitably; or

3. hope to find ways for people to receive more income from their own efforts and work.

Economic inequality is a growing problem worldwide. A shocking one percent of the world's population holds 40 percent of its entire wealth, and 10 percent hold 85 percent of its wealth. At the other end of the continuum, one percent of the world's wealth is shared by 50 percent of its population—three billion people (Davies, Sandstrom, Shorrocks, & Wolff, 2009). The richest one per cent of Canadians now receives 12 percent of all tax-able income (Statistics Canada, 2015b). According to a study published in *Perspectives on Labour and Income*, the top 20 percent of families in Canada held 75 percent of total household wealth in 2005, compared to 73 percent in 1999 and 69 percent in 1984. The study was based on the results of the 1984 Assets and Debts Survey and the Surveys of Financial Security conducted in 1999 and 2005 (Statistics Canada, 2010c). The share of all income going to the richest one percent in Canada increased significantly between 1982 and 2012, rising from 7.9 percent to 11.3 percent, respectively—with a peak of 13.7 percent being reached in 2007 (Statistics Canada, 2015b). In addition, economic inequality, measured by income or consumption, seems to be worsening in Canada and throughout much of the westernized world (Heisz, 2007).

According to one recent study commissioned by the Canadian Centre for Policy Alternatives:

"The growth in net worth between 1999 and 2012 has been nothing short of breath-taking for Canada's wealthiest families. With the exception of affluent families in their thirties, Canada's wealthiest have doubled the amount of wealth in real terms today compared to 1999:

In 1999, the most affluent families in their twenties held $280,000 in wealth (in 2012 dollars). Today they hold $540,000 in wealth — 95 per cent real growth since 1999.

In 1999, the most affluent families in their thirties held $740,000 in wealth (in 2012 dollars). Today they hold $980,000 in wealth — 33 per cent real growth since 1999.

The gains for the most affluent families in their fifties and sixties have been even more extreme in dollar terms. For instance in 1999, affluent families in their sixties held $1.8 million in wealth. Today they hold $3.4 million in wealth — a $1.6 million wealth gain (93 per cent) in real terms.

Across most age groups, middle class families also saw wealth gains between 1999 and 2012, although they were much more modest in percentage terms and quite small in dollar terms compared to the wealthiest:

Middle class families in their thirties actually have slightly less wealth today. In 1999, they held $68,000 in wealth but today they hold $63,000 in wealth—a 7 per cent drop since 1999.

Middle class families in their twenties, forties and fifties saw real wealth increases of less than 40 per cent since 1999. At best, middle class families in these age groups saw increases of less than $100,000. By comparison, the wealthiest at these ages were seeing real increases of well over a $1 million since 1999.

Middle class families in their sixties and seventies saw wealth increases of close to 80 per cent, closer to the proportional gains of the wealthiest. However, on a dol-lar basis, the gains of the wealthiest at those older ages dwarfed those of the middle class." (MacDonald, 2015, p. 6).

As another report notes: "Canada's richest 20% of families take almost 50% of all income. But when it comes to wealth, almost 70% of all Canadian wealth belongs to Canada's wealthiest 20%. Move higher up the income spectrum and the wealth gap is even greater.

Over a 13-year period, there has seen a pronounced increase in wealth in Canada, but that wealth has flowed into the hands of a concentrated few. For every new dollar of real wealth generated in Canada since 1999, 66 cents of that dollar has gone to the wealthiest 20% of families. For every new dollar in real wealth generated in Canada since 1999, the upper middle class captured 23 cents, while the bottom 60% of families had to settle for the last dime.

The level of wealth inequality in Canada has reached such extremes that in 2012, according to figures derived from *Canadian Business* magazine, the 86 wealthiest Canadian-resident individuals (and families) held the same amount of wealth as the poorest 11.4 million Canadians combined." Another way of stating this same point: "The Wealthy 86 represent only 0.002% of Canadians, but they hold the same amount of wealth as the bottom 34% of the population" (Macdonald, 2014, pp. 5–6).

These trends have been longstanding. A Statistics Canada study revealed that inequality in after-tax family income increased between 1976 and 2004, driven by widening differences in family market income (the sum of earnings from employment and net self-employment income, investment income, and private retirement income, for all family members). Indeed, the report concludes that "This increase occurred at the same time as a reduction in the generosity of several income transfer programs, including the Employment Insurance and Social Assistance Programs (in some provinces), and decreases in income tax rates. This potentially reflects a weakening of the redistributive role of the Canadian state" (Heisz, 2007, p. 5). As discussed later in this chapter, income security programs and the income tax system still help to moderate these income inequalities. A final point: the average family market income among the 10 percent of families with the highest incomes rose by 22 percent from 1989 to 2004. Meanwhile, among the 10 percent of families with the lowest incomes, it fell by 11 percent (Heisz, 2007). A recent study showed that during the 1981–2007 period, the Gini coefficient of after-tax income increased by 12.9 percent, from 0.348 in 1981 to 0.393 in 2007, indicating increasing inequalities among Canadians, even when studies are based on after-tax income (Sharpe & Arsenault, 2009).

Some scholars attribute this growing inequality to the deregulation of financial markets and industry, and the reduction of taxes for the rich (Hacker & Pierson, 2010). The impact of economic inequality on society is profound. Over the past 30 years, social science has provided convincing evidence that a variety of health and social problems are significantly worse in societies that have greater economic inequality: physical health, mental health, drug abuse, education, imprisonment, obesity, social mobility, trust and community life, violence, teenage pregnancies, and child well-being (Wilkinson & Pickett, 2009). In part, these problems occur because unequal societies have less economic redistribution and less commitment to social and health programs for people with lower and middle incomes. Many people, it should be pointed out, are assuming greater personal debt, as noted in Figure 4.4 (Statistics Canada, 2015d). The same is true of governments and other institutions. Figure 4.5 compares Canada's debt with that of other countries (McKinsey Global

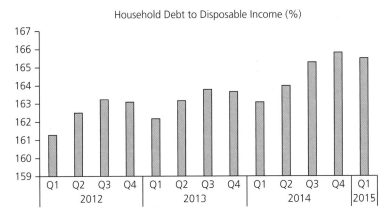

Household Debt to Disposable Income (%)

Figure 4.4 Household Indebtedness

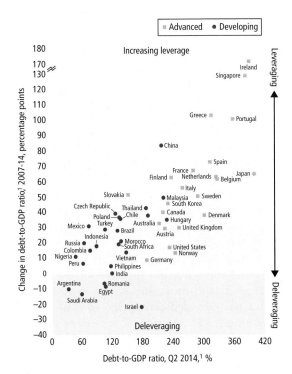

[1] Debt owed by households, nonfinancial corporations, and governments; Q2 2014 data for advanced economies and China; Q4 2013 data for other developing countries.

Figure 4.5 Debt to GDP Ratio

From "Debt and (not much) deleveraging", February 2015, McKinsey Global Institute, www.mckinsey.com. Copyright © 2015 McKinsey & Company. All rights reserved. Reprinted by permission.

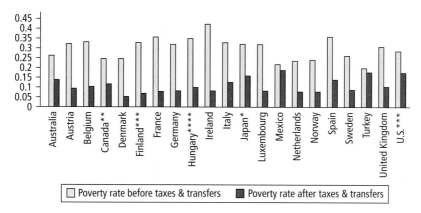

Figure 4.6 Poverty in Canada Compared with Other OECD Countries—Gini Coefficients (Higher numbers indicate greater income inequality)

Institute, 2015). Figure 4.6 compares poverty in Canada with other OECD countries, illustrating income inequality with Gini Coefficients.

According to a reputable source, one in seven Canadians, or a little under five million, live in poverty (Canada without poverty). Moreover:

- "21% of single mothers in Canada raise their children while living in poverty (7% of single fathers raise their children in poverty).
- People living with disabilities (both mental and physical) are twice as likely to live below the poverty line.
- 1 in 5 racialized families live in poverty in Canada, as opposed to 1 in 20 non-racialized families.
- Nearly 15% of elderly single individuals live in poverty." (Canada without poverty).

Child poverty rates continue to be a great concern. As noted in Figure 4.7, Canada's child poverty rates are higher than those of many other advanced industrialized countries.

The implications for food insecurity, access to health, housing, and other basic rights are all imperilled due to poverty. The longer that one is poor, the more difficult it is to escape poverty. In examining poverty dynamics (i.e., the poverty flow patterns that underlie the observed poverty rate at a point in time) between the North American countries and their European counterparts, Valletta (2006) found that poverty persistence is high in Canada, where transfer payments lift a smaller share of individuals from working-age families out of poverty than do social transfers in Germany and Great Britain.

Since the economic downturn starting in the fall of 2008, there has been considerably more unemployment, underemployment, and precarious employment (forms of work that involve such things as atypical employment contracts, limited social benefits or statutory entitlements, job insecurity, low job tenure, low wages, or high risks of ill health).

Education remains an important factor in distinguishing the poor from the non-poor, as shown in Figures 4.9 and 4.10. Social policies that encourage people to stay in school

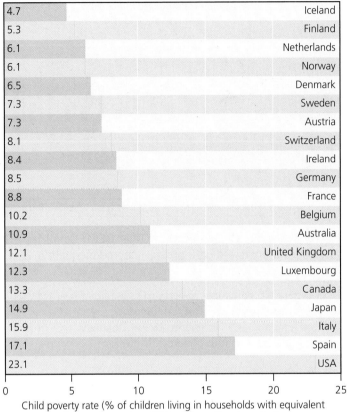

4.7					Iceland
5.3					Finland
6.1					Netherlands
6.1					Norway
6.5					Denmark
7.3					Sweden
7.3					Austria
8.1					Switzerland
8.4					Ireland
8.5					Germany
8.8					France
10.2					Belgium
10.9					Australia
12.1					United Kingdom
12.3					Luxembourg
13.3					Canada
14.9					Japan
15.9					Italy
17.1					Spain
23.1					USA

0 5 10 15 20 25

Child poverty rate (% of children living in households with equivalent income lower than 50% of the national median)

Figure 4.7 Relative Child Poverty, Selected OECD Countries

Source: Figure from "Innocenti Research Centre, Report Card 10", p.11. Published by United Nations Children's Fund, © 2012.

and that encourage post-degree continuous learning are potentially useful in reducing lifelong poverty.

SOCIAL POLICY AND ECONOMIC POLICY

Chappell (2006) suggests that Canadian social and economic policies are related in three ways and that these characteristics reflect the Canadian experience of economic insecurity.

1. The state of the economy determines which social programs are needed. For example, in times of high unemployment, the demand for such social services as social assistance, mental and physical health, and child welfare increases.

2. Recent patterns of social spending have been dependent not on need but on the government's economic priority of fiscal restraint in order to reduce deficit spending.

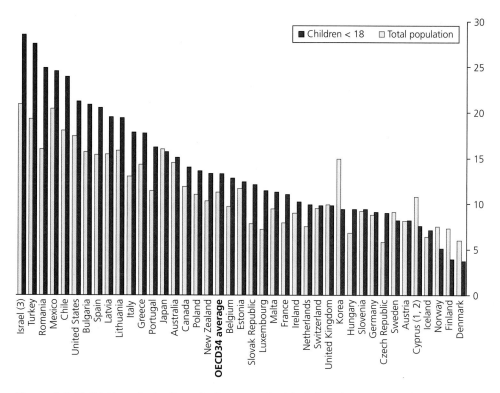

Figure 4.8 Child Poverty in Canada Compared with Other Countries, 2010

Source: Figure from OECD Family Database, p.2. Copyright © 2014 by Organisation for Economic Co-operation and Development.

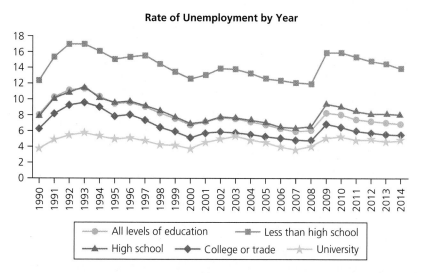

Figure 4.9 Rates of Unemployment Compared with Highest Education Attained

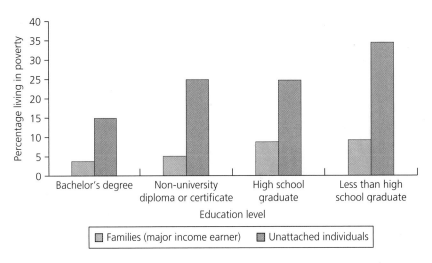

Figure 4.10 Education Makes a Difference

Source: Figure Library and Archives Canada/Poverty Profile/2007/issue 9. Copyright © Government of Canada. Reproduced with the permission of Library and Archives Canada.

3. Some people believe that social programs discourage economic growth because they decrease the spending power of working individuals and increase the debt/deficit situation. This point, however, is highly debatable. Indeed, several observers argue that social programs promote economic growth by putting more money into more hands (Battle, 1993; Mendelson, 1993).

Income Redistribution

The *Gini coefficient* is a means of comparing three types of income distribution levels with one another across time. In the Gini coefficient, 0 indicates perfect equality of income, where every Canadian receives the same amount of money. A score of 1 represents perfect inequality, where one person gets all the income and everyone else receives nothing. Both of these are ideal or theoretical scenarios that would probably never occur. The value of the Gini coefficient is that it provides the extreme parameters (0 and 1) between which we can make comparisons. Canada's Gini coefficient values from 1971 to 2011 are presented in Figure 4.11.

Figure 4.11 highlights the influence of income security programs and the tax system as tools of income redistribution. The highest line, which is also the one that shows the least equal income distribution, represents "earned income" prior to taxes. Individuals who do not have income from work are assigned an income of zero. The next highest line shows what happens when "earned income" is combined with income derived from such income security programs as Social Assistance, CPP, and Employment Insurance. This line reveals the equalizing effect of income-security social policies. The third line, which tends to a greater state of income distribution, represents income after taxes, demonstrating the greater equalizing effects of the income tax system.

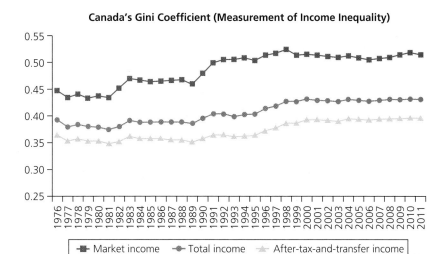

Canada's Gini Coefficient (Measurement of Income Inequality)

Legend: ■ Market income ● Total income ▲ After-tax-and-transfer income

Figure 4.11 Income Distribution in Canada: The Gini Coefficient

However, the income tax system does not benefit all Canadians equally. Scholars and policy analysts insist that many tax credits and tax deductions are used more by higher income earners than by the poor, and benefit higher income earners more than the poor. Two write-offs that favour well-to-do individuals are Registered Retirement Savings Plan (RRSP) contributions and child-care expenses. Far more high-income earners claim RRSP contributions than do low-income earners (Statistics Canada Pensions and Wealth Surveys Section, 2005). A second example is the federal government's child fitness tax credit; albeit this tax credit has been reduced in half for the 2016 budget year and will be eliminated entirely in 2017. A third example is the federal Medical Expense Tax Credit, which reduces the cost of a designated list of disability supports. Such non-refundable tax credits "have serious limitations. Their main shortcoming is that they are of little value to modest- and low-income households, which pay little or no income tax and therefore cannot benefit from a tax reduction" (Torjman, 2015, p. 6). While the current federal Liberal government has made efforts to phase out many of the tax credit programs created during the previous Conservative government, the most recent federal budget has similarly aimed to create benefits for those that earn higher incomes. In the 2016 federal budget, those that might be considered 'middle income' earners (i.e., those with annual income between $45,282 and $90,563) will have a reduction in their income tax rate from 22% to 20.5%.

Moreover and more generally, tax breaks to individuals and corporations drain billions of dollars from government budgets and thereby contribute to the retrenchment of social programs (Torjman & Battle, 1995a, 5; Guest, 1997, 188–189; Muszynski, 1987). For example, tax break measures implemented in the 2007–08 Federal Budget resulted in just over $3 billion in forgone government revenue in that fiscal year alone (Department of Finance Canada, 2007). More recently, it is estimated that the current federal government's new income tax changes will lower revenue by $8.9 billion over the next six years (Office of the Parliamentary Budget Office, 2016). These tax reductions will have serious implications if the government plans to erode funding for social programs, which in turn hurts all Canadians, particularly those who are poorer and hence particularly vulnerable.

A third and final example captures the way in which history can change inequities. The 1930 Income Tax Act changes, discussed in Chapter 2, had carried over the original 1917 flat tax deduction of 10 percent. As a historian points out, Let's consider a scenario, in which a taxpayer made a donation of $100 to charity. If the taxpayer is taxed at a rate of 50%, the donation would cost him or her $50, and the taxing authority would forego that $50. In other words, tax deductions have very real consequences for how much revenue a government may obtain. On the other hand, if a $100 donation is taxed at a 20% rate, the donor would save $20, and therefore real cost to the donor would be $80. There two scenarios – 50% versus 20% – provide a telling lesson. At a 50% tax rate, it is less expensive to make a charitable donation (Prichard, 2011, p. 2). Things changed, however, in the 1970s, with the National Voluntary Organizations lobbying the federal government to change federal legislation on charitable donations. And in 1988, a new scheme was established, in which the first $250 of charitable donations would create a credit of 17%, and donations exceeding this amount create a credit of 29%. These 1988 changes were more progressive than those schemes that came before, but only somewhat: higher incomes continued to benefit disproportionately from tax credit savings (Prichard, p. 2). It had become a little less regressive, but not entirely so. Again, the terms "progressive" and "regressive" are relative.

Paying Taxes

Death and taxes are claimed to be the two things in life that are unavoidable. Typically, Canadians are most aware of two types of taxes: personal income tax and consumption taxes, especially the goods and services tax (GST) and provincial sales tax (PST). In some provinces, there is a harmonized sales tax (HST), which combines the GST with the PST. Personal income tax is the largest source of government revenue in Canada (Martineau, 2005). Figure 4.12 illustrates the amount of income tax paid as a percentage of personal income for the years 1980 through 2008.

During the 2013–2014 fiscal year, Canada's federal government spent $276.8 billion (Department of Finance, 2014). Personal income tax revenues stood at about 48 percent of total revenues collected by the government. Corporate taxes account for 14 percent, and the Goods and Services Tax (GST) for 11 percent. Other revenues from crown corporations, and the sale of goods and services, account for 11 percent (Department of Finance Canada, 2014, p. 22). Although the GST and PST are the most noticeable forms of consumption taxes, "sin taxes" on such consumer items as tobacco and alcohol have received increased public attention.

Tax systems generally operate on either regressive or progressive principles (or on a combination of both). *Regressive tax systems* impose the same tax level on all citizens, which, in effect, imposes the greatest burden on those least able to pay (Muszynski, 1987). The PST is a Canadian example of a regressive tax. It is levied on a particular good at the same percentage regardless of a person's income. Because they have less disposable income, persons with low incomes pay a greater portion of their incomes in PST payments than do those in higher income brackets.

A *progressive tax system* bases the level of taxation on a person's ability to pay, such that those with higher incomes pay proportionately higher taxes. Canada's current

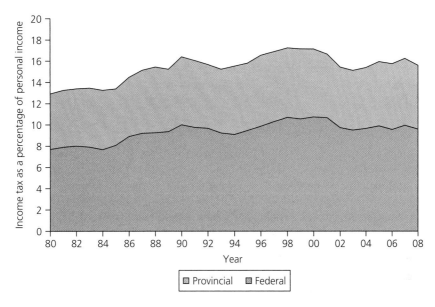

Figure 4.12 Income Tax Payment in Canada

Source: Statistics Canada, CANSIM database, Copyright © 2010, Reproduced and distributed on an "as is" basis with the permission of Statistics Canada.

income tax system contains both progressive and regressive elements. It is progressive insofar as it has multiple tax brackets, with a progressive increase in the percentage of taxable income paid as one's income rises (see Figure 4.13). In this sense, the income tax system differentiates between those with less money (and in lower tax brackets) and those with more (and in higher brackets). But critics point out that it could still be *more* progressive, with richer people and corporations paying more. Because poor people pay a greater proportion of their income to taxes than do rich people, the system has definite regressive elements. If well-to-do individuals and corporations paid more, the system would be more progressive and less regressive.

A recent income tax option that is not based on this progressive principle is the "flat tax." The 2015 election of the New Democratic Party changed Alberta's provincial income tax to make it more progressive. Prior to this, the provincial tax in Alberta had been a certain percentage of personal income, across the board; in 2009, it was 10 per-cent of taxable income (hence a flat tax) above the personal exemption of $16 775 per

- 15% **on the first** $44,701 of taxable income, **+**
- 22% **on the next** $44,700 of taxable income (on the portion of taxable income over $44,701 up to $89,401), **+**
- 26% **on the next** $49,185 of taxable income (on the portion of taxable income over $89,401 up to $138,586), **+**
- 29% of taxable income **over** $138,586.

Figure 4.13 Federal Tax Rates for 2015

year (it had retained a small progressive aspect in that people under the threshold are not responsible for the 10 percent payable) (Canada Revenue Agency, 2010). A flat tax brings a simplicity and efficiency to the current complex tax system with less emphasis on tax loopholes than the present system. But it tends to make the income tax system less progressive, and hence a less powerful instrument of income redistribution.

Changing Demographics

An international trend reflects what is described as a "vast gulf in birth and death rates amongst the world's countries" (Kent & Haub, 2005, p. 5). The wealthier, more urban nations—particularly in Europe—have shrinking and aging populations, while poorer, rural countries—particularly in Asia and Africa—have demographic growth and younger populations (Kent & Haub, 2005). Largely because of Latin immigration, the United States does not face as strong a demographic pressure as Europe. But Canada is close, experiencing the twin themes of birth rate decline and the aging of its population. In partial response to both, immigration has become increasingly important to the growth of the Canadian population over the last 30 years (Figure 4.14). Immigration rates appear to have been steady between 2003 (when it was 7.0 immigrants per 1000 population) and 2010 (8.2 immigrants per 1000 population) (Chagnon, 2013, p. 2). According to the 2006 Census, the most recent immigrants represented one in five (19.8 percent) of the total population of Canada (Statistics Canada, 2007). As Figure 4.14 illustrates, immigration will become increasingly more important to the sustainability of population growth in Canada in the future. This is not to downplay the problems of population growth, particularly as outlined in the next chapter in its comments about sustainable economic growth.

Age and retirement have become a topic of focus in national and international contexts over the last decade. Some critics describe the situation as a "demographic crisis" in which people throughout the developed world are not bearing enough children to sustain

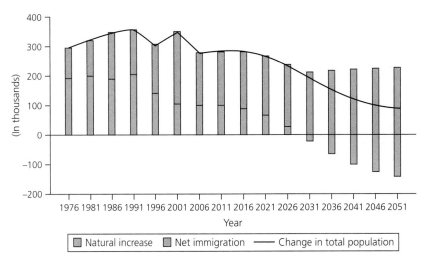

Figure 4.14 Change in Total Population in Canada, 1976 to 2051

themselves economically (Cohen, 2006). Today, nearly half of the world's population lives in countries with fertility at or below replacement levels. Further, by the mid-twenty-first century, three of four countries now described as *developing* are projected to reach or slip below replacement fertility rates (Morgan & Taylor, 2006).

Another major demographic factor is that people in advanced industrialized countries are living longer and retiring earlier (Townson, 2006; United Nations, 2002). During the Palaeolithic era, life expectancy at birth was 20 years. Ten thousand years later, for those in the Roman Empire, it had risen to 27 years. People living in fifteenth-century England and Wales had a life expectancy of 33 years; by the mid-nineteenth century, life expectancy had risen to 40 years and, by 1900, to 50 years (Usher, 2003, p. 5). Major changes in life expectancy occurred during the twentieth century. In 1920, Canada had life expectancies of 59 for men and 61 for women: the average person was not expected to make it to 65, the age of retirement that emerged as an OECD gold standard several decades after Bismarck's Germany introduced an old age social insurance program in 1889 (Germany originally set the age at 70). By 1950, average Canadian life expectancies were 66 for men and 71 for women. In 2009, they were over 82 years for women and 78 for men—and rising yearly (Statistics Canada, 2015b). In the early 1970s, working age people (18–64) accounted for 57 percent of the population, climbing to 64 percent in 1995 (Chui, 1996). All growth scenarios considered, and using the population estimates for July 1, 2009, the proportion of the working age population aged 15 to 64 is projected to decline steadily from about 70 percent to about 60 percent in 2036 (Statistics Canada, 2010c). The culmination of these two factors (low fertility and longer life expectancy) has created a situation known as *demographic aging* (Cheal, 2002). In response to this challenge, in 1998, the OECD published a report suggesting that national governments throughout the developed world need to reform legislation to remove incentives for early retirement to reduce the economic implications of an aging population (Townson, 2006). The Canadian government needs to make such adjustments soon to avoid a clash of generations—that is, fewer working age people will have to support the greater number of people born between 1945 and the early 1960s, who are sometimes known as the *baby boomers*. The baby boomers have a good portion of society's wealth, but as the baby boomers age, younger workers will have the burden of contributing to their retirement funds, health costs, and other age-related expenditures, which are destined to grow over time (Willetts, 2010).

Many Canadians, particularly when the issue came to the media's attention in the 1990s, wondered how social programs and retirement funds (private and public) could be sustained. Available projections show that people aged 65 and above will account for between 23 percent and 25 percent of the total population by 2036, nearly double the 13.9 percent figure from 2009 (Statistics Canada, 2010c). A similar study, using 2006 as the base year, shows that the ratio of the population aged 65 and over to the population of traditional working age (18–64) will rise from 20 percent to 46 percent in 2050 (Guillemette & Robson, 2006, p. 1). A further possibility looms on the horizon. Future projections in labour market characteristics suggest that between 2006 and 2015, 70 percent of all newly available jobs will result from people retiring (Lapointe et al., 2006; Human Resources and Skills Development Canada, 2007; KPMG, 2015). A combination of factors—the shrinking proportion of available workers to retired people and the increase in available jobs as a result of retirement—could essentially lead to higher numbers of jobs than there will be available or than there will be qualified workers to fill them (Lapointe et al., 2006). What is the future of the notion of "unemployment," as well as such social programs as health care and retirement, both of which are heavily used by retired people but are funded particularly by those who work (through the income tax system and payroll deductions)?

SOME CONSEQUENCES OF SOCIAL POLICY

Paradoxes of intervening in the economic life of some Canadians have long been recognized. For example, financial assistance programs may sometimes decrease the incentive to paid work for some recipients; that is, some programs contain inherent labour force participation disincentives. The authors of this textbook, like other progressive observers, insist on the need for plentiful jobs offering meaningful employment and decent wages; and plentiful, affordable childcare. More than any other factor, decent jobs and plentiful child care for working parents would alleviate much of the problem of such labour force participation disincentives (Clarke, 1997). In addition, some observers blame social policies themselves for the absence of a full-employment economy. The following components of social welfare programs continue to act as disincentives to paid work:

- the decreased purchasing power of current "minimum wages";
- health-care benefits that exceed those of many jobs;
- insufficient coverage for back-to-work expenses;
- high tax-back rates for earning exemptions; and
- lack of affordable, accessible childcare (National Council of Welfare, 1993).

Canada's transition from an institutional approach towards a market-state approach has reduced the scope and impact of such programs as Employment Insurance. As a result of successive cutbacks in eligibility criteria and benefit amounts for other income programs such as Workers' Compensation and Employment Insurance, "social assistance has moved from its original intent. It has grown into a major front-line program—larger than Employment Insurance in some provinces. An unpopular and stigmatizing program, it nonetheless has proved stubbornly resistant to reform" (Torjman, 2007, p. 1). Some proposed changes would particularly assist the unemployed who can seek work, as well as the precariously employed. These changes include making social assistance a genuine program of last resort; providing earnings supplementation measurements separate from social assistance; making work more remunerative than welfare; improving minimum wage levels; introducing working income tax benefits for the working poor; improving childcare benefits for the working poor (National Council of Welfare, 2007; Torjman, 2007, 2015); and improving accessibility to affordable daycare.

For over a generation, other critics have stressed that the demoralization of Canadians receiving welfare should be addressed by mandatory workfare programs as a condition for receiving social assistance and EI services (Handler & Hasenfeld, 1991). Proponents of workfare suggest that it promotes the "moral merit of work" in a "failed system of subsidized poverty" (Sirico, 1997). Self-respect, taking responsibility, the development of a "worker" identity, and the acquisition of work skills and work experience are among the moral benefits suggested by advocates of workfare programs. Such programs are based on separating out the able-bodied recipients from those who are unable to work. To some, this division seems a throwback to the nineteenth-century Poor Laws and their delineation of the deserving and undeserving poor. These laws were heavily influenced by the moral overtones of the view that poverty was a state resulting from idleness and immoral behaviour.

One of the key points to analyzing social policy is determining the extent to which individual versus societal factors can be conceived as a source and solution to social problems. Sociologist C. Wright Mills (1959) frames it well, suggesting an inextricable link between the private troubles of an individual and the public issues of which they form a part. He believed that private troubles "have to do with an individual's character and with those limited areas of social life of which s/he is directly and personally aware." Public issues "have to do with matters that transcend these local environments of the individual and the limited range of his/her life. They have to do with the organization of institutions of society" (Mills, 1959, pp. 395–396). One can infer from Mills and like-minded thinkers that both society and the individual are implicated in the construction, definition, and solution of social problems. Thus, difficulties that some social work clients experience getting off income security programs represent both individual trouble *and* a public issue. Some authors—particularly those from the political right—emphasize the individual component. Political scientist Tom Flanagan, as an example, was campaign manager and has been mentor to University of Calgary alumnus Prime Minister Stephen Harper. To Flanagan, the locus is the individual and family:

> There is no mystery about the road to success; it can be summarised in six rules: Go to school and graduate. Get a job and stick with it till you find a better one. Get married and stay married. Have children and invest in their future. Don't acquire a criminal record. Don't drink too much, use illegal drugs, or gamble excessively. Anyone who follows these Six Rules of Success cannot help but thrive in Canada. The rules are not absolutely inflexible. Some successful people are divorced, or never married, or childless, or alcoholics, or high-school dropouts. But all of the Six Rules are correlated with success, and anyone who violates several of them is headed for trouble. (Flanagan, 2007, 177)

Similar discourse is common in published reports commissioned by such organizations as the Atlantic Institute for Market Studies, the Canadian Council of Chief Executives, the Fraser Institute, or various banks. Other institutes to the left, such as the Caledon Institute for Social Policy, the Canadian Centre for Policy Alternatives, and the Canadian Council on Social Development, tend to emphasize societal issues as more prevalent causes of social problems.

CONCLUSION

As this chapter has discussed, a variety of ideological, economic, and social factors influence the nature of social policies, the contexts in which they were conceived and carried out, and the reasons why they change over time. The next chapter sheds light on important additional phenomena—globalization, the environmental movement, and social inclusion—which are now rightly seen as crucial considerations for social policies.

Chapter 5
Social Policy and Emerging Realities

The issues discussed in this book affect everyone: What level of entitlement is considered fair when determining benefit rates for income security programs such as social assistance? What should be the minimum number of weeks of paid employment to enable a claimant to obtain Employment Insurance benefits? How much money per capita should the state allocate to daycare programs? Should health insurance programs be universal, selective, or a combination of both? These questions and others like them reflect societal values and determine the basic structures of social policies.

The answers vary from place to place and over time. The welfare state of early twenty-first-century Canada is manifestly different from that of the early twentieth century.

As difficult as predictions into the future are to make, this chapter considers the following four essential issues that we expect to shape Canadian social policies in the new millennium:

1. the environmental imperative;
2. globalization;
3. social welfare retrenchment; and
4. changing conceptions of social welfare in relation to citizenship and social inclusion.

THE ENVIRONMENTAL IMPERATIVE

Rachel Carson's *The Silent Spring*, first published in 1962, was one of the earliest modern-day environmental treatises. Since then, an emergent environmental movement has sought to change social consciousness and legislation in developed countries, such as Canada, and in the developing nations of Asia, Central and South America, and elsewhere. Critical evidence of the ecological crisis throughout the globe is found in the staggering yearly figures of species extinctions (both animal and plant). A recent publication reports that the rate of species extinction is approximately 3000 per annum, a figure that is continually increasing (Meyer, 2006). Oceans cover almost three-quarters of Earth's surface and contain 97 percent of the world's water. Sediments, oils, wastes, and a damaged ozone layer, among other phenomena, increasingly assault them. The annual tonnage of fish caught in the world's oceans increased 1600 percent over the twentieth century (Sachs, Loske, & Linz, 1998, p. 74). This increase reflects the advent of industrial fishing in the 1950s; as a result of which, by 2003, big-fish stocks had been reduced globally by

90 percent over those five decades (Myers & Worm, 2003). Evidence from global bird and mammal species supports the hypothesis that large-bodied species are indeed more susceptible to extinction (Olden, Hogan, & Zen, 2007). The tragic decline and fall of a once-prolific cod fishery is well-known to the Atlantic provinces in Canada.

In more global terms, at the end of the twentieth century, one-third of the world's tropical forests, one-quarter of its available fresh water, and one-quarter of its fish resources were gone (World Wildlife Fund, 2006). To some extent, as Meyer (2006), Lovelock (2006), Sale (2006), and others argue, overpopulation is the problem. The current global population is more than 7 billion people, compared to 1 billion in 1850 and 2 billion in 1930.

But, as relevant as overpopulation, and of particular significance to this textbook, is the fact that the current ecological crisis is a problem largely caused by the developed world. The *ecological footprint* represents the impact of each person on the environment, through consumption of fossil fuels, agricultural production of food and other products, misuses of forests and water, human settlement, and so on. Canadians have an average ecological footprint of 7.01 global hectares per person, and Americans have an ecological footprint of 8.00 global hectares per person (Global Footprint Network, 2010). Likewise, throughout Europe, ecological footprints range from approximately 1.4 to 8.4 global hectares per person; while for Asian countries, they range from 0.6 to 10.7 global hectares per person and African countries have ecological footprints of between 0.7 and 4.3 global hectares per person (Global Footprint Network, 2010). For example, the consumption of fossil fuels alone illustrates the severity of the crisis. Carbon dioxide (CO_2) is released into the atmosphere through the burning of fossil fuels in cars and industries, by forest fires, and through other natural and human sources, causing a greenhouse effect in the atmosphere that steadily increases the world's temperature. The results are potentially calamitous: the possibility of the polar ice caps melting, resulting in the massive flooding of a considerable portion of Earth's land mass, not to mention the drought conditions created in many regions throughout the Global South, which results in the loss of economic and social sustainability for some of the world's poorest people (United Nations Development Programme, 2006). Today, 3 billion people live on less than US$2/day, and of these, over 1 billion live on less than $1/day.

How can Canada respond? With today's world population of more than 7 billion and levels of annual emission of CO_2 close to 29 billion tonnes (in 2007) (United Nations Statistics Division, 2010), an "equal rights of emission" worldwide would assume 5 tonnes per person annually. But in Canada, current annual domestic production of CO_2 (726 million tonnes in 2013) (Environment and Climate Change Canada, 2015) is equivalent to approximately 20 tonnes per person. Assume, as is the consensus among many demographers, current projections of a world population of 10 billion by 2050. In this scenario, Canada would need to diminish CO_2 emissions by 80 percent over the next 50 years to achieve even the objective of equal utilization rights with other countries (Flannery, 2006; Sachs, Loske, & Linz, 1998, p. 30).

Such a reduction would require a profoundly different approach to economic arrangements. *Sustainability* is an economic, political, and environmental world view that promotes present and future generations of stewardship of the physical world. Sustainable development, a resulting concept, "creates a process that ensures that natural resources are replenished, and that future generations continue to have the resources they need to meet their own needs" (Van Wormer, 1997, p. 650). Myriad nonprofit organizations—such as Greenpeace, Friends of the Earth, and the world scientific community—continue to influence public debate. The 1987 Brundtland Report, commissioned by the United Nations (UN), was an important document in the evolution of this latter concept. The Brundtland Report clearly links economic and environmental development issues. Also significant was the 1992 Rio de Janeiro Earth Summit, a UN conference that produced a 500-page document elaborating global partnerships that could achieve sustainability. This summit led to the 1997 Kyoto Protocol on Climate Change, which now has more than 160 signatories, Canada included. Canada's inability to honour its Kyoto commitments has garnered international media attention.

But the temptations to continue apace are strong. Consider that one barrel of oil is the equivalent in kilojoules of energy to 12 people working for you year-round, or 25 000 hours of human labour. Readily available energy has become intrinsic to all aspects of our lives, from travel to home heating, to consumer good transportation and personal transit. If the world were to immediately stop using hydrocarbons and convert, say, to nuclear energy, it would require 10 000 nuclear plants to meet the demand that oil is supplying now; and were this to happen, some predict that within 10 years the world's uranium reserves would be depleted. Other alternatives—biomass, ethanol, biodiesel, wind, solar, and tidal power—are small players in the world's energy markets (Tertzakian, 2006). Current research suggests massive changes in lifestyle and reductions in consumption will be required; yet the political will to realize these changes seems elusive, as does the public opinion required to make the changes happen.

Oil resources are finite. Yet the world uses approximately 1000 barrels of oil per second, or 87 million barrels of oil per day (Tertzakian, 2006). Canadian consumption is approximately 2.3 million barrels per day (Central Intelligence Agency, 2010; U.S. Energy Information Administration, 2010) or 24.86 barrels per capita per annum. In the 1950s, geophysicist M.K. Hubbert predicted that the world's discovery of finite oil resources would peak in the form of a bell curve, after which point oil and gas would become more expensive in direct proportion to their diminishing abundance. Some scholars think we have already hit "Hubbert's Peak" and are going to experience a difficult, impoverishing transition to a post-oil economy (Deffeyes, 2006). Geographer Jared Diamond (2005) argues convincingly that ecological factors have led to the collapse of many human societies in the past. Meanwhile, Wright (2004) worries that our species may be prone to ecologically induced self-destruction. In either case, the significance of physical ecology to social policy development is significant. The institutional period of social welfare went hand in glove with the coal- and oil-based economies of massive industrial capitalism. The Canadian market state is liberal in ideology, capitalist in economy, and continues to be powered by hydrocarbons. Will the stage of social welfare that proceeds from the market state be both post-oil in energy and sustainable in philosophy? Will there be a choice?

To the extent that sustainability challenges previous notions of economic growth, the attending basis upon which social policies are conceived may also need rethinking. Moreover, the crisis of worsening public and environmental health concerns is, to stress an important point, an international phenomenon, not just a Canadian one (Garret, 2000). This crisis influences international political and economic relationships too.

Perhaps a necessary condition of sustainability is a new world view that equates spiritual growth and self-realization with stewardship of Earth (Lonergan & Richards, 1988; Schumacher, 1973, pp. 54–57).

The 1974 "Group of 77" developing countries (now numbering more than 100) proposed to the UN General Assembly a new international economic order (NIEO) that would address North–South inequalities (the developed world and the developing world, respectively). Thinking about sustainability in that context, Sachs and other environmentalists propose significant changes to the way in which ordinary Canadians think about and act on their patterns of consumption:

- sharing such goods as skis, cars, and other commodities that are not required on a daily basis;

- using and further developing public transportation infrastructures, rather than roads, highways, and other car-oriented patterns of movement;

- planning cities in ways that revive notions of greater densities of population and greater built-in proximity among homes, schools, places of work, entertainment, and leisure (Sachs, Loske, & Linz, 1998, pp. 123, 133); and

- reducing, reusing, and recycling consumer products.

Several other low-cost strategies that could reduce Canadian greenhouse gas emissions by 50 percent over 30 years include use of increased insulation in houses, increased efficiency in the engineering of heating and cars, and increased use of more efficient, smaller power plants in place of larger-scale plants (Torrie, 2000).

Beyond these immediate courses of action, social policies have scarcely begun to integrate issues of social justice for people with the imperative of physical ecology. Indeed, many social welfare organizations have had only very loose connections with environmental nonprofits. Greater collaboration might be useful. According to one Canadian research report, Canada ranks among the worst five OECD nations on 25 environmental indicators (with a ranking among OECD nations of 28th out of 29), including greenhouse gas emissions, air pollution, water consumption, energy consumption, energy efficiency, fertilizer consumption, and generation of hazardous and nuclear waste (Boyd, 2001). A 2006 report by Canada's environment and sustainable development commissioner (Commissioner of the Environment and Sustainable Development, 2006) is likewise critical of the federal government's lack of resolve in implementing larger programs to reduce the amount of greenhouse gases emitted by individuals and industry. Among other concerns, the country's environment commissioner points out, are problems of unregulated livestock sewage and nitrogen in farm fertilizers contaminating water tables (Mittlestaedt, 2001) and pharmaceutical and cosmetic residue traces in water sources (Mittlestaedt, 2006). A recent study released by Simon Fraser University and the David Suzuki Foundation shows that if Canada's environmental policies were strengthened so they reflected the guidelines used in such developed countries as Sweden and Norway, Canada's environmental ranking would move from almost dead last to first place (Gunton & Calbick, 2010). Many observers are worried about government cutbacks to departments that monitor and ensure safe drinking water; such cutbacks, it is argued, are part of the wider phenomenon of government retreat from the social milieu.

GLOBALIZATION

Globalization refers to the current, pervasive trend of internationalized finance, communication, ideology, and political arrangements. As a result of globalization, money is invested quickly and easily across national borders. Corporations follow principles of transnational competition for lucrative markets and actively pursue inexpensive labour. What is more, in the absence of powerfully constraining national legislation or intranational structures, multinational corporations achieve growing sovereignty to pursue these objectives. Globalization has contributed to the rise of the market-state era of social welfare, as discussed in Chapter 2.

The Economic Context of Globalization

Two aspects of globalization need to be examined: economics and politics. Global economics is vastly different from any of the economic systems that preceded it. In the sixteenth, seventeenth, and eighteenth centuries, the European economic system was a system of mercantilism: colonial powers created foreign empires to cultivate worldwide systems of primary extraction abroad and production at home. Late-eighteenth-century England—and nineteenth-century France, Canada, the United States, and other countries—underwent an industrial revolution, featuring increased urbanization, steam manufacturing, coal extraction, and railway and other industrial infrastructures. As shown in Chapter 2, capitalism was further transformed in the 1930s, with the advent of an interventionist state and the post–World War II comprehensive welfare state of the institutional era. These structures started to unravel in the 1970s. In the 1990s, a very different basis for economic arrangements emerged: the market state. The market state, in turn, has experienced a profound transition after the severe stock market crash and credit crunch beginning in the fall of 2008.

Like all things, political and economic power are capable of change. In 1000, Chinese per capita incomes were slightly higher than Europe's. In the succeeding period, China lost growth, and Europe surged, so that by 1820, Chinese per capita income levels were half of Europe's (King, 2010, p. 30). Our economy is in perpetual pursuit of novelty and renewal; the basic roots of capitalism are a type of "creative destruction": as some things (e.g., the horse and buggy) become obsolete, new things (e.g., the automobile) rise in their stead.

One school of thought argues that the basic workings of capitalism started to change in the 1970s. At this time, as we shall elaborate in the next several pages, with the encouragement of government, capital started to flow more freely across national boundaries. As a result, production moved to less-expensive labour markets, depressing workers' incomes in the West. Money loans—credit—became progressively easier to obtain, which in part helped workers and the middle class in the West to reduce the impact on a diminishing standard of living (as discussed in Chapter 4). Beginning in the 1990s, the finance sector proliferated worldwide and a variety of increasingly complicated, and unregulated, trading instruments were developed, among them derivatives, futures, hedge funds, options, and swaps (Harvey, 2010). A real estate boom flowered in growing economies, fuelled by greed, low interest rates, and abundant credit. In some countries, such as the United States, income tax policies encouraged the purchase of mortgages, allowing filers to reduce taxes on the basis of their mortgages. Mortgage brokers, operating without sufficient regulation, and solely on the number of mortgages sold, encouraged people to buy housing they could not afford, passing on the bad debt to others in a dizzyingly complex finance sector. In many instances, these same bad loans in the United States and elsewhere were carved up into collateralized debt obligations (CDOs) and sold on international markets under the false impression that they were secure investments. When the credit crunch set in, in 2008, these CDOs became more difficult to sell and lost trading value.

Quite a few governments (Canada is a notable exception) failed to regulate their financial sectors properly; some financial institutions, particularly in the United States and the United Kingdom, were impervious to self-regulation. Greed overtook large portions of the financial sector and many ordinary investors, particularly those who sought mortgages they could not realistically afford. When the financial bubble burst in the fall of 2008, as it was destined to do at some point, many U.S. and U.K. banks discovered they had insufficient reserves to cover costs. Panic swelled quickly across markets, and historic government bailouts of major companies, which were previously deemed too big to fail, became prevalent. A widespread economic depression was avoided.

Another school of thought sees this several-decade change in economic relations as part of a shift of power from the West to other parts of the world (King, 2010). In the 1960s, the Japanese economy grew stronger, followed by the economies of South Korea, Taiwan, Singapore, and Hong Kong in the 1970s, and then by China in the 1980s. The Organization for Petroleum Exporting Countries (OPEC) was established in 1960. In the 1970s, its member states—including Algeria, the Arab states of the Persian Gulf, Nigeria, and Venezuela—expanded their wealth and influence in the wake of the growing scarcity and costs of oil and gas. Between 1990 and 2008, the middle class in some parts of the developing world increased markedly; by one estimate, their numbers grew from one-third to more than one-half of the world's population ("Burgeoning Bourgeoisie," 2009). (Ways of calculating the middle class in the Global South are different from the methods we would deploy in Canada. One estimate, for instance, claims anyone earning more than US$10/day in some Global South contexts may be considered middle class.) Considerable economic growth occurred in Brazil, China, India, and Indonesia and, to a lesser extent, in Bangladesh, Russia, and elsewhere. This increase may be seen as the third most significant surge of the middle class in modern history; the first surge was the rise of the middle class in nineteenth-century Europe, and the second, the baby boom in the West from 1945 to the early 1960s. When the poor start to enter the middle class in the millions, social and economic changes occur; as Marx and Engels (1848, trans. 1998) put it more than 160 years ago, the bourgeoisie "cannot exist without constantly revolutionizing the instruments of production, and thereby the relations of production, and with them the whole relations of society" (3). The middle class is able to allocate some of its discretionary income and to cease living hand-to-mouth, day-to-day, and season-to-season. They develop expectations for the present and the future. Between 1981 and 2007, the World Values Survey and the European Values Study carried out five waves of representative national surveys in many countries, covering almost 90 percent of the world's population (www.worldvaluessurvey.org). These studies show that when the poorest in a society become middle class, their beliefs and motivations change. They are more likely to seek education for their children, to desire prosperity, to insist on greater accountability from those who govern, and to be less deferential to prevailing structures of authority (Inglehart & Welzel, 2009).

The results of a growing middle class are therefore not universally undesirable. Indeed, many contemporary political scientists see economic modernization as the gateway to improvements in social and political arrangements:

> Modernization is a syndrome of social changes linked to industrialization. Once set in motion, it tends to penetrate all aspects of life, bringing occupational specialization, urbanization, rising educational levels, rising life expectancy, and rapid economic growth. These create a self-reinforcing process that transforms social life and political institutions, bringing rising mass participation in politics and—in the long run—making the establishment of democratic political institutions increasingly likely. (Inglehart & Welzel, 2009, p. 33)

But as several scholars emphasize, modernization and its positive consequences are not automatic; they need to be nurtured continuously (Hufbauer & Suominen, 2010; Rodrik, 2011). Volatile world economies make peoples' lives unpredictable, particularly the lives of the people who are most economically and socially vulnerable. Regimes in Bangladesh, Nigeria, the Philippines, Russia, and Thailand may stall democratic reform; but, in the long run, modernization tends to promote change, making democratization increasingly possible. Change does not occur linearly; it is rooted to a country's history. Nor is *change* synonymous with *Westernization*. Finally, as part of globalization, the experiences of one country influence another's. Worldwide inflationary food prices, to cite one example, are in part a product of a growing international middle class that possesses greater resources to purchase food.

The 1980s and 1990s saw the ushering in of trade blocs, or free-trade agreements. The most comprehensive example of this was the emergence of the European Union (EU), which included a common Parliament, an extensive legal system that often overrides domestic legislation, a court of justice, a common currency, and a central bank. In addition, people within the EU have the right to invest, live, travel, and work in other member states. On this continent, the United States and Canada struck the Free Trade Agreement (FTA) in 1989, after four years of intense negotiations involving the governments of Brian Mulroney in Canada and Ronald Reagan in the United States. As the economy continues to falter after the fall of 2008, and our ties to the U.S. economy are so profound, some wonder whether we might seek greater trade alliances with China, India, Brazil, and Indonesia: those countries that are seen as emerging economies. In any case, it is important to remember that countries have political choices. Indeed, some political leaders, such as Hugo Chávez in Venezuela, assert active resistance to American hegemony and the myriad global social movements that challenge globalization.

The Political Context of Globalization

Politically, globalization has profoundly transformed international relations during the past two and a half decades. The Cold War, which began with the cessation of World War II, came to an abrupt end with the series of collapsed Communist governments in the former Soviet Bloc during the late 1980s and early 1990s. In the aftermath, the old antagonism between the United States and its allies (sometimes referred to as *the West*), and the Soviet Union and its allies (sometimes referred to as *the Eastern or Soviet Bloc*), ceased to be *the* defining facet of global affairs. Commentators such as Fukuyama (1992) declared that liberal democracy had triumphed over communism; many others agreed, implying that the West had "won" the Cold War.

Immediately following World War II, there was a relatively widespread consensus in favour of a universal welfare state and an interventionist government. But by the 1990s, social democratic governments in France, Canada, and other countries appeared to have lost touch with their ideological roots, and globalization proponents eagerly sought opportunities to transform Eastern European societies into capitalist enclaves. (So, too, have other marketplaces—in Asia and in Central and South America—become heightened targets for international capitalism.)

After the fall of 2008, however, it became increasingly apparent that the West's victory in the Cold War—if that is what it was—was brief. We are entering a new era of global political arrangements in which China, in particular, but also other emerging powers such as Brazil, India, and Indonesia, are exerting greater prominence economically and politically.

One of the main problems with the U.S. economy is consumer debt, the balance of trade deficit and indebtedness through government bonds to other countries, such as China. This deficit is particularly important, given the growing importance of international finance structures on the global economy. The sheer volume of money crossing borders daily has increased exponentially since the 1960s. Figure 5.1 identifies trends for the past

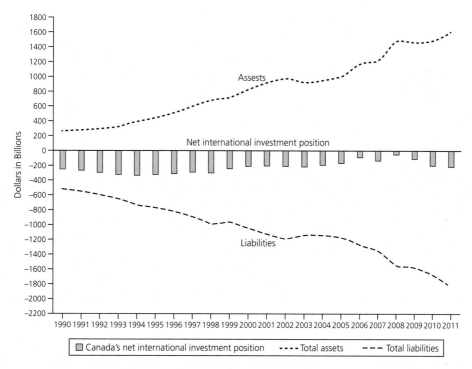

Figure 5.1 Canada in the Global Economy

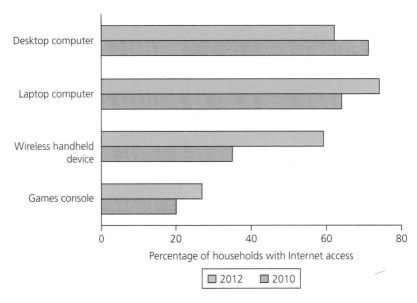

Figure 5.2 Devices Used to Access the Internet

Source: Statistics Canada, Canadian Internet Use Survey, Copyright © 2012. Reproduced and distributed on an "as is" basis with the permission of Statistics Canada.

two decades, but some of these patterns began as early as the 1970s. It shows the increase in Canadian assets abroad, particularly since the late 1980s, despite evidence indicating that the volume of trading of international currencies increased during that period. Meanwhile, as Figure 5.2 demonstrates, the proportion of households using the Internet for a multitude of tasks—unheard of in mass consumption prior to the 1990s—is now very significant, as is the considerable reduction in costs of long-distance phone calls and the increased use of faxes and other media to reduce global distances. Figure 5.3 shows current Internet usage in Canada, and the reasons for Internet access at home. However, there remains some disparity in Internet usage based on household income in Canada. Almost all households in the top income quartile (98%), or those with household incomes of $94,000 or more, have home Internet access, compared with 58% of households in the lowest income quartile, or those with household incomes of $30,000 or less (Statistics Canada, 2013b).

Finally, foreign direct investment—the amount of money invested outside of an individual country—increased fivefold worldwide over the course of the 1980s. By the early 1990s, the world's 300 largest multinational corporations—the major players in foreign direct investment—had gained control of one-quarter of the world's total capital (Marfleet, 1998, p. 15). More recently, "a third of wealth is now in the hands of some 200 corporations" (Mackey, 2003, p. 72). As a result of these trends, the world has entered an era of "turbo-capitalism," in which efficiency, insecurity, and uniformity prevail. Also prevalent—in a temporary way at least—is the generation of new wealth as older forms of practices, companies, and entire industries give way to the new (Luttwak, 1999). These forces create profound workplace changes, as discussed above.

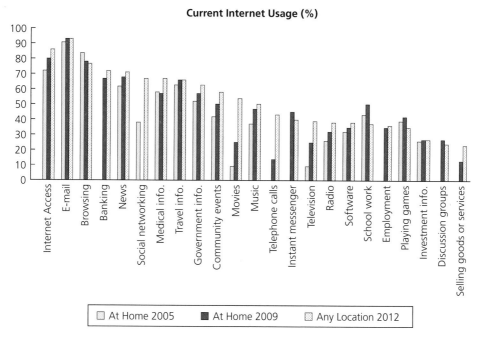

Current Internet Usage (%)

Legend: □ At Home 2005 ■ At Home 2009 ▨ Any Location 2012

Figure 5.3 How Canadians are Wired

As for the assumptions underpinning this global financial network, the changes in ideology are nothing short of revolutionary. As one scholar points out, globalization "redefine[s] all the fundamental reference points of human society.... and requires a modification of all existing paradigms" (Robinson, 1996, as cited in Marfleet, 1998, p. 2). Gone are the previous principles of a mixed economy during the institutional era of social welfare, where governments of nation-states extensively regulated capitalism. Indeed, in the market-state era, capital often tries to elude any countervailing forces, such as governments, unions, public interest groups, and populations. In Canada, several neo-liberal institutions that actively advocate for corporate interests are entirely aligned with the market-state approach to social welfare described in Chapter 2 and are increasingly influential in policy development. These institutions consist of business associations (e.g., Canadian Association of Petroleum Producers, Canadian Bankers Association, the Canadian Chamber of Commerce, Canadian Council of Chief Executives, and Canadian Manufacturers and Exporters), think tanks (e.g., Atlantic Institute for Market Studies and the Fraser Institute), groups speaking on behalf of citizens (Canadian Taxpayers Federation and National Citizens Coalition), and various private and corporate lobbyists (Abelson, 2009). These groups have enormous power and scope; the Canadian Council of Chief Executives, for example, represents the top 150 leading corporations in Canada, which hold $4.5 trillion in assets (CCCE, 2010). Some of these organizations object to government funding for civil society groups speaking on behalf of women, people with disabilities, or other communities, calling them *interest groups* (and perhaps not seeing themselves under the same moniker).

Between the 1980s and the fall of 2008, corporations' major remaining check was the marketplace itself. After the autumn of 2008, it became apparent in the United States, the United Kingdom, and other economies that government needed to regulate the private sector, particularly the financial sector, to ensure that major banks did not crash. Canada's situation, thanks largely to Liberal governments of the 1990s and the early part of the 2000s, was far more favourable. In any case, public–private sector relations have most certainly evolved over time. Prior to the first labour legislation, described in Chapter 2, nineteenth-century capitalism during the Industrial Revolution was similarly unhindered by safety and health regulations, urban zoning codes, environmental regulations, and a strong trade union tradition, "and so could send ten-year-olds into coal mines" (Gwyn, 1995, p. 98). Today, "transnational corporations… can make their products in a 'hands-off' plant in some underdeveloped country," where workplace and environmental standards may be profoundly lax (Gwyn, 1995, p. 98). Moreover, as Gwyn and others argue, the threat of transnational corporations moving production to plants in developing countries "tames governments, and workers of developed nation-states," such as Canada, into reducing environmental, workplace, and social policy standards to compete for jobs (Gwyn, 1995, p. 98). The very powers of the nation-state—and the extent to which governments can exercise choices—have become highly contested.

Associated with these factors is the growing fetishism about and fascination with the rich. Corporate evidence that Canada long ago left the institutional stage of social welfare for the market state can be found in Peter C. Newman's *The Canadian Establishment* (1975), a biography of major business leaders in Canada at that time. Corporate leaders of the country's institutional welfare-state period frequently complained that politicians were hostile to business and that the public did not understand the needs of business (Newman, 1975). Not so today. Take Alberta, where—as former premier Ralph Klein discovered as he took employment in the oil sector within months of resigning as premier—the transition from government to business is seamless: Alberta's elected governments take many of their marching orders from the oil sector, which is responsible for 40 percent of provincial revenues, as well as for provisioning healthy campaign coffers for the political parties on the right (Nikiforuk, 2007).

Throughout and beyond the OECD, corporate graft (the high salaries of corporate leaders) has been increasing at appalling rates. A recent study of 292 companies in the S&P 500 Index shows that the average annual compensation of CEOs in 2009 stood at $9.25 million (American Federation of Labor—Congress of Industrial Organizations, 2010). Meanwhile, in 2010, there were 24 billionaires in Canada, with David Thomson controlling US$19 billion, thus leading the pack in Canada and taking the title of the twentieth richest person in the world ("The World's Billionaire," 2010). But the question remains: Where precisely does power reside? Political scientist Donald Savoie (2010) argues that because organizations and institutions have become so complicated and because the extent of the problems they deal with are so complex, we seek individuals to create solutions to major social problems, be they "rock star" development economists who hang out with Bono, or CEOs of major companies. The hyper-rich and hyperconnected of today's world—such as Bill Gates and David Thomson—have more power than the capitalists of the Gilded Age (1860s to 1900), during which time industrialization took root and a small cabal controlled critical economic sectors (Cannadine, 2006). Most concerning of all, the new corporate elite has the power to transform and control consciousness. The popular media, which are owned either by corporations or by governments supporting corporations, rarely question the values of the corporate world; governments and civil society increasingly imbibe the corporate world's values, methods, and terminologies (Amernic & Craig, 2006). With the seamless transition of people between corporate and political sectors, boundaries and norms become blurred, and government power is diminished. Moreover, as anarchist scholar Noam Chomsky puts it, "With services privatized, democratic institutions may exist, but they will be mostly formalities because the most important decisions… will have been removed from the public arena" (2010, as cited in Pearson, 2010, 25).

Chomsky has long criticized democracy in advanced industrial nations, including the ability of corporate, political, and other leaders to divert attention away from true power within societal structures. As he wrote, "One fundamental goal of any well-crafted indoctrination program is to direct attention elsewhere, away from effective power, its roots, and the disguises it assumes" (1991, p. 303). On strictly ideological grounds, many advocates of globalization extol its virtues: the promotion of new wealth and competition, and competition equated with human freedom. And yet all of these assumed virtues can be challenged. With the forces of global capitalism weakening governments, trade unions, and social policy legislation, "corporations, above all transnational ones, [remain] free to reshape the world to suit their convenience" (Gwyn, 1995, p. 262). Unlike governments, corporations are not democratically answerable to a mass electorate; they are accountable only to their shareholders, boards of directors, and to some extent the consumers who buy their products, as well as whatever forms of legislation remain to constrain them. The single operating principle of a corporation is accumulation (Bakan, 2004). Stock market guru and multimillionaire George Soros sounded an important alarm in his 1997 article in *Atlantic Monthly* and his 1998 follow-up book. "Market fundamentalism," he argues, "is a greater threat to an open society than any totalitarian ideology" (3). Like the communism of closed societies, Soros contends, the ardent belief that markets can solve all social, economic, and political questions has become hegemonic—all-powerful. The free flow of ideas, the bedrock of an open society, falls by the wayside.

A 2016 Oxfam study noted that 62 billionaires, world-wide, own the same wealth as the world's poorest 3 billion people (Oxfam, 2016, p. 1). This number is declining yearly: in 2014, it was 85 people; in 2015, it was 80. Extreme concentrations of wealth are particularly felt in countries such as the United States of America—whose political and economic force has world-wide impact. In that country, mainstream media are owned by fewer and fewer entities; American journalists censor their writing and thinking so as to avoid offending major corporate interests who own them or who provide advertising revenues (Hedges, 2011). Mainstream politicians are likewise beholden to these same economic forces; although there could be exceptions. As this book nears completion, Republican billionaire Donald Trump appears to be largely self-financing his campaign, and Democratic candidate Bernie Sanders is a self-declared democratic socialist who relies heavily on crowd funding. Journalist Chris Hedges argues that the pillars of the American liberal class have collapsed; its media, churches, labour unions, the Democratic Party, and various universities—all of which used to uphold the rights of the majority through critical, liberal critique—have been co-opted into quiet subservience to the norms and values of the country's richest people (2011). Mainstream opinion increasingly equates growing economic inequality with such prosaic claims that the tiny elite with enormous wealth are in fact responsible for economic growth.

Anarchist anthropologist David Graeber provides a critical perspective on income inequality and debt. He argues that increasing economic inequality is nothing more than a wealth transfer from lower and middle income people to the wealthy; and by inference, he is critical of widespread claims that this wealth redistribution has fairly gone to the wealthiest in society (Graeber, 2011, 2013, 2015). The past 40 years has seen a simple redistribution of wealth from poor and middle class to a tiny elite within the 0.01%—aided and abetted by corporate welfarism (governments providing large contracts and other incentives to various companies), huge bailouts (on and after 2007–08), and a political system that the elites own/influence: media outlets, superPACs (pools of large campaign contributions that fund select politicians) in the U.S., and political influence more generally across and beyond a given society (Woolin, 2010; Hedges, 2015). One may also apply a critical perspective on mainstream claims that greater social welfare expenditures will create a problem of debt. "Debt," Graeber argues, is a constant in human history; just as some forms of post-2007–08 American corporate debt could be forgiven, so too could other forms of debt—the debt of poorer individuals, or even of governments (Graeber, 2011, 2013, 2015; Hedges & Sacho, 2012).

The political system in the United States has become so dominated by elite economic actors that one political scientist has coined the term "inverted totalitarianism." Classic political totalitarian systems such as Mussolini's Italy used political means to take over economic forces. In the inverse totalitarianism of today, the argument has it, economic elites have *de facto* ownership of political systems in countries like the U.S.: hence it is an "inverse" form of totalitarianism (the economic systems taking over political systems, and not the other way around) (Woolin, 2010).

SOCIAL WELFARE RETRENCHMENT

Since the advent of the market state, a clear trend across Canada over the past 30 years has been the withdrawal of both federal and provincial governments from commitments to social welfare programs. This withdrawal has not appreciably changed since the fall of 2008 and the resulting credit and economic crisis. Common themes in the past 30 years have included political platforms based on program cuts and public pronouncements that the welfare state has proven too expensive and is a cause of "dependency." Programs affecting even the most vulnerable populations are being cut, privatized, or redesigned to reduce usage and eligibility. Some familiar programs have been renamed to signify this shift. Unemployment Insurance, previously a hallmark of the social safety net, is now known as Employment Insurance. This new name, and indeed the entire program, is intended to emphasize the enhancement of employment opportunities, rather than the subsidization of unemployment. Social assistance programs have been renamed and restructured to focus on paid employment (such as Ontario Works, the new name for what was previously known as General Welfare Assistance) and to "target" those most in need (such as the Assured Income for the Severely Handicapped program in Alberta). Health-care programs and services have suffered harsh cuts, and hospitals are being closed across the country. Although homelessness has become an increasingly visible problem in Canadian cities, until 2009, the federal government had largely withdrawn from social housing commitments; however, the January 2009 Federal Budget provided more funding in support of social housing than we had seen in a generation. At the same time, homelessness represents a case example of the multiple sectors that are involved in social policy: local, provincial, and federal governments, as well as a battery of nonprofits, including locally based initiatives to end homelessness, which are sometimes the genesis of nonprofits and sometimes collaborations with government and the nonprofit and voluntary sector.

Governments are using several strategies to justify this reduction in public resources for social welfare. One is the device of targeting resources only to those presumed to be most in need, a strategy illustrated by the Canada Child Tax Benefit (CCTB). Through this policy, federal and provincial income security programs are integrated, creating a single benefit paid to all low-income families with dependent children. This program was the latest effort to replace universal family allowances with resources targeted to low-income families.

Another justification of reduced public spending is an increased focus on job training and "social preparation" for employment, expressed in the idea of workfare. Workfare programs take a variety of forms but are generally characterized by requirements that employable recipients of social assistance either provide "approved" labour or participate in activities designed to increase their employment possibilities in return for benefits. Examples of participation requirements are job searches and active preparation for work, such as training and "upgrading" programs (Evans, Jacobs, Noel, & Reynolds, 1995). Penalties for failure to comply can include being cut off from assistance or having benefits reduced. This scheme, which is being operated in some form in virtually all Canadian provinces (Evans, 1995), has deep roots in the tradition of the worthy and unworthy poor, and in the concept of less eligibility (Schragge, 1997). Researchers are critical of workfare programs in relation to their stated objectives. So far, workfare does not appear to improve employment prospects for most participants, to reduce their poverty, or to remove the stigma of being on welfare.

CHANGING CONCEPTIONS OF SOCIAL WELFARE IN RELATION TO CITIZENSHIP AND SOCIAL INCLUSION

How are notions of social welfare changing in the face of the realities of globalizing economies and retrenching welfare states? Examination of this question involves exploration of the changing nature of citizenship.

Social Citizenship

Current trends in economic and social welfare policy constitute an important change in the way social citizenship is perceived and experienced, and in particular the relationship between citizens and the government. The work of T.H. Marshall is widely acknowledged as the starting point for discussion of social citizenship. His 1949 essay, "Citizenship and Social Class," examines the meaning of citizenship, which he thought had developed in three stages. The first stage, forged in the eighteenth century, established the civil rights of citizenship, leading to property and legal rights, due process, and so on. During the nineteenth century, the second stage developed the political rights of citizenship, including the franchise and the right to hold office. In the twentieth century, citizenship expanded to include social rights, through which the developing welfare state administered basic social and economic security (Morrison, 1997). Many critiques of Marshall's work have pointed out the unevenness of access to these rights for all but reasonably well-off white males. Nevertheless, the creation of the welfare state during the twentieth century certainly involved the emergence of entitlements through social citizenship, although these entitlements were often more tenuous than is generally realized.

In Canada, the social rights of citizens have been protected to some extent through federal social programs. The Canada Assistance Plan (CAP), for instance, obligated provinces to provide for people in need, included prohibitions against workfare and discrimination, and required the development of appeals systems at the provincial level. But when the Canada Health and Social Transfer (CHST) replaced the CAP in 1996, the federal government ended its commitment to a social "floor" below which federal funding for provincially administered social programs would not be cut (Morrison, 1997). The repatriation of the Constitution and development of the 1982 Charter of Rights and Freedoms might seem to provide new protections, but in fact the Charter contains no explicit protections of social rights. Further, hopes for additional Charter protections via legal challenges now being mounted do not appear to hold much promise for protection of social rights. Some social advocates fear that a two-tiered system of citizenship is being advanced—one tier for those who depend on public resources and another (superior) system for those whose main relationships are with the marketplace.

Considerable concern about this shift in direction has been expressed for several decades. Pascal (1993) noted that the logical endpoint of such a shift is that even the most basic needs of able-bodied adults and their dependent children might eventually fail to constitute legitimate claims to entitlement. Schragge and Deniger (1997) concluded their discussion of workfare with a warning that these programs may herald an era of profound social change and inequality, in which large sections of the population will be excluded from stable, meaningful, and reasonably paid employment, as the recession beginning in 2008 has clearly demonstrated. As a result, Swift and Callahan (2009) suggested, the alternative is to insist on formulating and evaluating social programs not with efficiency principles but with principles of social justice.

As noted earlier, a primary concern has been whether the nation-state itself—and therefore its ability to develop distinct social welfare policy—is under threat of demise. As trade zones and agreements proliferate and supersede national law and policy, we need to question to what extent national governments can control internal economic forces (Delaney, Brownlee, & Sellick, 2001) and whether states can retain the capacity to provide basic welfare provisions for their citizens. Most social critics now recognize that powerful transnational corporate interests actually do not wish for the demise of the state but rather hope for the reshaping of states to better support their profit-based interests.

As Barlow (2001) argues, national governments still provide the security forces required to protect global economic interests. Lamarche (1999) points out that the state is also needed to manage the problems of poverty, which intensify with globalization. This kind of state management, however, transforms the notion of "good governance" from ensuring equality, citizenship, rights, and benefits to the project of producing better consumers. The "citizen" in this scenario becomes less a rights-bearing individual and more a "functional citizen," whose goal is intended to be success in the new and changing global market.

Conversations about citizenship used to assume the existence of the welfare state, along with the justice system, as the grounds within which claims and entitlements were legitimized. Unions were among the beneficiaries, because the resources, stability, and power of the welfare state provided the conditions for unions to build strength and credibility during the mid-1900s (Hargrove, 1999). The benefits of the "rights revolution" of the 1960s (Ignatieff, 2000) appeared to be thoroughly entrenched in the Canadian consciousness and embedded in social institutions.

Current developments have brought this assumption into doubt. Of course, the September 11, 2001, attack on New York's World Trade Center led directly to new federal legislation curtailing a variety of accepted civil and legal liberties in the name of security. But well before that event, research had noted that the reorganization and delegitimization of many traditional welfare-state functions were rapidly eroding citizenship rights, especially for the poor (Little, 1999; Swift, 2001). Marshall and many others believed that the welfare state laid the foundation for full social citizenship. Those who agree with this belief decry the dismantling or diminution of welfare-state structures. Others, however, argue that the welfare state, with its "false universalism" (Hansen, 1999), was never capable of developing either the conditions or the content of authentic citizenship because it does not recognize the unique differences among individuals. The claims of diverse groups for increased entitlements and recognition, discussed at more length in Chapter 6, reflect this problem. Further, social welfare does not encourage the associative ties implied by the idea of full citizenship. Social welfare serves, but it does not identify, nor does it involve. It creates "clients," Hansen argues, not citizens.

In any case, recent examinations of welfare-state activities suggest that they are shifting away from service to a function of assessing "risk" and mediating accountability for risk. The goals of this new welfare ideology are calculating and managing risk for individuals deemed unable to exercise self-management. Certainly, widespread use of risk-assessment tools has become standard practice in health, justice, and child welfare, to name a few domains of the welfare state (Swift & Callahan, 2009). In this conception of welfare, even the service function, already in doubt as useful grounds for promoting citizenship, has diminished.

Recently, discussions have linked citizenship to the idea of "civil society" rather than to the welfare state. But traditional theorists conceptualized the idea of civil society differently. Marx, for instance, saw *civil society* as synonymous with *bourgeois society* (Hansen, 1999). In this view, civil society is the site of market transactions for personal, self-serving activity and therefore a space to be challenged and replaced. Hegel regarded civil society as a social space, developed to address the tensions between individual autonomy and communal interests, a tension that Hansen (1999) suggests is reflected in the welfare state. Feminists raise the question of whether "family" is separate from or included in the civil society (Howell & Mulligan, 2005). Most contemporary activists equate civil society with "the third sector"—neither government nor market.

This non-governmental, non-profit, associational sector is estimated by some to be the fastest-growing sector of society. Many organizations formerly grounded either in particular countries or in international organizations, are transcending these boundaries to become coalitions of groups claiming the right to have input into wide-ranging decisions in both government and corporate arenas (Florini, 2000). As this trend continues, the natures of civil society and of citizenship are shifting, along with ideas about the nature and auspices of social welfare.

Edwards (2005) defines civil society broadly as "collective" activity that acts as a counterweight to individualism. He suggests incorporating a variety of views into the definition, with the intent of strengthening associational life, and he offers several proposals for the promotion of a healthy civil society. His first proposal is an attack on all forms of discrimination and inequality, which he describes as "poison" for civil society. Second, he recommends supporting innovations to encourage citizen action, including the creation of links between policy groups and across different interests to break down the "silos" that discourage collective action. Finally, he suggests openness to "surprises," meaning the powerful action occasionally seen from unexpected sources. For instance, we do not ordinarily expect mothers to create global interest in an issue, but the Mothers of the Plaza de Mayo, through their persistence and passion, managed to create globally backed resistance to military dictatorship in Argentina several decades ago through demonstrations on behalf of their "disappeared" children.

Rebick (2000) describes in some detail the idea of "active citizenship"—the participation of individuals not only in voting rights, but also in political, social, economic, and cultural decision-making. Thus, while some social critics have predicted the narrowing and even the demise of social citizenship, especially for vulnerable populations, others are now beginning to reconceptualize its possibilities with more breadth and depth. These are themes that are discussed in further detail in Chapters 7 and 9. Reduced citizenship will surely mean a concomitantly reduced social welfare arena, one much more likely to be shaped in support of economic interests. An expanded concept of citizenship, however, might result in forms of social welfare that are more responsive to diversity and social justice. In this potential scenario, the relationship of social welfare to civil society would have to be renegotiated to account for the needs of "active citizens."

Social Inclusion

In the last several decades, the issues of "belonging" (implied in Hansen's critique of the welfare state) and of active citizen participation (as examined by Edwards and Rebick) have become issues for Western nations with advanced welfare states, as various groups have identified themselves as "excluded" from society and its opportunities. Social exclusion and social inclusion have consequently become useful concepts in contemporary discussions of the meanings of citizenship.

The concept of social inclusion arises from discussions about its opposite: social exclusion. This term was first used in France in the 1970s to identify people unprotected by social insurance programs. Through the 1980s and 1990s, the term's meaning expanded to include those left behind by the effects of globalizing economies. These discussions about social exclusion were generally undertaken with a goal of enhancing possibilities of social cohesion. In both Europe and North America, the notion of exclusion has begun to replace the discourse of poverty, because it captures not only the conditions of the poor, but also the underlying social and economic processes leading to marginalization of many populations, including areas relating to health, education, debt, access to services, housing, and overall quality of life (Good-Gingrich, 2003).

Barata (2000), on the one hand, has argued that there are several advantages to moving toward the language of social exclusion and social inclusion instead of using the old language of poverty lines, disadvantaged populations, and underclass. The language of exclusion/inclusion (1) includes power relations in the analysis; (2) has the potential to incorporate many levels of experience, for instance, health, quality of life, and rights; (3) involves "the social," implicating society in general as the focus of discussion rather than just "the poor"; and (4) stresses process over established outcomes, such as contentious "poverty lines." Mitchell and Shillington (2005), on the other hand, argue that the focus should remain on poverty and inequality to emphasize the responsibility of society to develop inclusive circumstances.

Concerns with and critiques of the language of exclusion include the obvious problem of deciding what it is that people are excluded from and what they should be included in. If not used with care and precision, exclusion could imply that the goal is conformity with the status quo and a homogeneity of experience. In addition, critics warn that important analysis of poverty levels could be lost altogether in an imprecise discourse of exclusion.

Implementing a process of social exclusion involves processes, policies, and practices that "assign value, determine entitlement and judge legitimacy" (Good-Gingrich, 2003, 12). Good-Gingrich emphasizes that assimilation, exploitation, domination, abandonment, and indifference are all processes that lead to exclusion. She argues for a framework that is dynamic, multidimensional, and relational as opposed to approaches that focus on the individual as the unit of analysis and concentrate on attachment to the labour force as the primary concern (Good-Gingrich, 2008).

Many theorists are working to sharpen and clarify meanings of exclusion. Klasen (1998), for example, has identified four different sources of exclusion. One source is economic exclusion, relating to the problems of unemployment and poverty captured in previous examinations of disadvantage. A second type is social exclusion, based, for instance, on neighbourhood or family type. Exclusion by birth or background is another source, referring to such issues as disability. Finally, Klasen identifies socio-political exclusion, referring, for instance, to discrimination by race, culture, or gender. Good-Gingrich (2003) has expanded on these categories of exclusion to include political exclusion, which refers to an inability to participate in political processes; geographic exclusion, which consists of labelling places and spaces as, for instance, economically deprived or high-crime areas; and subjective exclusion, which means personal internalization of judgments.

The apparent opposite of social exclusion is *social inclusion*, a term that has come into common usage in North American social policy discourse, and one that Freiler (2000) argues has the capacity to bridge social and economic policy. A major contributor to the international discussion of social inclusion is Amartya Sen (1992). Sen explores the notion of "capability enhancement" as a feature of inclusionary policies. In this case, *capability* means having access to resources necessary for the creation of a life one values. Sen identifies two levels of capability, basic and complex, each important in itself. According to Sen, social welfare goals, now often framed in "risk" terminology, should focus instead on enhancing basic capabilities, such as food security and literacy, as well as complex capabilities, such as civic participation. Capability may be enhanced by social, economic, cultural, and political structures. Analysis of social welfare and social policy then becomes an examination not of risk and accountability, but of the way legislation and policy enhance or inhibit capacity building for individuals and identity groups.

Critics of the widespread use of social inclusion point out that this terminology can be used to support any political position. Silver (1994) has investigated this issue, identifying three ideological uses of this discourse: neo-liberal, social democratic, and social change. Her analysis shows that both British and North American usages of these terms are primarily neo-liberal. In Canada, *The Senate Report on Social Cohesion* (The Standing Senate Committee on Social Affairs, Science and Technology, 1999), for instance, developed strategies for inclusion that relied on neo-liberal terminology such as *investing in human capital* and *removing barriers to social and economic participation*. These objectives signal workfare and other programs designed to enforce participation in a labour force that is increasingly insecure.

Used with specificity and caution, however, the ideas of social exclusion and social inclusion have produced useful tools for reconceptualizing social citizenship, and they are also helpful in considering how social welfare might be redesigned. Jenson's (1998) conceptual framework identifying dimensions of social cohesion provides an example. She shows five continua useful for analyzing inclusion:

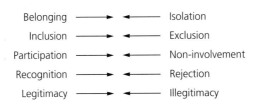

This framework identifies life possibilities and capabilities that allow individuals to become fully participating members of a society. As Hansen points out, the welfare state falls short on some of these dimensions, such as in its capacity to legitimize its users and to involve its "clients" as active participants. The notion of inclusion may help to provide new language and analytical tools that enhance the possibility for recognizing what is needed for authentic citizenship for a diverse population.

Richmond and Saloojee (2005) explore dimensions of inclusion related to specific groups, including women, children, visible minorities, First Nations, and people with disabilities. One author in this collection (Bach, 2005) argues that a "social solidarity" agenda is needed as a way of enabling currently devalued voices to be heard and to promote change that creates new paths to well-being. Good-Gingrich (2003) suggests that "Change is possible, as the dynamic relations of power that work to inscribe boundaries marking difference and exclusion are interrupted and contested with tenacious acts of collective resistance" (21). Amid the changing dynamics of social citizenship and the increasingly exclusionary processes within the global economic system, it becomes apparent that citizen participation is becoming the catalyst for improved social welfare. After performing a thorough review of relevant literature, Good-Gingrich (2003) suggests that resistance has become a significant concept within the present system and that evidence suggests the need to reject binaries, form alliances with other individuals and groups that are excluded, increase the role of civil society, and undermine the homogenization of the excluded group in order to reject the exclusion of people and groups within the present system.

CONCLUSION

Historically, social policies have reflected the national will to some extent. Yet globalization influences the range of choices exercised by governments. As companies compete in an increasingly international marketplace, the demands upon governments to restrict the welfare state may grow. Some corporate leaders, for example, seek minimalist tax structures and minimal corporate contributions to income security, health insurance, and other forms of publicly administered programs. Canadians are also subject to American political, cultural, and economic values (Grant, 1965, 1969). Given its growing presence, in part reinforced by the North American Free Trade Agreement, Canadian politicians, particularly those on the right, have looked to the United States for political precedents. Many policy analysts, in fact, are struck by the strongly American influences in contemporary Canadian social welfare retrenchment and workfare (Torjman, 1997, 1998b).

The influence of citizenship and social inclusion, likewise, will have a strong bearing on future social welfare development. But given the growing forces of globalization and North American political and economic integration, will the social policy choices Canadians make reflect what they agree as a society *should* be their destiny?

Chapter 6
Diversity and Social Policy

This chapter considers three questions. First, what is meant by *diversity*? Second, what are the relationships between diversity and social policy? And third, what is the "correct" balance between recognition of the interests of specific groups and the needs of Canada's population as a whole?

Three premises, in turn, guide the chapter. One premise is that social workers need to avoid thinking too universally about social policy. "Minority" groups have often been treated differently in social policy terms. Different groups of people, for instance, received the franchise at different times, some very recently. In the early part of the twentieth century, women were not recognized as "persons," and lesbians and gay men have only recently begun to achieve access to benefits long since accorded other Canadians and permanent residents.

A second basic premise is that a major goal of Canadian social policy has always been the goal of equity. However, social policy that purports to be equitable and potentially universal is being challenged for being too crude when universally applied and for failing to reflect the particularities of human experience. This is not a challenge to the idea of equality but a recognition that the provision of the same services for all is not always appropriate or desired.

The third premise is that Canadian social policy has been built on principles drawn from European and especially British traditions. A focus on paid "work" and a concomitant notion of the "dependence" of those who are not breadwinners are basic to our social policy framework. Basic principles also include the somewhat contradictory traditions of individual initiative and "the family" as the building blocks of society. The groups discussed in this chapter have in various ways challenged the relevance of these principles in contemporary times. The goals of these populations often do not fit well with tradition, and challenges to traditions, policies, and practices are the result.

WHAT IS MEANT BY *DIVERSITY*?

In everyday usage, *diversity* refers to characteristics of individuals such as race, culture, ability, age, gender, and sexual orientation. These characteristics are those that especially affect access to opportunity and resources. Consequently, the term *minority group* does not necessarily reflect the size of the membership but rather the relative social and economic power of the group. In relation to social policy, the term *diversity* reflects the reality that different people in Canada occupy different statuses and social locations in relation to the state and its policies. In this sense, diverse groups become categories and are often treated this way in social policy. One problem with this approach is that it tends to focus on people as members of categories. A related problem is that it becomes difficult to see that people fit into more than one kind of category.

Kallen (2004) speaks of "diverse" groups as subordinate populations. She views society as socially stratified, with unequal group relations constitutionally predicated on the inegalitarian notion of special group status. She endorses a human rights perspective based on "universal" ideals of equality and social justice, as expressed in such international documents as the United Nations Charter (1945) and the International Bill of Human Rights (1978, 1988). She explores the tensions between individual and community rights and considers how these tensions might be resolved by adopting a human rights approach based on the common humanity of all people, rather than on any single attribute of a person or group. Marumba (1998) elaborates this idea by suggesting that in the globalizing twenty-first century, people should adopt conceptions of human rights that include both the individual and group culture when defining what it means to be human.

Previous chapters have discussed basic provisions of Canadian social policy. However, people's different physical, mental, emotional, and experiential attributes mean they have different needs and variable access to these general social provisions. Further, the recognition of diverse needs in the Canadian population has produced social policies specific to the issues of different groups. Social workers need to be aware not only of basic policy and welfare provisions, but also of the related policies that reflect needs not addressed by these policies and/or that affect access to basic social provisions by specific groups.

Two British traditions have influenced Canadian social policy. One is the tradition of the British Poor Laws, which continue to inform social welfare policy. The Poor Laws, as noted in Chapter 2, established the concepts of deserving and undeserving poor, concepts that apportion blame to individuals for their own problems. Poor Laws also implied different expectations of males and females from the outset. A second tradition infused into social policy is social Darwinism (Christensen, 1995), which justified suppression and resource extraction from non-white populations and supported racial hierarchies. This ideology has shaped both immigration policy and majority–minority relations, and in turn has created the need for anti-discriminatory policies and protections. Along the way, built into social policy of almost every kind has been "familism" (Williams, 1989), a belief that strong families ensure a stable society. The so-called traditional family, embedded in Canadian thought and policy, is that of the heterosexual nuclear family, with a male breadwinner, a female engaged in reproductive work, and children who are "in training" to become productive and reproductive members of society.

Canada does not really have a set of coherent family policies. Rather, implicit assumptions and understandings about "the family" are infused into its laws and policies. Because there is no coherent family policy, there are some contradictions among policies and levels of government. Many policies have sought to define the family for purposes of benefit eligibility. Such definitions are currently subject to challenges from different quarters. For example, in the early 1990s, immigration policy attempted to enforce a very narrow definition of the family for purposes of sponsorship: a person could sponsor only an opposite-sex spouse or a child. This nuclear family model continues to be criticized by many cultural communities for whom the family is an extended kinship network (grandparents, adult siblings, aunts, etc.). An additional example includes women who have spent significant parts of their lives caring for others; they are concerned that their own pension benefits will be inadequate to support them in old age because they have not contributed to employee pension programs.

During the 1980s, various groups began to criticize the welfare state and its policies. "Interest groups," formed around cultural, racial, gender, and other "identities," have brought new demands and pressures for change and different directions in policy. In addition, because people are more aware of their identities, many have challenged policies previously assumed to be equitable and accessible to everyone. The 1982 Constitution also had an impact on the way Canadians think about social policy. Court challenges based on the Charter of Rights and Freedoms have brought new attention to the issue of rights. In turn, new rights have influenced policies and the way they are implemented (Canadian Council on Social Development, 1991), bringing attention to the identification and enforcement of anti-discriminatory policies.

Lessard (1997) and Kallen (1995; 2010) argue that despite these advances, entrenchment of rights may also have the effect of entrenching existing relations of subordination. Kallen has shown that the Charter entrenches the rights of three different specific populations in the Constitution, and that different and hierarchical sets of rights have been developed to protect these groups. The group with the most rights protection is termed the *founding peoples*, who are mainly of French and British extraction. Founding peoples are guaranteed positive rights that obligate the state in specified ways. Their rights are spelled out in some detail, involving, as an example, protection of Protestant and Catholic denominational educational rights. The second group is Aboriginal peoples, who are guaranteed collective rights under the Charter, but the rights guaranteed are "negative" ones, often involving non-interference rather than specific obligations of the state. The third group comprises other ethnic minorities, who are not specifically named, or *enumerated*, and who are protected only by negative, unspecified, and undefined rights. Furthermore, because certain minorities are enumerated in the Charter, and others are not, a hierarchy of rights has been established between these two groups.

HISTORY AND SOCIAL CONTEXT OF DIVERSE POPULATIONS IN CANADA

Canada's social policy was developed to redress specific inequalities, mainly those of class, income level and source, age, and family type. In general, state interventions were designed to mitigate poverty arising from problems with the market economy system (Williams, 1989). These policies generally related to the ability of an individual or family to access income and resources and were based on two principles: (1) ensuring that vulnerable populations did not fall below an established quality-of-life level and (2) acting to effect some redistribution of wealth from those with sufficient resources to those in need. For several decades, the building blocks of social policy addressing these issues were considered sufficient and at times path-breaking. The health care system is an example.

In reality, social policy has never been "the same for all" in Canada. Different social policies and limitations in access to resources have always existed for specific populations. This chapter describes several specific groups and the policies that affect them. These are certainly not the only populations representing the diversity of Canadians, but they do represent major groups around which social policy has been developed. It is important to keep in mind that these groups are not mutually exclusive. An individual may belong to one or more of these groups and identify with other diversities as well. Nor are these groups homogeneous; many within-group differences and disagreements are apparent. This reality, not always overtly acknowledged in policy discussions, is one of the significant features of contemporary social policy development. This chapter describes historical differences among various populations with a view to making visible their particular relationships to and claims upon the state. The discussion is intended to elaborate information presented in previous chapters, as well as to examine some challenges to the traditional foundations of Canadian social policy.

Ethno-racial Minorities

References to diversity often focus on racial and cultural groups. This may be because Canada's cultural and racial groups have been changing rapidly over the past several decades. In 2011, approximately 6.25 million Canadians identified themselves as a visible minority (19.1% of the Canadian population) (Statistics Canada, 2013c). In comparison, 16.2% of the population identified as a visible minority in 2006 (Statistics Canada, 2013c). Changes in immigration policy account for this shift. Until 1967, immigration to Canada was restricted to "preferred nations." Immigrants seeking and allowed entry varied somewhat, depending on world events and the needs of the country; however, they were overwhelmingly white Europeans, since Europe, and especially Northern and Western Europe, comprised the most preferred countries. British immigrants remained the largest group until World War II. During this period, immigrants were differentiated largely by language, and they tended to settle in regional concentrations of ethnocultural groups (Christensen, 1995).

In 1967, a new liberalized immigration policy came into force, one that focused not on source country—by then considered discriminatory—but on the characteristics of individual immigrants. During the 1970s and 1980s, source countries of immigrants to Canada changed dramatically—from European to Asian, African, South American, and Caribbean. The result has been a change in Canadian demographics. Immigrants now come from several dozen different source countries. According to the Statistics Canada 2011 National Household Survey, about one in five people in Canada, or 20.6 percent of the total population, are foreign-born (Statistics Canada, 2013c). Between 2006 and 2007, most of these immigrants were from Asia (56.9 percent), including the Middle East. Europeans were the second-largest group at 13.7 percent. Toronto, Montreal, and Vancouver are the primary settlement areas; 62.5 percent of recent immigrants settled in one of these three cities in 2011. However, increasing numbers of people are now choosing to settle in smaller cities.

As noted in Chapter 2, major policy responses to these population changes were announced in 1971 and again in 1988 legislation (An Act for the Preservation and Enhancement of Multiculturalism in Canada). The 1988 Act recognizes diversity as a basic characteristic of Canada and promotes participation of people of all origins in Canadian society. The legislation and policy provide an ideal espoused by many majority and minority Canadians, rather than a guarantee of equality. Legal protection of rights, however, was established in the Charter of Rights and Freedoms (1982), which is intended to guarantee cultural and racial pluralism and provide anti-discrimination mandates for social welfare law, policies, programs, and practices (Herberg & Herberg, 1995). The forerunners of this policy were laws after World War II that mandated "fair" access to housing, education, and employment for minorities. In the 1960s, these laws evolved into more comprehensive federal and provincial human rights codes. Kallen (1995, 2010) suggests that even these guaranteed rights are stratified for various groups of Canadian citizens and residents, with immigrants near the bottom.

Figures 6.1 and 6.2 illustrate historical trends for immigration to Canada. Figure 6.1 shows that the numbers of people immigrating to Canada have varied over the second half of the twentieth century. Since 2008, the number of new permanent resident immigrants in Canada has remained relatively stable. For the period between 2008 and 2014, the average number of newcomers was 259 822 per year, ranging from as high as 280 687 in 2010 to 248 747 in 2011 (Citizenship and Immigration Canada, 2015). Figure 6.2 shows that the number of immigrants was quite low at the beginning of the twentieth century and has gradually increased from the 1950s to the present. As of 2011, there were about 6.7 million immigrants in Canada.

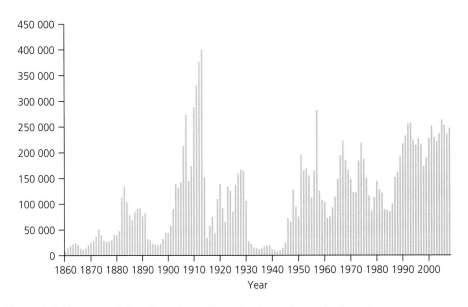

Figure 6.1 Number of Immigrants to Canada, from 1860 to 2008

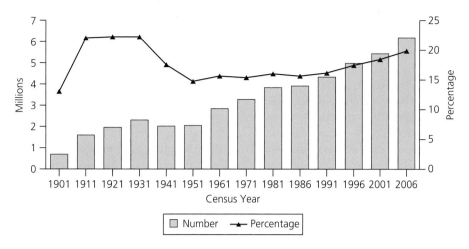

Figure 6.2 Number and Share of the Foreign-Born Population in Canada, 1901 to 2006

Source: Statistics Canada, censuses of population, 1901 to 2006. Copyright © 2015. Reproduced and distributed on an "as is" basis with the permission of Statistics Canada.

One major change in recent immigration policy is the source countries. In the 1950s, more than 80 percent of immigrants arriving in Canada were from Europe, with many from the United Kingdom. In 1994, only 17 percent were European, while 64 percent were from Asian countries. In that year, six percent were from Africa and four percent each were from South America and the Caribbean (*The Daily*, April 2, 2008). In 2011, Asian countries remained the greatest source of immigration; however, 12.3 percent of new immigrants between 2006 and 2011 were from the Caribbean, Central America, or South America, and 12.5% of newcomers in this same timeframe were migrating from Africa. Prior to 1970 only 1.9% of immigrants were from Africa, and only 5.4% were from the Caribbean, Central America, or South America (Statistics Canada, 2013c).

Another important change in immigration patterns is the classes of immigrants now arriving. In the 1950s and 1960s, the majority of arrivals were "family-class" immigrants— that is, sponsored by relatives already established in the country. In 1994, 46 percent of new arrivals were "economic" immigrants. In 2014, economic immigrants accounted for 63.3% of the 260 404 permanent residents admitted to Canada (Citizenship and Immigration Canada, 2015). These are the applicants demonstrating the requisite skills, education, work history, or money to enable entry into the country. That same year, only about 25.6% of immigrants entered the country as family-class immigrants, about nine percent entered as refugees, and a small percentage arrived in a catch-all "other" category that includes temporary residents and people admitted on "humanitarian grounds" (Citizenship and Immigration Canada, 2015).

Anderson and Marr (1987) acknowledge the importance of immigrants by calling them the "third force" in Canadian politics, not only because of their numbers, but also because many recent immigrants come from different cultural backgrounds and languages than either of the two "founding groups" and therefore bring different social policy issues to the fore. Furthermore, many newcomers settle in urban areas and are substantially changing the racial composition of cities. It is estimated, for example, that by 2031, people of colour could make up 29 to 32 percent of the entire population (*The Daily*, March 9, 2010). These demographic changes not only put pressure on service organizations to adapt to different kinds of needs, but also call into question the policy frameworks that have traditionally guided service development and delivery. In past decades, social workers often worked as though cultural differences were a small side issue. That is, approaches to professional social work could be considered generalizable to all populations. This belief was given credibility by the fact that the clients social workers interacted with were often born in Canada or were of European descent. Today's diversity of source countries makes this approach much more difficult to justify. In reality, of course, there have always been diversities that social workers might have noticed.

The federal government sets policy determining classes and levels of immigration and provides several settlement and adjustment programs from federal sources. The Adjustment Assistance Program, for instance, provides financial assistance for basic needs of socio-economically vulnerable immigrants on arrival. The Immigrant Settlement and Adaptation Program directs the federal government to contract services through voluntary agencies for basic settlement services, such as translation and counselling. Changes in immigration policy have included specification of access to services.

In 2002, Canadian immigration law was revised somewhat through passage of Bill C-11, the Immigration and Refugee Protection Act. This legislation requires that immigration policy fulfill Canada's international obligations (George, 2006). This law permits three basic groups to enter Canada as permanent residents: economic immigrants, family-class immigrants, and refugees. Each of these groups is positioned differently in relation to the state and its resources. Economic immigrants are allowed into the country on the basis of financial assets and/or skills considered important to the country and have generally been granted permanent resident status before arrival. Recent changes in immigration qualifications for skilled workers place more emphasis on employment "flexibility" based on education and language skills, rather than on specific occupations. The introduction of the Provincial Nominee Program, first adopted by Manitoba in 1999 and then by other provinces, and the Canadian Experience Class (created in 2008) mean that an increasing number of these immigrants will arrive and work in Canada for a minimum of two years prior to receiving permanent status (Gates-Gasse, 2010), after which they will have access to the same social programs as Canadian citizens.

Family-class immigrants, on the other hand, are permitted entry into the country on the basis of their relationship to a citizen or permanent resident already in the country. Entry of family members is contingent on a promise that the sponsoring relative will provide for the arriving family member(s) for three years (previously 10 years) following arrival. Arriving family members are therefore not eligible for many programs and resources available to other residents. In some provinces they are not eligible for welfare, even if the sponsoring relative abdicates responsibility for them. These immigrants can, however, access health care through provincial auspices. These restrictions present some difficult problems for social workers, who may be attempting to assist people ineligible for services otherwise available to others. In addition, the new law expands the temporary worker program, which allows temporary residence status for foreign workers, students, and some people on humanitarian grounds.

In 2015, the federal government passed Bill C-24, also known as the Strengthening Canadian Citizenship Act. This legislation provides the legal grounds for the federal government to revoke citizenship status of dual Canadian citizens, if those individuals are found guilty of committing treason, terrorism, or other serious criminal offences. At present, the governing federal Liberal party has indicated they intend to rescind this law.

Canadian immigration law defines two types of refugees. "Convention" refugees are those designated under the terms of the United Nations Convention Relating to the Status of Refugees. They may be selected either in Canada or abroad and are accorded full participation rights. A range of basic programs, including housing and financial assistance, are available to government-sponsored refugees in their first year in Canada. The other refugee group consists of people in need of protection. These claimants enter Canada without documentation with the hope of establishing a "credible claim" to stay in the country. Those who pass successfully through an initial screening become eligible for work permits and some provincial and municipal services, including health care.

Aboriginal Peoples

Aboriginal peoples, including those of mixed origin, constitute about 4.3 percent of Canada's population (Statistics Canada, 2013a). However, they are often overrepresented as clients in the service sector. Of relevance to social work and social policy is the fact that many different First Nations groups exist; for instance, there are 11 Aboriginal language families in Canada (Morrison & Willson, 1986, as cited in Frideres & Gadacz, 2005), several dozen dialects among these language groups, and 634 recognized First Nations governments or bands. Also, different Aboriginal peoples stand in different relationships to the Canadian state. The term *Aboriginal* came into common usage following passage of the Constitution Act, 1982. It can refer both to status Indians, who are registered by the federal government, and to non-status Indians, who are not registered. Inuit are Aboriginal people who are culturally and legally distinct from Indian peoples and who are not considered to be registered Indians. Métis people are those whose heritage is mixed Aboriginal and non-Aboriginal. Métis do not have rights under the Indian Act. However, recent legal challenges in a Federal Court case in 2013 and an Appeals Court case in 2014 have determined that Métis people are classified as 'Indian' under section 91(24) of the Constitution Act, which was recently affirmed by the Supreme Court of Canada in 2016. No clear policy solutions have been negotiated at the time of writing this new edition.

It is generally acknowledged that most of Canada's Aboriginal peoples live in difficult and often impoverished conditions and that they have for many decades experienced severe structural inequities. This reality is the result of events of the past as well as continued relations between First Nations and the Canadian state. Before contact with Europeans, Aboriginal peoples generally lived in small communities, and although there are significant variations among groups, many operated on principles that all members of the community would share resources and have a valued role in the group (Mawhiney, 1995). Contact with Europeans, who were determined to dominate both Aboriginal peoples and their land, resulted in severe damage to and reorganization of Aboriginal cultural forms (Bourgeault, 1988). Currently, more than one-half of status Indians, now more often called *First Nations* people, reside on reserves, most of them quite small. The Aboriginal population is projected to increase substantially more than the general population over the next two decades, and the population of registered Indians is expected to increase by 40 percent by 2029 (Indian and Northern Affairs, n.d.). This growth is due to several factors, including rising birth rates, reinstatement or inheritance of status, and migration.

The Indian Act of 1876—passed shortly after the British North America Act (1867), now known as the Constitution Act, 1982—marked the end of Indian self-government, which was replaced by federal control over the cultural, social, economic, and political activities of those defined in the Act as registered Indians. This definition was limited; those who fell outside this category became ineligible for the benefits of health, education, and social services provided in the Indian Act. Until recently, the definition of status was patrilineal: Indian women who married non-registered men lost their status. In February 1985, legislation was brought to Parliament to establish more gender equality in the Act. The changes allowed bands in Canada to determine their own eligibility criteria for band membership and assured the protection of rights for those who are band members. Aboriginal women who married non-registered men now have their status back and have access to federal programs as well as services off the reserves (Castellano, 2002). Further, in 2008, Bill C-21 repealed Section 67 of the Canadian Human Rights Act, which shielded the federal and First Nations governments from human rights complaints related to actions arising from the Indian Act. Section 67 was seen as especially prejudicial to Aboriginal women deprived of their status through marriage.

Aboriginal peoples who fall under the Indian Act access many programs and funding sources differently than other Canadians do. In fact, the Indian Act of 1876 gave the federal government jurisdiction over Indians and their land (Patterson, 1987), and agents employed by, as it is known now, Aboriginal Affairs and Northern Development, administered both benefits and sanctions. Also regulated by the Indian Act were legal rights, inheritance, taxation, wills, and many other matters. Until 1960, registered Indians who voted in a Canadian election lost their Aboriginal status and rights under this Act. Unlike for other citizens and residents of Canada, the health and welfare services received by registered Indians flow through the federal rather than the provincial governments, which otherwise claim these areas as their jurisdiction. Over time, exceptions to this rule have been worked out by intergovernmental arrangements (McGilly, 1998, p. 7).

These measures have had profound effects on Aboriginal peoples in Canada. For example, education, which is provided provincially to other Canadians, used to be administered entirely by the federal government for registered Indians. Residential schools were the required form of education for Aboriginal children between the late nineteenth and mid-twentieth centuries, with the result that many Aboriginal children were removed from their families at an early age and sent to boarding schools outside their own communities. Similarly, child welfare, normally a provincially administered service, was supposed to be delivered by the federal government to registered Indians. But since many children attended residential schools, a large part of the year, little service was provided (Johnston, 1983). In 1951, the Indian Act was revised to recognize provincial law as applying to First Nations (Mawhiney, 1995). Aboriginal children were increasingly encouraged to attend provincially funded schools and access provincial services. After 1951, child welfare services were increasingly extended to reserves, with the result that many children over the next several decades came into the care of child protection authorities (Johnston, 1983). Many of these children were adopted by families outside the province or even the country, and records of the whereabouts of many of these children disappeared. Others were raised in non-Indian care and became alienated from their own parents and communities. Today, most child welfare services on reserves are administered by bands through a variety of funding mechanisms (Indian and Northern Affairs, 2007).

Other services to Aboriginal peoples came primarily from the federal government after 1951; however, these services existed at a very low level, as revealed by the 1966 Hawthorn Report. The Hawthorn Report revealed that the ideal of equality among different groups of people in Canada was not being met for Aboriginal peoples. Subsequently, a 1969 White Paper recommended that Indian people receive services through the same channels and government agencies as other Canadians; but this proposal was rejected by Indian leaders and organizations because it implied the phasing out of rights guaranteed by the Indian Act. Currently, with the exception of child welfare, most provincial governments do not extend services to reserves. In the North, where about half the population is Aboriginal but where there are few reserves, services are generally delivered by the territorial governments (Indian and Northern Affairs, 2007). The funding and delivery of health, education, and welfare services to registered Indians on reserves is a federal responsibility. Section 91(24) of the Constitution gives the federal government the power to provide universal welfare benefits to registered Indians without encroaching on provincial powers. Access to services is at the band level. Bands are empowered under Section 81 of the Indian Act to enact and administer bylaws. In addition, most bands have developed sufficient administrative structure and capacity to deliver federally funded programs and services (Shewell & Spagnut, 1995). There are wide variations in how these tasks are accomplished, but generally speaking, service delivery through the bands has replaced administration by employees of Aboriginal Affairs and Northern Development Canada (AANDC) across Canada.

In addition, under the auspices of the Indian Act, the federal government funds the Social Development Program, which administers several services. These include child and family services; adult care, involving basic homemaker services for the chronically ill and elderly; and social assistance. The latter continues to be governed primarily by AANDC, a situation that symbolizes a continuing "dependent" relationship of First Nations peoples on the government of Canada. At the start of the twenty-first century, AANDC social services formed the sole source of support for many Aboriginals. A recent study shows the median incomes of Aboriginal people living on reserve are no more than $15 000 (Wilson & Macdonald, 2010). Since the 1960s, the federal government has made many efforts to implement economic development programs intended to increase First Nations self-sufficiency. These programs, however, have not resulted in improvements to the economic fortunes of many reserves across Canada (Shewell, 2007).

Since the early 1800s, the overall policy of the federal government has been the assimilation of Aboriginal peoples into the general population. Many efforts to achieve this goal have been made, but Aboriginal peoples have been determined to avoid this outcome. Over the past three decades, Aboriginal organizations and leaders have pressed for increasing rights and self-government. Advances in this direction have been made—for instance, in control of education and child welfare in particular locations. The Constitution Act of 1982 recognizes Aboriginal rights, specifically identifying Indian, Inuit, and Métis peoples. The wording of the Act places Aboriginal peoples in a new relationship with both federal and provincial governments, and represents a new phase in the long relationship between Canada and First Nations (Patterson, 1987).

Three main themes have been pursued in the recent political activities of First Nations peoples: (1) ending the paternalistic relationship that is the legacy of the Indian Act; (2) devolving social programs from federal and provincial auspices to First Nations' control; and (3) working toward self-government (Shewell & Spagnut, 1995). Another significant goal is the "revitalization" of Aboriginal communities (Castellano, 2002). The scope of self-government negotiations concerned with social welfare is inclusive—health, justice, education, housing, social security, child welfare, and social services are all "on the table." Control of child welfare has been of particular importance to First Nations peoples, to stem the outflow of their children from their communities and to control the socialization of their children.

Women

Social work has traditionally focused on women as clients, and the field is dominated by women as workers. However, until the "second wave" of feminism in the 1970s, many social workers were not aware of the special interests of women as a group. Of course, this lack of awareness is no longer the case. Social workers work more often with women than men because women are more disadvantaged in relation to social welfare and face different kinds of life tasks than men do, tasks that often involve dependents as well as themselves. As a result of these differences, policies addressing women's particular needs have been promoted and in some cases adopted. Social workers need to be aware of these policies and the debates surrounding them to work effectively with both male and female populations.

Changing demography is a different issue with respect to gender than with some other minority groups. Females generally compose just over half of the total Canadian population. However, females tend to dominate in older age groups. In 2011, about 55.5 percent of the population aged 65 and over were female (Statistics Canada, 2015n).

In addition, until relatively recently, women have been situated quite differently from men in relation to the law. Eichler (1987) notes that women were not considered to be "persons" under English Common Law. Following this tradition, the Dominion Elections Act (1906) contained a clause stating that "no woman, idiot, lunatic, or criminal shall vote" (CBC, 2000). Not until 1918 were Canadian women accorded the federal vote. In 1929, they were granted legal identity as "persons," and it remained for the 1982 Charter of Rights and Freedoms to guarantee women equality before the law.

Women have also been situated differently from men in relation to the paid labour force and its programs and benefits. The arrangements of industrial capitalism led to separation of the public and the private worlds of labour in the early part of the twentieth century. While men came increasingly to occupy the public and higher-status domain of paid work, women were consigned to the private world of unpaid and often invisible caring and household labour. Historically, there has been meagre support for women who were not attached to a breadwinning male. While a succession of policies has addressed this situation, the separation of the public and private worlds continues to have repercussions for women (and men) today. As Eichler (1987) notes, the husband as breadwinner was the statistical norm until the 1980s. More recently, women have entered the paid labour force in large numbers. Many of these women are employed part time, however, often because of child care or other responsibilities, and most women continue to work in female-dominated occupations, which provide lower status and pay (Statistics Canada, 2015d).

A report developed for the Canadian Research Institute for the Advancement of Women (Morris, 2007) confirms that women make up the majority of the poor in Canada, noting that even the United Nations has commented on the high rate of Canadian women who live in poverty. Today, one in seven Canadian women, or 2.4 million, is poor. The report demonstrates how membership in more than one disadvantaged group increases women's vulnerability. Women with disabilities are especially vulnerable to poverty. Those living in a household rather than an institution earn an average of $13 000 per year. Recent figures show that the average annual income for Aboriginal women is $21 733, compared to $30 110 for Aboriginal men (Indigenous and Northern Affairs Canada, 2013). Visible minority women fare slightly better than Aboriginal women, with an annual average income of $23 300 (Statistics Canada, 2015n).

There were substantial changes in the relationship of women to the paid labour force during the twentieth century. At the beginning of the century, women made up 13.3 percent of the total labour force. In 2011, women constituted 48 percent of the labour force (Statistics Canada, 2013e). Along with this change have come other changes in women's life paths. Women marry later and on average have their first baby at a later age. Availability of consumer goods has increased the possibility of spending less time doing domestic labour, thus freeing women to enter the paid labour force. At the same time, the rising cost of basic needs has come to require increased paid labour to cover expenses. Women have often taken paid jobs to close the gap between expenses and income, but their earnings continue to lag behind those of men. In 1967, women earned 58 percent of men's wages; in 1981, the ratio between women and men's average hourly wage was 77 percent, and in 2011 women's hourly wage was 87% that of men's average wage (Morissette, Picot, & Lu, 2013). Morissette et al. (2013) further find that "when gender differences in industry, occupation, education, age, job tenure, province of residence, marital status, and union status are taken into account, women' wages amounted to 92% of men's in 2011" (14). Although women made strides in public sector labour force participation during the 1980s and early 1990s, they are still placed differently in the labour market than men. Women have been historically highly overrepresented in the 10 lowest-paid occupations and underrepresented in the 10 highest-paid occupations (Pay Equity Task Force, 2004, Tables 1.4 and 1.5). Also, women represent a majority proportion of all part-time employees, about the same proportion as in the 1970s (Statistics Canada, 2015d).

Historically, there have been social policies specific to women, especially in their roles as mothers of dependent children. The provincially created "mothers' pension" program, initiated in Manitoba in 1916, is an example. This selective policy provided benefits to mothers only if they were raising children alone and were deemed "worthy." The universal Family Allowance (1940–92), a federally financed and administered direct transfer to mothers for each child in their care on a monthly basis, was another example. Contemporary assistance policies are couched in gender-neutral terms; however, women continue to be the primary recipients of assistance claimed on the basis of providing care for young children. In fact, it was not until 1984 that single fathers were able to access assistance benefits on the same terms as single mothers.

Over the past several decades, a range of policy initiatives dealing with the special concerns of women have been developed. Provincial policies funding women's shelters and other supports for victims of domestic violence are specific to women. Policies dealing with child care, pornography, sexual assault, sexual harassment, and sexual abuse are not necessarily confined to women but arose from women's concerns and experiences and are generally considered to apply to females much more often than to males. Equal pay legislation and policies are specifically aimed at reducing salary inequalities for women. These policies provide the legal framework to enforce equal pay for women who do the same work as men or who do work of "equal value." In addition, there are calls to redress policy directions that leave women in old age at a disadvantage in terms of pensions and benefits (Sayeed, 2002). Wages for housework and some form of pension credit for women whose labour has primarily been in the home are examples of suggested policy directions. The Pay Equity Task Force noted that women of colour, Aboriginal women, and women with disabilities suffer "double discrimination" in their wages and recommended that the framework for examining pay equity be broadened to focus on these groups. Recommendations have also been made for more proactive pay equity legislation (National Association of Women and the Law, 2007), but the federal government has so far refused to act on this recommendation.

Over the past three decades, the federal government has created an elaborate structure for incorporating women's issues into public policy. During the 1970s and 1980s, this structure came to include a minister responsible for the status of women, an Advisory Council on the Status of Women (SWC) at "arm's length" from the government, and a Women's Program at the Secretary of State, which funded many women's organizations (Eichler, 1987). In 2006, the federal government announced a 40 percent ($5 million) funding cut to SWC. In 2007, the funding was restored, although only a small amount is allocated to existing programs (Status of Women Canada, 2007). In addition, provinces have their own organizational structures specific to women's issues and concerns. In the era of downsizing and downloading, women's groups are concerned that these structures and the funding for women's groups they have supported are diminishing. In 2010, the federal government defunded or reduced funding for a number of women's groups, including the Canadian Research Institute for the Advancement of Women (CRIAW) and the Sisters in Spirit initiative, which brought to public attention the number of Aboriginal women who are murdered or missing (Airdrie, 2010). It is unclear at the time of writing if the situation for funding women's groups will improve under the recently elected federal Liberal government.

Women's participation in the paid labour force increased dramatically during the twentieth century and especially in the past three or four decades. In spite of this, most recent studies suggest that women continue to perform most of the labour in the household, including child care. In addition, women are increasingly required to compensate for the recent downsizing of many former programs and services by caring for vulnerable and dependent family members. For many years, women's organizations have lobbied for a national child-care policy that would support supervised, safe care for children while their mothers are in the paid labour force. Although repeatedly promised, as of now there is no such policy, a situation that continues to disadvantage women in the labour force. Instead, the federal government created the "child care allowance" in 2006, which provides $1200 per year for each child under the age of six to support costs of care, a mere fraction of the real cost. This program has been criticized by many as insufficient for this purpose. Under the Universal Child Care Plan this amount was extended to $1920 per year for children under the age of six, and was enacted in July 2015. Only Quebec has an accessible child-care program, one offering subsidized child care spaces at a rate of $7.30 per day.

Sexual Orientation

Not all groups in Canada have historically viewed same-sex relationships in negative terms. Some Aboriginal people, for instance, recognize the existence of people who combine aspects of both female and male. These "two-spirited" people are regarded as especially fortunate and associated with power and generosity. In contrast, European settlers, both English and French, adopted punitive positions toward same-sex relations. At times, Canadians of European background have shown tolerance toward same-sex relationships—for instance, in all-male situations of long duration, such as lumbering or mining camps (O'Brien & Weir, 1995). The general Canadian climate regarding homosexuality, however, has been one of hostility, with discrimination of many kinds evident in both public and private life. In recent years, the identification of sexually diverse populations has expanded to include not only lesbians and gays, but also bisexual, transgendered and transsexual people, two-spirit, intersex, queer, and/or questioning individuals (LGBTTTIQQ, or LGBTQ for short), thus disrupting the binaries of sexual orientation (female/male, gay/straight) and somewhat complicating our understanding of what social policies may need to account for.

Canada has long had a single national law governing same-sex sexual activity: the Criminal Code. As recently as 1967, men engaging in sexual activity with other men were considered "dangerous sexual offenders" under the Code and were subject to imprisonment. In 1969, provisions of the Code dealing with this issue were amended to decriminalize sexual behaviour between consenting adults.

Since the end of World War II, challenges to discrimination against gay, lesbian, and bisexual individuals have been increasingly raised at every level of government around the world, including at the United Nations (Wintemute, 1995). Representatives of these populations have been trying to establish a general principle that discrimination based on sexual orientation is inherently wrong. The adoption of such a principle would place the onus of responsibility on those who practise discrimination to demonstrate why such discrimination should be permitted. In Canada, two strategies can be used to establish this principle. One is the political advocacy strategy designed to create, change, or repeal laws in order to develop a non-discriminatory legislative framework. The second strategy is a legal one, carried out through courts and human rights tribunals designed to demonstrate that a particular instance of discrimination violates existing human rights legislation.

Through the 1970s and into the 1980s, several legal battles, some at the level of the Supreme Court of Canada, were fought concerning issues of discrimination against, or unequal treatment of, gay and lesbian individuals and groups. The advent of the Charter of Rights gave the Court the power to strike down laws depriving individuals of their rights. Section 15 of the Charter guarantees equal treatment under the law without discrimination. Although sexual orientation is not specifically enumerated in this section, court challenges have produced precedents confirming sexual orientation as grounds for protection under Section 15 (Young, 1994). The Charter of Rights and Freedoms has also helped to produce new debates, litigation, and directions concerning issues of sexual orientation (Woodford, Newman, Brotman, & Ryan, 2010).

Over the past several decades, there has been increased acceptance of gay and lesbian people, decreasing discrimination, and progress on social policy issues (O'Neill, 2006). For instance, Canada's Immigration Act at one time did not permit entry of gay people into Canada. This provision was dropped in 1977, but gay people were still prevented from sponsoring same-sex partners. In 2002, Bill C-11, the Immigration and Refugee Protection Act, replaced the old law. The new law allows sponsorship of a same-sex partner and additionally allows the admission of refugees on grounds of discrimination based on sexual orientation. A 1998 Supreme Court decision concerning employment discrimination because of sexual orientation ordered Alberta to include the words *sexual orientation* in its discrimination statute (*Vriend v. Alta*, 1998). As L'Heureux-Dubé (2000) noted, this decision shows the importance of looking beyond the Charter in the search for protection of equality rights. There have also been many political campaigns and court challenges over several decades based on the goal of including sexual orientation in human rights codes. All provinces and territories now include sexual orientation in their codes, and the Canadian Human Rights Act was amended in 1996 to include protection for gay and lesbian people (O'Neill, 2006).

Undoubtedly, the most significant policy shift in the last few years has been the legalization of same-sex marriage. In the past, both social policy and discourse tended to pose "the family" as separate and different from homosexuality, with the family symbolizing stability, responsibility, and happiness, and homosexuality representing a threat to this valued institution (O'Brien & Weir, 1995). Legal and social precedents defined *marriage* as inherently involving opposite-sex couples, with at least the theoretical possibility of procreation. In the 1990s, advocates mounted challenges to these traditional ideas about the family. From a social policy perspective, a central issue was whether "the family" can or ought to include lesbian and gay couples. From a human rights standpoint, the issue was whether it was discriminatory to deny same-sex couples benefits and entitlements enjoyed by heterosexual couples.

The Charter of Rights, Section 15, has been successfully used to challenge traditional laws related to marriage. In 2002, the House of Commons Justice Committee debated the question of gay marriage, finding a majority of witnesses in favour. By 2003, most provincial jurisdictions had passed laws allowing same-sex marriage, based on Section 15 of the Charter guaranteeing equal treatment under the law. The following year, the Supreme Court of Canada decided that the federal government had the power to legislate on the issue. The Civil Marriage Act, Bill C-38, permitting legal marriage between same-sex partners, was passed in 2005 by a narrow but convincing majority vote in Parliament. The Conservative government revisited the issue the following year, initiating a free vote on whether to reopen discussion on the legality of same-sex marriages, essentially with the intention of revoking the law. The initiative failed by a decisive margin, the subject was declared to be settled, and gay marriage remains the law of the land. The law means that same-sex partners have equal rights, obligations, and benefits of the marital relationship. Some issues continue to be challenged. The Supreme Court decision on the Hislop case in 2007 reiterated that surviving same-sex partners are eligible for equal CPP benefits, but it did not sanction retroactive payments past the preceding year (Egale, 2006).

While this policy shift received much national and international attention and has been advocated by many gay and lesbian people and groups, it is not viewed by some members of this demographically defined group as the most important or even an appropriate social goal. Inclusion in law on the same basis as heterosexual couples is referred to by Cossman (1996) and many others (e.g., Mulé, 2010) as an assimilationist position. There are substantial differences among advocates concerning whether assimilation is the most advantageous policy direction. Mulé (2005) describes the assimilationist position as a pursuit for equality leading to tolerance and legitimization of a sexually diverse population by the mainstream society. It is based on liberal notions of equal rights and tends to equate legal change with social change. In contrast, he describes a "liberationist" position held by many gay and lesbian people and groups as a challenge to existing social codes, freedom from traditional constraints, and self-fulfillment based on the creation of new forms of social organization, including the notion of registered domestic partnerships (RDPs), a proposal involving the replacement of government-sanctioned marriage with registration schemes allowing "private ordering of both conjugal and non-conjugal relationships" (Mulé, 2010, 76). Mulé cautions against too rigid a division between the assimilationist and liberationist positions, noting that each position exists on a continuum and each applies the strategies of the other at times.

Gay and lesbian people currently have other policy issues on their agenda. One relates to consultations and proposed legislation dealing with "sex laws" (Mulé, 2005). Proposed changes would include revision of laws dealing with definitions of "indecent acts," the age of consent for sexual activity, and the definition of a "common bawdy house." Parliamentary discussion of such issues as solicitation began a few years ago. Bill C-2, first introduced in 2005, was intended to alter sections of the Criminal Code related to exploitation of children and age of consent for sexual activity. Advocacy groups were divided somewhat along assimilationist and liberationist lines on provisions in this Bill, especially with respect to the age of consent for sexual activity. The Bill was passed in 2008, as Part 2 of the Tackling Violent Crime Act, in which the age of consent was changed from 14 to 16. Health policy, especially at the organizational level, is also an issue documented in literature (Mulé et al., 2009; Ryan, Brotman, & Rowe, 2000). Public policy awareness of gay and lesbian health issues has typically not gone beyond acknowledgment of HIV/AIDS. Issues relevant to gay and lesbian people include recognition of the impact on health of their status as a group subject to homophobia, as well as problems specific to this population, such as family planning, certain cancers, and barriers to accessing health care.

These challenges raise questions about social policy. One is why minorities such as those included in the LGBTQ communities have not been more readily recognized by social policy experts. Fiona Williams (1989) argues that social policies have always been intertwined with subordinations based on gender and race, but that these diversities have been hidden by the more universal categories of the social policy field, such as class and poverty. Certainly, those discriminated against on the basis of sexual orientation remain a marginal voice in social policy discourse, and the policy-based literature focused on them remains very small.

Another question is what constitutes social policy itself. Writing from a feminist perspective, Linda Gordon (1990) criticizes traditional approaches to social policy for being preoccupied with legislation and formal programs. Many writers in the field, she contends, do not understand that policy is constructed of practices as well as written legislation. This reality, as O'Brien (1998) notes, challenges traditional assumptions that the state is the primary site of power. Other critics suggest instead that state power is more fragmented and less coherent than the traditional field of social policy has assumed. However, it is important to note that much of the policy discourse related to sexual orientation, as well as policies themselves, are shaped through such state-sponsored processes as court challenges, rather than through traditional processes of policy analysis and development. In fact, in the case of sexual orientation, court challenges currently appear to be the primary instrument for change.

Sexual orientation is now included in the Social Work Code of Ethics (CASW, 2005). This addition means that the profession now formally recognizes the existence of these groups and bears some responsibility for taking action to reduce discrimination against them. However, Mulé (2008) argues that the profession needs to push harder for social policy that recognizes and addresses the specific needs and issues of members of these groups, rather than continuing to rely on human rights legislation.

Ability

People disabled by the physical and social environment have at different times in history been seen as symbols of divine punishment, as sacred beings, and as members of the deserving poor (Roeher Institute, 1996). In ancient Greek philosophy, disability was viewed as a deficit to humanness. In Western liberal thinking, disability has constituted a reason for exclusion from society and civil life. Canada's first residential institution for people with intellectual disabilities opened in 1859 in Ontario. Over the following century, institutional care dominated as the preferred form of service (Roeher Institute, 1996). The eugenics movement in the early part of the twentieth century, spawned partly by new technology, led to very punitive measures for people with both physical and intellectual disabilities, including institutionalization, sterilization, segregation, and medication (Stainton, 1994). Only within the past four decades have community-based services become the preferred service policy.

Canada is signatory to a number of international laws guaranteeing protection for human rights generally and for rights for people with disabilities particularly. The Universal Declaration of Human Rights (UDHR, 1948) is based on three principles: freedom, equality, and dignity. A subsequent U.N. document, the International Bill of Human Rights (IBHR, 1978), articulates rights of access to the economic resources required for participation in social and economic life, participation in decisions affecting one's own life, and affirmation of the worth of each person. Two further relevant U.N. documents are the Declaration on the Rights of Mentally Retarded Persons (1971) and the Declaration on the Rights of Disabled Persons (1975). Although not legally binding, these documents provide a moral basis for the formation of national legislation and policy commitments to people with disabilities. They express the principles of care, economic security, guardianship when necessary, freedom from exploitation, and rights of consent to the full extent possible given individual circumstances. A variety of more recent U.N. documents, most of which are not binding, indicate a trend in the direction of an international human rights framework for addressing issues related to disability (Rioux & Samson, 2006).

Critics of these international instruments note that the framers represent Western philosophy and attention to the individual, largely ignoring collective interests and rights (Rioux & Samson, 2006). Nevertheless, it is clear that both national and international human rights movements have strongly influenced relations between people with disabilities and the state (Stainton, 1994). Significant support and publicity for disability issues resulted from the U.N. designation of 1981 as the International Year of Disabled Persons. Later, the United Nations announced the International Decade of Disabled Persons, leading to a sustained focus on issues of disability rights for a longer period of time. Part of the Canadian response to this attention was a report tabled in 1981 called *Obstacles*, written by a Special Committee on the Disabled and the Handicapped. In it, three aspirations by and for people with disabilities were articulated: (1) respect and dignity; (2) empowerment to participate in decisions regarding their own lives and futures; and (3) accommodations providing the *means* to participate.

Also in the early 1980s, the Canadian Charter of Rights and Freedoms was adopted. Section 15 of the Charter, which enumerates specific groups protected under the Charter, includes those with a "mental or physical disability." Although Kallen (1989) notes that no right is beyond encroachment by state action, she also describes inclusion of disability in the Charter as a "monumental constitutional breakthrough." Inclusion provides rights protection as well as the potential for specific legal challenges based on this section.

In addition, persons with disabilities are one of four designated groups specifically mentioned in Canada's Employment Equity Act of 1986. This legislation requires federally regulated employers to implement equity programs and report annually on their results. In 1987, the Standing Committee on Human Rights and the Status of Disabled Persons was established by the House of Commons; and in 1991, the federal government launched the five-year National Strategy for the Integration of Persons with Disabilities. Both initiatives have been instrumental in advocacy efforts. Disability is also included in the human rights legislation of the provincial, territory, and the federal governments.

In the 1990s, several reports issued at the federal level provided more focus and commitment to policy relevant to ability. In the mid-1990s, the Federal–Provincial–Territorial Council on Social Policy Renewal considered this area a major focus. In 1996, the Scott Task Force, representing several federal departments, was charged with the task of defining the role of the federal government as it relates to the disability community. *In Unison: A Canadian Approach to Disability Issues*, a vision paper following up recommendations of the Scott Report, was issued in 1998. This document includes principles for ensuring full citizenship, including removal of barriers to full civic participation, for the estimated 14.3 percent of Canadians who identified themselves in 2006 as having a disability (Gilmour, 2010; Human Resources and Skills Development Canada, 2009). In 2005, the federal government announced improvements to tax measures related to disability, including the Disability Tax Credit. While important, critics also say that fairness and inclusion for people with disabilities must also involve investment in technical and personal supports for this population (Torjman, 2005).

Rioux and Samson (2006) suggest that two basic approaches to disabilities have shaped social policy over the past few decades. The most prominent is the biomedical model, which assumes an individual "abnormality" that can be prevented or ameliorated through intervention by qualified professionals. In one version of this approach, people with disabilities are positioned as "other" (113) and may then be considered as having little to contribute to society. Another version of this approach focuses less on the impairment itself and more on the limitations imposed on an individual's functional capacity. This idea leads to a goal of living as "normally" as possible. Second, a more recent approach to understanding disabilities is a focus on the social and economic conditions that impede full participation in social, political, and economic life. One aspect of this approach is to focus on sites for state intervention, resulting in the adaptation of the social and physical environments that act as barriers to participation. A "human rights" model, which is the most recent version of this approach, looks beyond specific contexts to examine broad underlying factors that prevent "some groups from participating in society as equals" (Rioux & Samson, 2006, p. 115). Impairment is then one of many determinants of exclusion. This idea leads to a much broader policy approach, one requiring a paradigm shift and substantive policy changes at many levels.

Bickenbach (2006) argues that anti-discrimination laws should be based on particular definitions of disability. He suggests that the International Classification of Functioning, Disability, and Health (ICF), a document of the World Health Organization, provides a solid framework of "body, personal capacity and social functioning" (79). In this view, disability is universal because functional capacity is universal: "disability is normality" (82), something everyone shares at some point. Social inequality as it relates to disability then becomes an issue of distributive justice—or injustice.

Canadian social policy concerning ability is quite diverse, involving all three levels of government and reflecting both the medical and social models described above (Rioux & Samson, 2006). Bickenbach (1993, p. 5) lists 14 distinct policy areas through which services related to ability are considered and delivered:

1. biomedical services;
2. employment programs;

3. autonomy protection;

4. rehabilitation and institutional care;

5. independent living;

6. housing;

7. income security;

8. physical access;

9. compensation;

10. communications and access to information/education;

11. health and safety legislation;

12. research;

13. human rights; and

14. anti-discrimination.

A 1990 report issued by the House of Commons Standing Committee on Human Rights and the Status of Disabled Persons noted the fragmentation of policy concerning disability. The report, *A Consensus of Action: The Economic Integration of Disabled Persons*, demonstrated that policy in this arena is inconsistent, ambiguous, contradictory, and often merely an "add-on" to other social policy.

Prior to the 1970s, disability of any kind was generally viewed as illness or abnormality in Canadian policy. Since that time, perceptions of disability have changed as a result of the advocacy efforts of Canadians with disabilities. Advocacy has been pursued in the form of three challenges to Canadian society and government (Valentine, 2001). One asserts the right of people with disabilities to organize autonomously, outside of the health care and policy sectors. The second asserts the right of disabled people to equal treatment as individuals with full citizenship. The third develops the argument that disability is a social construction, often more reflective of the fears and feelings of others than of the experiences of people with disabilities.

In Canada, as in the United States, a policy of deinstitutionalization has been in effect for more than three decades. Stroman (1989) identifies three dimensions to this historic process of deinstitutionalization: (1) the release of people from institutions; (2) specific practices designed to prevent people from entering institutions; (3) and modification of institutional practices to make them less institutional in character. Five forces converged to guide the movement away from institutional care:

- the growth of an advocacy movement, involving parents and organized associations;

- indictment and exposure of large institutions as dehumanizing and harmful;

- acceptance of the "normalization" principle—that people with disabilities can and should have access to normal living conditions;

- development of community-based services; and

- escalating costs of care in institutional settings.

Community services to supplement and replace institutional care were initiated largely by local organizations, often with funding from federal or provincial governments. In this era of cutbacks, developing a sufficient funding base and service infrastructure (as well as the social commitment required) for the wide range of community-based services required for people with disabilities to participate to the fullest extent possible in public life has become a serious policy issue. There is now a disability tax credit designed to provide tax relief to individuals with impairments who need assistance with basic daily living activities. The credit amount is fully indexed to inflation. The CPP also has a component intended to protect "working Canadians" (Lawand & Kloosterman, 2006, p. 268) against loss of income from any kind of disability, provided the disability is "severe" and "prolonged." Requirements to qualify for benefits are quite stringent, and although there has been a recent trend to encourage beneficiaries to return to work, most receive benefits for long periods of time, often until they are 65 years of age, when they become eligible for other benefits. Quebec operates a similar program under the QPP (Lawand & Kloosterman, 2006). There are also programs designed to enhance the employability of Canadians with disabilities (Jongbloed, 2006). In spite of these programs, employment rates of Canadians with disabilities remain far below those without (49 percent versus 79 percent, respectively) and incomes of Canadians with disabilities are only about two-thirds of those without (Statistics Canada, 2015f).

Increased attention to children with disabilities is currently being encouraged by community advocates. Available research shows that about 1.7 percent of Canadian children aged 0 to 4 have disabilities, and 4.6 percent of children aged 5 to 14 have disabilities (Employment and Social Development Canada, 2013). This percentage is expected to increase as medical technology helps to save the lives of more infants compromised at birth and in early childhood. Valentine (2001) shows that many of these children have multiple disadvantages. For instance, he found that children with disabilities are more likely than other children to live in poor families and in "problem" housing. However, there is as yet no integrated and clear policy focus on this population. Valentine (2001) recommends three "enabling conditions" for improving services: (1) adequate income; (2) sufficient services for effective parenting to occur; (3) and a supportive community environment.

Advocacy groups generally articulate the most important social policy goals as being self-determination and equality. Self-determination for people with disabilities should mean the same thing it does for the non-disabled: the opportunity to participate in making decisions about matters that affect their lives and support in developing the capacities enabling them to reach their goals. Equality means having the support needed (including special accommodations where necessary) to provide all people with an equal claim on society's offerings (Roeher Institute, 1996). Stainton (2005) distinguishes the current approach from the past. The concern now is capacity rather than outcome—with how choices are made rather than what choices are made. Also, the ability to act on that choice is key. Finally, Stainton calls attention to the "difference dilemma," referring to the issue of what people require to achieve full participation in civil/social life. Different people, he notes, require different treatment to achieve the same capacity for participation. Some critics warn that these goals may be difficult to achieve in a neo-liberal era that places more responsibility on individuals to guide their own fates. In this context, "ableness" may increasingly be seen as a necessary condition of inclusion and participation (Chouinard & Crooks, 2005).

Geography

A final area of diversity, of particular significance to Canada given the country's vast size, is geography. Historian Maurice Careless (1954) aptly describes the Canadian experience as a tension between metropolis and hinterland. Externally, much of our history has been that of a colony, subject to the norms and will of a faraway political/economic system, be it Great Britain, or, more recently, the United States. Internally, powerful centres—economically, socially, and politically—have dominated those areas that are farther removed from such power (Careless, 1954). Toronto, and Southern Ontario in general, has been the metropolis to the hinterland, resource-based Northern Ontario (Nelles, 1974). Central Canada may be seen to have been a metropolis to Western provinces and to Atlantic Canada (Morton, 1969). But these hinterland areas, too, have their own complex networks of metropolis–hinterland relationships within them. St. John's, as an example, has been a metropolis to the rest of Newfoundland and Labrador; Calgary and Edmonton are metropolises to Northern Alberta.

In social work, much literature has been imported from other countries, the United States in particular. In social policy, as we have seen, many factors existing outside the country have influenced Canadian developments. Social policies and the way in which social policies are conceived have had other biases beyond these. They have been overwhelmingly urban in orientation and have overlooked important differences relevant to rural, northern, and remote Canada (Delaney & Brownlee, 1995; Delaney, Brownlee, & Zapf, 1996; Delaney, Brownlee, & Graham, 1997). As Zapf (1999) points out, in one social policy textbook published many years ago, "rural areas were dismissed as exhibiting 'all the same problems as their larger metropolitan counterpart'" (345), and more generally still, "few pages" within any social policy text delved into "Native issues" (346), among other areas of concern to the country's traditional hinterlands.

Canada's population dispersion patterns are striking. A century ago, about half the population lived in rural areas. In 2011, only 19 percent were classified as living in a rural area (Statistics Canada, 2011). Only 1 percent of the population occupies the northern 80 percent of the country's land mass. And 80 percent of the population lives within 400 kilometres of the United States border, with a significant proportion in a narrow, and largely urban, corridor between Quebec City and Windsor. In Canada's North, small, disparate communities numbering under 250 are scattered across a territory as large as Europe, with only a handful of these small settlements approaching 10 000 inhabitants (Zapf, 1999, 348–349). In northern regions too, like their remote and rural counterparts, differential policy needs have been overlooked, and metropolis assumptions and metaphors have been systematically—and inappropriately—applied. As Zapf (1999) remarks, "Social policy and program planners have tended to view their own separate northern regions as variations of the south posing some service delivery problems" (349). Hinterland regions continue to be economically exploited, and when their natural resources are depleted or no longer valued, problems of unemployment, poverty, and limited labour mobility are intensified. Social policies have tended to reinforce metropolis–hinterland power imbalances and inequalities, so much so that some authors refer to areas of northern and rural Canada as a domestic Third World (Zapf, 1999, 349).

Soon after Confederation, the federal government began to implement economic policies and programs that affected regions of the country in different ways (Chappell, 2006). However, it was not until the 1940s and 1950s that serious examination of the way policies affected different parts of the country were undertaken. The Rowell–Sirois Commission of 1940 marked the beginning of the idea of equalization payments from richer to poorer provinces, based on recognition that uniform national tax rates did not provide equal services to all Canadians. The later Gordon Commission (1957) examined regional disparities further, especially those that persisted over time. A long-standing problem has been whether to define the issues in relation to provinces, regions, or subregions. Generally, provinces have been the identified unit of policy, since data are organized by province.

Since the 1960s, the federal government has run regional development programs in some parts of the country. These were initially aimed at depressed rural regions, but the mandate was later broadened. A Department of Regional Economic Expansion (DREE), established in 1969, was integrated in 1982 into the Department of Regional Industrial Expansion (DRIE). DRIE was dismantled in 1988. Critics of these federal efforts have generally felt that these policies placed inappropriate emphasis on the manufacturing sector and on job creation to spur economic growth in rural areas, rather than creating plans for sustainable economic development. DRIE was replaced by four regionally based agencies: Western Economic Diversification (WD); Atlantic Canada Opportunities Agency (ACOA); Canada Economic Development for Quebec Regions; and Federal Economic Development Initiative in Northern Ontario (FedNor). These agencies have attempted to promote local industries through financial supports to local firms and entrepreneurs and through previously established government programs. As one economist points out, regional development programs "encompass a broad range of policies, including grants, special depreciation allowances and loans to encourage the location of firms in designated areas. Federal departments and agencies have also entered into general development agreements with the provinces, which can include infrastructure programs, mineral exploration, industrial restructuring incentives, rural development schemes, etc." (Polese, 1998).

Collier (2006) examines the nature of social policy relevant to Canada's rural areas in relation to the differences among foraging, agricultural, and industrial economies. Foraging, or hunting and gathering, societies involved all members in subsistence provision. Kinship systems were of primary importance for survival, and decision-making was carried out by the whole group, rather than by representatives of the group, creating a relatively egalitarian society. Agricultural economies involve more permanent residence than foraging. Also, some people will be employed by others, and some will become much richer than others. Institutions like the church, schools, and charities emerge as supports and keepers of social order. As industrial economies developed and expanded, urbanization increased, and the modern state was born. Today, Canada's rural areas, Collier maintains, cannot escape the incursions of industrialism, and they are likely subject to various kinds of exploitation by industrial centres. They become, in his words, "peripheral" economies that are often subject to the needs of monopolies and multinational businesses rather than to local needs. Of course, welfare services and supports are present, although not necessarily as accessible as in cities. Collier recommends a "generalist" approach for social workers in remote regions where aspects of a foraging economy still exist and in rural agricultural societies. Knowledge of social forms and histories that still shape life in these regions is required, and a wide variety of skills is necessary, ranging from counselling to political and organizing expertise. As Zapf (1999) notes, a sense of community and local identity helps to create and sustain a worker mindset that will lead to advocating more geographically sensitive social policy practices.

HOW DIVERSITY CHALLENGES SOCIAL POLICY

Traditionally, treating everyone alike or with like intentions has been a valued social goal in the service sector. Diversity raises the question of whether these are appropriate objectives. The extension of equal child welfare services onto reserves, for example, has produced unequal results in terms of children taken into care (Swift, 1995). And, as many feminists point out, assumptions of gender neutrality are embedded in policies. In reality, the consequences of social policies have proven to be different for women than for men and different in many cases for minorities as well. Issues concerning definitions of the "family" are especially at issue. Lesbians and gay men have challenged the meaning of the family as being necessarily heterosexual, and members of various cultures, especially of non-European cultures, do not necessarily see the family as nuclear.

A related challenge involves the relationship of labour to social policy. This issue is especially relevant to work traditionally done by women in the private household. The caring labour performed mostly by women is a crucial and assumed piece of Canada's social structure. Current examples include the return to "family care," which translates into invisible free care often given by women. In fact, without this unpaid and usually invisible labour, most of our social policies would not be at all workable. If this form of labour were compensated, even at minimum-wage rates, the costs of social programs would substantially escalate. And as Eichler (1987) points out, until caring responsibility is equally shared—in actual practice—by men and women, social policy will necessarily be accessed by and affect men and women quite differently, with potentially different policy outcomes.

At a fundamental level, diversity challenges the concepts, assumptions, and structure of the Canadian social policy framework, including conventional ideas of need. In the combined neo-liberal and embedded liberal context of contemporary social welfare in Canada, the idea of need is increasingly personalized and attached to individual problems and failings, in the tradition of the Poor Laws. An alternative and useful way to think about social policy and diversity is in relation to the concept of "thick" and "thin" needs, introduced by Fraser (1989) and elaborated by Kerans (1994). We will examine thin needs first.

A thin need is characterized as "objective, universal, and abstract" (Kerans, 1994, 45). A thin need is rooted either in human physiology or in obligations imposed on the individual by society. This concept of need has been crucial in the development of social welfare policy because, as Kerans points out, the idea of universal need carries the moral weight required to justify redistribution of resources. Most social policy shaping the welfare state has been based on a notion of thin needs. Programs flowing from this idea were socially supported because of the presumed universality of the needs they were intended to meet.

Of course, universality of need does not translate directly into universality of claims on the public purse. Western societies, as Kerans notes, assume the market as the "normal" route for need fulfillment (1994, p. 48). Claims on the state are legitimized through evidence showing that the special circumstances of individuals and families mean that their needs cannot be met through this usual route. These circumstances typically include age, disability, caring responsibilities, job loss, and so forth. Nonetheless, a concept of thin need is an important assumption underlying social policy because it allows the possibility of claims by those in need. Thin needs as the basis for provision also enhance the possibility for justice and equity. An important characteristic of Canadian social policy is impersonal provision for socially legitimated needs. That is, it is not supposed to be patronage, or payoff, or promises of votes that justify provision; rather, it is the universality of need that justifies resource distribution. The goal is to ensure "standard treatment of all individuals, regardless of their ethnic identity, class position, or gender, as the basis for intervention with disadvantaged persons and populations" (Mawhiney, 1995, p. 223). This quotation should, of course, be expanded to include other characteristics of diversity, such as ability, age, and sexual orientation.

A problem with using thin or universal need as a basis for social provision, as Kerans notes, is that it is necessarily abstract. Thin need is an idea assumed to apply to all. Since it is not grounded in variations of real life, it cannot account for or express the multiplicity of experience and collective and individual differences that shape and give meaning to *need* in the everyday world. This reality has accounted for substantial dissatisfaction with social policies intended to address need as a universal experience. Bureaucratic procedures that objectify need for purposes of resource distribution (one-size-fits-all) have become sources of frustration for both receivers and providers of social programs. In other words, the attempt to create policy that addresses universally experienced needs runs the risk of "universalizing" human experience in unacceptable ways. Also, social policy is not created by all people. Policy formulation in fact is dominated by white males. Policy has a tendency to represent the viewpoints of its authors, which may erroneously appear as "universal" ideas.

Thick needs, in contrast, represent needs within a particular cultural context. Diversity is central to this concept of need. Thick need is not objectified and measurable but rather is viewed as subjective. Its meaning is constructed by individuals or groups through their particular experiences. As Kerans notes, neither category of need is as clear as definitions presume, and neither can stand on its own as the basis for social policy. However, the application of thick and thin ideas of need can help us explore the relationship between diversity and social policy. Challenges to the welfare state by diverse groups can be understood as insistence upon recognition of "thick" conceptions of need. That is, diverse groups are insisting upon their particular history and experience as factors in defining need and in satisfying it through social policy initiatives.

CONCLUSION

Fraser and Honneth (2003) pose two important understandings of injustice. One is socioeconomic, which is rooted in the political-economic structure of society. This is the primary kind of injustice addressed by redistributive social safety net policies discussed in other chapters of this book. The other kind of injustice, referred to as insufficient "recognition", is cultural and symbolic rather than material. Members of subordinated demographically defined groups (Kallen, 2004) are subject to both kinds of injustice, which frequently interact to reinforce each other.

Fraser (1995) argues that in the current era, class has become decentred; group identity and calls for recognition have to some extent supplanted class interests as the "chief medium of political mobilization" (11). The goals of recognition politics stand in some contradiction to the goals of the first form of injustice. Whereas redistributive forms of redress call for dissolving differences in the quest for equality, groups seeking recognition of identity seek acknowledgment of their differences from others. Fraser's challenge is to acknowledge both forms of injustice and to better understand the kinds of redress needed for each of them. She concludes that a transformative social and political agenda is the only way to address the goals of both kinds of injustice.

Chapter 7
Social Policy and Social Work Practice

Throughout this text we have provided an overview of the social welfare context in Canada in contemporary and historical periods (Chapters 1 and 2), current public policy efforts to address aspects of individual and group level social well-being (Chapter 3), along with ideological, social, political, economic, cultural, and environmental factors that act to frame social policy efforts at government and organizational levels of practice (Chapters 4, 5, and 6). By this point in the text you might be considering the question: How do we social workers influence social policy and more broadly the development of equitable social welfare efforts? This chapter seeks to answer this overarching question that many students of social work will have when engaging with this curriculum content.

IMPACT OF SOCIAL POLICY ON SOCIAL WORK PRACTICE: A CASE STUDY OF DEVELOPMENTALLY DELAYED ADULTS

As mentioned in Chapter 1, social policy pertains to provincial, federal, or municipal government legislation or service delivery frameworks that guide methods of intervention in direct practice. Social policy has a great deal of influence on how programs are focused and delivered in direct social service organizations, where social workers like yourselves might find employment. With this case example of services for developmentally delayed adults, we highlight the impact of social policy on social work practice. These services have been shaped by income security programs, eligibility criteria, and practice frameworks that aim to support the social inclusion of individuals in society. This social inclusion has been aimed at a range of social institutions—such as the labour market, the post-secondary education system, the health care system, within neighbourhoods or local jurisdictions, and within family life, among others. Each province has a distinct tapestry of social services, as elaborated in Chapters 2 and 3. For illustrative purposes, we are going to discuss briefly Alberta's policy in the *Persons with Developmental Disabilities Services Act* (2000). This policy outlines the government mandate to support developmentally delayed adults through the provision of services. This *Act* gives legislated authority to provide services to this group of service users. The application of this *Act* is manifested in several practice frameworks that guide practice. These include outlines for home living supports, employment supports, community access supports, and specialized community supports (see: Government of Alberta, 2015a).

Some programs provide services to individuals to live independent lives in their own housing, while other services include group home models with varying measures of restriction and security. These services generally aim to support individuals to maintain good mental and physical health and to participate actively in society through social interaction and engagement, along with labour market attachment. As social workers, it is imperative to consider the effectiveness of these practice models in achieving the desired social outcome of social inclusion, but also the desired individual outcomes for members of this service user group. For example, you might question: Is this model of practice ideal? And if not, what model of practice could be better, and in what ways could these practice frameworks be adapted to support improved social outcomes for this (or other) service user groups? It becomes essential for social workers to consider, on an ongoing basis, the relationship between public policy and the implementation of these policies at the organizational level.

Services for this group of service users is also impacted by benefit rates allocated through the Alberta government's *Assured Income for the Severely Handicapped (AISH)* income security program. Similar income security programs exist in every Canadian provincial and territorial jurisdiction (Chapter 3). Income security programs have significant implications for where people can afford to live, what they can afford to eat, and the extent to which people can engage in social and recreational life. Income security programs can have a significant impact on the level or quality of social inclusion that this group of service users experiences.

Furthermore, social policies that define eligibility for this group of service users impact who qualifies to receive these services. Following from the example in Alberta, policy has been established that individuals must meet criteria related to their adaptive ability and intellectual capacity. For adaptive ability, this policy has determined that individuals unable to undertake six adaptive skills among a list of 24, without the support of another person, would qualify as developmentally delayed; for intellectual capacity, an intellectual quotient below 70 and demonstrated lower intellectual capacity during childhood similarly qualify individuals (see: Government of Alberta, 2015b).

Through this one case example, it is apparent how social policy can affect the lives of members of a specific service user group. Likewise, for all service user groups there exists a range of public policy and practice frameworks that guide practice that impact service user outcomes. Furthermore, it is apparent that there are a number of contradictions between the different social policy domains. For example, there is widespread discrimination within the labour market. This discrimination reduces the opportunities of developmentally delayed adults to participate fully in income-earning roles to support their further social inclusion. Furthermore, the limited financial resources that income security programs provide impairs the level of social inclusion that members of this group can achieve. Without adequate income, individuals within this service user group may become more isolated from active social life, which is opposite to what is stated in the policy as a goal for this group of service users.

Likewise, the nature of programming (in group home and staffed service models)—which is also defined and mandated by government practice frameworks—can have an impact on the extent to which the general goal of social inclusion is promoted and achieved. Beginning in the 1970s, Independent Living emerged as a movement in which disabled people and professionals working in this direct service field began advocating for community-based support programs for this group of service users (Williams, 1983). The movement was a response to an inequity of participation in society and the inadequate supports available to disabled people following the de-institutionalization of major psychiatric institutions throughout North America and Europe. Formal institutional models of rehabilitation and treatment for disabled people were replaced by community-based support and independent living programs. In recent years, this community support model of service delivery has come under criticism for not fulfilling the earlier missions of the movement. Scholars and advocates have highlighted aspects of service delivery and social systemic factors that presently continue to maintain inequality in society for disabled people (Morris, 2004; Piastro, 1999; Shier, Sinclair, & Gault, 2011).

Generally, social service delivery programs for developmentally delayed adults have been criticized for being paternalistic, overly focused on individual deficits, and for aiding in maintaining expert control of everyday life (Miller & Rose, 2008; Scott et al., 2006). In fact, both models of institutionalized (in-patient) support and community support have focused on psychiatric rehabilitation (Baronet & Gerber, 1998; Barton, 1999; Pratt et al., 1999). The presence of the psychiatric hospital model has declined as a result of the perceived structural (or socially systemic) hardship affecting those individuals mandated to reside in institutions. In essence, a socio-political and socio-cultural rationale was applied to shut down these institutions (i.e., human rights, social exclusion, and individualism-based arguments). The alternative service delivery model, though, remains manifested in an agency-based approach, ignoring (in many ways) those structural elements that sparked this transition in service delivery models (see, for example: Cnaan et al., 1988; Becker et al., 1996; Rutnam, 1993). Further evidence of this individualistic focus is manifested in the principles of psychiatric rehabilitation: a model of intervention that is primarily concerned with individual goals, preferences, functioning, and treatment. This has led to community models of practice like traditional or intensive case management and assertive community treatment approaches (Boyer & Bond, 1999; Ellison et al., 1995; Rapp, 1998; Schaedle & Epstein, 2000).

This case example provides a general overview of the relationship between social policy and direct social work practice. As was described, it is not just government-mandated income security policies or eligibility requirements that impact service user experiences. The programs and the focus of efforts of the organizations that act as sites for social work are affected by government-mandated service delivery frameworks along with organizational policies that structure service provision for this group of individuals.

Social policy students and practitioners in Canada may be more aware of these relationships between policy and practice like this previous case example, than they had been in previous decades. An overall shift in general policy from support for the welfare state to the dismantling of programs and the restricting of access to social services has made social workers aware of the ways policy affects direct practice. Since the 1990s, social workers have seen the effects of job loss and long-term unemployment on Canadians. Many have found themselves in the position of refusing clients services previously offered; many have observed substantial withdrawal of funding and cutbacks to the programs they run. Yet social work training programs and literature often maintain a sharp division between the ideas and skills of direct practice and those of social policy development and analysis. This suggests—wrongly, in our view—that there are two distinct areas of social work practice: that is, direct work with individuals and social policy practice. However, as is demonstrated in the previous case example, each is mutually reinforcing. Government initiated service delivery frameworks and social policy areas like income security programs and program and service delivery legislation that outlines licensing and eligibility criteria all impact the way that social workers engage with individuals and families at a micro-level of practice.

One of the unique features of social work is its focus on the individual in a wider context (within a family system, an organizational system, a community, or a society), as well as the complex relationships between the individual and these broader structures. This emphasis on appreciating the individual in broad contexts is sometimes called understanding "the person in environment" approach —a key skill that social workers must cultivate.

In the early years of social work, this "environment" clearly included social policies and the requirement to use, develop, and change them for the benefit of clients. Pioneers of social work, such as Mary Richmond, Bertha Reynolds, and Jane Addams, focused on both the personal and the social context when framing ideas about the new profession. As Wharf (1990) notes, agencies such as settlement houses, located in inner cities, provided appropriate settings for social workers to observe the effects of social policies on individuals and to apply their efforts to individuals and to social causes simultaneously. In fact, these early social workers became leaders because of their commitment to social causes. "They cared desperately about people, they had a vision of the good life, and they were morally indignant about social evil" (Burns, as cited in Wharf, 1990, 16). These leaders considered social action, along with the promotion of legislation that would alter the conditions of life for individuals they cared about, to be a natural part of their work. But in 1915, Abraham Flexner, addressing a social work conference, issued a stinging indictment of social work. He urged social workers to enhance their own status as a profession by emulating the medical profession. Flexner said that if social work wanted to become a "real" profession, its members would have to develop a recognizable technology as doctors had done and would have to demonstrate this technology in their everyday practice with individuals where it could easily be seen.

As Popple and Leighninger (2001) argue, after Flexner, the social work profession focused on individuals and families as the route to professional success and largely abandoned social action. Flexner's work was important for highlighting the individualism that pervaded social work through the rest of the twentieth century. Certainly, by the 1920s, casework had established itself as the "nuclear skill" of social work (Lubove, 1965). Supported by the curriculum of most schools of social work, the majority of social workers have since been directed toward and trained in interventions with individuals and families. This trend reached a peak in the psychoanalytic training of the 1950s. During the 1960s and early 1970s, intense focus on social issues shifted emphasis back toward social action for many members of the profession.

However, social workers have continued to find pressing reasons to maintain their focus on individuals. One reason is that individuals and families present themselves directly to us; they are immediately available as the focus of possible changes, whereas policy changes are slow. In the political climate of the new millennium, many social workers may even believe that larger social change is beyond possibility. In *The Cult of Impotence*, McQuaig (1998) explores the widespread belief that social forces affecting individuals are now too powerful and overwhelming to be changed. Such disempowering myths reinforce for social workers the idea that the only useful point of intervention is the individual.

The welfare state era discussed in Chapter 2 tended to emphasize the active role of government in supporting the social well-being needs of the population. Scholars in that era did not consider, the way contemporary thinkers do, the broader influences of civil society/third sector and private sector roles. Social workers traditionally understood social policy to be developed and enacted by government and in turn shaping direct practice, and addressing substantive issues such as economic inequality. Contemporary thinkers continue to look at these machinations, but they also focus on the mezzo-level of social work practice—i.e., organizational level factors and practice roles related to social work manager, social welfare leader, and agent of social change. This level of practice, in fact, has always had a great deal of influence in shaping the application of social policy in practice along with engaging in activities that shape social policy development in both historical and contemporary periods of welfare state development. The following section elaborates further, addressing the somewhat narrow focus on the individual that our discipline finds itself, and emphasizing the diverse efforts that social workers can undertake to achieve improved social outcomes of service users. One point to keep in mind throughout this discussion: organizational level practice acts as a bridging agent between macro-level change tactics and improved micro-level social outcomes for service users.

HUMAN SERVICE ORGANIZATIONS AND CONTEMPORARY SOCIAL WELFARE

During the 1990s, scholars began to speculate about how the social welfare systems in advanced industrialized nations would evolve due to the enactment of changing economic principles associated with neo-liberalism, and hypothesized about the forces that would have the greatest impact on that transition. Social scientists across a range of disciplines favoured economic explanations. Some argued that things would balance out in the market: through market practices and measures the social welfare needs of people would be met. Social welfare state advocates attested to the important role that the public sector had in meeting the social welfare needs of people. They argued for a more elaborate federally directed social policy framework guaranteeing people economic equality and human rights (Powell, 2007). Other social welfare scholars began arguing for a possible "third-way" to social welfare provision. Those scholars began to highlight how many of these earlier discussions missed two fundamental aspects of our social welfare system: they disregarded the existence of a vibrant third sector that began emerging in more formal contexts since the 1970s, but had been around long before that; and social welfare was only considered in a macro-structural context. For instance, emphasis has largely been placed on systemic issues like poverty or homelessness, or large scale social policies, such as multiculturalism or income security measures. These discussions disregarded the role of mezzo-level social work (i.e., the efforts of organizations as a unit of analysis) in meeting the social welfare needs of people diverse in socio-economic status, psycho-social functioning, and demographically defined characteristics.

As an alternative to this traditional social welfare perspective, more recently, and in particular within the nonprofit and public administration literature, discussions related to the role of civil society and social capital to support social welfare development have gained momentum and favour. Primarily this has been because of a more recent realization or acceptance of the market system failure, and in many ways the failure of the government systems method of social welfare provision—with its primary focus on income security and other redistributive measures (Mayer, 2003). As a result, many social welfare theoreticians have begun to renegotiate the term social welfare in relation to the present social environment (defined by a wide range of political, economic, cultural, and social characteristics that have redefined the way in which the social well-being needs of citizens are addressed; see, for example: Castles, 2007; Clasen & Siegel, 2007; Powell, 2007). Many of these authors, following from post-modern traditions, have articulated the emergence of a deconstructive and re-constructive process of social welfare, primarily in relation to the third sector (i.e., nonprofit organizations and other forms of association such as grassroots initiatives or individual acts of reciprocity, such as donating or volunteering) (see, for example: Leibfried & Mau, 2008; Maloney & van Deth, 2008; Powell, 2007). Literature on the third sector, in relation to social welfare specifically, has highlighted the central role of nonprofits in influencing both public policy and acting as agents for the development of civil society (Anheier, 2004; Powell, 2007; Putnam, 2000). These discussions are important for social workers to understand. Since many social workers are employed by direct service nonprofits, their role in social welfare and social policy development becomes tied to their day-to-day work efforts with service user groups.

These contemporary discussions of the role of civil society organizations in shaping social welfare and social policy have followed from both neo-Tocquevillian (i.e., those that follow the earlier works of Alexis de Tocqueville) and Gramsci traditions (i.e., those that follow the earlier works of Antonio Gramsci) (Anheier, 2009). Focusing on the work of Alexis de Tocqueville (2004 – translated version), social scientists have presented the belief that social issues are rooted in a lack of social ties. This has led to a series of discussions about a phenomenon popularly known as "social capital" as it relates to nonprofit organizations and the voluntary sector (Putnam, 2000). What this research suggests is that nonprofits create opportunities for individuals to participate and can aid in reducing the social exclusion of segments of the population. Other scholars have followed the work of Antonio Gramsci, who has argued that the role of civil society is to mobilize popular discontent, to promote empowerment, and to create systemic change (Anheier, 2009). In this regard, nonprofits are seen as active agents that seek to address issues of inequality and mobilize groups to create social change within local jurisdictions. The role of third sector organizations generally follows in both of these ideals; that is, nonprofits promote social networking, democratic development, and prosperity, and they challenge existing authorities. In fact, within the literature there are many case study examples of direct service nonprofits undertaking these social development roles (Boyd & Wilmoth, 2006; Choco et al., 2004; Cnaan & Vinokur-Kaplan, 2015; Cohen & Hyde, 2014; Gulati & Guest, 1990; Kline, Dolgon, & Dresser, 2000; Nichols, 2006; Shier & Graham, 2013; Shier & Handy, 2015a; Spergel & Grossman, 1997; Wei-Skillern et al., 2007).

Scholars discussing the importance of mezzo-levels of social work practice and civil society/third sector and private roles are not universally claiming that the government should abandon its role in improving overall social well-being. We certainly do not, either. Instead, following Powell (2007), the argument is that civil society may offer a new social policy agenda because it may open up the state to citizen participation. It has the potential to render social policies more responsive to the local needs of the citizens. Chapter 4 outlines ideological differences amongst political parties; these same differences are found among individuals, and between the entire range of public, private, and civil society sectors that are part of social welfare (Harvey, 2005). There may be collaboration, but there may also be conflict (Brown & Troutt, 2003; Phillips, 2003; Phillips & Graham, 2000).

The importance of direct service nonprofits in contemporary social welfare is four-fold. First, in many areas of direct social work practice it is often nonprofit organizations where practitioners are exposed to the day-to-day needs of service users (such as in local neighbourhood associations, child welfare organizations, hospitals, universities, etc.). As a result, nonprofits are in a position to undertake ongoing local community needs assessments based on the experiences of those people that are made vulnerable by the social system, and provide meaningful solutions to improve social outcomes (Mulroy, 2004; Shier & Graham, 2013).

Second, there is a historical context in which social change emerges from the local level. There are many examples: the social movements beginning in the 1800s, such as the settlement house movement, social reform movement, or prison reform movement; those from the early to mid-1900s, which include institutionalized long-term care for the elderly, and independent living for people with serious mental illness; and more recently in the 1970s and 1980s, the recovery house movement, the development of domestic violence shelters, and community supports for people living with HIV/AIDs (Beard, Propst, & Malamud, 1982; Cohen, 1974; Dincin, 1975; Emery & Emery, 1999; Graham, 1992; 1996; Sowell & Grier, 1995; Splane, 1965; Tobin, 2003). As this literature suggests, direct service nonprofits have had a fundamental role in shaping the progress of social welfare (Shier & Graham, 2014).

Third, there have been structural changes within the social welfare system in most advanced industrialized countries in recent decades, where neo-liberal governments have moved away from traditional *welfarism* (characterized by extensive government income security support beginning around 1941 through to the mid-1970s) (see Chapters 2 and 3). Scholars have identified two key characteristics of this regrettable change: local community initiatives have become increasingly important for bringing to the forefront social justice related issues; and there has been a slow progression towards less government involvement in the direct provision of services, resulting in community-based organizations becoming potentially more responsible for providing direction for the development of quality services that are meeting service user (and community member) need (Bloemraad, 2006; Castles, 2007; Clasen & Siegel, 2007; Erickson, 2009; Leibfried & Mau, 2008; Maloney & van Deth, 2008; Powell, 2007; Salamon, 2002; van der Platt & Barrett, 2006).

Fourth, and finally, there are approximately 170 000 nonprofit organizations in Canada; or one organization for every 210 people (the second largest per capita nonprofit sector in the world) (Imagine Canada, 2015). The nonprofit and voluntary sector in Canada provides employment to 11.1 percent of the actively employed population and represents 8.1 percent of the country's gross domestic product (Imagine Canada, 2015). Recent data from 2010 show that Canadians donated over $10 billion in that year, and that nearly 85 percent of Canadians donated money (Imagine Canada, 2015). Also, approximately 47 percent of Canadians engage in volunteer activities. The number of volunteer hours in 2010 equated to nearly 2.1 billion hours (Imagine Canada, 2015). In relation to full-time work, this number of hours represents the equivalent of 1.1 million full-time jobs. Together, these numbers highlight the significant social, economic, and political impact of the nonprofit and voluntary sector by meeting emergent (such as new challenges associated with changing demographics) and persistent (such as ongoing challenges with housing loss or labour market vulnerability) social needs, by supporting labour market and general economic growth, and by providing opportunity for active citizenship through advocacy efforts and volunteerism. Likewise, as Shier and Handy (2014) argue, "in the United States, United Kingdom, Netherlands, Australia and many other developing and developed countries, there is a burgeoning growth in the nonprofit sector, and in many cases governments are turning to nonprofit organizations to partner with them in the provision of many collective goods and services (i.e., those goods and services that aim to benefit the general populace)" (p. 814).

As these points highlight, nonprofits, and the voluntary sector more generally, as key institutional entities within the contemporary welfare state, are in a position to create meaningful social change, and are actively pursuing efforts of social development beyond their direct service roles. However, research investigating the ways that these social change efforts are manifested within direct service nonprofits tends to focus on the political advocacy role of this organization type (Almog-Bar & Schmid, 2014; Shier & Handy, 2015a). This narrow focus does not fully capture the range of roles espoused by nonprofits in their efforts at shaping or creating social development, and certainly has had a significant impact on shaping the perspective of the role of social work in relation to social policy and social welfare development. Through emerging practices and perspectives of social entrepreneurship and social innovation, direct service nonprofits have been redefining their relationship with public policy and finding new ways to influence and shape social welfare development for service user groups (Shier & Handy, 2015a). One area has been through direct engagement in advocacy-related activities, although nonprofits are limited by Canada Revenue Agency regulations (informed by the Income Tax Act and Canadian common law) on the amount of resources nonprofits are able to allocate to such activities. Similarly, nonprofits have been actively engaged in developing and adapting existing programs to improve service user outcomes. The following elaborates further on how social workers engaged at a mezzo-level of practice through organizational management and leadership can shape social policy and social welfare development.

SHAPING SOCIAL POLICY AND SOCIAL WELFARE DEVELOPMENT

Social workers and other leaders in direct service organizations engage in a range of organizational level activities that not only shape how social policy is implemented at a practice level, but also shape contemporary policy discussions to improve existing legislation. Across Canada, direct social service organizations are typically nonprofits, although there are many for-profit, direct social service organizations throughout Canada as well, and in some jurisdictions or areas of social policy, governments still provide services—such as in the form of provincial income security programs or child welfare departments. For the latter, in many instances there are partnerships between government services and nonprofits or for-profit service-providing organizations to carry out the full scope of the intervention prescribed in a particular policy or practice framework. For example, in many Canadian jurisdictions child welfare services are provided by the government; however, some aspects of these services are also provided by direct social service nonprofits and for-profits—such as adoption services, respite services, and behavioural treatment programs, among others.

Similarly, many direct service nonprofits throughout Canada are engaging in market-based efforts (such as the development of social enterprise initiatives) to generate revenues (whether as a result of government funding cutbacks or to secure funding to undertake socially innovative programs and initiatives—that is, those programs and initiatives that aim to improve the macro quality of life of groups of service users) (Shier & Handy, 2015b). A social enterprise is a business that has a social mission, where the profits and assets accrued are utilized to achieve a particular social purpose (Quarter, Mook & Armstrong, 2009; Quarter, Ryan, & Chan, 2015a; Quarter, Ryan, & Chan, 2015b; Spear, 2006; Yunus, 2007). According to Social Enterprise Canada (2014), social enterprises are "businesses owned by nonprofit organizations that are directly involved in the production and/or selling of goods and services for the blended purpose of generating income and achieving social, cultural, and/or environmental aims."

These efforts of engagement between nonprofit and for-profit entities may highlight the emerging role of direct service nonprofits in shaping the focus of service delivery efforts beyond the focus of existing public policy. Nonprofits that engage in market-based efforts of revenue generation are able to develop programming and new methods of intervention beyond the sometimes narrow focus of existing government initiatives. Likewise, many nonprofits are increasingly relying on other civil society actors to address limitations in government funding and to undertake new efforts that aim to improve service user outcomes. These efforts have been manifested in philanthropic campaigns, applications for one-time project funding through philanthropic foundations and government departments, and engagement with volunteer workforces. This interrelationship between government, nonprofit, and for-profit providers is characteristic of the emerging model of third-sector governance mentioned in Chapter 1, and suggests a deeply embedded cross-sector (i.e., between government, for-profit, and nonprofit sectors) arrangement in the provision of contemporary social welfare efforts. This arrangement is depicted in Figure 7.1.

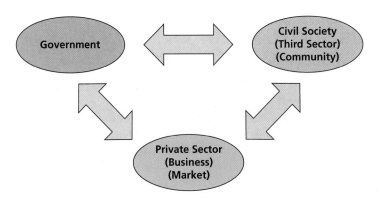

Figure 7.1 Contemporary model of governance.

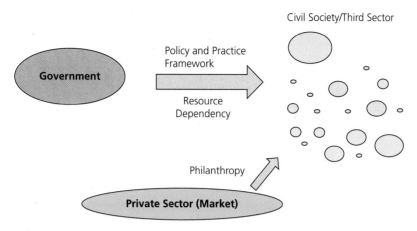

Figure 7.2 Cross-sector relationship characteristics of traditional welfarism.

The image in Figure 7.1 highlights the interrelationship between these three dominant societal sectors with regard to the administration and provision of social welfare. As previously mentioned, nonprofit service providing organizations are engaging more and more with the private sector through market-based activities (such as social enterprise initiatives) to fund programs and services that have a social good purpose. Likewise, the government and civil society sector are in a mutually engaged relationship through the application of public policy and the provision of government mandated services. This is a distinctive model of contemporary social welfare than what has been typically prescribed by traditional welfare state theorists. Figure 7.2 provides an image of what has typically been defined as a traditional welfare state model.

Figure 7.2 depicts one-sided relationships between the government and nonprofit organizations and between the private sector and nonprofit organizations. Furthermore, nonprofit organizations, from a traditional welfare state perspective, are not considered a collective sector of civil society actors, but instead are viewed in silos of distinct service areas. The relationship between the government and these organizations has been viewed in terms of policy and practice frameworks and resource allocation. Similarly, the relationship between these organizations and the private sector is also one of resource dependency, by way of engagement in philanthropic campaigns. From this traditional welfare state perspective, the relationship between social workers, public policy, and social welfare development has been conceptualized through the construct of political advocacy, which has tended to be the general focus within the literature (Almog-Bar & Schmid, 2014), and is depicted in Figure 7.3.

Political advocacy refers to those efforts made to change or adapt existing public policy legislation. As depicted in Figure 7.3, existing literature has widely suggested that the only role nonprofits and other civil society actors play in shaping social policy and social welfare development is through political advocacy efforts. However, not all civil society

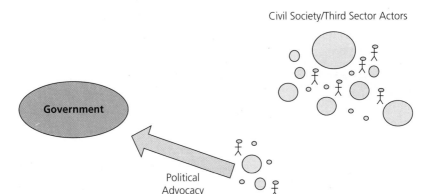

Figure 7.3 The traditionally viewed relationship between civil society actors and government policy.

actors play the same role. The depiction illustrates that only some civil society actors are engaged in such activities. Shier and Handy (2015a) summarize this point:

> "The dominant stream of literature has mainly investigated the political advocacy role of nonprofits (Child & Gronbjerg, 2007; Kimberlin, 2010; Mellinger, 2014; Mosley & Ros 2011; Schmid, Bar & Nirel, 2008). Almog-Bar and Schmid (2014) provide some evidence of this narrow focus in their recent literature review in the meaning and role of advocacy when applied to nonprofits. For instance, they defined advocacy as an effort to change public policy or influence decisions of government, and to protect individual socio-political rights and freedoms (Almog-Bar & Schmid 2014). This perspective begets the following question: Is this the only way that these nonprofits create social change?" (p. 2583).

Existing empirical and experiential evidence relating to the behaviour of organizations (inclusive of direct service nonprofits and advocacy-based organizations) highlights an evolving and more complex interrelationship between nonprofits (and other civil society actors) with government and the private sector. Nonprofits are not just silos of direct practice with some organizations engaging in acts of political advocacy. Instead, civil society (i.e., the third sector or the community) is the combined collective relationships between nonprofits and people. These associations happen on a continuum aimed at creating social change and generally represent various forms of community practice. These associations are formed by collective identities, geographies, interests, and cultures, and in the social services formed around service delivery areas, social and economic challenges, and the needs of specific social groups. Figure 7.4 provides a visual depiction of this collective association among civil society actors.

Figure 7.4 highlights a range of efforts that social workers working in organizations and engaging with individuals in the community use to shape social policy and social welfare

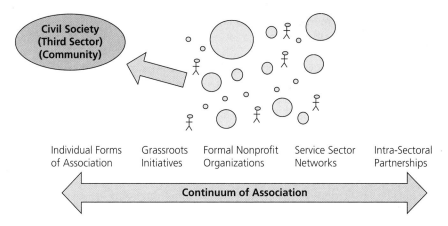

Figure 7.4 The collective association of civil society actors.

development. In particular, organizations (and the social workers working within them) might support engagement in grassroots initiatives that aim to improve the well-being of residents in a particular neighbourhood. Similarly, they might work in collaborations or partnerships (whether through resource sharing or collaborative service delivery models) with other nonprofits to achieve improved social outcomes for groups of service users. Evers (2009) conceptualizes this emergent trend in social welfare as a move away from traditional social welfare to an empowerment and participation based model. Characteristics of this model include a diversity of locally based services where service users and other citizens are encouraged to be active participants within society. Nonprofit organizations not only take on a role in political advocacy-based efforts, but they also assess need, adapt services, create social inclusion, promote public education and awareness, and promote citizenship through volunteerism and other forms of civic engagement (Evers, 2009; Shier & Handy, 2015a).

It is important for social workers to understand this interrelationship between these dominant societal sectors, and the mezzo-level context of social work practice—comprised of a range of organizational entities and other civil society actors. Through this lens, social workers are not just implementers of social and public policy in practice, but are key actors in creating social change through the adaptation of direct services and organizational processes, along with efforts to change public policies or laws that marginalize, exploit, and/or oppress social groups in society (such as general groups of service users, gay and lesbian people, transgendered people, women, ethno-racial minority groups, and disabled people, among others) (Bellefeuille & Hemingway, 2005; Cnaan & Vinokur-Kaplan, 2015; Handy & Cnaan, 2000; Karabanow, 2003; Lacroix & Shragge, 2004; Mulvale, 2001; Shier & Handy, 2015b; Shragge & Toye, 2006). The following section utilizes the emerging concepts of social innovation and social entrepreneurship to highlight the various ways that human service organizations (and the social workers who work in these organizations) act to shape social policy and social welfare development in contemporary Canadian society.

SOCIAL INNOVATION AND SOCIAL ENTREPRENEURSHIP

Social innovation and social entrepreneurship are relatively new concepts that have emerged within the scholarly and practice literatures to describe the various ways that nonprofits (and social workers and allied human service professionals who make up these organizations) embark on social change efforts, with the intention of addressing the emergent and persistent social welfare needs of the population. Social entrepreneurship refers to "innovative and effective activities that focus strategically on resolving social market failures and creating new opportunities to add social value systemically by using a range of resources and organizational formats to maximize social impact" (Nichols, 2006, p. 23). Thus, from the lens of social entrepreneurship, nonprofits are seen as dominant actors in creating social change through social innovations within local, national, and even international communities amidst the economic (resources) and political (power) conditions in a given country's context. In recent years, there have been many socially entrepreneurial efforts that have emerged in Canada through the development of new nonprofit organizations responding to persistent social problems in new ways, and through the development of new patterns of engagement with the private market (such as through the creation of social enterprise initiatives). However, developing new nonprofit organizations is just one way in which social workers can shape social policy and social welfare development in Canada. The concept of social innovation provides a more holistic assessment of the various ways that social workers (at least at a mezzo-level of practice) undertake this role.

Shier & Handy (2015c) note that "Social innovation refers to 'any new idea with the potential to improve either the macro-quality of life or the quantity of life', where macro-quality of life is defined as 'the set of valuable options that a group of people has the opportunity to select'" (Pol & Ville, 2009, p. 882). In relation to direct social service non-profits, the "group of people" refers to the population of people accessing services, and/or the population of people excluded from services due to the current structure and focus of service provision (Shier & Handy, 2015a). Therefore, among direct social service non-profits, a socially innovative program or initiative is one that aims to support improved social outcomes and/or address emergent social issues that have a negative impact on general *groups* of service users (e.g., people experiencing housing loss or developmentally delayed adults, etc.)" (pp. 2–3). This definition seems relatively abstract; however, Shier & Handy (2015a) conducted a study among direct social service nonprofits in Alberta, to aid in operationalizing this model. Figure 7.5 provides a summary of their empirically tested conceptual model.

Shier and Handy (2015b) describe process-based social innovations as "those internal organizational adaptations to the structure or procedures utilized within an organization to create better social outcomes for service users (Jaskyte & Lee, 2006; Perri 6, 1993)" (p. 8). From the operationalized descriptions presented in Figure 7.5, process-based social innovations within direct social service nonprofits include adaptations to organizational procedures and processes, along with adaptations to the methods of engagement with key stakeholder groups. These adaptations can impact social policy and social welfare development in several ways. For example, adapting organizational procedures to service delivery has an impact on the interpretation and application of mandated service delivery

Socially Transformative Social Innovations	Product Based Social Innovations	Process Based Social Innovations
Creating public awareness	Creating more inclusive programming	Adaptations to methods if engagement with key stakeholder groups
■ Education initiatives		
■ Promoting community engagement	■ New programs to meet emerging needs	■ Service users
■ Change public perceptions	■ Establishing new organizations	■ Other organizations
		■ Funders/donors
Influencing policy direction	Adapting existing services to attain better outcomes	■ Organization staff
		■ Community members
■ Bringing information forward	■ Incorporating new methods of intervention	Adaptations to organizational procedures, processes, and structure
■ Undertaking research	■ Restructuring existing programs	
■ Discussions in networks		■ Creating new positions
■ Invited participation in formal policy gatherings	Changing focus of service delivery efforts	■ Refocusing training efforts
	■ Seeking to attain different outcomes	■ Adapting focus of interaction with service users
	■ Aligning service delivery to client described need	

Source: From Human Service Organizations: Management, Leadership & Governance, Volume: 39, Issue: 01, pp: 06-24 by Michael L. Shier & Femida Handy. Copyright © 2015 by Taylor & Francis Group. Used by permission of Taylor & Francis Group.

Figure 7.5 Conceptual framework of the ways that direct service nonprofits create social change.

frameworks. An example could be the creation of a new position within an organization that seeks to act as a coordinator among multiple organizational departments in a multi-service organizational setting to better address the intersecting challenges that service users experience. For example, in housing supports, coordinated efforts are needed to link methods of intervention to support re-housing, but also labour market support and addictions treatment.

Product-based social innovations are "those where new programs and services are created to meet emerging or unmet demand (Perri 6, 1993)" (Shier & Handy, 2015b, p. 8). Figure 7.5 describes a range of ways in which direct social service nonprofits engage in product-based social innovations. These are exemplified by creating more inclusive programming (such as extending eligibility criteria) or by creating entirely new organizations that address unmet needs within community. Similarly, organizations might embark on initiatives that adapt existing services to help achieve improved social outcomes among existing service users, or change the focus of service delivery efforts (see also Shier & Graham, 2013).

Socially transformative social innovations "are those that seek to create wider systemic social change within the community more generally (Netting, O'Connor, & Fauri, 2007)" (Shier & Handy, 2015b, p. 8). Figure 7.5 highlights two key ways that direct social service nonprofits engage in these activities to shape social policy and social welfare development. The first is through public awareness initiatives. Organizations might seek to address socio-cultural perceptions in society that act to oppress or marginalize a particular service user group, such as individuals experiencing domestic violence or those with mental health issues (see also Guo & Saxton, 2014). The second is that direct social service nonprofits engage in activities that influence public policy directly. This is achieved, for example, by engaging in outcome-based research and by participating in formal and informal partnerships and collaborations with other nonprofits and government actors, along with engaging in direct social action.

Together, this collective model of social innovation suggests that direct social service nonprofits (and the social workers within those organizations) shape social policy and promote social welfare development in complex and intentional ways. While political advocacy remains a part of this framework of social innovation, it is only one component of a larger spectrum of organizational practices and procedures that can act to shape social policy and social welfare development in Canada. Through organizational leadership and management skill development, social workers may be able to take a more active role in shaping social policy in Canada's contemporary social welfare system.

There are a number of methods of engagement that social workers can deploy in this social welfare context to shape social policy and social welfare development. Following from notions of political advocacy, social workers (and their organizations) can engage in social action campaigns—such as letter writing or protesting to try to get their government representatives' attention to a particular issue. Likewise, social workers can support self-advocacy efforts among service user groups and their families or other affected stakeholders of a particular policy or practice. Social media has become a common approach to share information and mobilize groups in society. Likewise, legal measures can be undertaken to challenge existing legislation in the judicial system. However, many direct social service nonprofits have realized their independent role in contemporary social welfare in Canada, and have begun to work in collectives, through partnerships and collaborations, to find ways to better allocate resources and improve outcomes for service user groups. Likewise, they have found themselves in a context where the dynamics between the third sector and the private sector are being challenged and reshaped. An increasing number of organizations have begun to engage in market-based activities to generate revenue to pursue socially innovative initiatives in the absence of a public policy framework to support such efforts. New models of social finance (note the change in language from "funding") are emerging (such as Social Impact Bonds, Social Investment Funds, and Pay for Performance Contracts) that provide greater flexibility for nonprofits to focus their efforts and their methods of intervention, which are further reshaping the role of direct social service nonprofits in social welfare development.

As we have emphasized in previous chapters, the decline in scope and funding of governmental participation in social welfare is troubling. But as things change, there are also points of optimism that emerge. Indeed, a number of benefits from the new social financing procedures are emerging. They have the potential to: target investments to specific social issues in specific local communities; create job opportunities and local community economic development; reduce income inequality by diverting profits from investment income earned by large financial and corporate institutions to local communities (i.e., social economy development); and involve local community stakeholders to develop socially innovative solutions to persistent social problems. There is also, however, much uncertainty around the utility of these new social financing initiatives. For instance: public policy in Canada has not kept pace with this changing social welfare landscape through legislation to support such investment and to minimize risk; a dominant ideological shift is needed in society around the role of citizenship in creating and sustaining a social welfare regime; and it is unclear who determines how resources are to be allocated and for what purposes. These points will be elaborated on further in Chapter 9.

What is clear is that social workers—particularly through their work in direct service nonprofits with service users and in positions of organizational management and leadership—have been taking on an increasingly diverse role in shaping social policy and social welfare development beyond the traditional political advocacy notion that has framed social work's policy practice in recent decades. Through their organizational practice, social workers can actively shape program focus and organizational processes to significantly improve social outcomes for service user groups. Likewise, they are finding themselves working in more partnership and collaborative arrangements with other nonprofits, service delivery sectors, different levels of government, and the market to influence social welfare development in Canada.

CONCLUSION

This chapter provided an overview of the relationship between social work practice and social policy. Current social policies have an impact on how service users experience the social environment. They have an impact on their day-to-day well-being. However, social workers working in nonprofits and engaged in other civil society forms of association have a direct role in shaping social policy and social welfare development in Canada. A conceptual model of contemporary social welfare was described, along with an empirically tested model of social innovation. Together, these frameworks provide the means to understand the role of contemporary social work in addressing emergent and persistent social problems and challenges. New relationships are forging within and between sectors—and in particular between nonprofits and the private sector through the formation of social enterprise initiatives—that are allowing direct service nonprofits (and the social workers they employ) to have a greater influence in shaping social policy and social welfare. This is achieved through the development of new programs and initiatives, adaptations to organizational processes, and by embarking on socially transformative efforts to change public perceptions and adapt public policy. For social workers to be effective in this contemporary era of social welfare, new professional identities need to be developed; they could include social entrepreneur, social innovator, social welfare leader, social financier, social economist, and social change agent.

Chapter 8
Social Policy Analysis

The previous chapter highlighted the relationship between social work practice and social policy, and described the key ways in which social workers engage with and shape social policy in their direct service work and in their positions of leadership within organizations and through community practice. This present chapter focuses on social policy analysis, which is a key component of identifying the ways in which social policies are having an impact on the social wellbeing of service user groups and within society more generally, along with identifying applicable policy solutions to solve or alleviate persistent and emerging social problems.

Chapter 1 included a discussion of the various elements of social well-being, which was inclusive of the socio-economic, socio-political, socio-cultural, and psycho-social well-being of social groups or the population more generally. Each of these components of social well-being has been investigated and analysed extensively by social scientists, and in this chapter we consider the processes of analysis of the social policies that aim to improve the situation of the population on these various indicators of social welfare. For example, social policies have implications for the socio-economic well-being of the population in several ways. From Chapter 3 of this book you were introduced to a range of income security programs that have implications for the financial well-being of the population. A social policy analysis of these income security programs might investigate the extent to which benefits for low-income older adults affect levels and experiences of poverty within this segment of the population. Socio-political well-being includes aspects of human rights. Social policy analysis might investigate the extent to which employee rights legislation has an impact on supporting the equal participation of groups—such as developmentally delayed adults—in participating in the labour market. Socio-cultural well-being includes policies that support multiculturalism or prevent discrimination. Social policy analysis might consider the experiences of discrimination among ethno-racial minority groups in key public institutions—such as in the health-care system or within post-secondary education. Psycho-social well-being includes aspects related to individuals' intra-personal functioning, such as experiences of psychological distress. Social policy analysis might investigate employee support policies within private businesses that best support worker mental health. We might also consider the implications of social policy on the socio-spatial well-being of the population. For example, the relationship between service user groups and the spatial components of programming at a local homeless shelter; such as where service users line up to gain entrance or the physical location of shelter buildings in relation to available job opportunities.

One key aspect of social policy analysis is weighing different options for intervention (at different levels of social policy implementation—such as at a government level or at an organizational level). As was described in Chapter 4, social policy choices are impacted greatly by general societal values and beliefs, along with dominant ideological perspectives. However, social policy decisions should be made through an evidence-based investigation of the implications of a particular policy choice on individual, group, or community outcomes. Furthermore, there have been changing dynamics in governance (outlined in Chapter 1), where a range of actors are now making decisions on behalf of the well-being of individuals, groups, and the population more generally (inclusive of government, for-profit, and third sector or civil society actors). As a result, it has become even more important for social workers to develop skills to undertake social policy analysis. Such analysis would enable practitioners to make evidence-informed decisions at an organizational level (such as through organizational missions and mandates and where to allocate resources), and it would help to inform efforts to change or adapt social policies at a government level (whether through involvement in political advocacy efforts or through engagement in cross- and intra-sector partnerships and task groups with other nonprofits, and with for-profit and government actors).

PURPOSE OF SOCIAL POLICY ANALYSIS

Policy analysis has been defined as the "the disciplined application of intellect to public problems" (Pal, 1987, 19). Following from this definition, social policy analysis includes the application of research methods and approaches to solve problems aimed at improving the social well-being outcomes of individuals, groups, or within the community more generally. Pal describes the policy analysis process as the implementation of rational techniques (which is inclusive of a range of research methods—both quantitative and qualitative alike) to understand if a particular policy is having the intended effect. We would also extend the purpose of social policy analysis to include the implementation of rational techniques to understand the scope of general social problems and the ways in which current social policies are having a negative effect on specific social groups in society. This would suggest that social policy analysis is not just about investigating the effect of a particular social policy, but also aims to identify meaningful solutions that will have an impact on improving the social well-being of individuals.

For example, recently the first two authors of this book, along with colleagues, have undertaken research on how to better target supports to reduce the duration of housing loss among vulnerable populations, such as Indigenous people and recent immigrants (Shier, Graham, Fukuda, & Turner, 2014, 2015). Considering the predominantly episodic nature of homelessness, more tailored approaches of support are needed to minimize the duration of housing loss as people transition to more stable housing situations. In 2009 and 2010, data from a large sample (n=4160) of individuals in Alberta's seven cities were collected among 39 nonprofits providing housing and other related social supports. The findings provided some important insight into the situation of adequately addressing the housing needs of vulnerable populations. The descriptive results of the study sample are not particularly surprising. For instance, 77 percent of the study sample were living in a precarious housing situation (e.g., homeless, couch surfing, or transitional/temporary housing). Of those experiencing precarious housing, 30 percent were Aboriginal, and

10 percent were recent international migrants. Of the total sample, there were high prevalence rates (approximately 40 percent for each) of mental health, addictions, and physical health issues. It is widely documented that these are all risk factors associated with housing loss. However, further analysis provides some clearer insight into those aspects of social service support efforts that are having an impact, and what areas need to be scaled up to improve outcomes and reduce the duration of housing loss.

For instance, the results of the analysis show that the present efforts of social service support are effectively reducing the incidences (and possibly duration) of precarious living for individuals that have a mental or physical health-related illness, or are a recent international migrant. These results demonstrate areas of strength within our service delivery and social welfare system in supporting vulnerable individuals to maintain adequate housing. However, the results also highlight areas that could use improvement. Our study results show that Indigenous people are *two times* more likely to be living in a precarious housing situation when compared to the total study sample, and those of the total sample with an active addiction were 2.684 times more likely to be living in a precarious housing situation. Efforts to improve the situation of precarious housing require further targeted funding and direct service efforts to address treatment for active addiction and support for the unique needs of Indigenous people. Those might include preventative measures, such as pre-urban migration support in helping to find employment and housing.

There are finite resources within our social service delivery system, and later in this chapter we provide a discussion of cost-benefit and *cost-effectiveness analysis* to help support a better understanding of how monetary issues complicate the social policy analysis process. This policy analysis case example suggests the need for more targeted and strategic support to effectively reduce the incidences and duration of periods of homelessness. This can be achieved in two ways. First, it requires developing a knowledge base of the areas that need to be scaled up for targeted social investment based on the unique local needs of the precariously housed in Canada's municipal and provincial jurisdictions. In Alberta, Indigenous people and those with active addiction are at particular risk of housing vulnerability. More aggregated analysis is required in Canada's other jurisdictions to adequately target resources to those areas of vulnerability that prevail in those local regions.

Second, a strategic plan in local municipalities among direct service nonprofits and municipal departments is necessary to offer specific targeted programming to address the identified needs of local populations. One way this might be achieved is through purposeful efforts that support strategic cross-sector partnerships between nonprofits and local municipal governments. Meaningful and mutually beneficial partnerships are a foundation for social innovation within our cities. However, there is no social policy framework supporting the development of these partnerships: a point that is elaborated on further in Chapter 9 when we discuss future areas of social policy development in Canada.

Perhaps, the most useful finding from this case example of social policy analysis is that it helps to figure out the diverse nature of homeless populations (for example: Indigenous people, international migrants, individuals from a wide spectrum of age categories, or those with addictions), as well as ways in which policy and practitioners could focus resources on particular subsets of the entire homeless population. With more focused and specifically targeted services there is a greater hope of alleviating the social epidemic of homelessness.

This case example demonstrates that the purpose of social policy analysis focuses on understanding the effects of social policy (at government and organizational levels) and identifying meaningful solutions based on an understanding of the context in which a particular adverse social situation emerges and is dealt with. The following section describes in greater detail how this social policy analysis process unfolds, and provides a social policy analysis framework to aid engagement and understanding of the rationalistic process of evaluating social policy and identifying meaningful solutions.

A SOCIAL POLICY ANALYSIS FRAMEWORK

Understanding social policy and how it affects the lives of service users is an important aspect of social work practice and is a component of all undergraduate and graduate social work training in Canada. The authors of this book have had the pleasure of teaching social policy to social work students. However, within this task is the challenge of teaching the subject of social policy in a tangible way. It is more than just teaching students about the social problems created by social policy or the governmental policies that make up Canada's welfare state (such as income security programs). The task is to teach students of social work how they contribute to the implementation of existing policies through their positions in organizations and when interacting with service users, and more importantly, how they can influence, shape, and create social policies that have a meaningful impact on the lives of service user groups; that is, individuals and groups that are made vulnerable due to current political, economic, cultural, social, and spatial conditions in society.

Fundamental to this effort, and subsequently to social work practice in general, are efforts of social policy analysis. The process of engaging in these efforts can be captured in a social policy analysis framework. Figure 8.1 provides an image of a social policy analysis framework, which helps to identify the types of information needed and the varied areas of analysis that can help lead to rational social policy solutions or alternatives to existing social policy.

Among social policy scholars there have been many attempts to describe this social policy analysis process, which is described in greater detail later in this chapter. A common distinction between approaches has to do with the comprehensiveness or degree of incrementalism in the approach to understanding the general social problem that the social policy response seeks to address. The framework in Figure 8.1 was developed based on the processes of analysis and interpretation from several research studies conducted by the first two authors of this book. The focus of those studies was to investigate the relationship between social policy and the lived experiences of vulnerable and marginalized groups in Canadian society (such as individuals with long-term labour market attachment difficulties, people experiencing housing loss, and youth and young adults experiencing un- and under-employment). The social policy analysis framework is composed of eight stages of information gathering, interpretation, and analysis that can aid social work practitioners to understand the scope of a particular social problem, including the context of the problem, the current policy environment, and how the problem and policy response or focus can impact the experience of service user groups.

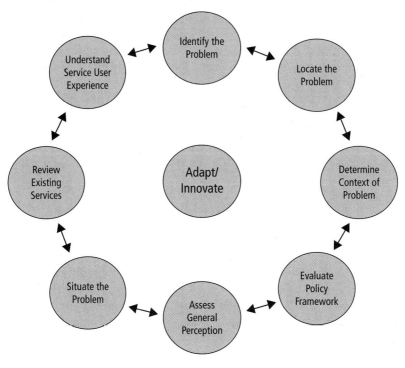

Figure 8.1 Social Policy Analysis Framework

The policy analysis framework presented here follows neither a wholly comprehensive nor wholly incremental approach to the policy-making process. Instead, it blends aspects of each of these traditional areas of theory on the policy-making process, but favours a more pragmatic approach to understanding the process of policy analysis. The intention of such a pragmatic approach is to make the policy-analysis process seem less abstract. Each of the components of this policy analysis framework is discussed in greater detail utilizing a case example of research conducted by the first two authors and colleagues. The research was qualitative and quantitative in approach and sought to better understand the challenges that young adults experience when engaging with the labour market, with the intention of providing policy recommendations to address the persistent social problem of young adult un- and under-employment, a social issue that many readers of this book have likely experienced or will experience.

The Case of Young Adult Un- And Under-Employment

The social policy analysis framework presented in Figure 8.1 depicts a circle with an isolated outcome at the centre. The circle helps to illuminate for the reader that there is no one segment that is the starting point in the social policy analysis process. Depending on the social workers' experiences or position, the starting point might differ. For example, social workers that work in leadership positions within nonprofits might be connected with other organizations or government actors and have a perspective on an issue that is more macro in focus; whereas those that work directly with service users might start at a point of better understanding the service user experiences with a particular social issue. Here we start by *identifying the general problem and intended outcomes of intervention*. In relation to the example of young adult un- and under-employment, the general problem is the fact that young adults experience higher rates of un- and under-employment than those that are over the age of 25. Through a review of publicly available statistics, this disparity is apparent in every Canadian provincial jurisdiction and has not changed in over 50 years, despite the presence of many community and government programs to support young adult employment.

Once the problem is understood through a demonstration of prevalence rates, it is important to *locate the problem in wider discussions of our changing social environment*. In relation to the situation of young adult un- and under-employment, we must investigate the social and economic context in which this situation exists. To do so, we have highlighted theories of labour market change. These changes have direct implications for young adults who are seeking attachment to the labour market. They define what types of jobs are available to them and should define the types of programs and interventions that are provided to young adults in support of their successful attachment to meaningful, full-time work. There are two general theories of labour market change: the skills mismatch and labour market polarization theories. The skills mismatch theory suggests that the labour market has a supply and demand problem. That is, there are more skilled labour jobs than there are people to fill them. Alternatively, the polarization debate suggests that there might be an increasing divide between high-skill/high-pay and low-skill/low-pay labour market opportunities, which suggests that jobs that might fit within the middle of this skill-based spectrum are diminishing.

The next step in this social policy analysis framework is to *determine which context best explains our contemporary reality* in Canada. Figure 8.2 provides the results from a descriptive analysis of Canadian census data starting in 1971 through 2010, and focuses on the occupational classifications of the jobs that Canadians have held during that 40 year time period.

The results from Figure 8.2 show that the theoretical context that best explains the Canadian situation is the increasing polarization of Canada's labour market. The occupational classifications of Groups 2 and 3 represent the professional occupational groups, whereas Group 5 represents service workers and market sales. In Canada's labour market, Groups 2 and 3 tend to be higher paid and require a higher skill set (mostly requiring some occupational specificity through post-secondary education and training), while those in Group 5 tend to be paid minimum wage or fill temporary or part-time positions. The remaining occupational groups have converged to levels below 10 percent for each of the available job opportunities, many of which would provide more middle income earnings, and likely would provide opportunity for young adults who may not yet have sufficient occupational specificity to work in the professional sector.

Understanding the problem in relation to the current context provides necessary information to *evaluate the current public policy and initiative framework* that aims to support young adults in their labour market attachment pursuits. In particular, it aids in assessing whether or not the current social policy focus (at both a government level and at a programmatic level within service delivery nonprofits) can effectively address the problem given the current context of the issue. In relation to the problem of the disparity

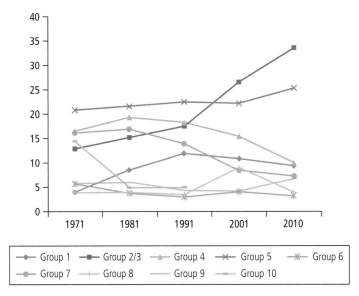

Figure 8.2 Proportion of employed Canadians between 16 and 65 years old by occupation group* for each census year (1971, 1981, 1991, 2001) and 2010

Source: All data was extracted from the Canadian census for the years 1971, 1981, 1991, and 2001 accessed through the Minnesota Population Centre at: http://www.ipums.org/ and Statistics Canada. *Table 282-0010 - Labour force survey estimates (LFS), by National Occupational Classification for Statistics (NOC-S) and sex, annual (persons unless otherwise noted),* CANSIM (database), Using E-STAT (distributor). http://estat.statcan.gc.ca/cgi-win/cnsmcgi.exe?Lang=E&EST-Fi=EStat/English/CII_1-eng.htm (accessed: December 15, 2012)

between young adult unemployment and the unemployment rate of those over the age of 25, a wide network of public social policies exists to support young adults in attaining meaningful full-time work. Some specifically target youth and young adults, while others would provide employment support services to youth or young adults who have a particular experience with vulnerability (such as being disabled or have poor English language ability). For example, at the federal government level there is the Aboriginal Skills and Employment Training Strategy, the Youth Employment Strategy, Correction Canada's

---

*Occupation groups are determined by the International Standard Classification of Occupations. Groups include: 1 – Legislators, senior officials, and managers; 2 – Professionals; 3 – Technicians and associate professionals; 4 – Clerks; 5 – Service workers and shop and market sales; 6 – Skilled agricultural and fishery workers; 7 – Crafts and related trades workers; 8 – Plant and machine operators and assemblers; 9 – Elementary occupations; 10 – other

Reprinted with permission from Shier, M.L., Graham, J.R., &Eisenstat, M. (2015). Psychosocial characteristics and successful labour market attachment among young adults: The internalization of individual inadequacy as explanations for failure within the labour market. *Canadian Journal of Family and Youth, 7*(1), 27–54.

National Employability Skills program, the Labour Market Agreements for Persons with Disabilities, and the Adult Learning, Literacy, and Essential Skills program. At the provincial government level, there are different programs throughout Canada. In Ontario, for example, programs specifically targeted to youth and young adult employment include the Youth Employment Fund and the Ontario Labour Market Partnership. It is important to evaluate the focus of these current public policies and initiatives. For young adult unemployment, the evaluation of these policies leads to a determination that the focus is on basic skill development and career planning. For example, the Youth Employment Strategy with the Canadian federal government focuses on basic skill development, summer internship training, and career focus (see http://www.youth.gc.ca/eng/common/yes.shtml). However, within the context of Canada's increasingly polarized labour market, this focus on basic skill development is insufficient to adequately address the challenges young adults face in transitioning from the low-skill/low-pay service sector labour market to the high-skill/high-pay professional sector. Basic skills and career planning are out of touch with the realities of Canada's contemporary labour market.

The question that emerges is why are social policies focused in a way that do not provide the needed benefit to support the social well-being needs of this particular group in society? We can answer this question through the next stage in this social policy analysis framework, which is to *assess the general perception towards your population of service users*. The general perceptions in society held of a service user group can shape the policy discourse. In relation to our case study example here, within current research there is a general emphasis on individual level outcomes as barriers to young adult employment (Matsuba, Elder, Petrucci, & Marleau, 2008; Miller & Porter, 2007; Naccarato, Brophy, & Courtney, 2010). What this research suggests is that young adults do not have adequate human capital (such as sufficient experience and education); they may have been involved in criminal behaviour or abuse drugs and alcohol; they may have made choices, such as having children, that limit their labour market opportunities; or that they may have a poor psycho-social orientation of self (such as low self-esteem or lack of confidence). Together, these individually rooted factors constrain young adults' transition to meaningful, full-time employment. However, it has also been shown in population-based research that young adults are generally orientated towards successful labour market attachment (Devadason, 2008), they generally maintain a sense of hope for upward social mobility (Reeskens & Oorschot, 2008; Taylor, 2011), and they perceive employment-related successes as contributing to their overall life satisfaction (Khattab & Fenton, 2009). At the same time, lack of employment or education opportunities results in young adults having a diminished sense of hope and reduced sense of their own individual agency (Rose et al., 2012), and internalizing their lack of success in attaching to the labour market (i.e., they believe they have some deficiency) (Bourgois, 2003; MacLeod, 1987).

Throughout this social policy analysis process, we begin to get a richer and deeper understanding of a particular social problem, and the possible solutions to help improve upon the problem through a particular social policy focus. The next stage in this process continues to magnify the problem by *situating the problem within your own area of local practice*. The qualitative research in this case study was conducted in the Jane and Finch neighbourhood in the City of Toronto. This neighbourhood has a high level of concentrated poverty, in some parts of which the poverty rate is four times greater than the metropolitan Toronto average. This neighbourhood also has one of the highest rates of affordable/subsidized housing units in all of Toronto's neighbourhoods, and it has higher unemployment rates for young adults in comparison to the Toronto metropolitan average. With a broader understanding of the problem—one that considers the local and institutional contexts, along with the focus of policy efforts—social workers can propose efforts, whether engaged in political advocacy efforts or adapting programs and services, that will have a meaningful social impact on vulnerable service user groups.

As a service provider/social work practitioner you would next want to *review your existing services* in this general context of the problem. For this particular study, the respondents were all participating in employment support programs; many of them had completed post-secondary education (suggesting that they had basic skills and goal setting abilities). The community-based nonprofits providing support focused their efforts (as many similar programs do), on resiliency, and providing programming to youth through outreach, group work, and skill development. The aims of these efforts are to support youth to reengage with goal setting and the pursuit of upward social mobility, with emphasis on providing support to the individual to more equitably access education and employment opportunities. Many of these efforts are defined by the current focus of government policy and programming. However, through this policy analysis framework, it has become apparent that these efforts are disconnected from the macro-level realities of the contemporary labour market and existing research on the situation of young adult un- and under-employment. This leads to a final stage in the policy analysis framework: *understand the experiences that service users might have when accessing your services.*

Understanding the experiences of the service user group is an important component in all social policy analysis. The research conducted in this case example identified four general themes that impact the transition of young adults to meaningful, full-time work (for more details about this study, see: Graham, Shier, & Eisenstat, 2014, 2015; Shier, Graham, & Eisenstat, 2015; and Shier, Graham, Goitam, & Eisenstat, 2014). These themes include: 1) the various ways in which young adults internalize their inability to attach to the labour market; 2) experiences of discrimination when seeking work or engaged in employment; 3) inadequate social networks supporting the transition to meaningful work opportunities; and 4) a disconnect between post-secondary education supply and labour market demand. Each of these themes is more nuanced than what is presented here. However, together they provide a perspective of some of the challenges that young adults might experience when trying to attach to the labour market. They also provide a perspective on the ways in which social policies and practice can *adapt and innovate* (the central feature of this policy analysis framework) to better meet the needs of this social group. Given the comprehensive context of this particular social problem, and the more in-depth understanding from the macro (i.e., institutional and public policy context), mezzo (i.e., the organizational and service delivery context), and micro (i.e., the neighbourhood and individual service user context) levels that impact this particular social problem, some examples of social policy solutions might be:

1. Provide programming in secondary schools that supports youth in making post-secondary decisions based on labour market demand, and not on post-secondary

supply. This would allow young adults to make more informed decisions about post-secondary education programs and the applicability of those programs in Canada's contemporary labour market.

2. Adapt the focus of existing youth and young adult employment support programs so that young adults have more opportunities to transition to the higher-skill/higher-pay labour market sector.

3. Create programming that aims to develop relationships between nonprofit providers and employers of young adults. The outcome might improve the degree of social support and social capital that young adults have, leading to future upward social mobility.

This is just a brief list of possible solutions. With a more comprehensive understanding of this context, what other social policy solutions would you suggest to address the overarching disparity in employment rates between young adults and those over the age of 25? Furthermore, you might ask yourself, how would your perspective on possible solutions change if you did not follow through each of the stages of this social policy analysis framework?

This case study demonstrates the complex process of identifying a social policy focus. Through the use of this social policy analysis framework one is able to identify areas in which new policies can be developed and how existing policies can be adapted. However, to undertake this rational process, it is necessary to have a background in a range of research methods and to consider a range of data sources before coming to a conclusion on a specific social policy response. For instance, in this one case study, census data were analysed, qualitative data were collected among program participants where inductive analytical techniques were utilized, existing policies were evaluated, current empirical literature was assessed, and an environmental scan was performed to assess the focus of current efforts in direct service nonprofits.

These research methods go beyond the scope of this book, and are a component of other courses in social work education at the undergraduate and graduate level. And certainly, the research approaches utilized in this case study analysis are not inclusive of all the different research approaches and analytical techniques that can be utilized for social policy analysis. For example, quantitative methods—such as survey research—can be used to assess group level experiences with specific policies. One example is a time series research design, where researchers have some social indicator or outcome measure for a group of people at various time points before the implementation of a particular policy, and then scores of the same social indicator or outcome measure after the implementation of a specific policy. This research approach would aim to assess the level of change on the social indicator or outcome measure from before the policy was implemented to after it was implemented in order to assess the level of change associated with the new or adapted policy.

Furthermore, as previously mentioned, while we have presented a more pragmatic social policy analysis framework, other scholars have discussed this process of identifying applicable, meaningful, or solution-oriented social policies in other ways. We provide an overview of these discussions as they—like our own research—have shaped how we perceive this process. You will find characteristics of each of these different approaches in the previously described social policy analysis framework.

The Comprehensive Approach

When comparing the social policies of different countries, researchers often use social indicators representing quality-of-life measures. These social indicators reflect how public policies, social institutions, social programs, and social services work in each country, and how they influence the various elements that make up a society of people. For example, countries may be compared to each other based on child poverty, the social equality of women, the quality and availability of educational institutions and health (physical and mental) resources, social welfare spending as a percentage of gross national product, criminality and correctional resources, child welfare services, and income security levels, among others. As such, social indicators provide a comprehensive overview of each nation's social policies in practice and, in turn, allow nations to be ranked based on the various social indicators.

This approach is called the *comprehensive approach* to policy-making because it begins with global objectives based on social values and then translates those policies into public policies, social institutions, social programs, and social services. The advantage of this highly centralized approach is that policy is equally applied to all parts of a country. The following summaries of representative approaches of social policy analysis will be helpful to review and revisit as you proceed through this section of the chapter.

The Rational Model (Simon, 1957) The rational decision-making model uses the following sequence of tasks:

a.   identify and clarify a social problem;

b.   identify and rank goals with respect to that problem;

c.   develop strategies that can remedy the problems (or achieve the goals);

d.   carefully examine all possible consequences; and

e.   decide on which policy best achieves government/organizational goals.

The Incremental Model (Braybrooke & Lindblom, 1963) The incremental model suggests that the rational model fails because it cannot account for everything and therefore must be incomplete at the design level. This model instead views policy-making as "muddling through" by making incremental adjustments to existing policies. This model directly contrasts the comprehensive approach, and is described in further detail in the following subsection of this chapter.

The Mixed-Scanning Model (Etzioni, 1968) The mixed-scanning model suggests that substantive (political or social) issues need to be addressed by rational decision-making; then adjustments need to be made to the policy to reflect unforeseen social realities and unintended consequences. This model, like the rational social policy analysis framework presented earlier in this chapter, blends aspects of both the comprehensive and incremental approaches to social policy analysis.

The following summaries are examples of social policy analysis and development processes that follow from this comprehensive approach.

Values Competition Model (Rein, 1974) The values competition model suggests that social policy is, above all, concerned with choice among competing values. Society consists of people holding diverse values (world views) who are in competition with one another and, consequently, with one another's values, in an effort to achieve maximum power. Values are so ingrained in every aspect of social, economic, and public policies that a major role of policy-makers is to learn how to control their own values and prejudices.

Social Justice and the Comprehensive Model of Social Policy (Gil, 1970; 1992)
This model suggests that social policies are guidelines for behaviours that have evolved through societal processes. They specify, maintain, or transform the structures, relations, values, and dynamics of a society's particular way of life. As such, comprehensive and rational social policies govern societal life and are therefore of great concern to social workers and other human-service personnel. Good social policies should be concerned not only with life-sustaining activities that ensure minimum basic needs, but also with life-enhancing activities that stimulate human potential.

The Value Criteria Model (Haskins & Gallagher, 1981; Wharf & Mackenzie, 2004)
The value criteria model suggests that after determining what the problem is and what policy alternatives are available to address the problem, policy-makers must use value criteria, informed by universal and selective values, and *cost–benefit analysis* to evaluate each policy alternative. In short, the best policy is the one that maximally reflects these value criteria.

The Garbage Can Model (Kingdom, 1995)
The garbage can model suggests that the three types of policy processes—problems, solutions, and politics—operate individually and independently until a crisis occurs that requires all three to come together. Resolving the crisis is dependent on: (1) how the public perceive the problem; (2) what the current political agenda is; and (3) who the participants are. Getting an issue on the policy agenda becomes a function of whether or not there is a crisis or situation that creates a need for the three processes to come together.

This summary of existing social policy analysis framework approaches provides an introductory overview of the various theoretical or conceptual debates that shape the social policy development process. For example, some advocates believe that social policy should be analysed and developed along the lines of the garbage can model. Politicians and policy analysts should determine what each country's social policies should be and then put these policies into practice. Social policy is thus the aggregate of all social indicators, and a statement about society's values. The comprehensive view of social policy analysis and the process of social policy development maintain that a scientific, rational approach to social policy-making is feasible and desirable. The following two examples of comprehensive approaches—Rein's and Gil's models—provide greater detail on the variation in application of this comprehensive approach to the policy-making process.

Rein's Model

Social and public policies are often about struggles between value preferences and how some values become dominant and why. Rein (1974) suggests that social policy is about choice between competing values. From his perspective (see Figure 8.3), the social policy analysis process stresses the interaction between values (input), *operating principles* (conversion process), and outcomes (output).

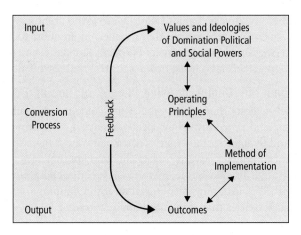

Figure 8.3 Rein's Overview of the Policy-Making Process

People who hold positions of political and/or social power disproportionately influence which values (input) win. When the debate about values is limited to ideology and worldviews, rather than the real world and the needs of real people, then the social policy analysis process suffers from what Rein calls *detached ideology*—that is, choices are made strictly in accordance with values, regardless of the outcome and consequences to others. Statements such as "It is important to reduce employment in order to control inflation;" "Adjustments to the safety net are required if Canada is to overcome its national debt"; or "Social services must be limited to what a country can afford" are simply instances of the values of the people in power (in this case, economic well-being) being used to justify reduced opportunities and services (i.e., reductions in another value) for the average Canadian (social well-being).

Input for social policy design and analysis consists of the values and ideologies of dominant political and social powers. In Canada and all democratic societies, governments are elected by the people to lead the nation. Part of that leadership is the implementation of the "political platform," which states the vision the party has for the country or the province. This vision reflects the worldviews and ideologies that constitute the value base for that political party. In other words, different political parties—such as the Liberal Party, the Bloc Québécois, the New Democratic Party, and the Conservative Party—inform the public of what they will do if elected. Once in power, a majority government can pass legislation that creates new social policies and alters existing policies. These policies, called *public policies*, are a purposive course of government action designed to deal with issues of public concern (Anderson, 1990). Berkowitz (1980) notes that social choices made in the policy process only rarely benefit the interests of all without being adversely consequential to some. Thus, the political influence held by various alliances and interest groups in Canada can limit universality. These influential groups can include the economic/business sector; special interest groups, such as the elderly, women, or people with disabilities; and international monetary institutions.

From this perspective social policies are based on operating principles, which combine with implementation methods and create a *throughput* or *conversion process*. *Operating principles* are "attempt[s] to integrate various social ideals with a practicable rule of application" (Rein, 1974, 297–298). These ideals include universality, citizen participation, housing and in-kind benefit subsidies, earned access, equity, and other such principles that are held to be of value by society. Not all of these principles support a social work value system, and it is incumbent on social workers to carefully analyze and articulate the operating principles associated with social policy decisions and positions. The *methods of implementation* consist of organizations, including social agencies, specifically designed or altered to provide the services prescribed by implemented social policies. For example, social policies and public policies regarding children have resulted in the establishment of myriad social agencies, such as schools, children's aid societies, children's mental health clinics, and young offender facilities. However, many of these agencies and the professionals within them can prefer a particular value (e.g., children/youth should or should not be involved in agency policy-making; family is or is not the primary institution in a child's life; or children have or do not have the same human rights as adults) or a particular practice methodology (e.g., psychotherapy, brief therapy, task-centred therapy, or community-based practice). This prescribed value or practice methodology can in fact compromise the policy and operating principles to the extent that they become congruent with the prevailing value or practice methodologies. In effect, the agency or staff members could be doing the same thing but under a different name and could be acting in a manner that is counterproductive to the values and objectives of the new policy. This debate about the principles of implementation is known as *doctrinaire insulation* (Rein, 1974, 298). In Canada, other examples of doctrinaire insulation include situations where southern-based practice methodologies and specializations are applied directly to northern environments without adaptation or citizen consensus, and situations where public policies do not account for the values and views of groups other than the policy-makers, such as women's groups, ethnic groups, or religious groups (Delaney & Brownlee, 1995).

The output of social policy is its outcome. The importance of outcome centres on whether the outcome and the purpose of the social policy are congruent and *in whose estimation*. Often social policy success is measured by social impact studies or by feedback from those whom the social policy was intended to benefit. However, the degree to which citizens are allowed to give feedback and influence social policy is in itself a fundamental issue for social policy analysis.

Rein views values, operating principles, and outcomes as inseparable and in fact completely interrelated. Rein (1974) explains this interrelationship in the following manner:

> Policies are in fact interdependent systems of: (1) the abstract values we cherish; (2) the operating principles which give these values form in specific programs and institutional arrangements judged acceptable for public support; (3) the outcomes of these programs which enable us to contrast ideals and reality; and (4) the often weak linkages among aims, means, and outcomes, and the feasible strategies of change this pattern suggests. (298)

Gil's Model

Another social policy theorist who supports a comprehensive approach to the social policy analysis and development process is David Gil (1998; 1992). Gil maintains that human beings and human development should form the basis of social policy. Gil believes that throughout history, systemic inequalities have resulted in social arrangements that benefit selected members of society and disadvantage the remaining members of society. He calls this process *patterned inequalities* and suggests that, over time, people do not even recognize the injustice or the inequalities. The result is the creation of social institutions that serve to benefit the interests of the few, while dehumanizing, marginalizing, discriminating against, and/or oppressing the many. Gil believes that most societal violence stems from the damage these social institutions do to people.

Gil argues that social policy must promote and enhance human development and potential and in doing so, serve as "guidelines for behaviour, evolved through societal processes, which specify and maintain or transform the structures, relations, values, and dynamics of a society's particular way of life" (Gil, 1992, 21–22). Gil defines social policy as a set of guiding principles that govern societal life and that therefore must be of great concern to social workers and other human service personnel. In effect, social policies should control all other public policies, excluding religion and foreign trade, but including economic policies.

From this perspective, social policy should reflect long-range visions of what a just and non-oppressive society would look like (Gil, 1998). Gil's vision also stresses values and ideologies affirming equality, individuality, liberty, cooperation, community, and global solidarity, rather than the currently prevailing values and ideologies that support inequality, individualism, selfishness, domination, competition, and disregard for community. For example, if Canada and other nations used the Universal Declaration of Human Rights, as adopted by the United Nations in 1948, as the centrepiece for all social policy, then all social policies would have to conform to this declaration to be established as public policies. By signing the U.N. document, Canada committed itself to eradicating poverty and ensuring basic human rights—and then did not do it.

Gil's comprehensive view of the social policy-making process suggests that social policies should govern natural and human-created resources; all aspects of employment, including human issues; the production of life-sustaining and life-enhancing resources; social, political, and civil rights; mechanisms for the distribution of rights and privileges; and mechanisms for the assignment of social status (Gil, 1992, 24–25). Therefore, all social problems are the result of a flawed social policy; thus, the policy, not the problem, needs to be redressed. As such, social policies are "potentially powerful instruments for planned, comprehensive, and systematic social change rather than reactive measures designed to ameliorate (in a fragmented fashion) undesirable circumstances" (Gil, 1970, 413).

For social workers, Gil's notion of social policy conforms to the profession's value and ethical base. Having social policy address the challenges and realities of the human condition is certainly an ideal worth seeking. Making the interests of all people, their families, and the community the first principle for societal governance emphasizes the *common good* rather than the *public* or *private interest*. As social welfare philosopher Frederic Reamer (1993) puts it, there is a substantive difference between the common good and the public interest, with commensurate implications to social policies. The common good refers to "that which constitutes the well-being of the community—its safety, the integrity of its basic institutions and practices, the preservation of its core values," and human end-states such as human flourishing and moral development (35). While originally referring to national security and prosperity goals, because of the neo-liberal world view, the *public interest* has now come to mean "a rational alliance of primarily self-interested individuals whose collective good is constituted by the collection or aggregation of private interests" (Reamer, 1993, 35). Thus, powerful groups can argue that they are promoting public interest by enhancing the individual pursuit of self-interest, while social workers, who have a particular commitment to social justice for society's most marginalized, must hold notions of the common good as sacrosanct, despite changing notions about the public interest.

Implementing Gil's approach would require society to agree on what set of values should govern social policies. But in societies where political, ideological, and economic power is in the hands of fewer and fewer people (Bishop, 2002), this degree of social transformation is unlikely to occur. In the neo-liberal world view, life enhancement is something to earn, and society is responsible only to provide the minimal life-sustaining needs.

The Incremental Approach

Other social policy theorists do not take as comprehensive a view of social policy analysis and development as Rein and Gil do. Wharf (1992) distinguishes between the *ordinary* and *grand issues of social policy*. *Grand* issues are "those pertaining to the fundamental structure of political–economic life" (14), including distribution of income and wealth, political power, and corporate prerogatives. *Ordinary issues of social policy* include "the governance of child welfare services, deinstitutionalization, and the development of community support programs, the struggle to raise social welfare rates in Ontario, and the debate about abortion politics in Nanaimo" (15). Wharf argues that *ordinary* issues should be of concern to social workers because these issues directly affect the lives of people, can be managed and redressed by community-based organizations, and are sometimes the unintended consequence of earlier reforms.

When dealing directly with the *ordinary* issues of social policy, social workers often employ the rational decision-making model used by incrementalists. The incremental model views the social policy-maker as having to do the following:

- define and rank governing values;
- specify objectives compatible with these values;
- identify all relevant options or means of achieving these objectives;
- calculate all the consequences of these options and compare them; and
- choose the option or combination of options that would maximize the values earlier defined as being important (Hogwood & Gunn, 1984, 46–47).

Wharf (1992) makes note of the "goal-directed-muddling-through" approach to the policy process (where goals emerge in a way that might not be clear at the outset of the intervention) that social workers use. This inductive approach allows the social worker to ensure that the people's interest is known and that the policy process is "anchored in a philosophical position and a vision for change" (233). Because it permits a high degree of flexibility, practice wisdom, and discretion in pursuing objectives, Wharf believes it is an adaptive approach to policy-making. For most social workers, who will only rarely be exposed to global social policy issues, the values and ethics of social work are often the only firm base they have in policy.

A criticism of the incremental approach is that social workers and other human service workers become too preoccupied with resolving local or immediate issues stemming from social policy and do not pay sufficient attention to the social issues that may be creating the problem in the first place.

The Mixed-Scanning Model

Etzioni (1968) argues that there may be a method of reconciling the differences between a comprehensive policy-making process and an incremental policy-making process. The mixed-scanning model can bridge the gap between these two approaches. After making a rational, comprehensive policy decision, policy-makers adjust the policy incrementally, based on information gained from its implementation. Thus, policy-makers can focus on the greater issues without becoming bogged down in details (Hess, 1993).

Table 8.1 shows that each theory has its strengths and weaknesses. Anderson's sequence is rational and easy to understand, but it fails to address who is benefiting from these policies and why policies are directed to their benefit (Mason, Talbott, & Leavitt, 1993). While Wharf's sequencing appears similar to Anderson's, his approach is much more analytical and substantive, with a very clear community-organization perspective. Wharf's sequence addresses concern about which people are involved in the policy-initiation process; whether the problem the policy is addressing is correctly defined or whether it can be redefined; and whether sufficient resources, including people and funding, are available. Like Wharf, Rein recognizes that the policy-making process is not linear and that each stage is subject to problems and to political manipulation.

In the mixed-scanning model, policy-makers choose different paths through the sequence. They can start with Wharf and McKenzie's value criteria model (2010), which requires them to evaluate costs, benefits, and alternatives after defining the problem and the policy alternatives. Or they can use the garbage can model's three types of policy

Table 8.1 Sequencing the Policy-Making Process			
Anderson (1990)	**Wharf (1992)**	**Wharf & McKenzie (2010)**	**Rein (1974)**
Policy agenda	Initiation	Problem identification	Values
Policy formulation	Formation	Identification of value criteria	Operating principles
Policy adaptation	Execution	Assessing alternatives	Method of implementation
Policy implementation	Implementation	Feasibility assessment	
Policy evaluation	Evaluation	Recommendations	Outcomes

processes (problems, solutions, and politics), allowing them to operate independently until a situation or crisis arises. If a particular issue does not get on the policy agenda, then it may have to wait until a new opportunity arises or have to be removed if it appears to be resolved. In other words, whenever there is a public concern, such as those being expressed over water quality in Ontario or farm subsidies in the Western provinces, then all components come together. When the crisis is over, they separate again, only to be re-engaged when another crisis strikes. While these processes are separated, there is little opportunity for social change.

The mixed-scanning approach is important because it allows social workers to understand both the anticipated and unanticipated impacts of social policy, as well as potential or actual shifts in social policy in Canada. Pierce (1984) notes, "Social workers also need to be able to identify policies that actually constitute a part of their practice world. If policy is to be used in generalist practice, its definition must come from the practice parameters and perspectives of line social workers".

However, the policy analyst should be aware of Wharf's (1990) cautions regarding four limitations associated with generalist practice models based on the ecological systems perspective:

1. The mixed-scanning approach assumes that problems, once identified, will generate a demand for change—that is, change will occur and the problem will be solved.

2. This approach ignores power and its distribution in Canada—that is, goodness-of-fit for the rich is good to excellent, while the goodness-of-fit for the poor is bad to terrible. Who has the power and the will to change this—the rich who are benefiting?

3. This approach does not assign social workers responsibility to bring about change.

4. This approach does not address the issue of auspices—that is, the fact that social workers work in agencies that are given their mandates by those holding political power. The social worker's efforts to change the system are limited by each agency's political and social agenda.

COST BENEFIT AND COST EFFECTIVENESS ANALYSES

The previous sections of this chapter described the policy analysis process. The outcome of this process is the development of new policies or an adaptation to existing policies, with the intention of improving the well-being of the population or specific groups in society. Apparent in that previous discussion are differing views on the process of developing applicable policy-related solutions to general social problems and the roles of social workers in that process. However, one foundational consideration in all social policy analysis is the cost of one policy choice over another. Within contemporary literature these discussions of cost have been operationalized through cost-benefit and cost-effectiveness analyses.

Cost-related analyses follow from the pragmatic and rationalistic approach undertaken in this chapter to explain the social policy analysis process. When identifying meaningful social policy solutions to persistent social problems that are apparent in social work direct practice, it is important to recognize the costs of one option in comparison to another. In an environment where there are finite resources, spending on one area means that resources are not expended elsewhere. Likewise, when providing a recommendation for a new policy or an adaptation to an existing policy it is important to be able to demonstrate the relative costs associated with the new intervention or approach that the policy would legitimate. This will help to secure buy-in from individuals who are making a final decision of whether or not to implement the proposed solution.

Cost-benefit analysis (CBA) is an assessment of the various options that are available based on the monetary costs and monetary benefits (including, labour, time, and savings) of different approaches, policies, or practices. Some examples might include the comparative cost-benefit of providing in-patient hospital services versus community-based Assertive Community Treatment (ACT) programming for individuals with serious mental illness. The cost-benefit analysis would assess the monetary costs of operating each of these programs and compare that to the monetary benefits. The monetary benefits might include savings such as reduced acute care costs of mentally ill patients accessing emergency hospital services in an ACT programming team, the increased costs for housing and income security payments to recipients of community programming, and the increased wage earnings of individual service users that are able to participate in the labour market because they are in a community-based program and not hospitalized, among other considerations. The challenge with a cost-benefit analysis is identifying all the relative costs and assessing the monetary value of the benefits. Another example might be consideration of better housing options for individuals that are experiencing housing loss. The two options might be to continue to use short-term shelters or create more affordable housing units. The monetary costs and benefits would include a mix of infrastructure and maintenance expenses, human personnel expenses, and programming expenses, among others.

Cost-effectiveness Analysis (CEA) is a comparison of the relative costs and effects of choosing any of two or more outcomes. Similar to CBA, but in CEA the outcomes are not monetized. The typical way to determine the extent of the outcomes is through Quality Adjusted Life Years (or QALYs). The value of a QALY is determined by the number of healthy years of life gained by a particular intervention. For example, if someone were to receive a treatment for a disease, but the treatment results in the individual being bedridden most of the time, the result would by 0.5 Quality Adjusted Life Years (i.e., lived a full year of life but only had 0.5 functioning). The same goes for someone that were to receive a treatment that led to half a year of perfect health with full functioning; this too would result in 0.5 Quality Adjusted Life Years. In such a situation the determination of which intervention to fund becomes controversial. If a health-related intervention provides on average six months of extra life at 100% functioning and costs significantly less (determined by the amount of available resources) than an intervention that provides an extra year of life, but only at 50% functioning, which intervention would you choose?

The effects do not have to be QALYs; they can be any desirable outcome that you seek to achieve: for example, the number of people not experiencing a particular disease through immunization efforts; an increase in years of active life; a decrease in the number of days experiencing active addictions; a reduction in days unemployed; the duration of time spent away from acute care hospital service by individuals with serious mental illness; or the length of time newcomers find meaningful, full-time work, among others.

In cost-effectiveness analysis we determine the extra costs of a particular treatment in comparison to an alternative treatment or intervention approach, and in relation to a specific outcome associated with both treatment/intervention approaches. This is represented by the Incremental Cost Effectiveness Ratio (ICER). To calculate the ICER, we represent the ratio as: $(C_1 - C_2)/(E_1 - E_2)$, where C refers to cost for Options1 and 2, and E refers to the effect of Options 1 and 2. Cost-effectiveness analysis is used more frequently than CBE in the human services because many of the outcomes that we seek to achieve cannot be monetized, preventing us from undertaking a cost-benefit analysis. Furthermore, it is common in cost-effectiveness analysis to differentiate between different subpopulations of a group to help determine what intervention is the most cost-effective based on the specific situation of the distinct group members. For example, groups may be divided by age or gender or some other characteristic or quality that might signify having different needs that represent different proportions within a particular social group.

Table 8.2 provides a fictional cost-effectiveness analysis of various housing-related options for people experiencing housing loss in a particular geographic area. The effect (or outcome) that is sought is an increase in the number of days of housing loss that is prevented. The options are the use of transitional housing support, affordable housing, or intervention as usual (i.e., shelter services). This comparison could be complicated further with other alternative intervention recommendations, such as rent subsidy programs. Calculating a cost-effective analysis of interventions to support individuals that are experiencing housing loss is complicated by the different categories of housing loss (i.e., episodic or chronic) and the extent of service utilization of each of these distinct groups. Individuals experiencing episodic homelessness are those that periodically (for shorter time frames) experience homelessness. In this example, the average number of days of housing loss experienced by an episodically homeless person is 30 days. The majority of people that experience homelessness are the episodically homeless. The chronically homeless are those individuals that have been homeless for a longer period of time, and many have been homeless for several years in a row.

For this fictional area, 25% of the people experiencing housing loss are chronically homeless, and 75% are episodically homeless. There are approximately 500 shelter beds available in this area. Assuming that the shelters are at full capacity, the number of possible days in shelter (in any given year) for individuals experiencing homelessness is 182 500 (i.e., 365 days × 500 shelter beds). Of those 500 beds, 375 of them are utilized by people who are episodically homeless, and 125 of them are chronically homeless (who are homeless 365 days a year). Considering the average turnaround time for the episodically homeless is one month, there are approximately 4500 people who will experience episodic homelessness during the course of one calendar year in this area. In total, those that are chronically homeless experience 45 625 days homeless (125 people × 365), and those that are episodically homeless experience 136 875 days homeless (375 people × 365 days). One shelter bed costs about $2100 per month ($69/day). One transitional housing support bed/unit costs $6000 per month ($197/day). And one affordable housing unit costs $3200 per month ($105/day, accounting for maintenance and utility expenses, and assuming that these units have already been built and individuals will be provided with only 30 days of lodging).

Table 8.2 Cost-effectiveness Analysis of Housing Support Option for Episodically and Chronically Homeless Subgroups.

Episodically Homeless	Shelter Services	Affordable Housing	Transitional Housing Support
Cost for supporting the number of people experiencing homelessness (total: long term, short term, societal, medical)	$9 444 375 ($69/day × 365 days × 375 shelter beds)	$14 400 000 ($3200 for one month × 4500 people who will experience episodic housing loss during a year)	$27 000 000 ($6000 for one month × 4500 people who will experience episodic housing loss during a year)
Benefit (number of days homeless prevented)	50 000	100 000	125 000
ICER with previous category	—	$99	$504
ICER with shelter services	—	$99	$234
Chronically Homeless			
Cost for supporting the number of people experiencing homelessness (total: long term, short term, societal, medical)	$3 148 125 ($69/day × 365 days × 125 shelter beds)	$4 800 000* ($3200 per month × 125 people experiencing chronic homelessness × 12 months for the year)	$9 000 000 ($6000 per month × 125 people experiencing chronic homelessness × 12 months for the year)
Benefit (number of days homeless prevented)	0	20 000	40 000
ICER with previous category	—	$83	$210
ICER with shelter services	—	$83	$146

*For simplicity, this is an estimated cost for a 12-month period. In all likelihood the cost would be higher because the affordable housing would need to be offered for more than one year.

Common in cost-effectiveness analysis is that no clear decision will be apparent. In some instances there might be a decreasing cost and an increasing benefit. In such a case it would be clear that the new or alternative approach would be more desirable. The results in Table 8.2 do not clearly identify which of the three service delivery options are the most desirable from a cost-effectiveness perspective for either of the chronically or episodically homeless subgroups. The results are interpreted as follows:

- For the episodically homeless subgroup, it will cost $99 for each extra day of homelessness prevented by using affordable housing when compared to using shelter services. That is, it will cost $99 for each of the 50 000 extra days of homelessness prevented by using affordable housing for this subgroup.

- For the chronically homeless subgroup, it will cost $83 for each extra day of homelessness prevented by using affordable housing when compared to using shelter services. That is, it will cost $83 for each of the 20 000 extra days of homelessness prevented by using affordable housing for this subgroup.

- For the episodically homeless subgroup, it will cost $504 for each extra day of homelessness prevented by using transitional housing support when compared to using affordable housing. That is, it will cost $504 for each of the 25 000 extra days of homelessness prevented by using transitional housing for this subgroup.

- For the chronically homeless subgroup, it will cost $210 for each extra day of homelessness prevented by using transitional housing support when compared to using affordable housing. That is, it will cost $210 for each of the 20 000 extra days of homelessness prevented by using transitional housing for this subgroup.

- For the episodically homeless subgroup, it will cost $234 for each extra day of homelessness prevented by using transitional housing support when compared to using shelter services. That is, it will cost $235 for each of the 75 000 extra days of homelessness prevented by using transitional housing for this subgroup.

- For the chronically homeless subgroup, it will cost $146 for each extra day of homelessness prevented by using transitional housing support when compared to using shelter services. That is, it will cost $146 for each of the 40 000 extra days of homelessness prevented by using transitional housing for this subgroup.

These results can be used to help make decisions (whether in government or in non-profit service delivery organizations) about which approaches to take to solve a particular social problem in relation to the value of inputs—such as revenue. Available resources may allow for affordable housing, although there may be insufficient resources to fund transitional housing support programs, at least for the larger population of episodically homeless individuals. Therefore, a decision would need to be made to determine if the extra cost for each day of homelessness prevented is worth the benefit. The results also can shape decisions where the value of the increasing benefit is no longer deemed appropriate. For example, in the case presented above, if it were the case that transitional housing support only prevented a few thousand extra days of homelessness, then you might decide that the return on the investment was not feasible and instead seek alternative methods of intervention that may result in greater achievement of outcomes.

CONCLUSION

This chapter provided an introductory overview to social policy analysis. A pragmatic social policy framework was introduced to aid social workers in identifying problems and applicable social policy related solutions, and was demonstrated through a case example of the problem of young adult un- and under- employment in Canada's contemporary labour market. Social policy analysis and the policy planning process have been conceptualized by many scholars, and are inclusive of both comprehensive and incremental approaches. The social policy analysis framework presented here is inclusive of principles of each theorized approach. No matter the process in which new policies are developed or adapted, the monetary cost of the proposed initiatives is of equal importance, and can impact adoption of the proposed initiative. As a result, it is important to understand how costs and benefits are assessed. Two widely used techniques described in this chapter include cost-benefit analysis and cost-effectiveness analysis.

Chapter 9
Future Directions in Canadian Social Policy and Social Welfare

Throughout this introductory book, the reader has been introduced to a wide range of concepts related to historical and contemporary social welfare and social policy in Canada. We have included instances that illuminate the implications and application of social policy in direct practice contexts. While the examples provided throughout are not comprehensive of the range of social work practice areas, nor do they capture all of the specific provincial, territorial, or municipal applications of social policy, the content of the book provides a starting point for students to begin their own investigation of the relationship between social policy and their own practice area and jurisdiction.

In summary, Chapter 1 provided key definitional content for both social policy and social welfare. Distinctions were made between the notions of a welfare state and a welfare regime. In the latter, the social well-being needs of the population are not just met by government action (through legislated social policy, such as income security benefits), but also by the private sector, the third sector, and the family. Each has a fundamental role to play in social policy and social welfare development in contemporary Canadian society. Chapter 2 described the historical development of Canada's welfare state through four historical periods. Throughout this historical analysis the relationship between the three dominant societal sectors (i.e., the government, the market, and the third sector) in promoting the social well-being needs of Canada's population is apparent. This historical context has had implications for the development of social policy and social welfare in Canada, and has specific implications for how Canadians generally perceive social welfare and the focus of social welfare efforts. In the contemporary market-state era of social welfare development, emerging neo-liberal policies of less government intervention, increased privatization, decentralization of policies and programs to local jurisdictions, and increasing socio-cultural domination of the values of individualism, have begun to re-shape social policy and social welfare, requiring greater citizen participation in developing new programs and organizations to address the emerging and persistent social well-being needs of the population. Chapter 3 described key institutional characteristics of contemporary social policy in Canada. Emphasis was placed on key social welfare policy frameworks—such as the Canada Health Transfer and the Canada Social Transfer—along with current income security programs that aim to redistribute monetary resources. Chapter 4 highlighted ideological factors that act to shape the focus of government social policy efforts, and specifically how these forces have shaped general perceptions towards 'need' and 'socio-economic well-being' (i.e., poverty). Similarly, Chapter 5 overviewed major social, economic, and political trends that act to shape the focus and application of contemporary social policies. Key trends include the physical environment, global political–economic processes, and emerging theoretical perspectives related to citizen participation, such as social inclusion. Chapter 6 described how diverse social groups are impacted by and have themselves impacted social policy. The chapter highlights experiences of social, economic, and political inequality of diverse social groups, and describes the long historical tradition in Canada of political advocacy among citizens in supporting socio-political equality. Chapter 7 covered the relationship between social policy and social work practice. Emphasis was placed on the bridging role of organizational practice in shaping social policy. New theoretical notions of social innovation and social entrepreneurship were introduced, and provide a conceptual context of how this role has become manifested in contemporary Canadian social welfare and social policy practice. Finally, Chapter 8 highlighted key aspects of social policy analysis to support evidence-based decision making in both policy construction and direct practice. In particular, content focused on different approaches to social policy development, with some focusing on wider social change initiatives by addressing macro-level structural issues like social exclusion or social inequality, and others focusing on more incremental approaches, with specific focus on adapting practices or changing the social conditions of specific social groups.

You might have deduced by now that this material is complicated. Social welfare practices and policies are heavily influenced by general societal perception of how best to support the social well-being needs of the population. Likewise, it is apparent that much of this content is related to espousing a particular vision of societal well-being. Social scientists and social theorists have attempted to understand emerging contexts and have applied policy related solutions to address persistent social problems. It is also apparent that social policy is evolving, and as new realities emerge, social policies need to be amenable to changing contexts. The remainder of this chapter focuses on potential future directions of social policy and social welfare development in Canada. While there can be many specific areas of future social welfare development in Canada, limits of space allow us only to highlight four here that broadly capture a range of more specific actions. These include the continued pursuit for social and political rights for marginalized or oppressed social groups in Canadian society, addressing the disparity of socio-economic equality among Canadians, the further development and enhancement of Canada's social economy, and efforts to promote civic engagement.

FUTURE DIRECTIONS IN SOCIAL WELFARE AND SOCIAL POLICY DEVELOPMENT

Social Rights

Valuing diversity and the unique contributions made by diverse social groups has been an important component of Canadian social policy and social welfare development. Not all groups in Canadian society are, or have been, treated equally. This was elaborated on in greater detail in Chapters 2 and 6. Promoting the social rights of marginalized or oppressed groups will continue to be an important aspect in Canada's social welfare future. As the demographic population of Canada continues to change, advocacy efforts will need to be undertaken to promote greater equality among diverse social groups. For example, the Supreme Court of Canada has recently ruled in favour of allowing doctor-assisted death, and the federal and provincial governments have been charged to develop legislation to allow for this under Canada's current health-care system and criminal code. Certainly, as Canada's population continues to age, several other facets related to this social group will emerge, which will require policy adaptations to accommodate the needs. Furthermore, recently the Canadian federal government has increased its commitment to the Syrian refugees displaced from the Middle East. Efforts need to be made to support the integration and settlement of these and other groups of international migrants that come to Canada. Both of these situations represent recent, and ongoing, claims for individual and group level social rights in Canada. The list could be endless.

Recently, attention has been focused on the rights of gay and lesbian individuals, and the social rights of transgendered people. In 2015, the Truth and Reconciliation Commission of Canada released their report on the conditions of the residential school system and subsequent atrocities directed towards Indigenous people. Furthermore, in the absence of equitable housing policy in Canada, many Canadians experience housing loss throughout any given year. Efforts need to be made to address the degree of social exclusion of disabled people within the contemporary labour market. Each of these areas of social rights will lead to further action in the promotion of group level well-being.

The intention is not to suggest that certain groups require greater attention, but instead to highlight the need for ongoing efforts in all the areas in which social workers practice. As a result, social work has a continuing role in undertaking political advocacy efforts to support the changing needs of demographic groups in Canada. It is important to view our social, political, and economic systems with a critical lens, one that recognizes that some social groups have privilege due to the focus of current social policy efforts, whereas others are marginalized, oppressed, and without power to make changes that are more equitable. In many ways these efforts happen through large coalitions of interested stakeholders. These are collectives of not only individuals, but also organizations—direct service and advocacy-based organizations alike.

Socio-Economic Equality

A second area of future social policy and social welfare development includes efforts to address increasing socio-economic inequality in Canada. This has been manifested in large part due to Canada's changing labour market, which has changed considerably over the last 40 years. The result has been an increasing polarization between higher skill and higher pay employment opportunities and lower skill and lower pay employment opportunities (Shier, Graham, & Eisenstat, 2015). This trend has had significant implications on the socio-economic well-being of the population. For instance, in a less polarized labour market, there are more opportunities to make what might be considered a 'middle-income' salary, which would allow individuals to purchase housing and support their family. However, now many Canadian workers are constrained to the lower-pay labour market sector (which is primarily characterized by the sale of goods and services) and are unable to generate sufficient income to support their own individual and familial well-being. For example, Zuberi (2013) has described this situation for hospital workers in positions that have been outsourced to private companies. The result of outsourcing has been reduced wages for workers, resulting in the need to take on multiple employment positions to remain above the poverty threshold and effectively support oneself and their family. This example highlights the increasing precariousness within Canada's labour market. This precariousness is characterized by changes in the nature of work. For instance, there has been an increase in part-time, temporary employment opportunities, making full-time, permanent, meaningful work harder to attain. Social mobility becomes even more difficult, because of such forces as computerization, globalization, and technical innovations, which render insecure the future of many professions once deemed secure. Cab drivers are being made redundant by Uber, journalists by Internet-based bloggers. Computer algorithms can do many things that used to be the domains of accountants or lawyers. The work of these professionals, as well as those of architects, engineers, radiologists and many other professionals can be outsourced to people outside the country (Susskind & Susskind, 2015). Not surprisingly, there can be greater feelings of insecurity, particularly among younger people seeking to enter labour markets, or those who fear their jobs or careers may be imperilled by forces outside of their control. These same patterns of insecurity, not surprisingly, can also reinforce existing patterns of inequality, insofar as they block the mobility of people from lower income levels to higher levels.

Socio-economic inequality is a by-product of the inherent inequality within our social institutions, including the labour market (Vosko, 2006; Wallis & Kwok, 2008). Some recent works have begun to conceptualize the ramifications of a changing labour market (Ehrenreich, 2001; Zuberi, 2013) and social welfare system (Schneider, 2006) on socially and economically marginalized individuals and groups within society. For instance, Smith's (2006) *On the Margins of Inclusion* investigates the impact of changing labour markets and social policy frameworks on precariously employed people. Similarly, Iverson and Armstrong's (2006) *Jobs aren't Enough* is an interesting ethnographic study, investigating the experiences of low income families: people who work and are motivated to work. They argue for a more holistic and systemic social welfare and policy approach to understanding why these families remain in poverty and why more and more families are heading into poverty.

The two lead authors of this book along with colleague Marion Jones have investigated the intersection between two key institutional frameworks that create socio-economic inequality in Canada: the labour market and the housing market. The focus of this research has been on how these institutional contexts contribute to and maintain vulnerability among social groups in Canada, such as individuals experiencing housing loss and individuals with long-term labour market attachment difficulties (Graham, Jones, & Shier, 2010; Shier, Graham, & Jones, 2009; 2010; Shier, Jones, & Graham, 2012). Together, this research focuses not only on the economic mobility at an individual or familial level, but also on the systemic barriers within the labour and housing markets that lead to continued precarious living among marginalized, impoverished individuals. Together, this research offers a contemporary, structuralist theory of social and economic underclass, highlighting the barriers placed on the economic and social mobility of vulnerable social groups due to contemporary social institutions.

Together, this emerging body of scholarship has brought attention to the need for more specific policy initiatives that support upward social mobility of vulnerable groups in society. The result is the need for a widespread shift in the focus of contemporary labour market support policies that emphasize basic skill development. Current policy-related efforts largely aim to prepare individuals for employment in the precarious, lower skill and lower pay labour market sector. Instead, in the future, social policy efforts need to be made to support marginalized and vulnerable groups to transition to the higher skill, and subsequently higher pay, labour market sector. This could be achieved with more targeted programming that support post-secondary educational attainment among vulnerable groups (such as the creation of new legislation in Ontario that provides free tuition to students from low socio-economic status families), along with the development of specific occupational skills that are aligned with labour market demand. This is one example of a policy direction that takes an incremental approach to policy development (see Chapter 8). More comprehensive approaches to policy development might seek to create a living wage requirement, so that all individuals in Canada receive at the least a sufficient wage to achieve their individual and familial social well-being needs. However, in Canada's current political-economic context of *pragmatic liberalism* (inclusive of both embedded- and neo-liberal values and public policies), some observers prefer more incremental approaches to social policy development in relation to addressing socio-economic inequality.

Social Economy

Chapter 7 analysed current theoretical debates around contemporary social welfare, and the active role played by nonprofits in supporting social welfare development. These discussions suggest there is a need for increased efforts to support the development of Canada's social economy. Social economy refers to those economically productive parts of Canada's economy that support the achievement of social goods. Quarter (1992) described Canada's social economy in great detail, highlighting that Canada's economy is more than just a "mix of private ownership with some government ownership for selected services and industries" (ix). The term social economy "implies an integrated system of institutions working toward common social goals, rather than the current reality of relatively independent institutions, some financed through tax revenues and charitable donations, assisted by volunteers, and functioning within the shadow of an economy dominated by the private sector" (Quarter, 1992, x). While this seminal text on Canada's social economy was written more than two decades ago, the language in the previous quotation holds true within the current time. It is still widely believed within popular culture that the work that is undertaken within nonprofits (and other forms of association within Canada's social economy) is not economically productive. However, as was previously highlighted in Chapter 7, nonprofits and the voluntary sector in Canada contribute more than 8% to Canada's GDP and employ more than 10% of the actively employed population (Imagine Canada, 2014). This is an important consideration for the future direction of social welfare development in Canada. Furthermore, it is an important consideration given current demand for social goods (like social services) and the lessening availability of public funds to attain them.

In further developing Canada's social economy, there are two primary areas that we would like to highlight, and both relate directly to the relationship between Canada's third sector (or civil society) and the private market. These include: 1) legislation to support the development of social enterprise initiatives by nonprofits; and 2) a stronger commitment by Canadian governments to support social finance initiatives. You might recall from Chapter 7, we described in detail the relationship between the third sector and the other two dominant sectors of society (i.e., the government and the market), and the emergent role in recent decades played by social actors outside of government in addressing emergent and persistent social challenges. What this model demonstrates is that nonprofits are taking it upon themselves to engage in market-based activities to support the development of new programs and initiatives that aim to improve social outcomes for service user groups. The solution is no longer just to advocate for more financial resources from government, which is an unlikely outcome within Canada's current political-economic climate. Instead, resources can be sought by engaging in revenue-generating activities. The question remains: How do you support these efforts?

First, many nonprofits are engaging in social enterprise initiatives. However, there remains an absence of legislation and other government efforts to support these initiatives in Canada. In fact, Canada's policy landscape is relatively immature in this particular area when compared to other countries, such as the United States, the United Kingdom, Australia, France, Poland, and South Korea (Kerlin, 2009). For example, in the U.K. new organizational forms have been defined in legislation, providing legitimacy to these hybrid nonprofit and for-profit entities. These have been termed Community Interest Companies. Unlike a registered charity, these Community Interest Companies allow for a paid (rather than volunteer) board. The designation of these social enterprises is highly regulated to maintain the community interest aspect of the revenue-generating organization. Likewise, in the U.K. legislation has been created (i.e., the Social Values Act) which requires that when the government procures services that the social, economic, or environmental benefits are assessed adequately. This requires a great deal of attention to assessing the social impact of these market-driven activities, and creating a layer of accountability. The emergence of social enterprises, and government legislation to support such efforts, has been a global phenomenon (for an overview, see: Kerlin, 2009). However, in Canada, the government has remained absent in developing policies and practice frameworks that would support these efforts.

In Canada, there are some barriers that currently restrict the revenue-generating activities of nonprofits (whether they are nonprofit corporations or charitable nonprofits). For nonprofit corporations (i.e., those nonprofits registered only at the provincial level of government) to qualify for tax exemption, some profit-generating activity is allowable; however, the revenue cannot be excessive, cannot exceed the needs of the existing programs at the organization, nor can revenues be distributed to members. This places limitations on earning profits to fund future initiatives or to expand programming to new areas. For charitable nonprofits (i.e., those nonprofits registered with the federal government), their participation in revenue-generating activities are limited by the Canada Income Tax Act to those business activities that are related to the purpose of the charity, and cannot intentionally try to make a profit. This legislation is problematic, and quite restrictive in the establishment of social enterprises, and the further development of Canada's social economy. (For further discussion of this legal context see: Social Enterprise Canada, http://www.socialenterprisecanada.ca/en/toolkits/devtoolkit/nav/TheLegalContext.html).

The second area of potential policy direction in Canada related to the social economy is further support for the development and implementation of new social finance initiatives. Social finance can be defined as:

> an approach to mobilizing multiple sources of capital that delivers a social dividend and an economic return in the achievement of social and environmental goals. Social finance provides opportunities to leverage additional investments to increase the available dollars to scale up proven approaches that address social and environmental challenges. It also creates opportunities for investors to finance projects that benefit society and for community organizations to access new sources of funds. (Employment and Social Development Canada, 2014)

Recently, the Canadian federal government has shown some interest in further developing this aspect of Canada's social economy.

Examples of social finance initiatives include Social Impact Bonds, Pay for Performance Contracts, and Social Investment Funds. Social Impact Bonds (SIBs) refer to:

> SIBs combine a pay-for-performance element with an investment-based approach: private investors provide up-front capital to fund interventions, and can expect to get back their principal investments and a financial return if the results are achieved. This allows the government to use funds otherwise spent on services like counseling, health care or detention to reward investors who fund programs that reduce the need for these services in the first place. The initiative funded by the SIB must be proven, more beneficial than the existing program and both scalable and replicable. (Employment and Social Development Canada, 2014)

The implementation of Social Impact Bonds requires an extensive partnership effort between the government, nonprofit service providers, evaluators, and for-profit investors. One of the significant challenges of fully implementing Social Impact Bonds is the lack of risk protection for the initial investment. This model of social financing (much like efforts to support social enterprise) is underdeveloped compared to elsewhere in the world (such as in the U.K., U.S., Australia, Korea, and France).

Social Investment Funds "pool capital from investors to provide loans, mortgages and venture capital to nonprofits, social enterprises and social purpose businesses. SIF financing features less stringent repayment terms, allowing organizations to access 'patient working capital' (funding with a longer-term repayment schedule) as well as bridge loans" (Employment and Social Development Canada, 2014). Social investment funds, like social impact bonds, are relatively underdeveloped in Canada, at least at a government level. In contrast, in the United Kingdom there has been a great deal of effort made to support the development of social investment funds. For instance, in 2012 the U.K. government created Big Society Capital, which is the first social investment bank (as its sole purpose) in the world (see: http://www.bigsocietycapital.com/). This bank provides capital to undertake social investment initiatives, which include profit-generating ventures that have both social and financial returns. The term social investment has emerged in recent years to describe efforts that have blended financial and social returns, such as social enterprise initiatives. Similar efforts exist in Canada within the third sector, through the efforts of cooperatives, such as VanCity (see: https://www.vancity.com/AboutVancity/). However, this has not been a focus of public policy in Canada.

Finally, Pay for Performance Contracts is another possible social finance effort that could be developed further in Canada to support Canada's growing social economy. A Pay for Performance Contract is defined as "an agreement between a government and external organization in which the government identifies desired social results and commits to pay the external organization an agreed upon amount of money once these results are achieved" (Employment and Social Development Canada, 2014). Pay for Performance Contracts are similar to Social Impact Bonds. There is a requirement that organizations demonstrate a particular threshold of social impact to receive the pay associated with the contract. This requires a highly established network of evaluation and assessment among direct service nonprofits (and other organizational forms).

Together, these social finance possibilities highlight areas for social innovation and social entrepreneurship within the human services. They can have the potential to support new efforts and initiatives that are aimed at improving social outcomes for service user groups in comparison to the service delivery methods in common practice. They can also support local community economic development by creating employment opportunities and undertaking initiatives with investments that benefit local economies. Quarter (1992) critiqued the common practice of investing in large corporations that have demonstrated economic success (i.e., Blue Chip companies), in large financial institutions, and in overseas companies. Many of these investments do not support local community economic development, or even economic development in Canada anywhere. For instance, numerous manufacturers have closed offices and plants in Canada, moving their operations overseas (an outcome related to international trade deals between Canada and other countries). This has led to increasing unemployment and a loss of middle income jobs. Alternatively, social financing initiatives could create opportunity to develop local social enterprise businesses that create value in the local economy, and bolster the economic contributions of this sector. However, for these social financing initiatives to have such an impact, one or more levels of government in Canada have to find a way to minimize the risk of the financial investments. The current belief is that private sector investors will altruistically invest in various social finance initiatives, and carry the burden of the financial risk; Employment and Social Development Canada (2014) has referred to this as the "pay it forward" perspective. To significantly impact Canadians' well-being, further government efforts are needed to support these social finance initiatives, involving more than private sector investors, or at least increasing their scope of impact.

A final area of social policy development could support these social finance initiatives: a bilateral agreement between the governments in Canada and the nonprofit and voluntary sector. In direct practice, many government departments refer to nonprofits as their "contracted agencies". There is a resulting misperception among government actors about the independent role of the nonprofit and voluntary sector in Canada's social welfare system. Further policy needs to be developed that clearly outlines the relationship between the government and civil society. In the United Kingdom, this relationship has been documented in *The Compact*, which acts as an agreement between the nonprofit and voluntary sector and the government. Similarly, in Australia this relationship has been defined in a document titled *The National Compact*. In Canada, efforts were made in 2003 to create such an agreement. The result was the document *An Accord Between the Government of Canada and the Voluntary Sector*. This document does not represent an agreement, but rather a framework. No efforts since have been made to create a more formal agreement.

Several critical questions need to be raised within these discussions related to Canada's social economy. For instance, it is important to consider how social value or social impact is defined. That is, from whose perspective is the social value determined? From a social work lens, the perspective we are most interested in is that of the service user group. As a result, it becomes necessary for social work to begin joining these conversations, to provide the insight needed that might support the most optimal outcomes for service users.

Civic Engagement

The final theme for future social policy and social welfare development has to do with how citizens engage in supporting the social well-being needs of the population. "Civic engagement" is a broad term that refers to the various ways that individuals associate to promote some common societal benefit (Schneider, 2013). It includes the various ways that citizens participate in active social life with the intention of shaping the future of community and/or to improve the social, economic, or political conditions of social groups (Adler & Googin, 2005; Shier, McDougle, & Handy, 2014). As was highlighted in Chapters 5 and 7, citizen participation has become a key component of contemporary social welfare development in Canada, primarily through the active engagement and involvement of citizens in community-based initiatives (whether those are grassroots initiatives or more formal forms of association, such as nonprofit organizations).

Recently, scholars have emphasized the role of volunteering and donating in promoting civic engagement, and certainly this is one component part of the concept. Shier, McDougle, and Handy (2014) recently conceptualized the notion of civic engagement through a "civic footprint" metaphor. Taking the idea from the "environmental footprint" literature, they sought to investigate the various ways that nonprofits promote civic engagement within local jurisdictions, with the intention of understanding the ways in which nonprofits could maximize their "civic footprint". Their research highlights a number of ways that nonprofits engage with citizens to promote civic engagement. These include: 1) efforts to enlist volunteers and donors to participate in their programs—whether that is active participation in the day-to-day functioning of the organization, or by providing monetary or in-kind donations to support the organization's efforts; 2) engaging in activities that bring community members together, such as through program participation and community events; 3) participation in collaborative arrangements with other nonprofits and less formal community groups; and 4) activities that promote education and awareness within the community (Shier, McDougle, & Handy, 2015). As key actors in nonprofits, social workers can support the promotion of civic engagement by engaging in these activities within their organizations.

Only a very minimal public policy framework encourages Canadian civic engagement. One of the most impactful and longstanding policies is the allowance of tax deductions on charitable donations made to registered charities in Canada. While Canada has approximately 170000 nonprofit organizations, only approximately half of those are registered charitable nonprofits. For nonprofits to attain a registered charitable status, they must register their organization with the federal government of Canada, and in particular, with the Canada Revenue Agency (CRA). Those that do not register with the CRA do not have charitable status. Even if they are registered as nonprofit corporations with their respective provincial governments, they cannot receive tax deductible charitable donations. An important national institution is Imagine Canada, a nationally focused advocacy and research-based nonprofit representing the interests of the nonprofit and voluntary sector (www.imaginecanada.ca). Imagine Canada promotes greater civic engagement through the donation of financial resources. To this end, it advocates that the federal government extend the tax deduction allowance of financial donations to charitable nonprofits. It has termed the "Stretch Campaign", which is intended to increase the federal charitable tax credit on monetary donations to charitable nonprofits (Imagine Canada, 2016). There are several benefits of such an initiative. First, it provides opportunity for the federal government (through the loss of tax revenue) to support local community efforts and initiatives. Second, it allows for greater citizen participation in the development of social welfare efforts, and creates opportunities to provide solutions to local problems. However, such an effort could be criticized because it removes the government's role in creating consistent social welfare efforts throughout the entire country, and has the potential to introduce bias in resource allocation, based on general public perceptions towards specific service user groups and the extent to which they are "deserving" of services and support.

Furthermore, there are minimal efforts within Canada to promote more engaged participation in civic life among the general population. In particular, efforts to support volunteering are minimal. Some school jurisdictions have incorporated volunteering as part of the high school curriculum and/or as a component of the secondary school diploma credential. However, no other efforts have been developed to support such initiatives. One area of future policy direction could be efforts that support individuals to participate more actively in civic life. In some ways this could be manifested in resources allocated to direct service nonprofits (in their contract funding with government). Government funding focuses primarily on service delivery, with little to no resources for leadership activities, such as civic engagement initiatives that promote active participation. Likewise, efforts could be made to target the private for-profit sector to allocate some work time or resources to participating in the local community through volunteer initiatives.

CONCLUSION

This chapter has provided a summary of the key themes throughout this book along with a brief discussion of some possible future directions in social policy and social welfare development. These future directions should not be viewed as distinct social policy and social welfare paths. Instead, they are linked efforts that need to occur in tandem. They are informed by the experiences of vulnerable groups and the realities of our contemporary political–economic context.

Glossary

Aboriginal peoples: Native persons indigenous to Canada. Aboriginal communities consist of First Nations peoples (those Aboriginal peoples with treaty status), Métis (Aboriginal people who, following eighteenth- and nineteenth-century intermarriage of First Nations peoples with traders/settlers, founded distinct societies in Western Canada), and Inuit (Aboriginal peoples who live north of the tree line).

Alms: A historical term describing charity in cash or kind provided to the needy.

Block grant: A cash transfer provided by one level of government to another, the amount of the transfer being fixed independently of the purpose to which the funds are put. Also known as a general-purpose grant. Its opposite is a *specific-purpose grant.*

Breadwinner male: A term coined by scholars to describe the social construction of men as the principal income earners. Notions of the breadwinner male have had mutually reinforcing relationships with some social programs but have been challenged by feminist thinking and some contemporary social programs. See also *women's domesticity.*

Canada Assistance Plan (CAP): Introduced in 1966, this program allowed provinces and the federal government to cost-share on a fifty–fifty basis education, health care, and social welfare services. Provinces administered these services and received federal money, subject to federal standards. The CAP gradually eroded during the latter part of the 1970s, 1980s, and 1990s, and was ultimately replaced in 1996 by the Canada Health and Social Transfer (CHST), with looser federal standards.

Canada Health Act: Federal legislation enacted in 1984 that reaffirms five principles of our universal health care system: its universality, comprehensiveness, accessibility, portability, and public administration.

Canada Pension Plan/Quebec Pension Plan (CPP/QPP): Both pension plans were introduced in 1966. The CPP applies to all working Canadians except for those in Quebec, which has its own contributory pension plan, the QPP. Both are publicly administered and are based on employees' workplace contributions.

Canadian Charter of Rights and Freedoms: The only Charter of Rights entrenched in the Canadian Constitution. It came into force in 1982.

Canadian Constitution: A body of fundamental principles and established precedents on which the Canadian state operates and which determine legislative and administrative responsibilities among the three levels of government: federal, provincial, and municipal. Named the British North America Act in 1867, it was renamed the Constitution Act in 1982. Every law that is inconsistent with the Constitution is, to the extent of the inconsistency, of no force and effect.

Capitalism: An economic system in which the production and distribution of goods and services are controlled through private ownership and open competition.

Civic engagement: Citizen involvement in active community life through efforts that aim to have a societal impact.

Collectivism: A world view wherein the rights and welfare of the group or society are placed above those of the individual.

Comparative needs: Needs that are determined by comparing one individual or group to another.

Conditional grant: A transfer of money from one level of government to another, and tied directly to an expected type of service delivery. The Canada Assistance Plan (1966–96) is an example of a conditional grant. CAP provided federal transfers to provincial governments to cover the latter's delivery of health, education, and social services.

Corporate welfarism: Governments providing large contracts and other incentives to various companies.

Cost-benefit analysis: A method of analysis that supports decision making for the allocation of resources by comparing the monetary costs with the monetary benefits of different methods if intervention.

Cost-effectiveness analysis: A method of analysis that supports decision making for the allocation of resources by comparing the monetary costs with some non-monetary benefit.

Debt: A cumulative, multiyear calculation based on the total amount of money that is owed.

Deficit: A yearly calculation based on annual operating costs. It occurs when spending exceeds revenue.

Detached ideology: Those political values that create policy choices that are made strictly in accordance with one's values, regardless of the outcome and consequences to others.

Dictatorship of the proletariat: According to Marxist theory, the control of communist parties that begins immediately following a revolution. Marxist theory projects the dictatorship as ending with the development of a classless society.

Diversity: A concept that conveys differences between people on the basis of age, culture, ethnicity, gender, nationality, race, range of ability, religion, and sexual orientation, among other social factors.

Egalitarianism: A world view that values human equality politically, socially, and economically.

Elitism: A world view that sees society organized around groups that are unequal in power and resources.

Embedded liberalism: See Keynesianism definition.

Employment Insurance (EI): Formerly Unemployment Insurance (introduced 1940), this publicly administered, universal, employment-based contributory insurance program was initially intended to provide for the hazards of temporary unemployment but has been expanded to include other reasons for temporary cessation of work, including maternity and parental benefits. Renamed *Employment Insurance* in 1996.

Equalization payment: Also known as an unconditional grant, an equalization payment is a transfer of money from one level of government to another; no particular commitment by the recipient government to tie the grant to an expected type of expenditure is required. Its opposite is a *conditional grant.*

Expressed needs: Needs that are communicated to others.

Family Allowance (FA): A universal program, introduced in 1944 and withdrawn in 1992, that provided mothers a monthly payment for each child under their care. In 1992, the universal FA program was replaced by a refundable, income-tested (i.e., selective) tax credit.

Federal system of government: In this type of system, political power is divided between the national and provincial governments. Canada is a federal system. Most countries are unitary, meaning that political power is centralized in one national level of government.

Felt needs: Needs that are defined on a personal or subjective level.

Fiscal capacity: A particular level of government's ability to change the total or composition of its revenues (e.g., taxes) or expenditures (e.g., a social program).

Globalization: A current, pervasive trend of international finance, ideology, and political arrangements. As a result of globalization, money is invested quickly and easily across national borders. Principles of transnational competition for lucrative markets and inexpensive labour are actively pursued. In the absence of powerfully constraining national legislation or intra-national structures, multinational corporations have growing sovereignty to pursue their objectives.

Governance: A concept that describes the way that decisions are made and who is involved.

Grand issues of social policy: Those issues relating to the fundamental structures of political–economic life. Examples include distribution of income and wealth, political power, and corporate prerogatives. Grand issues are contrasted with *ordinary issues of social policy.*

Gross domestic product (GDP): A measurement of a country's economic productivity over time.

Horizontal imbalance: An unequal relationship in fiscal capacity between richer and poorer provinces.

Human rights: Those legal, social, and political entitlements that are justly claimed to belong to any individual in society. These include, but are not restricted to, the right to justice, equality of opportunity, and religious freedom.

Ideology: A pattern of ideas based on experiences, values, and beliefs, and profoundly influencing one's political views. Ideologies shape, organize, and justify a course of action, and are used to legitimize the power held by the active political party.

Individualism: A world view wherein freedom, worth, and self-determination are foremost attributed to the individual rather than a group.

Intergovernmental finance: The web of financial movement that links governments in a federal system.

Inverse totalitarianism: A political-economic system where economic elites have defacto ownership of political systems. It is an inverse situation to typical totalitarianism where political elites have ownership of economic systems.

Low-income cut-off (LICO): A relative measure of *poverty* and the standard *poverty line* used by the federal government since 1959. It is calculated based on information from a survey of family spending patterns conducted by Statistics Canada.

Keynesianism: A political economic orientation that values government intervention in the private sector market. It is a form of liberalism (referred to as embedded liberalism). Named after the economist John Maynard Keynes.

Market exchange: A form of economic integration characterized by the sale of goods and services, and principles of supply and demand.

Means of production: According to Marxist theory, the land, labour, and capital that are used by a society to produce material goods.

Neoliberalism: A political economic orientation that values minimal government intervention in the private sector market. It is a form of liberalism.

Nonprofit and Voluntary Sector: A dominant societal sector that includes the various forms association among citizens and acts of reciprocity. Also referred to as civil society, community, or the third sector.

Normative needs: Needs that are determined by someone other than the individual by applying some benchmark or standard to the individual case.

Old Age Security (OAS): Introduced as a selective, means-tested program in 1927, Old Age Security was transformed into a universal program in 1952, providing all Canadian senior citizens a monthly income. The introduction in the late 1980s of income tax "claw-backs" for individuals and couples having or surpassing a particular net income has called into question whether OAS may truly be considered a universal program today.

Operating principles: The policy results that occur when various social ideals are integrated with a practicable rule of application.

Ordinary issues of social policy: Those policy issues that directly affect the lives of people in a community and the technical operating principles of direct social work intervention. These are often managed and redressed by community-based organizations, and are sometimes the unintended consequence of earlier reforms. Examples include how child welfare service organizations are structurally administered, or the deinstitutionalization and development of community support programs. Ordinary issues of social policy are contrasted with *grand issues of social policy*.

Political advocacy: Efforts that aim to change the focus of public policy or to create new public policy.

Poverty: A state of deficiency in money or in the means of subsistence.

Poverty line: A measure representing a minimal level of human need. An absolute poverty line presumes that there is some fairly objective means for determining the absolute minimum an individual or household requires for food, shelter, clothing, and any other physical necessities. A relative poverty line assumes that poverty is to be defined relative to prevailing community standards, as opposed to absolute criteria.

Power: In social policy, power refers to the capacity to alter policies and decisions.

Pragmatic liberalism: A political economic orientation that combines values and elements of both embedded (or Keynesian) and neoliberal traditions.

Proletariat: According to Marxist theory, the proletariat consists of individuals and families who are members of the working class, particularly manual and industrial labourers.

Public policies: Legislated acts, regulations, and bylaws (including all associated policies in the ministerial, agency, and public arenas) at the federal, provincial/territorial, and municipal levels of government.

Reciprocal exchange: A form of economic integration where individuals, families, or social group help each other. Modern forms of reciprocal exchange include volunteering time or donating money.

Redistributive exchange: A form of economic integration where resources are allocated to individuals in need. Typically associated with income security programs funded through public tax revenue.

Selective programs: Social welfare programs implemented on the basis of assessed need. Eligibility for benefits is determined through means testing. Selective programs are distinct from *universal programs*.

Social assistance: An income security program that uses a "means" or "needs" test to determine eligibility.

Social economy: All forms of economic activity that has a social good purpose.

Social enterprise: A revenue generating business that supports a social cause, such as programming in a nonprofit service delivery organization.

Social finance: Approaches to support social benefit efforts that engage with for-profit businesses.

Social groups: Collectives of individuals that share something in common. The commonality is typically some similar characteristic, background, or experience.

Social entrepreneurship: A classification that characterizes the behavior of social welfare leaders that can generate resources or revenues to provide a service in a new way.

Social innovation: A new idea, process, or approach that improves the quality of life for general social groups.

Social insurance: An income security program in which eligibility for benefits is determined on the basis of a record of contribution and the occurrence of a foreseen contingency, such as injury, retirement, unemployment, or the death of an income-earning spouse.

Social policy: The statements of the selected social goals and objectives to which a group—be it professional, governmental, or private—is committed.

Social policy analysis: A rationalistic structured process of assessing the impacts of public policy.

Social welfare: A complex network of personal relationships, institutions, policies, and services that a society creates to contribute to the well-being, or welfare, of its members.

Specific-purpose grant: A cash transfer provided by one level of government to another. The amount of the transfer is tied to its intended purpose; an example would be a matched or shared-cost program. Its opposite is a *block grant*.

Standard of living: A term denoting the necessities and luxuries required for living in a particular circumstance.

superPacs: Pools of large campaign contributions that fund select politicians.

Sustainability: An economic, political, and environmental world view that promotes present and future generations of stewardship of the physical world.

Universal programs: Social welfare programs based on national and categorical membership. These programs are available to all persons regardless of need. They are distinct from *selective programs*.

Vertical imbalance: An unequal relationship in fiscal capacity between the federal and a provincial government.

Welfare regime: A more comprehensive system of social welfare than welfare state, that includes the contributions to social well-being made by the market, the family, government, and civil society actors.

Welfare state: A term coined by the Archbishop of Canterbury during World War II to describe those governments, such as Canada's, that were committing themselves to the use of resources and to the development of social policies for the collective well-being of all. Also referred to as 'traditional social welfarism' and the 'modern welfare state'.

Women's caring: A term coined by scholars to describe the social construction of women as principal caregivers in family and social relationships.

Women's domesticity: A term coined by scholars to describe the social construction of women in the domestic or home realm—daughters, mothers, wives, or widows. This term contrasts with the gendered social construction that encouraged men to take on economic, political, and social activities outside of the home. See also *breadwinner male*.

World view: An outlook drawn from religious, political, social, and physical information about humans and the societies they create.

References

Abelson, D. E. (2009). *Do think tanks matter?* (2nd ed.). Montreal: McGill-Queen's University Press.

Adams, R. (2002). *Social policy for social work.* Basingstoke, UK: Palgrave Macmillan.

Adler, R. P., & Goggin, J. (2005). What do we mean by "civic engagement"? *Journal of Transformative Education, 3*(3), 236–253.

Airdrie, K. (2010). *Canadian Aboriginal women's "Sisters in Spirit" funding cut.* Retrieved from http://www.suite101.com/content/canadian-aboriginal-womens-sisters-in-spirit-funding-cut-a306076

Alberta Health Services. (2010). *Becoming the best: Alberta's 5-Year Health Action Plan 2010–2015.* Edmonton: Alberta Health Wellness Communications.

Allen, R. (1971). *The social passion: Religion and social reform in Canada, 1914–1928.* Toronto: University of Toronto Press.

Almey, M. (n.d.). *Women in Canada: Work chapter updates.* Retrieved from http://www.statcan.gc.ca/pub/89f0133x2006000-eng.htm

Almog-Bar, M., & Schmid, H., (2014). Advocacy activities of nonprofit human service organizations: A critical review. *Nonprofit and Voluntary Sector Quarterly, 43*(1), 11–35.

American Federation of Labor—Congress of Industrial Organizations. (2010). *Executive paywatch.* Retrieved from http://www.aflcio.org/corporatewatch/paywatch/

Amernic, J., & Craig, R. (2006). *CEO speak: The language of corporate leadership.* Montreal: McGill-Queen's University Press.

Anderson, G., & Marr, W. (1987). Immigration and social policy. In S. Yelaga (Ed.), *Canadian social policy* (Rev. ed., 88–114). Waterloo, ON: Wilfrid Laurier University Press.

Anderson, J. E. (1990). *Public policymaking.* Boston: Houghton Mifflin.

Anheier, H. (2004). Third sector-Third Way: Comparative perspectives and policy reflections. In Surender, R., & Lewis, J. (Eds.), *Welfare state change: Towards a Third Way? (111–134).* Oxford: Oxford University Press.

Anheier, H. (2009). What kind of non-profit sector, what kind of society? Comparative policy reflections. *American Behavioral Scientist, 52*(7), 1082–1094.

Armitage, A. (1996). *Social welfare in Canada revisited: Facing up to the future* (3rd ed.). Don Mills, ON: Oxford University Press.

Armitage, A. (2003). *Social welfare in Canada* (4th ed.). Oxford: Oxford University Press.

Artibese, A. F. J., & Stelter, G. A. (1985). Urbanization. In *The Canadian encyclopedia* (Vol. 3, 1887). Edmonton: Hurtig.

Babbie, E. (1986). *Observing ourselves: Essays in social research.* Belmont, CA: Wadsworth.

Bach, M. (2005). Social inclusion as solidarity: Rethinking the child rights agenda. In T. Richmond & A. Saloojee (Eds.), *Social inclusion: Canadian perspectives* (126–154). Halifax: Fernwood.

Bailey, R., & Brake, M. (Eds.) (1975). *Radical social work.* London: Edward Arnold.

Bakan, J. (1997). *Just words: Constitutional rights and social wrongs.* Toronto: University of Toronto Press.

Bakan, J. (2004). *The corporation: The pathological pursuit of profit and power.* New York: Simon and Schuster.

Ball, O., & Gready, P. (2006). *The no-nonsense guide to human rights.* Toronto: New Internationalist Publications.

Banks, K., & Mangan, M. (1999). *The company of neighbours: Revitalizing community through action-research.* Toronto: University of Toronto Press.

Bannock, G., Baxter, R. E., & Davis, E. (Eds.). (1998a). Gross domestic product. In *The penguin dictionary of economics.* Retrieved from http://www.xreferplus.com.ezproxy.lib.ucalgary.ca/entry/445411

Bannock, G., Baxter, R. E., & Davis, E. (1998b). Gross national product. In *The Penguin dictionary of economics*. Retrieved from http://www.xreferplus.com.ezproxy.lib.ucalgary.ca/entry/445417

Banting, K. G. (1985). Institutional conservatism: Federalism and pension reform. In J. S. Ismael (Ed.), *Canadian social welfare policy: Federal and provincial dimensions* (48–74). Kingston/Montreal: McGill-Queen's University Press.

Barata, P. (2000). *Social exclusion in Europe: Survey of literature*. Unpublished paper. Toronto: Laidlaw Foundation.

Barker, J. (1999.) *Street-level democracy: Political settings at the margins of global power*. Toronto: Between the Lines.

Barker, R. L. (1991). *The social work dictionary*. Washington, DC: National Association of Social Workers.

Barlow (2001). *Global Showdown: How the New Activists Are Fighting Global Corporate Rule* (with Tony Clarke) – Stoddart, Toronto (2001).

Baronet, A., and Gerber, G. J. (1998). Psychiatric rehabilitation: Efficacy of four models. *Clinical Psychology Review, 18*, 189–228.

Barter, K. (1996). Collaboration: A framework for northern practice. In R. Delaney, K. Brownlee, & K. M. Zapf (Eds.), *Issues in northern social work practice* (pp. 66–78). Thunder Bay, ON: Centre for Northern Studies.

Barton, R. (1999). Psychosocial rehabilitation services in community support systems: A review of outcomes and policy recommendations. *Psychiatric Services, 50*, 525–534.

Battle, K. (1993). *Federal social programs: Setting the record straight*. Ottawa: Caledon Institute of Social Policy.

Battle, K. (2001). *Relentless incrementalism: Deconstructing and reconstructing Canadian income security policy*. Ottawa: Caledon Institute of Social Policy.

Battle, K. (2002). *Social policy that works: An agenda*. Ottawa: Caledon Institute of Social Policy.

Battle, K., & Mendelson, M. (1997). *Child benefit reform in Canada: An evaluative framework and future directions*. Ottawa: Caledon Institute of Social Policy.

Battle, K., & Torjman, S. (1993). *Federal social programs: Setting the record straight*. Ottawa: Caledon Institute of Social Policy.

Battle, K., & Torjman, S. (2014). *If you don't pay, you can't play: the children's fitness tax credit*. Ottawa: Caledon Institute of Social Policy.

Beach, C. M., Green, A. G., & Reitz, J. G. (Eds.). (2004). *Canadian immigration policy for the 21st century*. Montreal: McGill-Queen's University Press.

Beard, J. H., Propst, R. N., & Malamud, T.J. (1982). The Fountain House model of rehabilitation. *Psychosocial Rehabilitation Journal, 5*(1), 47–53.

Becker, D. R., Drake, R. E., Farabaugh, A., and Bond, G. R. (1996). Job preferences of clients with severe psychiatric disorders participating in supported employment programs. *Psychiatric Services, 47*, 1223–1226.

Bellefeuille, G., & Hemingway, D. (2005). The new politics of community based governance requires a fundamental shift in the nature and character of the administrative bureaucracy. *Children and Youth Service Review, 27*(5), 491–498.

Berkowitz, I. (1980). Social choice and policy formulation: Problems and considerations in the construction of the public interest. *Journal of Sociology and Social Welfare, 16*(2), 533–545.

Berman, M. (2000). *Wandering God: A study in nomadic spirituality*. Albany: State University of New York Press.

Bickenbach, J. E. (1993). *Physical disability and social policy*. Toronto: University of Toronto Press.

Bickenbach, J. E. (2006). *Canadian Charter v. American ADA: Individual rights or collective responsibilities*. In M. McColl & L. Jongbloed (Eds.), *Disability and social policy in Canada* (2nd ed., 77–86). Concord, ON: Captus Press.

Bill 56, Ontario Retirement Pension Plan Act, 2015. http://www.ontla.on.ca/web/bills/bills_detail.do?locale=en&BillID=3092. Accessed July 6, 2015.

Bishop, A. (1994). *Becoming an ally: Breaking the cycle of oppression*. Halifax: Fernwood.

Bishop, A. (2002). *Becoming an ally: Breaking the cycle of oppression* (2nd ed.). Halifax: Fernwood.

Bishop, A. (2005). *Beyond token change: Breaking the cycle of oppressive institutions*. Halifax: Fernwood.

Bissoondath, N. (1994). *Selling illusions: The cult of multiculturalism in Canada*. Toronto: Penguin.

Blackburn, R. (2002). *Banking on death, or investing in life: The history and future of pensions*. London: Verso.

Blake, R. B. (2009). *From rights to needs: A history of Family Allowances in Canada, 1929–92*. Vancouver: University of British Columbia Press.

Blake, R., Bryden, P., & Strain, F. (Eds.). (1997). *The welfare state in Canada: Past, present, and future*. Concord, ON: Irwin.

Bloemraad, I. (2006). *Becoming a citizen: Incorporating immigrants and refugees in the United States and Canada*. Berkeley, CA: University of California Press.

Bobbitt, P. (2002). *The shield of Achilles: War, peace, the course of history*. New York: Anchor Books.

Bopp, J., Bopp, M., Brown, L., & Lane, P. (1985). *The sacred tree*. Lethbridge, AB: Four Worlds Development Press.

Bornstein, D., & Davis, S. (2010). *Social entrepreneurship: What everyone needs to know*. New York: Oxford University Press.

Bourgeault, R. (1988). Race and class under mercantilism: Indigenous people in nineteenth-century Canada. In B. Bolaria & P. Li (Eds.), *Racial oppression in Canada*. (2nd ed., 41–70). Toronto: Garamond Press.

Bourgois, P. (2003). *In search of respect: Selling crack in El Barrio*, New York: Cambridge University Press.

Boychuk, G. W. (1998). *Patchworks of purpose: The development of provincial social assistance regimes in Canada*. Kingston/Montreal: McGill-Queen's University Press.

Boyd, A. S., & Wilmoth, M. C. (2006). An innovative community-based intervention for African American women with breast cancer: The Witness Project. *Health and Social Work*, *31*(1), 77–80.

Boyd, D. (2001, April 27). They're blowing smoke. *The Globe and Mail*, p. A19.

Boyer, S. L., and Bond, G. R. (1999). Does assertive community treatment reduce burnout? A comparison with traditional case management. *Mental Health Services Research, 1*, 31–45.

Brager, G., Specht, H., & Torczyner, J. (1987). *Community organizing*. New York: Columbia University Press.

Braybrooke, D., & Lindblom, C. E. (1963). *The strategy of decision*. New York: Free Press.

Brinkerhoff, J. M., & Brinkerhoff, D.W. (2002). Government-nonprofit relations in comparative perspective: Evolution, themes, and new directions. *Public Administration and Development, 22*, 3–18.

Broad, D., & Antony, W. (1999). *Citizens or consumers? Social policy in a market society*. Halifax: Fernwood.

Brown, L., & Troutt, E. (2003). Stability and stress in the relationship between government and the nonprofit sector: The case of Manitoba. In K.L Brock & Banting, K. G. (Eds.). *The nonprofit sector in interesting times: Case studies in a changing sector* (177–218). Kingston, Ontario: McGill-Queens University Press.

Bruce, M. (1961). *The coming of the welfare state*. London: B.T. Batsford.

Burgeoning bourgeoisie. (2009, February 12). [Special supplement]. *Economist Magazine, 390*(8618), p. 1.

Burns, T. J., Batavia, A. I., & DeJong, G. (1994). The health insurance work disincentive for persons with disabilities. *Research in the Sociology of Health Care, 11*, 57–68.

Callahan, M. (2004). Chalk and cheese: Feminist thinking and policy-making. In B. Wharf & B. McKenzie (Eds.), *Connecting policy to practice in the human services* (2nd ed., 128–140). Don Mills, ON: Oxford University Press.

Campaign 2000. (2007). *Raising the falling fortunes of young families of Canada*. Toronto: Family Service Association of Toronto.

Canada. (1966). *Canada Assistance Plan*. Ottawa: Queen's Printer (Repealed in 1995).

Canada. (1984). *The Health Act*. Ottawa: Queen's Printer.

Canada. (1985, 1995). *Federal-Provincial Fiscal Arrangements Act*. Ottawa: Queen's Printer.

Canada. (1997). *Canada Health and Social Transfer Regulations*. Ottawa: Queen's Printer.

Canada Revenue Agency. (2010, December 13). Canada Child Tax Benefit. Retrieved from http://www.cra-arc.gc.ca/bnfts/cctb/menu-eng.html

Canada Revenue Agency (2015a, June 1). CCTB: *Calculation and payment information*. http://www.cra-arc.gc.ca/cctb/.

Canada Revenue Agency (2015b, June 1). *Child Disability Benefit (CDB)*. http://www.cra-arc.gc.ca/bnfts/dsblty-eng.html.

Canada without poverty. http://www.cwp-csp.ca/poverty/. Accessed October 12, 2015.

Canadian Association of Gift Planners. (2010). Who gives: Statistics on giving Canada. Retrieved from Leave a Legacy website: http://www.leavealegacy.ca/program/who/

Canadian Association of Social Workers (CASW). (2005). Code of Ethics.

Canadian Broadcasting Corporation (2015). http://www.cbc.ca/news/business/taxes/retirement-savings-in-canada-by-the-numbers-1.1303371

Canadian Council of Chief Executives. (2010). About CCCE. Retrieved from http://www.ceocouncil.ca/en/about/about.php

Canadian Council on Social Development. (1991). *Social policy in the 1990s: The challenge*. Ottawa/Montreal: CCSD.

Canadian Institute for Health Research. (2014). National health expenditure trends, 1975 to 2014. Ottawa: Author. Retrieved May 18, 2016 from: https://www.cihi.ca/en/nhex_2014_report_en.pdf

Canadian Press, The. (2010, December 18). 2010 a tough year for charity scams, experts say. Retrieved from CTV.ca Ottawa website: http://ottawa.ctv.ca/servlet/an/local/CTVNews/20101218/social-scams-101218/20101218/?hub=OttawaHome

Canadian Union of Public Employees. 2015. http://cupe.ca/its-time-expand-cpp-sign-our-petition. Retrieved July 5, 2015.

Canel, E. (n.d.). *New social movement theory and resource mobilization theory: The need for integration*. International Development Research Centre. Retrieved from http://www.idrc.ca/en/ev-54446-201-1-DO_TOPIC.html

Cannadine, D. (2006). *Mellon: An American life*. New York: Allen Lane.

Careless, J. M. S. (1954). Frontierism, metropolitanism, and Canadian history. *Canadian Historical Review, 35*, 1–21.

Carniol, B. (1987). *Case critical: Challenging social work in Canada* (2nd ed.). Toronto: Between the Lines.

Carniol, B. (1995). *Case critical: Challenging social work in Canada* (3rd ed.). Toronto: Between the Lines.

Carson, R. L. (1962). *Silent Spring*. Boston: Houghton Mifflin/Mariner Books.

Carty, R. K., Cross, W., & Young, L. (2000). *Rebuilding Canadian party politics*. Vancouver: University of British Columbia Press.

Cassidy, F. (Ed.). (1991). *Aboriginal self-determination*. BC and Montreal: The Institute for Research on Public Policy and Oolichan Books.

CASSW. (1996). *The manual of standards and procedures for the accreditation of Canadian programs of social work education*. Ottawa: Author.

Castellano, M. (2002). *Aboriginal family trends: Extended families, nuclear families, families of the heart*. Ottawa: The Vanier Institute of the Family.

Castles, F. G. (Ed.) (2007). *The disappearing state? Retrenchment realities in an age of globalization*. London: Edward Elgar Publishing.

CBC. (2000). "Nellie McClung: The Sculpting of Angels." *Life and Times*. Retrieved from http://www.cbc.ca/lifeandtimes/mcclung.html

CBC News. (2008). *Canada votes*. Toronto: CBC. Retrieved from http://www.cbc.ca/news/canadavotes/story/2008/10/15/voter-turnout.html

Central Intelligence Agency. (2010). *The world fact book, 2010*. Washington: Author. Retrieved from https://www.cia.gov/library/publications the-world-factbook/

Chamberlin, J. (1997). A working definition of empowerment. *Psychiatric Rehabilitation Journal, 20*(4), 43–46.

Changon, J. (2013). Migration: International, 2010 and 2011. Ottawa: Statistics Canada. http://www.statcan.gc.ca/pub/91-209-x/2013001/article/11787-eng.pdf. Accessed October 12, 2015.

Chapin, R. K. (1995). Social policy development: The strengths perspective. *Social Work, 40*(4), 506–514.

Chappell, R. (1997). *Social welfare in Canadian society*. Scarborough, ON: ITP International Thomson Publishing.

Chappell, R. (2006). *Social welfare in Canadian society*. Toronto: Nelson Thompson Learning.

Cheal, D. (Ed.). (2002). *Aging demographic change in Canadian context*. Toronto: University of Toronto Press.

Child, C., & Gronbjerg, K. (2007). Nonprofit advocacy organizations: Their characteristics and activities. Social Science Quarterly, 88(1), 259–281.

Choca, M. J., Minoff, J., Angene, L., Byrnes, M., Kenneally, L., Norris, D., Pearn, D., & Rivers, M. M. (2004). Can't do it alone: Housing collaborations to improve foster youth outcomes. *Child Welfare, 83*(5), 469–492.

Chomsky, N. (1991). *Deterring democracy*. London: Verso.

Chomsky, N. (2010). *Hopes and prospects*. New York: Haymarket Books.

Chouinard, V., & Crooks, V. (2005). "Because *they* have all the power and I have none": State restructuring of income and employment supports and disabled women's lives in Ontario, Canada. *Disability and Society, 20*(1), 19–32.

Christensen, C. (1995). Immigrant minorities in Canada. In J. Turner & F. Turner (Eds.), *Social welfare in Canada* (3rd ed., 179–212). Scarborough, ON: Allyn and Bacon Canada.

Christian, W., & Campbell, C. (1990). *Political parties and ideologies in Canada* (3rd ed.). Toronto: McGraw-Hill Ryerson Ltd.

Chui, T. (1996). Canada's population: Charting into the 21st century. Catalogue No. 11-008-XPE. Ottawa: Statistics Canada.

Citizenship and Immigration Canada. (2009). *Facts and figures 2009: Summary tables—Permanent and temporary residents*. Ottawa: Author. Retrieved from http://www.cic.gc.ca/english/resources/statistics/facts2009-summary/permanent/01.asp.

Citizenship and Immigration Canada (2015). *Canada facts and figures: Immigrant overview permanent residents, 2014*. Ottawa, ON: Author. www.cic.gc.ca/english/resources/statistics/menu-fact.asp

Clarke, T. (1997). *Silent coup: Confronting the big business takeover of Canada*. Ottawa/Toronto: Canadian Centre for Policy Initiatives/James Lorimer & Co.

Clasen, J., & Siegel, N. A. (Ed.) (2007). *Investigating welfare state change: The 'dependent variable problem' in comparative analysis*. London: Edward Elgar Publishing.

Cnaan, R. A., Blankertz, L., Messinger, K. W., and Gardner, J. R. (1988). Psychosocial rehabilitation: Toward a definition. *Psychosocial Rehabilitation Journal, 11*(4), 61–77.

Cnaan, R. A., & Vinokur-Kaplan, D. (2015). Social innovation: Definitions, clarifications, and a new model. In R. A. Cnaan & D. Vinokur-Kaplan (Eds.). *Cases in Innovative Nonprofits: Organizations that make a difference*. Thousand Oaks, CA: Sage Publications.

Coggan, P. (2010, June 26). Repent at leisure [A special report on debt]. *Economist Magazine*. Retrieved from http://www.economist.com/node/16397110?story_id=16397110&source=hptextfeature

Cohen, E. S. (1974). An overview of long-term care facilities. In E. Brody, *A social work guide for long-term care facilities*. Rockville, MD: National Institute of Mental Health.

Cohen, E. (2006). Why have children? *Commentary Magazine*, June, 44–49.

Cohen, M. B., & Hyde, C. A. (2014). *Empowering workers & clients for organizational change*. Chicago, IL: Lyceum Books.

Collier, K. (2006). *Social work with rural peoples*. Vancouver: New Star Books.

Commissioner of the Environment and Sustainable Development. (2006). *2006 Report of the Commissioner of the Environment Sustainable Development*. Ottawa: Office of the Auditor General of Canada. Retrieved from http://www.oag-bvg.gc.ca/domino/reports.nsf/html/c2006menu_e.html

Cooke, M. (2003). The Canada Pension Plan goes to market. *Canadian Review of Social Policy, 51*, 126–131.

Copp, T. (1974). *The anatomy of poverty: The conditions of the working class in Montreal, 1897–1929.* Toronto: McClelland and Stewart.

Cornish, M., & Faraday, F. (2008). *Ontario's gender pay gap cheats women workers.* Retrieved from http://www.thestar.com/comment/article/500415

Cossman, B. (1996). Same-sex couples and the politics of family status. In J. Brodie (Ed.), *Women and Canadian Public Policy* (pp. 223–253). Toronto: Harcourt Brace and Company.

Crossley, T., & Curtis, L. (2006). Child Poverty in Canada. *Review of Income & Wealth, 52*(2), 237–260.

CUPE. (2007, November 16). Transfers to municipalities fell billions short in 2006. *CUPE economic brief.* Retrieved from http://cupe.ca/updir/Municipal_Transfer_Shortfall.pdf

Daily, The. (2006, March 7). *Women in Canada.* Ottawa: Statistics Canada.

Daily, The. (2007, July 17). *2006 census: Age and sex.* Ottawa: Statistics Canada.

Daily, The. (2007, December). *2006 census: Immigration, citizenship, language, mobility and migration.* Ottawa: Statistics Canada.

Daily, The. (2008, April 2). *2006 census: Ethnic origin, visible minorities, place of work and mode of transportation.* Ottawa: Statistics Canada.

Daily, The. (2010, March 9). *Study: Projections of the diversity of the Canadian population.* Ottawa: Statistics Canada.

Daily, The. (2011, January 7). *Latest release from the Labour Force Survey.* Ottawa: Statistics Canada. Retrieved from http://www.statcan.gc.ca/subjects-sujets/labour-travail/lfs-epa/lfs-epa-eng.htm

Dare, B. (1997). Harris' first year: Attacks and resistance. In D. Ralph, A. Regimbald, & N. St-Am (Eds.), *Open for business, closed to people* (20–26). Halifax: Fernwood.

Davies, J., Sandstrom, S., Shorrocks, A., & Wolff, E. (2009). The global pattern of household wealth. *Journal of International Development, 21*(8), 1111–1124.

Deffeyes, K. S. (2006). *Beyond oil: The view from Hubbert's Peak.* New York: Hill Wang.

Delaney, R. (1995). The philosophical base. In J. Turner & F. Turner (Eds.), *Canadian social welfare* (3rd ed., 12–27). Scarborough, ON: Allyn and Bacon Canada.

Delaney, R., & Brownlee, K. (Eds.). (1995). *Northern social work practice.* Thunder Bay, ON: Centre for Northern Studies.

Delaney, R., Brownlee, K., & Graham, J. R. (Eds.). (1997). *Strategies in northern social work practice.* Thunder Bay, ON: Centre for Northern Studies.

Delaney, R., Brownlee, K., & Sellick, M. (Eds.). (1999). *Social work with rural and northern communities.* Thunder Bay, ON: Centre for Northern Studies.

Delaney, R., Brownlee, K., & Sellick, M. (2001). Surviving globalization: Empowering rural remote communities in Canada's provincial norths. *Australian Rural Social Work, 6*(3), 4–11.

Delaney, R., Brownlee, K., & Zapf, K. M. (Eds.). (1996). *Issues in northern social work practice.* Thunder Bay, ON: Centre for Northern Studies.

Department of Finance Canada. (2006). The economic fiscal update 2006. Ottawa: Public Works and Government Services Canada. Retrieved from http://www.fin.gc.ca/budtoce/2006/ec06_e.html

Department of Finance Canada. (2007). *Restoring fiscal balance for a stronger federation.* Ottawa: Author. Retrieved from http://www.budget.gc.ca/2007/bp/bpc4e.html#equalization

Department of Finance Canada. (2010). *Canada's finance minister highlights tax breaks for Canadians.* Ottawa: Author. Retrieved from http://www.fin.gc.ca/n10/10-099-eng.asp

Department of Finance Canada. (2011). *Federal support for provinces and territories.* Ottawa: Author. Retrieved from http://www.fin.gc.ca/fedprov/mtp-eng.asp

Department of Finance. (2014). Your tax dollar. http://www.fin.gc.ca/tax-impot/2014/2013-14-e.pdf. Accessed October 12, 2015.

Department of Finance Canada (2015). *Federal Support to Provinces and Territories.* http://www.fin.gc.ca/fedprov/mtp-eng.asp. Accessed July 5, 2015.

Derbyshire, J. (2011, January 8). Internet activism: For and against. *New Statesman.*

Retrieved from **http://www.newstates-man.com/blogs/the-staggers/2011/01/morozov-internet-netroots**

de Schweinitz, K. (1943). *England's road to social security.* Philadelphia: University of Pennsylvania Press.

Desert, G. (1976). Une source historique trop oublié: Les archives hospitaliers. *Gazette des Archives, 94,* 145–164.

Desroches, C. (2009). For them but never really theirs: Finding a place for the "aged" within state-funded institutions in nineteenth century Nova Scotia. *Journal of the Canadian Historical Association, 20*(1), 57–84.

de Tocqueville, A. (2004 – translated version). *Democracy in America.* Translated by Arthur Goldhammer. New York, NY: The Library of America.

Devadason, R. (2008). To plan or not to plan? Young adult future orientations in two European cities. *Sociology, 42*(6), 1127-1145.

Diamond, J. (2005). *Collapse: How societies choose to fail or succeed.* New York: Viking Books.

Dincin, J. (1975). Psychiatric rehabilitation. *Schizophrenia Bulletin, 1,* 131–147.

Disability-Related Policy Website. (n.d.). *Disability 101.* Retrieved from **http://www.disability-policy.ca/policy/index.php**

Doern, B., & Aucoin, P. (Eds.). (1971). *The structures of policy-making in Canada.* Toronto: Macmillan.

Dolgoff, R., & Feldstein, D. (1984). *Understanding social welfare* (2nd ed.). London: Longman.

Dominelli, L. (1988). *Anti-racist social work.* London: Macmillan.

Dominelli, L. (1997). *Sociology for social work.* London: Macmillan.

Dominelli, L., & McLeod, E. (1989). *Feminist social work.* London: Macmillan.

Drover, G. (1988). Social work. In *The Canadian encyclopedia* (2034–2035). Edmonton: Hurtig.

Drover, G. (2000). Redefining social citizenship in a global era [Special issue on social work and globalization]. *Canadian Social Work Review, 17,* 29–49.

Drover, G., & Kerans, P. (1993). New approaches to welfare theory: Foundations. In G. Drover & P.

Kerans (Eds.), *New approaches to welfare theory* (pp. 3–32). Brookfield, VT: Edward Elgar.

Dutt, M. (2014). Affordable access to medicines: A prescription for Canada. Ottawa: Canadian Center for Policy Alternatives. **https://www.policyalternatives.ca/affordable-access medicines#sthash.ndUTv3FO.dpuf.** Accessed July 5, 2015

Easterbrook, W. T., & Aitken, H. G. J. (1956). *Canadian economic history.* Toronto: Macmillan.

Edwards, M. (2005). Civil society. In *The encyclopedia of informal education.* Retrieved from **http://www.infed.org/association/civil_society.htm**

Egale. (2006). *Equal marriage backgrounder.* Retrieved from **http://www.egale.ca**

Ehrenreich, B. (2001). *Nickel and dimed: On (not) getting by in America.* New York: Metropolitan Books.

Eichler, M. (1987). Social policy concerning women. In S. Yelaga (Ed.), *Canadian social policy* (Rev. ed., 139–156). Waterloo, ON: Wilfrid Laurier University Press.

Ellison, M. L., Rogers, E. S., Sciarappa, K., Cohen, M., and Forbess, R. (1995). Characteristics of mental health case management: Results of a national survey. *Journal of Mental Health Administration, 22,* 101–112.

Ellwood, W. (2006). *The no-nonsense guide to globalization.* Toronto: New Internationalist Publications.

Elson, P.R. (2011). *High ideals and noble intentions: Voluntary sector-government relations in Canada.* Toronto: University of Toronto Press.

Emery, G., & Emery, J. C. H. (1999). *A young man's benefit: The independent Order of the Odd Fellows and sickness insurance in the United States and Canada, 1860-1929.* Montreal and Kingston: McGill-Queen's University Press.

Emery, J. C. H., & Emery, G. (1999). *A young man's benefit: The Independent Order of Odd Fellows and sickness insurance in the United States and Canada, 1860–1929.* Montreal: McGill-Queen's University Press.

Employment and Social Development Canada (2006). *Disability in Canada: A 2006 profile. Retrieved March 19, 2016 from:* **http://www.esdc.gc.ca/eng/disability/arc/disability_2006.shtml**

Employment and Social Development Canada (2014). *Harnessing the power of social finance*. Ottawa, Government of Canada. Retrieved February 10, 2016 from: **http://www.esdc. gc.ca/eng/consultations/social_finance/ report//index.shtml**

Environment and Climate Change Canada (2015). *National greenhouse gas emissions*. Ottawa, ON: Government of Canada. Retrieved February 11, 2016 from: **https:// www.ec.gc.ca/indicateurs-indicators/default. asp?lang=en&n=FBF8455E-1**

Erickson, D. J. (2009). *The housing policy revolution: Networks and neighborhoods*. Washington, DC: The Urban Institute Press.

Esping-Anderson, G. (1990). *The three worlds of welfare capitalism*. Cambridge, UK: Polity Press.

Etzioni, A. (1968). *The active society*. New York: The Free Press.

Etzioni, A. (1975). *A comparative analysis of complex organizations* (2nd ed.). New York: Free Press.

Evans, B., & Wellstead, A. (2014). Tales of policy estrangement: Non-governmental policy work and capacity in three Canadian Provinces. *Canadian Journal of Nonprofit and Social Economy Research, 5*(2), 7–28.

Evans, P. (1995). Women and social welfare: Exploring the connections. In J. C. Turner & F. Turner (Eds.), *Canadian social welfare* (3rd ed., 150–164). Scarborough, ON: Allyn and Bacon Canada.

Evans, P. (1997). Divided citizenship? Gender, income security, and the welfare state. In P. Evans & G. Wekerle (Eds.), *Women and the Canadian welfare state: Challenges and change* (91–116). Toronto: University of Toronto Press.

Evans, P., Jacobs, L., Noel, A., & Reynolds, E. (1995). *Workfare: Does it work? Is it fair?* Montreal: Institute for Research on Public Policy.

Evers, A. (2009). Civicness and civility: Their meanings for social services. *Voluntas: International Journal of Voluntary and Nonprofit Organizations, 20*, 239–259.

Evers, A., Pilj, M., & Ungerson, C. (eds.). 1994. *Payments for Care*. Aldershot, UK: Avebury.

Fair taxes, not more taxes. (1995, February 13). *The Globe and Mail*, p. A12.

Federal/Provincial/Territorial Ministerial Council on Social Policy Renewal. (2003). *Three year review: Social union framework agreement*. Ottawa: Social Development Canada. Retrieved from **http://socialunion.gc.ca/ menu_e.html**

Federation of Canadian Municipalities. *The state of Canadian cities and communities 2012*. Ottawa: Federation of Canadian Municipalities.

Federico, R. (1983). *The social welfare institution* (4th ed.). Toronto: D.C. Heath.

Feehan, K., & Hannis, D. (Eds.). (1993). *From strength to strength. Social work education and Aboriginal people*. Edmonton: Grant MacEwan Community College.

Ferley, P., & Janzen, N. (2009). *Ontario budget 2009: Impact of the recession is evident but is it being sufficiently countered?* Royal Bank of Canada Economics Research.

Ferguson, B. (2007). The potential of private sector health care in Canada. Does it cause global warming? Canadian Health Care Consensus Group Background Paper Number 5. Retrieved from Halifax: Atlantic Institute for Market Studies. **http://www.aims.ca/site/ media/aims/CHCCGBP5E.pdf**. Accessed July 5, 2015.

Fernandez, L., & Smirl, E. (2013). Losing Ground How Canada's Employment Insurance system undermines inner-city and Aboriginal workers. Winnipeg: Canadian Center for Policy Alternatives. **https://www.policyalternatives.ca/ publications/reports/losing-ground#sthash. PPY8GoCR.dpuf**

Figuera-McDonough, J. (1993). Policy practice: The neglected side of social work interventions. *Social Work, 38*, 179–188.

Fingard, J. (1989). *The dark side of life in Victorian Halifax*. Porters Lake, NS: Pottersfield Press.

Finkel, A. (2006). *Social policy and practice in Canada: A history*. Waterloo, ON: Wilfrid Laurier University Press.

Finlayson, A. (1996). *Naming Rumpelstiltskin: Who will profit and who will lose in the workplace of the 21st century*. Toronto: Key Porter Books.

Flanagan, T. (2007). The six rules of success. In R. Griffiths (Ed.), *Great questions of Canada* (177–180). Toronto: Porter Publishing.

Flannery, T. (2006). *The weather makers: The history and future impact of climate change.* Berkeley, CA: Atlantic Monthly Press.

Florini, A. M. (2000). *Third force: The rise of transnational civil society.* Washington D.C.: Carnegie Endowment for International Peace.

Flynn, J. P. (1992). *Social agency policy* (2nd ed.). Chicago: Nelson-Hall.

Fook, J., & Gardner, F. (2007). *Practising critical reflection: A resource handbook.* Maidenhead, UK: Open University Press.

Forget, E. L. (2011). The town with no poverty. Using health administration data to revisit outcomes of a Canadian Guaranteed Annual Income field experiment. **http://public.econ.duke.edu/~erw/197/forget-cea%20%282%29.pdf**. Accessed July 5, 2015.

Forster, M., & d'Ercole, M. M. (2005). *Income distribution and poverty in OECD countries in the second half of the 1990s.* Paris: OECD Publications.

Foucault, M. (1972). *Power/knowledge: Selected interviews and other writings.* New York: Pantheon Books.

Frankl, V. (1969). *The will to meaning.* Scarborough: Plume.

Fraser Forum. (2009). *May 2009: The tax burden.* Retrieved from **http://www.fraserinstitute.org/research-news/research/display.aspx?id=13199**

Fraser, N. (1989). *Unruly practices: Power, discourse and gender in contemporary social theory.* Minneapolis: University of Minneapolis Press.

Fraser, N. (1995). From redistribution to recognition? Dilemmas of justice in a "post-socialist" age. *New Left Review, 212,* 68–93.

Fraser, N., & Honneth, A. (2003). *From redistribution to recognition? A political-philosophical exchange.* London: Verso.

Freeman, H., & Sherwood, C. (1970). *Social research and social policy.* Englewood Cliffs, NJ: Prentice-Hall.

Freiler, C. (2000). *What needs to change? Social inclusion as a focus of well-being for children, families, and communities.* Unpublished paper. Toronto: Laidlaw Foundation.

Freiler, C., & Cerny, J. (1998). *Benefiting Canada's children: Perspectives on gender and social responsibility.* Ottawa: Status of Women Canada.

Freire, P. (1968). *Pedagogy of the oppressed.* New York: Seabury Press.

Freire, P. (1985). *The politics of education: Culture, power and liberation.* South Hadley, MA: Bergin and Garvey.

Freire, P. (1994). *Pedagogy of hope.* New York: Continuum.

Frideres, J., & Gadacz, R. (2005). *Aboriginal peoples in Canada: Contemporary conflicts* (7th ed.). Toronto: Pearson Prentice Hall.

Fromm, E. (1955). *The sane society.* Greenwich, CT: Fawcett.

Fromm, E. (1967). The psychological aspects of the guaranteed income. In R. Theobald (Ed.), *The guaranteed income* (183–193). Garden City: Anchor.

Fukuyama, F. (1992). *The end of history and the last man.* New York: Avon Books.

Galabuzi, G. E. (2006). *Canada's economic apartheid: The social exclusion of racialized groups in the new century.* Toronto: Canadian Scholars Press.

Galarneau, D., & Fecteau, E. (2014). The ups and downs of minimum wage. Ottawa: Statistics Canada. **http://www.statcan.gc.ca/pub/75-006-x/2014001/article/14035-eng.pdf**. Accessed July 5, 2015.

Galbraith, J. K. (1983). *The anatomy of power.* Boston: Houghton Mifflin.

Galper, J. (1975). *The politics of social services.* Englewood Cliffs, NJ: Prentice-Hall.

Galster, G. (1996). *Reality and research: Social science and U.S. urban policy since 1960.* Washington: Urban Institute Press.

Garrett, L. (2000). *Betrayal of trust: The collapse of global public health.* New York: Hyperion.

Gates-Gasse, E. (2010). *"Two Step" immigration: Canada's new immigration system raises troubling issues.* Retrieved from **http://www.policyalternatives.ca/publications/monitor/two-step-immigration**

George, U. (2006). Immigration and refugee policy in Canada: Past, present, and future. In A. Westhughes (Ed.), *Canadian social policy: Issues and perspectives* (4th ed., 349–374). Waterloo, ON: Wilfrid Laurier University Press.

Germain, C., & Gitterman, A. (1980). *Social work practice, people, and environments: An ecological perspective*. New York: Columbia University Press.

Germain, C., & Gitterman, A. (1996). *The life model of social work practice: Advances in theory practice*. New York: Columbia University Press.

Giddens, A. (1998). *The third way: The renewal of social democracy*. Cambridge: Polity Press.

Gil, D. (1970). A systematic approach to social policy analysis. *Social Service Review, 44* (4), 411–426.

Gil, D. (1990). Implications of conservative tendencies for practice education in social welfare. *Journal of Sociology Social Welfare, XVII* (2) 5–27.

Gil, D. (1992). *Unravelling social policy* (5th ed.). Rochester, NY: Schenkman Books.

Gil, D. (1998). *Confronting injustice and oppression: Concepts and strategies for social workers*. New York: Columbia University Press.

Gilbert, N., & Specht, H. (1974). *Dimensions of social welfare policy*. Englewood Cliffs, NJ: Prentice-Hall.

Gilmour, J. (2010). Retrenchment not Reform: Using Law and Policy to Restrict the Entitlement of Women with Disabilities to Social. In S. Gavigan & D. Chunn (Eds.), *The legal tender of gender* (pp. 189–216). Onati International Series in Law and Society. Oxford: Hart Publishing.

Giugni, M. (1999). Introduction: How social movements matter. Past research, present problems, and future developments. In M. Giugni, D. McAdan, & C. Tilly (Eds.), *How social movements matter* (iii–xxxiii). Minneapolis: University of Minnesota Press.

Global Footprint Network. (2010). *Humanity's ecological footprint biocapacity through time*. Retrieved from http://www.footprint-network.org/en/index.php/GFN/page/ecological_footprint_atlas_2008/

Gonthier, N. (1978). Dans le Lyon médiéval: Vie et mort d'un pauvre. *Cahiers d'Histoire, 23*(3), 335–347.

Good-Gingrich, L. (2003). Theorizing social exclusion: Determinants, mechanisms, dimensions, forms, and acts of resistance. In W. Shera (Ed.), *Emerging perspectives on anti-oppressive practice* (pp. 3–23). Toronto: Canadian Scholars' Press Inc.

Good-Gingrich, L. (2008). Social exclusion and double jeopardy: The management of lone mothers in the market-state social field. *Social Policy and Administration, 42* (4), 379–395.

Gordon, L. (1990). The new feminist scholarship on the welfare state. In L. Gordon (Ed.), *Women, the state, and welfare* (pp. 78–89). Madison: University of Wisconsin Press.

Gormley, W. T. (2007). Public policy analysis: Ideas and impacts. *Annual Review of Political Science, 10*, 297–313.

Government of Alberta. (2002). *A framework for reform: Report of the Premier's Advisory Council on Health*. Edmonton: Author.

Government of Alberta (2015a). *Program purpose*. Retrieved April 10, 2016 from: http://www.humanservices.alberta.ca/pdd-online/program-purpose.aspx

Government of Alberta (2015b). *Developmental disability*. Retrieved April 10, 2016 from: http://www.humanservices.alberta.ca/pdd-online/eligibility-developmental-disability.aspx

Government of Canada. (2007). *Citizenship and Immigration Canada website*. Retrieved from (http://www.cic.gc.ca/english/information/applications/guides/E16000TOC.asp)

Government of Canada. (2008, October 8). *Newfoundland and Labrador offshore arrangements*. Retrieved from Department of Finance Canada website: http://www.fin.gc.ca/fedprov/na-eng.asp

Government of Canada (2015a, June 1). *Immigration & citizenship: Refugees and asylum*. http://www.cic.gc.ca/english/refugees/index.asp.

Government of Canada (2015b, June 1). *Justice Laws Website: Qualifying for Benefits*. http://laws-lois.justice.gc.ca/eng/acts/E-5.6/page-5.html.

Government of Canada: Labour Program (June 11, 2014). Union Coverage in Canada, 2013. Retrieved June 19, 2015 from: http://www.labour.gc.ca/eng/resources/info/publications/union_coverage/union_coverage.shtml#fnb1.

Government of Ontario. (2010, November 17). *Ontario guaranteed annual income system.* Retrieved from Ministry of Revenue website: **http://www.rev.gov.on.ca/en/credit/gains/**

Government of Ontario (2015). Ministry of Finance: Ontario Guaranteed Annual Income System. **http://www.fin.gov.on.ca/en/credit/gains/.**

Government of Quebec (2015). **http://www.budget.finances.gouv.qc.ca/Budget/outils/garde_en.asp.** Accessed July 5, 2015.

Government of Saskatchewan. (2010). *The seniors income plan.* Retrieved from **http://www.socialservices.gov.sk.ca/SIP-factsheet.pdf**

Government of Saskatchewan (2015, June 1). Personal and Family Support. *Financial help for seniors.* **http://www.saskatchewan.ca/live/personal-and-family-support/assistance-for-seniors/financial-help-for-seniors.**

Graeber, D. (2011). *Debt: The first 5000 years.* Brooklyn, N.Y.: Melville House.

Graeber, D. *(2013). The democracy project: A history, a crisis, a movement.* New York: Spiegel & Grau.

Graeber, D. *(2015). The utopia of rules: On technology, stupidity, and the secret joys of bureaucracy.* New York: Melville House.

Graham, J. R. (1992). The Haven, 1878–1930. A Toronto charity's transition from a religious to a professional ethos. *Histoire Sociale/Social History, 25*(50), 283–306.

Graham, J. R. (1995). Lessons for today: Canadian municipalities and unemployment relief during the 1930s Great Depression. *Canadian Review of Social Policy, 35,* 1–18.

Graham, J. R. (1996a). *A history of the University of Toronto School of Social Work, 1914–1970* (Doctoral dissertation, University of Toronto).

Graham, J. R. (1996b). A practical idealism: A theoretical values conception for northern social work practice. In R. Delaney, K. Brownlee, & J. R. Graham (Eds.), *Strategies in northern social work practice* (95–103). Thunder Bay, ON: Centre for Northern Studies.

Graham, J. R. (1996c). An analysis of Canadian social welfare historical writing. *Social Service Review, 70*(1), 140–158.

Graham, J. R. (2008). Canadian approaches to income security. In J. C. Turner & F. J. Turner (Eds.), *Canadian social welfare* (6th ed., 276–293). Toronto: Prentice Hall.

Graham, J. R., & Barter, K. (1999). Collaboration: A social work practice method. *Families in Society: The Journal of Contemporary Human Services, 80*(1), 6–13.

Graham, J. R., Jones, M. E., & Shier, M. (2010). Tipping Points: What participants found valuable in labour market training programs for vulnerable groups. *International Journal of Social Welfare, 19*(1), 63–72.

Graham, J. R., Shier, M. L., & Eisenstat, M. (2014). Misalignment between post-secondary education demand and labour market supply: Preliminary insight from young adults on the evolving school to work transition. *International Journal for Educational and Vocational Guidance, 14*(2), 199–219.

Graham, J. R., Shier, M. L., & Eisenstat (2015). Young adult social networks and labour market attachment: Interpersonal dynamics that shape perspectives on job attainment. *Journal of Social Policy, 44*(4), 769–786.

Graham, J. R., Trew, J. L., Schmidt, J. A, & Kline, T. B. (2007). Influences on the subjective well-being (SWB) of practicing social workers. *Canadian Social Work, 9*(1), 92–105.

Gramsci, A. (1971). *Prison notebooks.* New York: International Publishers.

Grant, G. (1965). *Lament for a nation: The defeat of Canadian nationalism.* Toronto: Anansi.

Grant, G. (1969). *Technology and empire: Perspectives on North America.* Toronto: Anansi.

Grant, T. (2010, October 21). "Excessive" personal debt a concern. *The Globe and Mail,* p. B4.

Greenaway, N. (2004, August 20). Fewer Canadians on welfare: Study. *The Globe and Mail,* p. A9.

Grob, G. (1992). How policy is made and how evaluators can affect it. *Evaluation-Practice, 13*(3), 175–183.

Guest, D. (1997). *The emergence of social security in Canada* (3rd ed.). Vancouver: University of British Columbia Press.

Guillemette, Y., & Robson, W. B. P. (2006). No elixir of youth: Immigration cannot keep Canada young. *CD Howe Institute Backgrounder, 96.* Toronto: CD Howe Institute.

Gulati, P., & Guest, G. (1990). The community-centered model: A garden-variety approach or a radical transformation of community practice? *Social Work, 35*(1), 63–68.

Gunton, T., & Calbick, K. S. (2010). *The Maple Leaf in the OECD: Canada's environmental performance.* Report for the David Suzuki Foundation Simon Fraser University.

Guo, C., & Saxton, G. (2014). Tweeting for social change: How social media are changing nonprofit advocacy. *Nonprofit and Voluntary Sector Quarterly, 43*(1), 57–79.

Gwyn, R. (1995). *Nationalism without walls: The unbearable lightness of being Canadian.* Toronto: McClelland and Stewart.

Haber, A., & Runyon, R. (1986). *Fundamentals of psychology* (4th ed.). New York: McGraw-Hill Company.

Hacker, J. S., & Pierson, P. (2010). *Winner-take-all politics: How Washington made the rich richer—and turned its back on the middle class.* New York: Simon & Schuster.

Hage, J., & Hollingsworth, J. R. (1977). The first steps toward the integration of social theory social policy. *Annals of the American Academy of Political and Social Science, 434,* 1–23.

Hall, M. H., de Wit, M. L., Lasby, D., McIver, D., Evers, T., Johnston, C., et al. (2004). *Cornerstones of community: Highlights of the national survey of non-profit and voluntary organizations.* Ottawa: Minister of Industry.

Handler, J. F. (1979). *Protecting the social service client: Legal and structural controls on official discretion.* New York: Academic Press.

Handler, J. F., & Hasenfeld, Y. (1991). *The moral construction of poverty: Welfare reform in America.* Newbury Park, CA: Sage.

Handy, F., & Cnaan, R. A. (2000). Religious nonprofits: Social service provision by congregations in Ontario. In K. G. Banting, K. G. (Ed.). *The nonprofit sector in Canada: Roles and relationships* (69–106). Kingston, Ontario: McGill-Queens University Press.

Hansen, P. (1999). The welfare state as political community. In D. Broad & W. Antony (Eds.), *Citizens or consumers? Social policy in a market society* (314–321). Halifax: Fernwood.

Hansmann, H. (1980). The role of non-profit enterprise. *Yale Law Journal, 90,* 835–90.

Hardesty, J., & Furdon, E. (2004). Policing civil society: NGO watch. *The Public Eye, 18,* 1.

Hargrove, B. (1999). Unions and social policy: Confronting a challenging future. In D. Broad & W. Antony (Eds.), *Citizens or consumers? Social policy in a market society* (73–82). Halifax: Fernwood.

Harischandra, K., & Palacios, M. (2007, March 15). Equalization reforms: Consensus disagreements. Retrieved from **http://www.fraserinstitute.org**

Harvey, D. (2005). *A brief history of neoliberalism.* Oxford, UK: Oxford University Press.

Harvey, D. (2010). *The enigma of capital and the crises of capitalism.* New York: Oxford University Press.

Haskins, R., & Gallagher, J. J. (1981). *Models for analysis of social policy.* Norwood, NJ: Ablex Publishing Corporation.

Healy, K. (2005). *Social work theories in context: Creating frameworks for practice.* New York: Palgrave Macmillan.

Hedges, C. (2011). *Death of the liberal class.* New York: Nation Books.

Hedges, C. & Sacho, J. (2013). *Days of destruction, days of revolt.* New York: Nation Books.

Hedges, C. (2015). *Wages of rebellion: The moral imperative of revolt.* New York: Nation Books.

Heisz, A. (2007). *Income inequality and redistribution in Canada: 1976 to 2004.* Catalogue No. 11F0019MIE – No. 298. Ottawa: Ministry of Industry, Government of Canada.

Herberg, D., & Herberg, E. (1995). Canada's ethno-racial diversity: Policies and programs for Canadian social welfare. In J. Turner & F. Turner (Eds.), *Social welfare in Canada* (3rd ed., 179–212). Scarborough, ON: Allyn and Bacon Canada.

Hess, M. (1993). *An overview of Canadian social policy.* Ottawa: Canadian Council on Social Development.

Hettne, B. (1995). Introduction: The international political economy of transformation. In Cox, R., Gill, S., Hettne, B., van der Pijo, K., Rosenau, J., & Sakamoto, Y. (Eds.).

International political economy: Understanding global disorder (1–30). Halifax, N.S.: Fernwood Publishing.

Hick, S. (2007). *Social welfare in Canada: Understanding income security* (2nd ed.). Toronto: Thompson Educational Publishing.

Hobsbawm, E. (1995). *Age of extremes: The short twentieth century 1914–1991.* London: Abacus.

Hodgson, G., & Browarski, S. (2008). *Harmonize consumption taxes to improve economic efficiency.* Ottawa: The Conference Board of Canada.

Hoffman, P. T. (2015). *Why did Europe conquer the world?* Priceton NJ: Princeton University Press.

Hogwood, B., & Gunn, L. (1984). *Policy analysis for the real world.* Toronto: Oxford University Press.

Holosko, M., Holosko, D. A., & Spencer, K. (2009). Social services in Sweden: An overview of policy issues, devolution, and collaboration. *Social Work in Public Health, 24*(3), 210–234.

Homan, M. (1994). *Promoting community change: Making it happen in the real world.* Pacific Grove, CA: Brooks/Cole Publishing Company.

Hoover, K. R. (1992). Conservatism. In M. Hawkesworth & M. Kogan (Eds.), *Encyclopedia of government and politics* (Vol. I, 139–154). New York: Routledge.

Horowitz, G. (1970). Red Tory. In W. Kilbourn (Ed.), *Canada: A guide to the peaceable kingdom* (254–260). Toronto: Macmillan of Canada.

Howell, J. & D. Mulligan, (Eds.). (2005). *Gender and civil society: Transcending boundaries.* London: Routledge.

Hufbauer, G. C., & Suominen, C. (2010). *Globalization at risk: Challenges to finance and trade.* New Haven, CT: Yale University Press.

Hum, D., & Simpson, W. (1993). Economic response to a Guaranteed Annual Income: Experience from Canada and the United States. *Journal of Labor Economics.* 11(1): 263–96.

Human Resources and Skills Development Canada. (2004). *Employment insurance and regular benefits.* Retrieved from http://www.hrsdc.ca

Human Resources and Skills Development Canada. (2007, January 29). *Looking ahead: 10-year outlook for the Canadian labour market (2006–2015).* Retrieved from http://www.hrsdc.gc.ca/eng/publications_resources/research/categories/labour_market_e/sp_615_10_06/future.shtml

Human Resources and Skills Development Canada. (2009). *Advancing the inclusion of people with disabilities.* Retrieved from http://www.hrsdc.gc.ca/publications

Human Resources and Skills Development Canada. (2010, January 15). *Union membership in Canada 2009.* Retrieved from http://www.hrsdc.gc.ca/eng/labour/labour_relations/info_analysis/union_membership/index2009.shtml

Human Resources and Social Development Canada. (2005). *Social security statistics Canada and provinces 1978–79 to 2002–03* Tables. Retrieved from http://www.hrsdc.gc.ca/en/cs/sp/sdc/socpol/tables/page02.shtml

Human Resources and Social Development Canada. (2006). *Low income in Canada: 2000–2002: Using the market basket measure.* Ottawa: Author. Retrieved from http://www.hrsdc.gc.ca/en/cs/sp/sdc/pkrf/publications/research/2002-000662/SP-628-05-06e.pdf

Human Resources and Social Development Canada. (2007). *Employment insurance program characteristics.* Ottawa: Author. Retrieved from http://srv200.services.gc.ca/iiws/eiregions/geocont.aspx

Ignatieff, M. (2000). *The rights revolution.* Toronto: Anansi.

Imagine Canada (2014a). Assets and giving trends of Canadian grant making foundations. Retrieved June 30, 2015 from: http://sectorsource.ca/sites/default/files/resources/files/trends-canadas-grantmaking-foundations-sept2014.pdf

Imagine Canada (2014b). Narrative core resource: The beginnings of a new discussion with Canadians about the charitable and nonprofit sector. Retrieved June 19, 2015 from: http://sectorsource.ca/sites/default/files/resources/files/narrative-core-resource-en.pdf.

Imagine Canada (2015a). *Key facts about Canada's charities.* Retrieved July 15th, 2015 from:

http://www.imaginecanada.ca/resources-and-tools/research-and-facts/key-facts-about-canada%E2%80%99s-charities

Imagine Canada (2015b). Sector Source: Resource for the charitable sector. Retrieved from: http://www.imaginecanada.ca/

Imagine Canada (2016). *Its time to stretch*. Retrieved February 10, 2016 from: http://www.imaginecanada.ca/our-programs/public-policy/its-time-stretch

Indian and Northern Affairs. (2007). *Annual reports, minister's message*. Retrieved from http://www.tbs-sct.gc.ca

Indian and Northern Affairs Canada. (n.d.). *Social development programs*. Retrieved from http://www.ainc-inac.gc.ca/ai/mr/is/sdpr-eng.asp

Indian and Northern Affairs Canada. (n.d.). *Registered Indian demography—Population, household and family projections, 2004–2029*. INAC Strategic Research and Analysis Directorate, CMHC Policy and Research Division.

Indigenous and Northern Affairs Canada (2013). Aboriginal Women in the Canadian Economy - The Links Between Education, Employment and Income. Retrieved March 19, 2016 from: https://www.aadnc-aandc.gc.ca/eng/1331046626766/1331046698685

Inglehart, R., & Welzel, C. (2009). How development leads to democracy: What we know about modernization. *Foreign Affairs, 88*(3), 33–48.

Inwood, G. J. (2000). Federalism, globalization, and the (anti-)social union. In M. Burke, C. Mooers, & J. Shields (Eds.), *Restructuring and resistance: Canadian public policy in an age of global capitalism* (124–144). Halifax: Fernwood.

Irving, A. (1987). Federal-provincial issues in social policy. In S. A. Yelaja (Ed.), *Canadian social policy* (326–349). Waterloo, ON: Wilfrid Laurier University Press.

Irving, A., Parsons, H., & Bellamy, D. (1995). *Neighbours: Three social settlements in downtown Toronto*. Toronto: Canadian Scholars Press.

Iverson, R. R., & Armstrong, A. L. (2006). *Jobs aren't enough: Toward new economic mobility for low-income families*. Philadelphia, PA: Temple University Press.

Jackson, A., & Robinson. D. (2000). *Falling behind: The state of working Canada, 2000*. Ottawa: Canadian Centre for Policy Alternatives.

Jackson, A., & Sanger, M. (1998). *Dismantling democracy: The multilateral agreement on investment (MAI) and its impact*. Ottawa: Canadian Centre for Policy Alternatives and James Lorimer & Co.

Jackson, A., & Sanger, M. (2003). *When worlds collide: Implications of international trade investment agreements for non-profit social services*. Ottawa: Canadian Centre for Policy Alternatives.

Jackson, A., & Schetagne, (2010). *Is EI working for Canada's unemployed?: Analyzing the great recession. Technical paper: Alternative federal budget 2010*. Ottawa: Canadian Center for Policy Alternatives.

Jansson, B. (1990). *Social welfare policy: From theory to practice*. Belmont, CA: Wadsworth Publishing Company.

Jansson, B. (2011). *Becoming an effective policy advocate*. Belmont, CA: Brooks/Cole.

Jaskyte, K., & Lee, M. (2006). Interorganizational relationships: A source of innovation in non-profit organizations? *Administration in Social Work, 30*(3), 43–54.

Jenson, J. (1998). *Mapping social cohesion: The state of Canadian research*. Canadian Policy Research Network Study No. F103. Ottawa: Renouf Publishing.

Jenson, J., & Saint-Martin, D. (2003). New routes to social cohesion? Citizenship and the social investment state. *Canadian Journal of Sociology/Cahiers Canadiens de Sociologie*, 77–99.

Jetté, C. et Y. Vaillancourt (2011). Social economy and home care services in Quebec: Co-production or co-construction. *Voluntas, 22*, 48–69.

Johnson, L. (1986). *Social policy: A generalist approach* (2nd ed.). Boston: Allyn and Bacon.

Johnston, P. (1983). *Native children and the child welfare system*. Toronto: James Lorimer and Company.

Jones, A., & Rutman, L. (1981). *In the children's aid: J. J. Kelso and child welfare in Ontario*. Toronto: University of Toronto Press.

Jones, L., Milligan, K., & Stabile, M. (2015). Child cash benefits and family expenditures:

Evidence from the National Child Benefit. Cambridge, Massachusetts: National Bureau of Economic Research. **http://www.nber.org/papers/w21101**. Accessed July 5, 2015.

Jongbloed, L. (2006). Disability income and employment policies in Canada: Historical development. In M. McColl & L. Jongbloed (Eds.), *Disability and social policy in Canada* (2nd ed., 243–253). Concord, ON: Captus Press.

Kadushin, A., & Martin, J. (1988). *Child welfare services* (4th ed.). New York: Macmillan.

Kahn, A. J., & Kamerman, S. B. (1998). *Big cities in the welfare transition.* New York: Columbia University School of Social Work.

Kallen, E. (1989). *Label me human: Minority rights of stigmatized Canadians.* Toronto: University of Toronto Press.

Kallen, E. (1995). *Ethnicity and human rights in Canada* (2nd ed.). Toronto: Oxford University Press.

Kallen, E. (2004). *Social inequality and social injustice: A human rights perspective.* New York: Palgrave Macmillan.

Kallen, E. (2010). *Ethnicity and human rights in Canada* (3rd ed.). Don Mills, ON: Oxford University Press.

Karabanow, J. (2003). Creating a culture of hope: Lessons from the street children agencies in Canada and Guatemala. *International Social Work, 46*(3), 369–386.

Kealey, G. S. (1980). *The working class response to industrial capitalism in Toronto, 1867–1892.* Toronto: University of Toronto Press.

Kealey, L. (Ed.). (1979). *A not unreasonable claim: Women and reform in Canada, 1880s–1920s.* Toronto: The Women's Press.

Kent, M. M., & Haub, C. (2005). Global demographic divide. *Population Bulletin, 60*(4), 1–25. Retrieved from **http://www.prb.org**

Kerans, P. (1994). Need and welfare: "Thin" and "thick" approaches. In A. Johnson, S. McBride, & P. Smith (Eds.), *Continuities and discontinuities: The political economy of social welfare and labour market policy in Canada* (44–59). Toronto: University of Toronto Press.

Kerlin, J. A (Ed.) (2009). *Social enterprise: A global comparison.* Hanover: University Press of New England.

Khattab, N., and Fenton, S. 2009. What makes young adults happy? Employment and non-work as determinants of life satisfaction. *Sociology, 43*(1), 11-26.

Kimberlin, S. E. (2010). Advocacy by nonprofits: Roles and practices of core advocacy organizations and direct service organizations. *Journal of Policy Practice, 9,* 164–182.

King, S. D. (2010). *Losing control: The emerging threats to Western prosperity.* New Haven, CT: Yale University Press.

Kingdom, J. (1995). *Agendas, alternatives, and public policies* (2nd ed.). New York: Harper/Collins.

Kingdon, G. G., & Knight, J. (2007). Subjective well being poverty vs. income poverty and capabilities poverty. In D. Hulme & J. Toye (Eds.), *Understanding poverty well-being: Bridging the disciplines* (115–140). London: Routledge.

Klasen, S. (1998). *Social exclusion and children in OECD countries.* Paris: OECD Publications.

Klein, N. (2007). *The shock doctrine: The rise of disaster capitalism.* Toronto: A. A. Knopf Canada.

Kleiss, K. (2010, December 9). Leaked document suggests health-care privatization for Alberta. *Edmonton Journal.* Retrieved from the Calgary Herald website: **http://www.calgaryherald.com/business/Leaked+document+suggests+health+care+privatization+Alberta/3907320/story.html**

Kline, M., Dolgon, C., & Dresser, L. (2000). The politics of knowledge in theory and practice: Collective research and political action in a grassroots community organization. *Journal of Community Practice, 8*(2), 23–38.

KPMG (2015). British Columbia 2022 labour market outlook. **http://www.workbc.ca/WorkBC/files/5f/5fc26f16-3c0f-4884-ab99-b475ca7448b7.pdf**. Accessed November 28, 2015.

Krieger, J. (Ed.). (1993). *The Oxford companion to politics of the world.* New York: Oxford University Press.

Kwok, S. M, & Tam, D. (2010). Rethinking the role of municipal governments on redistribution in Ontario, Canada. *Journal of Policy Practice.* 9(1):69–79.

Lacroix, M. & Shragge, E. (2004). Introduction: Globalization and community mental health. *Canadian Journal of Community Mental Health, 23*(2), 5–12.

Lafitte, F. (1962). *Social policy in a free society.* Birmingham, AL: Birmingham University Press.

Lamarche, L. 1999. New governing arrangements, women and social policy. In D. Broad & W. Antony (Eds.), *Citizens or consumers? Social policy in a market society* (5–72). Halifax: Fernwood.

Lapointe, M., Dunn, K., Tremblay-Cote, N., Bergeron, L. P., & Ignakzac, L. (2006). *Looking ahead: A ten year outlook for the Canadian labour market.* Ottawa: Human Resources Social Development Canada Publications Centre.

Lawand, N., & Kloosterman, R. (2006). The Canada Pension Plan Disability Program: Building a solid foundation. In M. McColl & L. Jongbloed (Eds.), *Disability and social policy in Canada* (2nd ed., 267–283). Concord, ON: Captus Press.

Laxer, J. (1997). *In search of a new left: Canadian politics after the neo-conservative assault.* Toronto: Penguin.

Lecomte, R. (1990). Connecting private troubles and public issues in social work education. In B. Wharf (Ed.), *Social work and social change in Canada* (31–51). Toronto: McClelland and Stewart Inc.

Le Grand, J. (2007). *The other invisible hand: Delivering public services through choice and competition.* Princeton University Press.

Leibfried, S., & Mau, S. (Eds.) (2008). *Welfare states: Construction, deconstruction, reconstruction.* London: Edward Elgar Publishing.

Leiby, J. (1978). *A history of social welfare and social work in the United States.* New York: Columbia University Press.

Leonard, P. (1975). Towards a paradigm for radical practice. In R. Bailey & M. Brake (Eds.), *Radical social work* (46–61). London: Edward Arnold, Ltd.

Leonard, P. (1984). *Personality and ideology: Towards a materialist understanding of the individual.* Atlantic Highlands, NJ: Humanities Press.

Leonard, P. (1997). *Postmodern welfare: Reconstructing an emancipatory project.* London: Sage Publications.

Lerner, M. (1997). *The politics of meaning: Restoring hope and possibility in an age of cynicism.* Don Mills, ON: Addison-Wesley.

Lessard, H. (1997). Creative stories: Social rights and Canada's Constitution. In P. Evans & C. Wekerle (Eds.), *Women and the Canadian welfare state: Challenges and change* (pp. 71–90). Toronto: University of Toronto Press.

Lewin, A. C., & Hasenfeld, Y. (1995). AFDC marital dissolution: Does welfare policy reduce the gains from marriage? *American Sociological Association Papers.*

Lewis, D., & Kanji, N. (2009). *Non-governmental organizations development.* London: Routledge.

L'Heureux-Dubé, C. (2000). A conversation about equality. *Denver Journal of International Law and Policy, 29*(1), 65.

Lightman, E. (2003). *Social policy in Canada.* Don Mills, ON: Oxford University Press.

Lipsky, M. (1980). *Street-level bureaucracy: Dilemmas of the individual in public services.* New York: Russell Sage Foundation.

Little, B. (2001, May 21). Remarkable progress cutting federal debt. *The Globe and Mail*, p. B7.

Little, M. M. (1999). The limits of Canadian democracy: The citizenship rights of poor women. *Canadian Review of Social Policy, 43*, 59–76.

Little, M. (2005). *If I had a hammer: Retraining that really works.* Vancouver: UBC Press.

Liverant, B. (2009). The incorporation of philanthropy: Negotiating tensions between capitalism and altruism in twentieth century Canada. *Journal of the Canadian Historical Society. 20*(1), 191-220.

LivingwageCanada (2015). http://www.livingwagecanada.ca/files/3913/8382/4524/Living_Wage_Full_Document_Nov.pdf. Accessed July 5, 2015.

Lonergan, A., & Richards, C. (Eds.). (1988). *Thomas Berry and the new cosmology.* Mystic, CT: Twenty-Third Publications.

Lovelock, J. (2006). *The revenge of Gaia: Earth's climate crisis and the fate of humanity.* New York: Basic Books.

Lower, A. (1958). *Canadians in the making: A social history of Canada.* Toronto: Longmans, Green, and Company.

Lubove, R. (1965). *The professional altruist: The emergence of social work as a career, 1880–1930.* Cambridge: Harvard University Press.

Lukes, S. (2005). *Power: A radical view* (2nd ed.). New York: Palgrave-Macmillan.

Luttwak, E. (1999). *Turbo-capitalism: Winners and losers in the global economy.* New York: Harper Collins.

Macarov, D. (1995a). *The design of social welfare.* New York: Holt, Rinehart and Winston.

Macarov, D. (1995b). *Social welfare: Structure and practice.* Thousand Oaks, CA: Sage.

MacDonald, D. (2014). *Outrageous fortune: Documenting Canada's wealth gap.* Ottawa, ON: Author. Retrieved May 4, 2016 from: https://www.policyalternatives.ca/sites/default/files/uploads/publications/National%20Office/2014/04/Outrageous_Fortune.pdf

Macdonald, D. (2015). *The wealth advantage: The growing wealth gap between Canada's affluent and the middle class.* Ottawa: Caledon Institute for Social Policy.

Macdonald, D., & Friendly, M. (2014). *The parent trap: Child care in Canada's biggest cities.* Ottawa: Canadian Center for Policy Alternatives.

Mackey, W. F. (2003). Forecasting the fate of languages. In J. Maurais & M. A. Morris (Eds.), *Languages in a globalising world* (72). Cambridge, UK: Cambridge University Press.

Mackinnon, D. (2011). *Dollars and Sense: A case for modernizing Canada's transfer agreements.* Toronto: Ontario Chamber of Commerce. http://www.occ.ca/portfolio/dollars-sense-a-case-for-modernizing-canadas-transfer-agreements/. Accessed July 5, 2015.

MacKinnon, J. (2013). *Health care reform from the cradle of medicate.* Ottawa: MacDonald Laurier Institute.

MacLeod, J. (1987). *Ain't no makin' it: Leveled aspirations in a low-income neighborhood,* Boulder: Westview Press.

Makarenko, J. (2007, April 1). 2002 Mazankowski Report on Health Care in Alberta. Retrieved from Maple Leaf Web website: http://www.mapleleafweb.com/features/2002-mazankowski-report-health-care-alberta

Makarenko, J. (2008, April 24). *Equalization Program in Canada: Overview and Contemporary Issues.* Retrieved from Maple Leaf Web website: http://www.mapleleafweb.com/features/equalization-program-canada-overview--contemporary-issues

Maloney, W. A., & van Deth, J. W. (Eds.) (2008). *Civil society and governance in Europe: From national to international linkages.* London: Edward Elgar Publishing.

Mannheim, K. (1936). *Ideology and utopia.* New York: Harcourt, Brace & World.

Marchak, M. P. (1988). *Ideological perspectives on Canada* (3rd ed.). Toronto: McGraw-Hill Ryerson Ltd.

Marfleet, P. (1998). *Against the globalist paradigm.* International conference on globalization: Political, social, and economic perspectives, held at Eastern Mediterranean University (TRNC), November 19–21, 1998.

Marshall, T. H. (1949). Citizenship and social class. Reprinted in D. Held et al., *States societies.* 1983. London: Open University.

Marshall, T. H. (1965). *Social policy.* London: Hutchinson.

Martineau, P. (2005). *Federal personal income tax: Slicing the pie.* Catalogue No. 11-621-MIE. Ottawa: Minister of Industry.

Marumba, S. K. I. (1998). Cross-cultural dimensions of human rights in the twenty-first century. In A. Anghie & G. Sturgess (Eds.), *Legal visions of the 21st century: Essays in honour of Judge Christopher Weeramantry* (201–240). The Hague: Kluwer Law International.

Maslow, A. H. (1954). *Motivation and personality.* New York: Harper.

Mason, D., Talbott, S., & Leavitt, J. (1993). *Policy politics for nurses* (2nd ed.). Toronto: W. B. Saunders Co.

Matsuba, M., Elder, G., Petrucci, F., and Marleau, T. (2008). Employment training for at-risk youth: A program evaluation focusing on changes in psychological well-being. *Child and Youth Care Forum, 37*(1), 15–26.

Marx, K., & Engels, F. (1947). The German ideology, parts 1 and 3, (C. J. Arthur, Trans). New York: International Publishers. (Original work published 1846)

Marx, K., & Engels, F. (1998). *The communist manifesto*. New York: Verso. (Original work published 1848)

Maurutto, P. (2009). Charity public welfare in history: A look at Ontario, 1830–1950. *The Philanthropist*, 19(3), 159—167.

Mawhiney, A. (1995). The First Nations in Canada. In J. Turner & F. Turner (Eds.), *Canadian social welfare* (3rd ed., 213–230). Scarborough, ON: Allyn and Bacon Canada.

Mayer, M. (2003). The onward sweep of social capital: Causes and consequences for understanding cities, communities and urban movements. *International Journal of Urban and Regional Research*, 27(1), 110–132.

McGilly, F. (1998). *An introduction to Canada's public social services*. Don Mills, ON: Oxford University Press.

McInnis-Dittrich, K. (1994). *Integrating social welfare policy and social work practice*. Pacific Grove, CA: Brooks/Cole Publishing Company.

McKenzie, B. (1997). Connecting policy and practice in First Nations child and family services: A Manitoba case study. In J. Pulkingham & G. Ternowetsky (Eds.), *Child and family policies: Struggles, strategies and options* (pp. 100–114). Halifax: Fernwood.

McKinsey Global Institute (February, 2015). Debt and (not much) deleveraging. Retrieved August 4, 2015 from: **http://www.mckinsey.com/insights/economic_studies/debt_and_not_much_deleveraging**

McMenemy, J. (1995). *The language of Canadian politics: A guide to important terms and concepts*. Waterloo, ON: Wilfrid Laurier University Press.

McNally, D. (2006). *Another world is possible: Globalization and anti-capitalism* (Rev. ed.). Winnipeg: Arbeiter Ring Publishing.

McPherson, D., & Rabb, D. (1994). *Indian from the inside: A study in ethno-metaphysics*. Thunder Bay, ON: Centre for Northern Studies.

McQuaig, L. (1993). *The wealthy banker's wife*. Toronto: Penguin Books.

McQuaig, L. (1995). *Shooting the hippo: Death by deficit and other Canadian myths*. Toronto: Viking.

McQuaig, L. (1998). *The cult of impotence: Selling the myth of powerlessness in the global economy*. Toronto: Viking.

Mellinger, M. S. (2014). Beyond legislative advocacy: Exploring agency, legal, and community advocacy. *Journal of Policy Practice*, 13(1), 45–58.

Mendelson, M. (1993). *Social policy in real time*. Ottawa: Caledon Institute of Social Policy.

Meyer, S. M. (2006). *The end of the wild*. Cambridge, MA: MIT Press.

Miller, C., and Porter, K. E. (2007). Barriers to employment among out-of-school youth. *Children and Youth Services Review*, 29(5), 572–587.

Miller, P. and Rose, N. (2008). *Governing the present: Administering social, economic and personal life*. Cambridge, UK: Polity.

Mills, C. W. (1959). *The sociological imagination*. Oxford: Oxford University Press.

Minoto, H., & Cross, P. (1991). The growth of the federal debt. *Canadian Economic Observer*, June, 3.1–3.17.

Mishra, R. (1981). *Society and social policy: Theories and practice of welfare* (2nd ed.). London: Macmillan.

Mishra, R. (1995). The political bases of Canadian social welfare. In J. Turner & F. Turner (Eds.), *Canadian social welfare* (3rd ed., 59–74). Scarborough, ON: Allyn and Bacon Canada.

Mitchell, A., & Shillington, R. (2005). Poverty, inequality and social inclusion. In T. Richmond & A. Saloojee (Eds.), *Social inclusion: Canadian perspectives* (33–57). Halifax: Fernwood.

Mittlestaedt, M. (2001, October 3). Commission throws water on Ottawa's lakes cleanup. *The Globe and Mail*, p. A13.

Mittlestaedt, M. (2006, March 6). Drug residue tainting water, report warns. *The Globe and Mail*, p. A5.

Moreau, M. (1989). *Empowerment through a structural approach to social work*. Ottawa: Carleton University School of Social Work.

Morgan, S. P., & Taylor, M. G. (2006). Low fertility at the turn of the twenty-first century. *Annual Review of Sociology, 32*, 375–390.

Morissette, R., Picot, G., & Lu, Y. (2013). *The evolution of Canadian wages over the last three decades*. Ottawa, ON: Minister of Industry.

Morissette, R., Schellenberg, G., & Johnson, A. (2005). Diverging trends in unionization. *Statistics Canada's Perspectives on Labour and Income, 17*(2), n.p. Retrieved from Statistics Canada website: http://www.statcan.ca/bsolc/english/bsolc?catno=75-001-X20050027827

Morissette, R., & Zhang, X. (2006). Revisiting wealth inequality. *Perspectives on Labour and Income, 7*, 12, December. Statistics Canada—Catalogue No. 75-001-XIE.

Morris, J. (2004). Independent living and community care: A disempowering framework. *Disability and Society, 19*(5), 427–442.

Morris, M. (2007). *Fact Sheet No 9: Women's experiences of social programs for people of low income*. Canadian Research Institute for the Advancement of Women.

Morrison, I. (1997). Rights and the right: Ending social citizenship in Tory Ontario. In D. Ralph, A. Regimbald, & N. St-Amand (Eds.), *Open for business, closed to people* (pp. 68–79). Halifax: Fernwood.

Morton, W. L. (1969). *The kingdom of Canada*. Toronto: McClelland and Stewart.

Mosley, J. E., & Ros, A. (2011). Nonprofit agencies in public child welfare: Their role and involvement in policy advocacy. *Journal of Public Child Welfare, 5*, 297–317.

Mulé, N. (2005). Equality's limitations, liberation's challenges: Considerations for queer movement strategizing. *Canadian Online Journal of Queer Studies in Education, 2*(1). Retrieved from http://jqstudies.library.utoronto.ca/index.php/jqstudies/article/view/3290/1419

Mulé, N. (2008). Demarcating gender and sexual diversity on the structural landscape of social work. *Critical Social Work, 9*(1). Retrieved from http://www.criticalsocialwork

Mulé, N. (2010). Same-sex marriage and Canadian relationship recognition—One step forward, two steps back: A critical liberationist perspective. *Journal of Gay & Lesbian Social Services, 22*, 74–90.

Mulé, N., Ross, L., Deeprose, B., Jackson, B., Daley, A., Travers, A., & Moore, D. (2009). Promoting LGBT health and wellbeing through inclusive policy development. *International Journal for Equity in Health, 8*,(18). Retrieved from http://www.equityhealthj.com/content/8/1/18

Mullaly, R. (1993). *Structural social work*. Toronto: McClelland and Stewart.

Mullaly, R. (2002). *Challenging oppression: A critical social work approach*. Don Mills, ON: Oxford University Press.

Mullaly, R. (2007). *The new structural social work*. Don Mills, ON: Oxford University Press.

Mulroy, E. A. (2004). Theoretical perspectives on the social environment to guide management and community practice: An organization-in-environment approach. *Administration in Social Work, 28*(1), 77–96.

Mulvale, J. P. (2001). *Reimagining social welfare: Beyond the Keynesian welfare state*. Toronto: Garamond.

Muszynski, L. (1987). *Is it fair? What tax reform will do to you*. Ottawa: Canadian Centre for Policy Alternatives.

Muukkonen, M. (2009). Framing the field: Civil society and related concepts. *Nonprofit and Voluntary Sector Quarterly, 38*(4), 684–700.

Myers, R., & Worm, B. (2003). Rapid worldwide depletion of predatory fish communities. *Nature, 423*, May 15, 280–283.

Naccarato, T., Brophy, M., and Courtney, M. E. (2010). Employment outcomes of foster youth: The results from the Midwest evaluation of the adult functioning of foster youth. *Children and Youth Services Review, 32*(4), 551–559.

National Association of Women and the Law. (2007). *Pay equity at the heart of equality*. Retrieved from http://www.nawl.ca/ns/en/is-wmnwrk-pe.html

National Council of Welfare. (1993). *Incentives and disincentives to work*. Ottawa: Ministry of Supply and Services Canada.

National Council of Welfare. (1995). *The 1995 budget and block funding*. Ottawa: National Council of Welfare.

National Council of Welfare. (2001). *Child poverty profile 1998*. Ottawa: National Council of Welfare.

National Council of Welfare. (2006a). *Poverty Profile, 2002 and 2003*. Catalogue No. SDZ5-1/2003E. Ottawa: Minister of Public Works and Government Services Canada.

National Council of Welfare. (2006b). *Welfare Incomes 2005*. Ottawa: Minister of Public Works Government Services Canada. Retrieved from http://www.ncwcnbes.net/en/research/welfare-bienetre.html

National Council of Welfare. (2007). *Solving poverty: Four cornerstones of a workable national strategy for Canada*. Ottawa: National Council of Welfare.

Naylor, C. D. (1986). *Private practice, public payment*. Montreal/Kingston: McGill-Queen's University Press.

Naylor, D., & Martin, R. (2005, February 10). A better way to share. *The Globe and Mail*, p. A23.

Nelles, H. V. (1974). *The politics of development: Forests, mines, and hydro-electric power in Ontario, 1849–1941*. Toronto: Macmillan.

Nelson, R., & Krashinsky, M. (1973). Two major issues of public policy: Public policy and the organization of supply. In R. Nelson & D. Young (Eds.). *Public subsidy for day care of young children* (47–69). Lexington, Mass.: D.C. Health.

Netting, F. E., O'Connor, M. K., Fauri, D. P. (2007). Planning transformative programs: Challenges for advocates in translating change processes into effectiveness measures. *Administration in Social Work, 31*(4), 59–81.

Newman, P. (1975). *The Canadian establishment*. Toronto: McClelland & Stewart.

Neysmith, S., Bezanson, K., & O'Connell, A. (2005). *Telling tales: Living the effects of public policy*. Halifax: Fernwood.

Neysmith, S., Reitsma-Street, M., Baker-Collins, S., Porter, E., & Tam, S. (2010). Provisioning responsibilities: How relationships shape the work that women do. *Canadian Review of Sociology, 47*(2), 149–170.

Nichols, A. (2006). Introduction. In A. Nichols (Ed.). *Social entrepreneurship: New models of sustainable social change* (1–35). Oxford: Oxford University Press.

Nikiforuk, A. (2007, June 11). Is Canada the latest emerging petro-tyranny? *The Globe and Mail*, p. A13.

O'Brien, C. (1998). *Sexual regulation and Ontario social policies in the 1990s* (Doctoral dissertation. Faculty of Social Work, University of Toronto.)

O'Brien, C., & Weir, L. (1995). Lesbians and gay men inside and outside families. In N. Mell & A. Duffy (Eds.), *Canadian families: Diversity, conflict and change* (111–139). Toronto: Harcourt Brace and Company.

OECD Stat (2015). Income distribution and poverty: By country. Retrieved August 3, 2015, from http://stats.oecd.org/Index.aspx#.

O'Neill, B. (2006). Toward inclusion of gay and lesbian people: Social policy changes in relation to sexual orientation. In A. Westhughes (Ed.), *Canadian social policy: Issues perspectives* (4th ed. pp. 331–348). Waterloo, ON: Wilfrid Laurier University Press.

Ontario Blue Cross. (2014). Annual Report, 2014. http://www.useblue.com/corporatif/a-propos/annual-reports.en.html. Accessed July 5, 2015.

Ontario Chamber of Commerce. (2015). Getting it right: The business perspective on the undersaving challenge in Ontario. Toronto: Ontario Chamber of Commerce. http://www.occ.ca/Submissions/GettingItRight_Submission_Feb18.pdf. Accessed July 6, 2015.

Ontario Ministry of Finance. (2015). Bill Strengthening Retirement Security for Millions of Workers Passes in Ontario Legislature. Accessed July 6, 2015. http://news.ontario.ca/mof/en/2015/04/bill-strengthening-retirement-security-for-millions-of-workers-passes-in-ontario-legislature.html

Obituaries, Bessie Touzel. (1997, April 26). *The Globe and Mail*.

Offe, C. (1984). *Contradictions of the welfare state*. Cambridge, MA: MIT Press.

Office of the Parliamentary Budget Office (2016). *The fiscal and distributional impact of changes to the federal personal income tax regime*. Ottawa, ON: Author. Retrieved May 4, 2016 from: http://www.pbo-dpb.gc.ca/en/blog/news/PIT

Olden, J., Hogan, Z., & Zen, M. (2007). Small fish, big fish, red fish, blue fish: Size-biased extinction risk of the world's freshwater and marine fishes. *Global Ecology & Biogeography, 16*(6), 694–701.

Oxfam. (2016). *An economy for the 1%.* http://policy-practice.oxfam.org.uk/publications/an-economy-for-the-1-how-privilege-and-power-in-the-economy-drive-extreme-inequ-592643. Accessed February 15, 2016.

Pal, L. A. (1987). *Public policy analysis: An introduction.* Toronto, ON; Methuen.

Palmer, B. D. (1979). *A culture in conflict: Skilled workers and industrial capitalism in Hamilton, Ontario, 1860–1914.* Montreal/Kingston: McGill-Queen's University Press.

Pascal, G. (1993). Citizenship—A feminist analysis. In G. Drover & P. Kerans (Eds.), *Welfare theory* (pp. 113–126). Aldershot, UK: Edward Elgar Publishing.

Pasma, C. (2010). *Ontario: Bearing the brunt.* Retrieved from Citizens for Public Justice website: http://www.cpj.ca/en/blog/chandra/ontario-bearing-brunt

Pateman, C. (1992). Equality, difference, subordination: The politics of motherhood and women's citizenship. In S. James & G. Bock (Eds.), *Beyond equality and difference: Citizenship, feminist politics, and female subjectivity* (pp. 17–31). New York: Routledge.

Patterson, E. (1987). Native peoples and social policy. In S. Yelaja (Ed.), *Canadian social policy* (Rev. ed., 175–194). Waterloo, ON: Wilfrid Laurier University Press.

Pay Equity Task Force. (2004). *Pay equity: A new approach to a fundamental right.* Ottawa: Minister of Justice and Attorney General of Canada, and the Minister of Labour.

Payne, J. (1998). *Overcoming welfare: Expecting more from the poor and from ourselves.* New York: Basic Books.

Payne, M. (2005). *Modern social work theory* (3rd ed.). Chicago: Lyceum Books.

Payne, R. K. (2010). *How much is enough? Buddhism, consumerism, and the human environment.* New York: Wisdom Publications.

Payne, S. (1992). Fascism. In M. Hawkesworth & M. Kogan (Eds.), *Encyclopedia of government politics* (Vol. I, 167–178). New York: Routledge.

Pearson, G. (1975). Making social workers: Bad promises and good omens. In R. Bailey & M. Brake (Eds.), *Radical social work* (13–45). London: Edward Arnold, Ltd.

Pearson, J. (2010, November 26). Empire lines. *Times literary supplement.* 5620, 25.

Penner, N. (1992). *From protest to power: Social democracy in Canada 1900–present.* Toronto: Lorimer.

Perri 6. (1993). Innovation by nonprofit organizations: Policy and research issues. *Nonprofit Management and Leadership, 3*(4), 397–414.

Philanthropic Foundation Canada (2014). *Assets and giving trends of Canada's grantmaking foundations: Key facts and figures.* Retrieved July 15th, 2015 from: http://pfc.ca/wp-content/uploads/key-facts-trends-canadas-grantmaking-foundations-sept2014-en.pdf

Philips, S. D. (2003). Voluntary sector-government relationships in transition: Learning from international experience for the Canadian context. In K.L Brock & Banting, K.G. (Eds.). *The nonprofit sector in interesting times: Case studies in a changing sector* (17–70). Kingston, Ontario: McGill-Queens University Press.

Phillips, S. D. (2012). Dual restructuring: Civil society and the welfare state in Canada, 1985-2005. *British Journal of Canadian Studies, 25*(2), 161–180.

Philips, S. D., & Graham, K. A. (2000). Hand-in-hand: When accountability meets collaboration in the voluntary sector. In K. G. Banting, K. G. (Ed.). *The nonprofit sector in Canada: Roles and relationships* (pp. 149–190). Kingston, Ontario: McGill-Queens University Press.

Piastro, D. B. (1999). Coping with the transitions in our lives: From "afflicted" identity to personal empowerment and pride. *Reflections: Narratives of Professional Helping, 5*(4), 42–46.

Picot, G., Hou, F., & Coulombe, S. (2007). *Chronic low income and low-income dynamics among recent immigrants.* Catalogue no. 11F0019MIE — No. 294. Ottawa: Statistics Canada.

Picot, G., Hou, F., & Coulombe, S. (2008). Poverty dynamics among recent immigrants to Canada. *International Migration Review, 42*(2), 393–424.

Pierce, D. (1984). *Policy for the social work practitioner*. New York: Longman.

Pierson, C. (1991). *Beyond the welfare state: The new political economy of social welfare*. University Park: Pennsylvania State University Press.

Pol, E., & Ville, S. (2009). Social innovation: buzz word or enduring term? *The Journal of Socio-Economics*, 38(6), 878–85.

Polese, M. (1998). Regional economics. *The 1998 Canadian and world encyclopedia* [CD ROM]. Toronto: McClelland and Stewart.

Polanyi, K. (1944). *The great transformation*. Boston, Mass.: Beacon Press.

Popple, P., & Leighninger, L. (2001). *The policy-based profession: An introduction to social welfare policy for social workers* (2nd ed.). Boston: Allyn and Bacon.

Powell, F. P. (2007). *The politics of civil society: Neoliberalism or social left?* Bristol: The Policy Press.

Pratt, C. W., Gill, K. J., Barrett, N. M., and Roberts, M. M. (1999). *Psychiatric rehabilitation*. San Diego, CA: Academic Press.

Prentice, A., Bourne, P., Cuthbert-Brandt, G., Light, B., Mitchinson, W., & Black, N. (1988). *Canadian women: A history*. Toronto: Harcourt, Brace, Jovanovich.

Prince, M. J. (2014). Locating a window of opportunity in the social economy: Canadians with disabilities and labour market challenges. *Canadian Journal of Nonprofit and Social Economy Research*, 5(1), 6–20.

Prichard, C. (2011). Charitable tax credits – who gives? ActiveHistory.Ca. http://activehistory.ca/2011/11/charitable-tax-credits-%E2%80%93-who-gives/. Accessed July 5, 2015.

Putnam, R. D. (2000). *Bowling alone: The collapse revival of American community*. New York: Simon Schuster.

Quarter, J. (1992). *Canada's social economy: Co-operatives, non-profits, and other community enterprises*. Toronto, ON: James Lorimer & Company Publishers.

Quarter, J., Mook, L., & Armstrong, A. (2009). *Understanding the Social Economy: A Canadian Perspective*. University of Toronto Press.

Quarter, J., Ryan, S., & Chan, A. (2015a). Social Purpose Enterprises: A Conceptual Framework. In J. Quarter, S. Ryan & A. Chan (Eds.). *Social Purpose Enterprises: Case Studies for Social Change* (1–16). Toronto: University of Toronto Press.

Quarter, J., Ryan, S., & Chan, A. (2015b). Social Purpose Enterprises: A Modified Social Welfare Framework. In J. Quarter, S. Ryan & A. Chan (Eds.). *Social Purpose Enterprises: Case Studies for Social Change* (214–222). Toronto: University of Toronto Press.

Raphael, D. (Ed.). (2004). *Social determinants of health: Canadian perspectives*. Toronto: Canadian Scholars' Press.

Rapp, C. A. (1998). The active ingredients of effective case management: A research synthesis. *Community Mental Health Journal*, 34, 363–380.

RBC, (May 1, 2015). Economics Research: Canadian federal and provincial fiscal tables. Retrieved June 19, 2015 from: http://www.rbc.com/economics/economic-reports/pdf/provincial-forecasts/prov_fiscal.pdf.

Reamer, F. (1993). *The philosophical foundations of social work*. New York: Columbia University Press.

Rebick, J. (2000). *Imagine democracy*. Toronto: Stoddart.

Reeskens, T., and van Oorschot, W. (2008). Those who are in the gutter look at the stars? Explaining perceptions of labour market opportunities among European young adults. *Work, Employment, & Society*, 26(3), 379–385.

Rein, M. (1974). Social policy analysis and the interpretation of beliefs. *The American Institute for Planners Journal*, September, 31(3), 297–310.

Rein, M. (1983). *From policy to practice*. Armonk, NY: M. E. Sharpe Inc.

Report for the Interprovincial Conference of Ministers Responsible for Social Services. (1980). *The income security system in Canada*. Ottawa: Canadian Intergovernmental Conference Secretariat.

Ricciutelli, L., Larkin, J., & O'Neill, E. (1998). *Confronting the cuts: A sourcebook for women in Ontario*. Toronto: Inanna Publications and Education Inc.

Rice, J. J., & Prince, M. J. (2000). *Changing politics of Canadian social policy.* Toronto: University of Toronto Press.

Rice, J., & Prince, M. (2013). Changing politics of Canadian social policy. 2nd edition. Toronto: University of Toronto Press.

Richmond, M. (1930). *The long view.* New York: Russell Sage Foundation.

Richmond, O., & Carey, H. (Eds.). (2005). *Subcontracting peace: The challenges of the NGO peacebuilding.* Aldershot, UK: Ashgate Publishing.

Richmond, T., & Saloojee, A. (Eds.). (2005). *Social inclusion: Canadian perspectives.* Halifax: Fernwood.

Rioux, M., & Samson, R. (2006). Trends impacting disability: National and international perspectives. In M. McColl & L. Jongbloed (Eds.), *Disability and social policy in Canada* (2nd ed., 112–142). Concord, ON: Captus Press.

Rodrik, D. (2011). *The globalization paradox: Democracy and the future of the world economy.* New York: Norton.

Roeher Institute. (1996). *Disability, community and society.* Toronto: Author.

Rooke, P. T., & Schnell, R. L. (1987). *No bleeding heart: Charlotte Whitton—A feminist on the right.* Vancouver: UBC Press.

Rose, H., Daiches, A., & Potier, J. (2012). Meaning of social inclusion to young people not in employment, education or training. *Journal of Community and Applied Social Psychology, 22*(3), 256–268.

Ross, D. P., Scott, K. J., & Smith, P. J. (2000). The Canadian fact book on poverty. The Canadian Council on Social Development.

Royal Canadian Legion Ontario Provincial Command. (2009). *WVA rates.* Retrieved from http://www.on.legion.ca/veterans/wvarates.asp

Royal Commission on Aboriginal Peoples. (1996). Highlights of the Report of the Royal Commission on Aboriginal Peoples http://www.aadnc-aandc.gc.ca/eng/1100100014597/1100100014637?utm_source=sgmm_e.html&utm_medium=url Accessed June 27, 2015.

Rutman, I. D. (1993). And now, the envelope please... Psychosocial Rehabilitation Journal, 16(3), 1–3.

Ryan, B., Brotman, S., & Rowe, B. (2000). *Access to care: Exploring the health and well-being of gay, lesbian, bisexual and two-spirit people in Canada.* Montreal: McGill Centre for Applied Family Studies.

Ryser, L., & Halseth, G. (2014). In the edge in rural Canada: The changing capacity and role of the voluntary sector. *Canadian Journal of Nonprofit and Social Economy Research, 5*(1), 41–56.

Sachs, W., Loske, R., & Linz, M. (1998). *Greening the North: A post-industrial blueprint for ecology and equity.* New York: Zed.

Sadava, M. (2010). More choice, less education. *Alberta Views, 13*(6), 28–30.

Sale, K. (2006). *After Eden: The evolution of human domination.* Durham, NC: Duke University Press.

Salamon, L. M. (1993). The marketization of welfare: Changing nonprofit and for-profit roles in the American welfare state. *The Social Service Review,* 16–39.

Salamon, L. (2002). *The state of nonprofit America.* Washington D.C.: Brookings Institution.

Sarlo, C. (November, 2013). Poverty: Where do we draw the line? Fraser Institute. Accessed August 14, 2015 from: http://ssrn.com/abstract=2354442. Sarlo Basic Needs updated 2009: Montreal Diet Dispensary updated 2010.

Saul, J. R. (1995). *The unconscious civilization.* Concord, ON: House of Anansi Press.

Savoie, D. (2010). *Power: Where is it?* Montreal: McGill-Queen's University Press.

Sayeed, A. (2002). *The 1997 Canada Pension Plan changes: Implications for women and men.* Ottawa: Status of Women Canada.

Schaedle, R., and Epstein, I. (2000). Specifying intensive case management: A multiple stakeholder approach. *Mental Health Services Research, 2,* 95–105.

Schansberg, D. E. (1996). *Poor policy: How government harms the poor.* Boulder, CO: Westview Press.

Schmid, H., Bar, M., & Nirel, R. (2008). Advocacy activities in nonprofit human service organizations: Implications for policy. Nonprofit and Voluntary Sector Quarterly, 37(4), 581–602.

Schneider, J. (2006). *Social capital and welfare reform*. New York, NY: Columbia University Press.

Schneider, J. (2013). Connections and disconnections between civic engagement and social capital in community-based nonprofits. *Nonprofit and Voluntary Sector Quarterly, 36*(4), 572–597.

Schorr, A. (1985). Professional practice as policy. *Social Service Review, 59*(June), 185–86.

Schragge, E. (Ed.). (1997). *Workfare: Ideology for a new under-class*. Toronto: Garamond Press.

Schragge, E., & Deniger, M. (1997). Workfare in Quebec. In E. Schragge (Ed.), *Workfare: Ideology for a new under-class* (59–84). Toronto: Garamond Press.

Schumacher, E. F. (1973). *Small is beautiful: Economics as if people mattered*. New York: Harper and Row.

Schwartz, W. (1974). Private troubles and public issues: One social work job or two? In P. E. Weinberger (Ed.), *Perspectives on social welfare* (2nd ed., pp. 22–43). New York: Macmillan.

Scott, K. (1998). *Women and the CHST: A profile of women receiving social assistance in 1994*. Ottawa: Status of Women Canada.

Scott, W. R., Deschenes, S., Hopkins, K., Newman, A., and McLaughlin, M. (2006). Advocacy organizations and the field of youth services: Ongoing efforts to restructure a field. *Nonprofit and Voluntary Sector Quarterly, 35*(3), 453–476.

Sen, A. (1992). *Inequality reexamined*. New York: Harvard University Press.

Senate Committee on Poverty. (1971). *Poverty in Canada*. Ottawa: Canadian Government Publishing Centre.

Service Canada. (2007). *Employment insurance regular benefits*. Ottawa: Author. Retrieved from http://www1.servicecanada.gc.ca/en/ei/types/regular.shtml#Qualifying

Service Canada (2015a, June 1). *Canada Pensions Plan payment amounts*. http://www.servicecanada.gc.ca/eng/services/pensions/cpp/payments/index.shtml

Service Canada (2015b, June 1). *Employment Insurance Regular Benefits*. http://www.servicecanada.gc.ca/eng/ei/types/regular.shtml#long.

Service Canada (2015c, June 1). *Old Age Security pension*. http://www.servicecanada.gc.ca/eng/services/pensions/oas/pension/index.shtml

Shah, P. J., & Smith, P. K. (1995). Do welfare benefits cause the welfare caseload? *Public Choice, 85*(1–2), 91–105.

Sharpe, A., & Arsenault, J. (2009). *Living Standards Domain Report. Canadian Index of Wellbeing*. CSLS Research Report (Vol. 4).

Shewell, H. (2007). *Gathering strength or just more welfare? The socio-economic situation of First Nations before and since the Royal Commission on Aboriginal Peoples*. Unpublished paper.

Shewell, H., & Spagnut, A. (1995). The First Nations of Canada: Social welfare and the quest for self-government. In J. Dixon & R. Scheurell (Eds.), *Social welfare with indigenous peoples* (1–15). London: Routledge.

Shier, M. L., & Graham, J. R. (2013). Identifying social service needs of Muslims living in a post 9/11 era: The role of community-based organizations. *Advances in Social Work, 14*(2), 379–394.

Shier, M. L., & Graham, J. R. (2014). Social policy in Canada. In C. Franklin (Ed.). *Encyclopedia of social work online* (1–13, online). New York, NY: Oxford University Press.

Shier, M. L., Graham, J. R., & Eisenstat, M. (2015). Psychosocial characteristics and successful labour market attachment among young adults: The internalization of individual inadequacy as explanations for failure within the labour market. *Canadian Journal of Family and Youth, 7*(1), 27–54.

Shier, M. L., Graham, J. R., Fukuda, E., & Turner, A. (2015). Risk and protective factors of precarious housing among Aboriginal people living in urban centres in Alberta, Canada. *Canadian Review of Social Policy, 72/73*, 1–29

Shier, M. L., Graham, J. R., Fukuda, E., & Turner, A. (2016). Predictors of living in precarious housing among immigrants accessing housing support services. *Journal of International Migration and Integration,17*(1), 173-192.

Shier, M. L., Graham, J. R., Goitam, M., & Eisenstat, M. (2014). Young adult experiences with employment: How perceived and actual discrimination hinder labour market attachment. *Canadian Review of Social Policy, 70*(1), 48–63.

Shier, M. L., Graham, J. R., & Jones, M.E. (2009). Barriers to employment as experienced by disabled people: A qualitative analysis in Calgary and Regina, Canada. *Disability and Society, 24*(1), 63–75.

Shier, M. L., Graham, J. R. & Jones, M.E. (2010). Social capital for vulnerable groups: Insight from employed people experiencing homelessness. *Journal of Social Distress and the Homeless, 19*(3/4), 132–155.

Shier, M. L., & Handy, F. (2014). Research trends in nonprofit graduate studies: A growing interdisciplinary field. *Nonprofit and Voluntary Sector Quarterly, 43*(5), 812–831.

Shier, M. L., & Handy, F. (2015a). From advocacy to social innovation: A typology of social change efforts by nonprofits. *Voluntas: International Journal of Voluntary and Nonprofit Organizations, 26*(6), 2581–2603.

Shier M. L., & Handy F. (2015b). Social change efforts of direct service nonprofits: The role of funding and collaborative networks in shaping social innovations. *Human Service Organizations: Management, Leadership & Governance, 39*(1), 6–24.

Shier, M. L., & Handy, F. (2015c). Cross-sector partnerships: Factors supporting social innovation by nonprofits. *Human Service Organizations: Management, Leadership & Governance,* online first. DOI: 10.1080/23303131.2015.1117556

Shier, M. L., Jones, M. E., & Graham, J.R. (2012). Employment difficulties experienced by employed homeless people: Labour market factors that contribute to and maintain homelessness. *Journal of Poverty, 16*(1), 27–47.

Shier, M. L., McDougle, L. M., & Handy, F. (2014). Nonprofits and the promotion of civic engagement: A conceptual framework for understanding the 'civic footprint' of nonprofits within local communities. *The Canadian Journal of Nonprofit and Social Economy Research, 5*(1), 57–75.

Shier, M. L., Sinclair, C., and Gault, L. (2011). Challenging 'ableism' and teaching about disability in a social work classroom: A training module for generalist social workers working with people disabled by the social environment. *Critical Social Work, 12*(1), 47–64.

Shirky, C. (2008). *Here comes everybody: The power of organizing without organizations.* London: Penguin Press.

Shragge, E., & Toye, M. (Eds.) (2006). *Community economic development: Building for social change.* Sydney, NS: Cape Breton University Press.

Silver, H. (1994). Social exclusion and social solidarity: Three paradigms. *International Labour Review, 1333*(5–6), 531–578.

Simon, H. (1957). *Administrative behavior: A study of decision-making processes in administrative organization* (3rd ed.). New York: Free Press.

Sirico, R. A. (1997, July 27). Work is moral and so is workfare. *New York Times,* p. E15.

Smiley, D. (1976). *Canada in question: Federalism in the seventies* (2nd ed.). Toronto: McGraw-Hill Ryerson.

Smith, D. M. (2005). *On the margins of inclusion: Changing labour markets and social exclusion in London.* Bristol, UK: The Policy Press.

Smith, P. K. (1993). Welfare as a cause of poverty: A time series analysis. *Public Choice, 75*(2), 157–170.

Smith, S. R. (2011). The nonprofit sector. In M. Edwards (Ed.) *The Oxford handbook of civil society* (pp. online resource). New York, NY: Oxford University Press.

Social Enterprise Canada. (2014). What is a social enterprise? Retrieved from **http://www .socialenterprisecanada.ca/en/learn/nav/ whatisasocialenterprise.html**

Soros, G. (1997). *The crisis of global capitalism: Open society endangered.* New York: Public Affairs.

Sowell, R. L. & Grier, J. (1995). Integrated case management: The AIDS Atlanta model. *Journal of Case Management, 4*(1), 15–21.

Spear, R. (2006). Social Entrepreneurship: A Different Model? *International Journal of Social 6 Economics 33*(5/6), 399–410.

Speech from the Throne. (2010, February 4). *Third Session of the Twenty-seventh Legislature.* Edmonton: Government of Alberta.

Spergel, I. A., & Grossman, S. F. (1997). The Little Village Project: A community approach to the gang problem. *Social Work, 42*(5), 456–470.

Spicker, P. (2006). *Policy analysis for practice: Applying social policy*. Bristol, UK: The Policy Press.

Splane, R. B. (1965). *Social welfare in Ontario 1791–1893: A study of public welfare administration*. Toronto: University of Toronto Press.

Stainton, T. (1994). *Autonomy and social policy*. Aldershot, UK: Avebury.

Stainton, T. (2005). Empowerment and the architecture of rights based social policy. *Journal of Intellectual Disabilities*, 9, 289–298.

Standing Senate Committee on Social Affairs, Science and Technology, (1999). *Final report on social cohesion*. Retrieved from http://www.parl.gc.ca/36/1/parlbus/commbus/senate/com-e/soci-e/rep-e/repfinaljun99part1-e.htm

Stapleton, J. (2015). Guaranteed annual income contains three words: Let's talk about the annual part. http://vibrantcanada.ca/blogs/john-stapleton/guaranteed-annual-income-contains-three-words-let%E2%80%99s-talk-about-%E2%80%98annual%E2%80%99-part. Accessed July 6, 2015.

Statistics Canada. (2003, December 16). *Total Income Groups in Constant. (2000) Dollars*. File no. 97F0020XCB2001073. Ottawa: Author. Retrieved from http://www12.statcan.ca/english/census01/proucts/standard/themes/RetrieveProductTable.cfm?Temporal=2001&PID=60960&APATH=3&GID=355313&METH=1&PTYPE=55496&THEME=54&FOCUS=0&AID=0&PLACENAME=0&PROVINCE=0&SEARCH=0&GC=99&GK=NA&VID=0&VNAMEE=&VNAMEF=&FL=0&RL=0&FREE=0

Statistics Canada. (2006, March 7). *Women in Canada*. *The Daily*. Retrieved from http://www.statcan.ca/Daily/English/060307/d060307a.htm

Statistics Canada. (2006a). *Low wage low income*. Catalogue no. 75F0002MIE. Ottawa: Author.

Statistics Canada. (2006b). *Population by selected ethnic origins, by province and territory*. Ottawa: Author. Retrieved from http://www40.statcan.ca/l01/cst01/demo26a-eng.htm.

Statistics Canada. (2007). *Income in Canada*. Catalogue no. 75-202-X. Retrieved from http://dsp-psd.tpsgc.gc.ca/Collection/Statcan/75-202-XIE/75-202-XIE2004000.pdf

Statistics Canada. (2009). *Population urban and rural, by province and territory*. Retrieved from http://www40.statcan.ca/l01/cst01/demo62a-eng.htm

Statistics Canada. (2010a). *Charitable Donors*. Retrieved from http://www40.statcan.gc.ca/l01/cst01/famil90-eng.htm

Statistics Canada. (2010b). *Government finance: Revenue, expenditure and surplus*. Retrieved from *The Daily*: http://www.statcan.gc.ca/daily-quotidien/090616/dq090616a-eng.htm

Statistics Canada. (2010c). *Latest release from the Labour Force Survey*. Retrieved from *The Daily*: http://www.statcan.gc.ca/subjects-sujets/labour-travail/lfs-epa/lfs-epa-eng.htm

Statistics Canada. (2010d). *Satellite account of non-profit institutions volunteering*. Retrieved from *The Daily*: http://www.statcan.gc.ca/daily-quotidien/101217/dq101217b-eng.htm

Statistics Canada (2011). Population, urban and rural, by province and territory. Retrieved: http://www.statcan.gc.ca/tables-tableaux/sum-som/l01/cst01/demo62a-eng.htm

Statistics Canada (2013a). *Aboriginal peoples in Canada: First Nations people, Metis, and Inuit*. Ottawa, ON: Minister of Industry.

Statistics Canada (2013b). Canadian internet use survey, 2012. Retrieved December 3, 2015 from: http://www.statcan.gc.ca/daily-quotidien/131126/dq131126d-eng.htm.

Statistics Canada (2013c). *Immigration and ethnocultural diversity in Canada*. Ottawa, ON: Minister of Industry.

Statistics Canada (2013d). Individual internet use and e-commerce, 2012. Retrieved December 3, 2015 from: http://www.statcan.gc.ca/daily-quotidien/131028/dq131028a-eng.htm

Statistics Canada (2013e). Occupation - National Occupational Classification (NOC) 2011 (691), Class of Worker (5), Age Groups (13B) and Sex (3) for the Employed Labour Force Aged 15 Years and Over, in Private Households of Canada, Provinces, Territories, Census Metropolitan Areas and Census Agglomerations, 2011 National Household

Survey. Retrieved: http://www12.statcan.gc.ca/nhs-enm/2011/dp-pd/dt-td/Rp-eng.cfm?TABID=2&LANG=E&APATH=3&DETAIL=0&DIM=0&FL=A&FREE=0&GC=0&GK=0&GRP=0&PID=105897&PRID=0&PTYPE=105277&S=0&SHOWALL=1&SUB=0&Temporal=2013&THEME=96&VID=0&VNAMEE=&VNAMEF=

Statistics Canada (2014). Employer pension plans (trusteed pension funds), second quarter 2014. http://www.statcan.gc.ca/daily-quotidien/141210/dq141210e-eng.htm

Statistics Canada. (2015a). Canada goes urban. http://www.statcan.gc.ca/pub/11-630-x/11-630-x2015004-eng.htm. Accessed July 5, 2015.

Statistics Canada (2015b). General social survey: Giving, volunteering and participating, 2013. Retrieved June 19, 2015 from: http://www.statcan.gc.ca/daily-quotidien/150130/dq150130b-eng.pdf

Statistics Canada, (2015c) http://www.statcan.gc.ca/tables-tableaux/sum-som/l01/cst01/health26-eng.htm. Accessed November 28, 2015.

Statistics Canada (2015d). *Paid work*. Retrieved March 19, 2016 from: http://www.statcan.gc.ca/pub/89-503-x/2010001/article/11387-eng.htm

Statistics Canada, (2015e). Pensions: the ups and downs of coverage. http://www.statcan.gc.ca/pub/11-630-x/11-630-x2015003-eng.htm

Statistics Canada (2015f). *Persons with disabilities and employment. Retrieved March, 19, 2015 from:* http://www.statcan.gc.ca/pub/75-006-x/2014001/article/14115-eng.htm

Statistics Canada (2015g). Population by broad age groups and sex, 2011 counts for both sexes, for Canada, provinces and territories. Retrieved: http://www12.statcan.gc.ca/census-recensement/2011/dp-pd/hlt-fst/as-sa/Pages/highlight.cfm?TabID=1&Lang=E&Asc=1&PRCode=01&OrderBy=999&Sex=1&View=1&tableID=21&queryID=1

Statistics Canada (2015h). *Study: The local unemployment rate and retirement, 1991-2007.* http://www.statcan.gc.ca/daily-quotidien/150422/dq150422a-eng.htm

Statistics Canada (2015i). *Summary of Charitable donors.* Table 111-0001. http://www5.statcan.gc.ca/cansim/a26?lang=eng&retrLang=eng&id=1110001&paSer=&pattern=&stByVal=1&p1=1&p2=31&tabMode=dataTable&csid=

Statistics Canada (2015j). Survey of household spending, 2013. Retrieved August 16, 2015 from: http://www.statcan.gc.ca/daily-quotidien/150122/dq150122b-eng.htm

Statistics Canada (2015k). Table 202-0501 http://www5.statcan.gc.ca/cansim. Retrieved September 17, 2015

Statistics Canada (2015l). Table 204-0001. High income trends of tax filers in Canada. Retrieved August 16, 2015 from: http://www5.statcan.gc.ca/cansim/

Statistics Canada (2015m). *Table 378-0123 - National Balance Sheet Accounts, financial indicators, households and non-profit institutions serving households, quarterly (percent),* CANSIM (database). Retrieved August 3, 2015 from: http://www5.statcan.gc.ca/cansim/

Statistics Canada (2015n). *Visible Minority Women.* Retrieved March 19, 2016 from: http://www.statcan.gc.ca/pub/89-503-x/2010001/article/11527-eng.htm

Statistics Canada (2015o). Unemployment rates of population aged 15 and over, by educational attainment, Canada, 1990 to 2014. Retrieved August 14, 2015 from: http://www.statcan.gc.ca/pub/81-582-x/2015002/tbl/tble3.1-eng.htm

Statistics Canada (2015p). Volunteering and charitable giving in Canada. Retrieved from: http://www.statcan.gc.ca/pub/89-652-x/89-652-x2015001-eng.htm#wb-tphp

Statistics Canada, Health Statistics Division. (2006). *Deaths, 2004.* Ottawa: Minister of Industry. Retrieved from http://www.statcan.ca/english/freepub/84F0211XIE/84F0211XIE2004000.htm

Statistics Canada, Income Statistics Division. (2006). *Low income cut-offs for 2005 and low income measures for 2004.* Catalogue no. 75F0003MIE. Ottawa: Statistics Canada.

Statistics Canada, Income Statistics Division. (2007). *Low-income cutoffs for 2006 and low income measures for 2005.* Income Research Paper Series, Catalogue no. 75F0002MIE. Ottawa: Minister of Industry.

Statistics Canada, Income Statistics Division. (2008). *Income security stability during retirement in Canada.* Income Research Paper Series, Catalogue no. 306 - 11F0019M. Retrieved from http://www.statcan.gc.ca/pub/11f0019m/11f0019m2008306-eng.pdf

Statistics Canada, Income Statistics Division. (2010). *2008 Survey of Household Spending.* Retrieved from *The Daily:* http://www.statcan.gc.ca/daily-quotidien/091218/dq091218b-eng.htm

Statistics Canada and the Council of Ministers of Education Canada. (2006). *Education indicators in Canada: Report of the pan-Canadian education indicators program 2005.* Ottawa: Author.

Statistics Canada Pensions and Wealth Surveys Section. (2005). *The wealth of Canadians: An overview of the results of the survey of financial wealth.* Catalogue No. 13—F0026MIE. Ottawa: Author.

Statistics Canada. Unionization rates falling. (2015). http://www.statcan.gc.ca/pub/11-630-x/11-630-x2015005-eng.htm. Accessed July 5, 2015.

Status of Women Canada. (2007). *Status report.* Retrieved from http://www.swc-cfc.gc.ca/index_e.html

Stedman Jones, G. (2004). *An end to poverty? A historical debate.* New York: Columbia University Press.

Stelter, G. A., & Artibese, A. F. J. (Eds.). (1977). The *Canadian city: Essays in urban history.* Toronto: McClelland and Stewart.

Stittle, M. (2010, March 4). *Budget fights deficit with freeze on future spending.* Retrieved from CTV News website: http://toronto.ctv.ca

Stroman, D. (1989). *Mental retardation in social context.* Lanham, MD: University Press of America, Inc.

Strong-Boag, V. (1976). *The parliament of women: The National Council of Women of Canada, 1893–1929.* Ottawa: National Museum of Man.

Struthers, J. (1983). *No fault of their own: Unemployment and the Canadian welfare state, 1914–1941.* Toronto: University of Toronto Press.

Struthers, J. (1994). *Limits to affluence: Welfare in Ontario, 1920–1970.* Toronto: University of Toronto Press.

Sun Life Assurance Annual Report, 2014. http://cdn.sunlife.com/static/global/files/Annual%20reports/2014/Annual_Report_2014_SLF_en.pdf. Accessed July 5, 2015.

Susskind, R., & Susskind, D. (2015). *The future of the professions: How technology will transform the work of human experts.* New York: Oxford University Press.

Swift, K. (1995). *Manufacturing bad mothers: A critical perspective on child neglect.* Toronto: University of Toronto Press.

Swift, K. (2001). The case for opposition: Challenging contemporary child welfare policy directions. *Canadian Review of Social Policy, 47,* 59–76.

Swift, K., & Callahan, M. (2009). *At risk: Social justice in child welfare and other human services.* Toronto: University of Toronto Press.

Taylor, S. (2011). Educational and vocational exploration in vulnerable youth. *Child & Youth Services, 32*(4), 355–379.

Teeple, G. (1995). *Globalization and the decline of social reform.* Toronto: Garamond Press.

Teilhard de Chardin, P. (1955). *The phenomenon of man.* New York: Harper & Brothers.

Tertzakian, P. (2006). *A thousand barrels a second: The coming oil break point and the challenges facing an energy dependent world.* Toronto: McGraw-Hill.

Thomlison, R., & Bradshaw, C. (1999). Canadian political processes and social work practice. In F. Turner (Ed.), *Social work practice: A Canadian perspective* (pp. 264–275). Scarborough, ON: Prentice Hall Canada.

Thompson, N. (1993). *Anti-discriminatory practice.* London: Macmillan.

Thyer, B. (2010). Social justice: A conservative perspective. *Journal of Comparative Social Welfare, 26*(2/3), 261–274.

Tilly, C. (1999). From interactions to outcomes in social movements. In M. Giugni, D. McAdan, & C. Tilly (Eds.), *How social movements matter* (253–270). Minneapolis: University of Minnesota Press.

Tillotson, S. (2008). *Modern charitable fundraising and the making of the welfare state, 1920-1960.* Toronto: University of Toronto Press.

Titmuss, R. M. (1958). *Essays on the welfare state.* London: George Allen & Unwin.

Titmuss, R. (1970). *The gift relationship: From human blood to social policy.* London: George Allen & Unwin.

Titmuss, R. (1974). *Social policy: An introduction.* London: George Allen & Unwin Ltd.

Tobin, S. S. (2003). The historical context of "humanistic" culture change in long-term care. *Journal of Social Work in Long-Term Care, 2*(1/2), 53–64.

Torjman, S. (1996a). *Workfare: A poor law.* Ottawa: Caledon Institute of Social Policy.

Torjman, S. (1996b). *History/hysteria.* Ottawa: Caledon Institute of Social Policy.

Torjman, S. (1997). *Welfare warfare.* Ottawa: Caledon Institute of Social Policy.

Torjman, S. (1998a). *Community-based poverty reduction.* Ottawa: Caledon Institute of Social Policy.

Torjman, S. (1998b). *Welfare reform through tailor-made training.* Ottawa: Caledon Institute of Social Policy.

Torjman, S. (1999). *Dumb and dumber governments.* Ottawa: Caledon Institute of Social Policy.

Torjman, S. (2005). *Disability tax: The budget's quiet little secret.* Ottawa: Caledon Institute of Social Policy.

Torjman, S. (2007). *Repairing Canada's social safety net.* Ottawa: Caledon Institute of Social Policy.

Torjman, S. (2014). *Paying for Canada.* Ottawa: Caledon Institute of Social Policy.

Torjman, S. (2015a). Renewing Canada's social architecture. Disability supports: Missing on the policy radar. Ottawa: Caledon Institute.

Torjman, S. (2015b). *The Canadian social report so far.* Ottawa: Caledon Institute for Social Policy.

Torjman, S., & Battle, K. (1995a). *Can we have national standards?* Ottawa: Caledon Institute of Social Policy.

Torjman, S., & Battle, K. (1995b). *The dangers of block funding.* Ottawa: Caledon Institute of Social Policy.

Torrie, R. (2000, May 19). A clear and present danger: We can cut greenhouse gasses by half and it won't hurt a bit. *The Globe and Mail,* p. A13.

Townson, M. (2006). *Growing older, working longer: The new face of retirement.* Ottawa: Canadian Centre for Policy Alternatives.

Trofimenkoff, S. M. (1983). *The dream of nation.* Toronto: McClelland and Stewart.

Trudeau, P. E. (1990). The values of a just society. In T. Axworthy & P. E. Trudeau (Eds.), *Towards a just society,* (357–385). Markham, ON: Viking.

Turk, J., & Wilson, G. (1996). *Unfair shares: Corporations and taxation in Canada.* Don Mills, ON: Ontario Coalition for Social Justice and Ontario Federation of Labour.

Turner, F. (1995). Social welfare in Canada. In J. Turner & F. Turner (Eds.), *Canadian social welfare* (3rd ed., 1–11). Scarborough, ON: Allyn and Bacon Canada.

United Nations, Department of Economic Social Affairs, Population Division. (2002). *World population ageing: 1950–2050.* New York: United Nations Publications.

United Nations Development Programme. (2006). *Human development report 2006. Beyond scarcity: Power, poverty, and the global water crisis.* New York: Author.

United Nations Development Programme. (2010). *Human Development Index and its components.* Retrieved from http://hdr.undp.org/en/media/HDR_2010_EN_Table1_reprint.pdf

United Nations Development Report, 2014. http://hdr.undp.org/en/2014-report/download. Downloaded November 29, 2015.

United Nations Statistics Division. (2010). *Millennium development goals indicators: CO2 emissions, 2007.* Retrieved from http://unstats.un.org/unsd/mdg/SeriesDetail.aspx?srid=749

Ursel, J. (1992). *Private lives and public policy: One hundred years of state intervention in the family.* Toronto: Women's Press.

U.S. Energy Information Administration. (2010). *Canada energy data.* Retrieved from http://www.eia.doe.gov/

Usher, D. (2003). *Political economy.* Oxford: Blackwell.

Vaillancourt, Y., & Tremblay, L. (Eds.) (2002). *Social economy, health, and welfare in four Canadian provinces*. Halifax: Fernwood Publishing.

Valentine, F. (2001). *Enabling citizenship: Full inclusion of children with disabilities and their parents*. Discussion paper No. F/13. Ottawa: Canadian Policy Research Network.

Valletta, R. (2006). The ins and outs of poverty in advanced economies: Government policy poverty dynamics in Canada, Germany, Great Britain, and the United States. *Review of Income & Wealth, 52*(2), 261–284.

van der Platt, M., & Barrett, G. (2006). Building community capacity in governance and decision-making. *Community Development Journal, 41*(1), 25–36.

Van Wormer, K. (1997). *Social welfare: A world view*. New York: Nelson Hall.

Veterans Affairs Canada. (2009, February 18). *Veterans affairs disability pension program*. Retrieved from **http://www.veterans.gc.ca/general/sub.cfm?source=Services**

Veterans Affairs Canada (2015, June 1). *Disability Pension: Rates*. **http://www.veterans.gc.ca/eng/services/after-injury/disability-benefits/disability-pension**.

Vosko, L. F. (2006). Precarious employment: Towards an improved understanding of labour market insecurity. In L. F. Vosko (Ed.), *Precarious employment: Understanding labour market insecurity in Canada* (3–39). Montreal/Kingston: McGill-Queen's University Press.

Waldi, P. (2006, November 16). Canadian firms and charity: Are they scrooges? *The Globe and Mail*, p. B2.

Wallis, M. A., & Kwok, S. (Eds.) (2008). *Daily struggles: The deepening racialization and feminization of poverty in Canada*. Toronto, ON: Canadian Scholars Press.

Weaver, R. D., Habibov, N., & Fan, L. (2010). Devolution and the poverty reduction effectiveness of Canada's provincial social welfare programs: Results from a time-series investigation of a Canadian national survey, *Journal of Policy Practice*, 9(1):80–95.

Webb, D. (1981). Radical and traditional social work. *British Journal of Social Work, 11*, 143–158.

Weber, M. (1958). *The Protestant ethic and the spirit of capitalism*, (T. Parsons, Trans.). New York: Charles Scribner's Sons. (Original work published 1930)

Wein, F. (1991). *The role of social policy in economic restructuring*. Halifax: The Institute for Research on Public Policy.

Weisbrod, B. A. (1975). Toward a theory of the voluntary non-profit sector in a three-sector economy. In E.S. Phelps (Ed.). *Altrusim, morality, and economic theory* (197–223). New York, NY: Russell Sage Foundations.

Wei-Skillern, J., Austin, J. E., Leonard, H., & Stevenson, H. (2007). *Entrepreneurship in the social sector*. Thousand Oaks, CA: Sage Publications.

Westhues, A. (Ed.). (2003). *Canadian social policy: Issues and perspectives*. Waterloo, ON: Wilfrid Laurier University Press.

Westhues, A. (Ed) (2006). *Canadian social policy* (4th ed.). Waterloo, ON: Wilfrid Laurier University Press.

Wharf, B. (1986). Social welfare and the political system. In J. Turner & F. Turner (Eds.), *Canadian social welfare* (2nd ed., 103–120). Don Mills, ON: Collier Macmillan.

Wharf, B. (Ed.). (1990). *Social work and social change in Canada*. Toronto: McClelland and Stewart.

Wharf, B. (1992). *Community and social policy in Canada*. Toronto: McClelland and Stewart.

Wharf, B., & Cossom, J. (1987). Citizen participation and social welfare policy. In S. Yelaja (Ed.), *Canadian social policy*. (Rev. ed., 266–287). Waterloo, ON: Wilfrid Laurier University Press.

Wharf, B., & McKenzie, B. (1998). *Connecting policy to practice in the human services*. Toronto: Oxford University Press.

Wharf, B., & McKenzie B. (2004). *Connecting policy to practice in the human services* (2nd ed.). Don Mills, ON: Oxford University Press.

Wharf, B. & McKenzie B. (2010). *Connecting policy to practice in the human services*. (3rd ed.). Toronto: Oxford University Press.

Wilensky, H. L., & Lebeaux, C. N. (1958). *Industrial society and social welfare*. New York: Russell Sage Foundation.

Wilkinson, R., & Pickett, K. (2009). *The spirit level: Why more equal societies almost always do better.* London, UK: Allen Lane.

Wilkinson, R., & Pickett, K. (2010). *The spirit level: Why equality is better for everyone.* London, UK: Penguin Books.

Willetts, D. (2010). *The pinch: How the baby boomers took their children's future—and why they should give it back.* London: Atlantic Books.

Williams, F. (1989). *Social policy: A critical introduction.* Cambridge: Polity Press.

Williams, G. H. (1983). The Movement for Independent Living: An evaluation and critique. *Social Science and Medicine, 17*(15), 1003–1010.

Wills, G. (1995). *A marriage of convenience: Business and social work in Toronto, 1918-1957.* Toronto: University of Toronto Press.

Wilson, D., & Macdonald, D. (2010). *The income gap between Aboriginal peoples and the rest of Canada.* Ottawa: Canadian Centre for Policy Alternatives.

Wintemute, R. (1995). *Sexual orientation and human rights.* Oxford: Clarendon Press.

Woodford, M., Newman, P., Brotman, S., & Ryan, B. (2010). Northern enlightenment: Legal recognition of same-sex marriage in Canada: Strengthening social work's advocacy efforts. *Journal of Gay & Lesbian Social Services, 22,* 191–209.

Woodsworth, D. (1986). Canadian realities. (44–66). In J. Turner & F. Turner (Eds.), *Canadian social welfare* (2nd ed.). Don Mills, ON: Collier Macmillan.

Woolin, S. (2010). *Democracy incorporated: Managed democracy and the specter of inverted totalitarianism.* New Jersey: Princeton University Press.

Workers' Compensation Board-Alberta, The. (2010). *What Workers' Compensation provides.* Retrieved from **http://www.wcb.ab.ca**

Workers' Compensation Board – Alberta (2015, June 1). Wage replacement and benefits. **http://www.wcb.ab.ca/workers/wage_replacement.asp**.

Workplace Safety and Insurance Board of Ontario (2015, June 1). *Operation Policy Manual: Benefit Dollar Amounts – Accidents from 1998.* **http://www.wsib.on.ca/**.

World Wildlife Fund. (2006). *Living planet report: 2006.* Gland, Switzerland: Author.

The world's billionaire. (2010). *Forbes Magazine.* Retrieved from **http://www.forbes.com/2010/03/10/worlds-richest-people-slim-gates-buffett-billionaires-2010_l.html**

Wright, R. (2004). *A short history of progress.* Toronto: Anansi.

Yalnizyan, A. (2010). The rise of Canada's richest 1%. *Canadian Centre for Policy Alternatives.* Retrieved from **http://www.collectionscanada.gc.ca/caninfo/ep036.htm**

Yelaja, S. (Ed.). (1987). *Canadian social policy* (Rev. ed.). Waterloo, ON: Wilfrid Laurier University Press.

Young, C. (1994). Taxing times for lesbians and gay men: Equality at what cost? *Dalhousie Law Journal, 17*(2), 534–559.

Yunus, M. (2007). *Creating a world without poverty: Social businesses and the future of capitalism.* New York: Public Affairs.

Zapf, M. K. (1999). Geographic factors. In F. Turner (Ed.), *Social work practice: A Canadian perspective* (344–358). Scarborough, ON: Allyn and Bacon Canada.

Zuberi, D. (2013) *Cleaning up: How hospital outsourcing is hurting workers and endangering patients.* Ithaca, NY: Cornell University Press.

Index

British North America, 26
colonization of Aboriginal peoples in, 29
former colonies of, 27
British North America Act (1867). *See* Constitution Act (pre. British North America Act)
Broadbent Report, 42
brokerage politics, 74
Brundtland Report (1987), 102
business associations, 109
business liberalism, 74
Byzantine East, 22

C

cab drivers, 188
Caledon Institute of Social Policy (CISP), 51, 99
Calgary, first Muslim mayor, 45
Callahan, M., 114
Campbell, C., 74
Canada
Aboriginal peoples, 127–130
carbon dioxide (CO_2) production, 101
deinstitutionalization policy in, 139
dispersion patterns of population, 141
doctrinaire insulation in, 175
ecological crisis in, 101
environmental policies, 103
family care, 143
family policy in, 121–122
federal government transfers in 2015-2016, 48–49
as federal state, 46
financial sector in, 105
former colonies of British North America, 27
GDP, 43
government debt, 40–41
greenhouse gas emissions, 101, 103
healthcare, 37–40
immigrants/immigration to, 123–127
income security programs, 147
industrial revolution, 104
local governments, 46–47
metropolis *vs.* hinterland, 141

military involvement in Afghanistan, 41
municipal powers in, 47
neoliberal institutions in, 109–110
Pay for Performance Contracts, 192
political power in, 46
Protestants' influence on, 24, 28
provinces, 46
public policy in, 161
refugees, 127
regional development programs, 142
rural/remote areas, 142–143
social enterprise initiatives, 190
social finance, 160, 191–193
Social Gospel Movement, 28
social policy structures in, 44–67
social rights, 186–187
social rights of citizens, 114
social spending in, 36
social work profession in, 30
tax system, 56–57
territories, 46
trade unions, 28, 29
traditional family in, 121
and United States, FTA between, 106
up to 1945, 25–30
voluntary sectors in, 34
welfare regime, 4
Canada Assistance Plan (CAP), 33–34, 36, 48, 51, 114
Canada Child Tax Benefit (CCTB), 40, 44, 54, 60–61, 113
Canada Economic Development for Quebec Regions, 142
Canada Health Act (CHA), 1, 37–38
Canada Health and Social Transfer (CHST), 36, 51–52
Canada Health Transfer (CHT), 49, 51–52
Canada Income Tax Act, 190
Canada Pension Plan (CPP), 23, 34, 44, 58–59
Canada Revenue Agency (CRA), 153, 194

Canada Social Transfer (CST), 49, 51–52
Canadian Association of Schools of Social Work (CASSW), 1
Canadian Association of Social Workers, 30
Canadian Business, 87
Canadian Census (2006), 96
Canadian Centre for Philanthropy, 42
Canadian Centre for Policy Alternatives, 99
Canadian Council of Chief Executives (CCCE), 99, 109
Canadian Council on Child Welfare, 30
Canadian Council on Social Development (CCSD), 32, 83, 99
on poverty line, 85
Canadian Criminal Code, 71
The Canadian Establishment (Newman), 110
Canadian Experience Class, 126
Canadian Human Rights Act, 128
Canadian Labour Union, 29
Canadian Research Institute for the Advancement of Women, 131
Canadian Research Institute for the Advancement of Women (CRIAW), 132
Canadian Union of Public Employees (CUPE), 66
Canadian Welfare Council, 32
capability enhancement, 118
capitalism
change in basic workings of, 104–105
creative destruction, 104
hegemonic position of, 3
nineteenth-century, 110
social policy and, 19
transformation, 104
carbon dioxide (CO_2), 101
Careless, Maurice, 141
Caribbean, immigrants/ immigration from, 123, 125
Carson, Rachel, 100
cash programs, 44
Cassidy, Harry, 32
CASSW. *See* Canadian Association of Schools of Social Work (CASSW)
CCTB. *See* Canada Child Tax Benefit (CCTB)

market basket measure (MBM)
to poverty, 85
market fundamentalism, 111
market state, 35–43
transition after 2008
economic crisis, 104
market system failure, 151
Marr, W., 126
marriage
defined, 134
homosexuality as threat
to, 134
Marsh, Leonard, 32
Marshall, T. H., 13, 114
Marsh Commission, 32
Marsh Report, 32
Marumba, S. K. I., 121
Marx, Karl, 71, 105
Marxism, 71
Marxists, 71
on welfare state, 77
Maslow, Abraham, hierarchy of
needs theory of, 79–80
McGill University, 30
McKenzie B., 9, 173, 178
McPherson, D., 11
means tests, 62
Medical Care Act, 33
Mental Health Act, 15
mercantilism, 104
Métis people, 127
as Indian, 127
Indian Act and, 127
metropolis vs. hinterland,
141
Meyer, S. M., 101
mezzo-level of social work, 150,
157
microfinance, 45
middle class
in developing world, 105
modernization and, 106
in West, 104
Middle East, 26
immigrants from, 123
Mills, C. Wright, 99
minimum-wage legislation,
44
Minister of Indian and Northern
Affairs Canada, 46
minority group, 120
Mishra, R., 12, 13
Mitchell, A., 117
Montreal, as primary settlement
area, 123
Morissette, R., 131

mortgages, United States,
104–105
mothers' pension program,
30–31, 132
Mother's Pensions, 30–31
Mulé, N., 135
Mulroney, Brian, 53, 106
multinational corporations, 108
Mulvale, J. P, 76
municipal governments, 46, 47
social services budget,
47
municipalities, 46, 47
municipal powers, 47
Muslims, 21
Mussolini, 73, 112
mutual aid societies, 22

N

National Action Committee on
the Status of Women,
42, 43
National Advisory Committee on
Voluntary Action, 42
National Child Benefit (NCB)
supplement, 61
The National Compact, 193
National Council of Women,
28
National Strategy for the
Integration of Persons, 137
natural disasters, 21
NCB. See National Child Benefit
(NCB) supplement
needs
comparative, 79
expressed, 79
felt, 79
hierarchy of (Maslow),
79–80
normative, 79
physiological, 80
special, 80–81
thick, 143, 144
thin, 143–144
neo-conservatism, 73
neoliberal institutions, and social
welfare, 109–110
neo-liberals, 73
Netherlands, HDI in, 82
New Brunswick
equalization payments to,
50
Poor Laws in, 26
New Democratic Party (NDP),
72, 75–76

Newfoundland
childcare spaces, 50
claw back in equalization
payments, 50
new international economic order
(NIEO), 103
Newman, Peter C., 110
New Testament, 21
New Zealand
HDI in, 82
NIEO. See new international
economic order (NIEO)
Nigeria, regimes in, 106
nonprofit organizations, 3, 45,
151–153
Canada Revenue Agency
regulations and, 153
charitable status for, 194
donations to, 42–43
employment offered by,
152
flexibility for, 160
government and, 153–154,
155, 156
importance of, 152–153
income sources of, 43
number of, 152, 194
political advocacy-based
efforts, 155–156, 157
private sector and, 154,
155, 156
social enterprise, 154, 190
normative needs, 79
North America
European heritage and,
25–30
exclusion in, 117
psychiatric institutions,
148
North–South inequalities, 103
Northwest Territories, 46
Norway
environmental policies,
103
HDI in, 82
not-for-profit organizations, 45
Nouvelle France, 25–26
colonization of Aboriginal
peoples, 29
Nova Scotia
childcare spaces, 50
claw back in equalization
payments, 50
federal support payments,
49
Poor Laws in, 26

nuclear family, 121, 122
Nunavut, 46

O

O'Brien, C., 136
Obstacles (Special Committee
    on the Disabled and the
    Handicapped), 137
occupational welfare measures, 44
oil resources, 102
Old Age Pensions Act (1927), 31
Old Age Security (OAS), 34, 40,
    44, 59
Old Testament, 21
Ontario
    children in, 50
    federal share of CAP
        transfers to, 36
    nurses per capita, 50
    Roman Catholic Church
        in, 26
    social assistance programs
        in, 24
    Social Housing Reform
        Act, 15
    Workers' Compensation
        (WC), 62
Ontario Blue Cross, 67
Ontario Chamber of Commerce,
    50
Ontario Disability Supports
    Program (ODSP), 15
Ontario Guaranteed Annual
    Income System (GAINS), 65
Ontario Labour Market
    Partnership, 169
Ontario Works, 24
On the Margins of Inclusion
    (Smith), 188
OPEC. *See* Organization
    for Petroleum Exporting
    Countries (OPEC)
operating principles, social policy,
    175
ordinary issues of social policy, 177
Organisation for Economic
    Co-operation and
    Development (OECD)
    healthcare ranking, 38–39
    ranking of countries on
        environmental issues,
        103
Organization for Petroleum
    Exporting Countries (OPEC)
    establishment, 105
    member state, 105

Orthodox Christian patriarchs, 22
outdoor relief, 24
output/outcomes of social policy,
    176
outsourcing, 187–188

P

Pal, L. A., 163
Parti Québécois, 53, 76
Pascal, G., 114
patriarchy, 29
patterned inequalities, 176
pauperism, 24
Pay for Performance Contracts,
    192
Payne, S., 73
Pembina Institute, 42
Penner, Jacob, 71
pensions
    federal programs, 57–62
    private sector, 65–67
    provincial programs, 62–67
    See also income security
        programs
People in Action Report, 42
people of colour, 126
peripheral economies, 142
Persons with Developmental
    Disabilities Services Act,
    146
Perspectives on Labour and Income,
    86
pharmacare, 67
philanthropy, 3, 42
Philippines, regimes in, 106
physical force, 16
physiological needs, 80
Pierce, 179
Polanyi, Karl, 3
policy analysis, 162–184
    CBA, 164, 179–183
    CEA, 164, 179–183
    defined, 163
    evidence-informed
        decisions, 163
    framework, 165–179
    implementation of rational
        techniques, 163
    incrementalist approach,
        11
    key aspect of, 163
    purpose of, 163–165
    research methods and
        approaches, 163
    understanding service user
        group experience, 170

policy-making process, 166
    comprehensive approach
        to, 172–173
    garbage can model, 173,
        178–179
    Gil's model of, 176–177
    goal-directed-muddling-
        through approach,
        177–178
    incremental approach to,
        172, 177–178
    mixed-scanning model,
        178–179
    rational decision-making
        model, 172
    Rein's model, 173–175
    sequencing, 178
    social justice and
        comprehensive model,
        173
    value criteria model, 173,
        178
    values competition model,
        172–173
political advocacy, 155–156,
    157
    defined, 155
    nonprofits/civil society
        actors efforts, 155–156
political exclusion, 117
political parties, 74–76, 174
    Bloc Québécois, 76
    Conservative Party of
        Canada, 75–76
    Liberal Party of Canada,
        73, 74–75
    NDP, 72, 75–76
political platform, 174
political power, 16, 46
political rights of citizenship,
    114
polycentric perspective, 10–11
Pooled Registered Pension Plans
    (PRPP), 61–62
Poor Law Reforms of 1834,
    24, 27
Poor Laws, 22, 23, 26, 121
Popple, P., 149
population
    Aboriginal peoples, 127
    dispersion patterns, 141
    immigrants/immigration
        in, 96
    women in, 130
populations, homeless, 163–164
postsecondary student loans, 44

S

Sale, K., 101
sales tax, 57
Saloojee, 118
same-sex marriage, 134–135
    legality of, 135
        Supreme Court on, 135
same-sex relations, 133
Samson, R., 138
Sanders, Bernie, 111
Sanger, Matthew, 34
Savoie, Donald, 110
school jurisdictions, volunteering
    and, 194
Schragge, E., 114
Scott Task Force, 138
Section 67 of the Canadian
    Human Rights Act, 128
selective programs, 56
self-interest, 177
Semaines sociales, 28
Sen, Amartya, 118
*The Senate Report on Social
    Cohesion*, 118
Seniors Income Plan (SIP), 65
September 11, 2001 attack, 115
service delivery frameworks, 149
service delivery organizations, 2
settlement houses, 28
sexual abuse, 132
sexual orientation, 133–136
    Charter of Rights and
        Freedoms and, 134, 135
    Social Work Code of
        Ethics and, 136
    Supreme Court decision of
        1998 on, 134
shelters, 44
Sherwood, C., 14
Shier, M. L., 156, 158–159, 193
Shillington, R., 117
The Silent Spring (Carson), 100
Silver, H., 118
Simon Fraser University, 103
single parents, 62
SIP. *See* Seniors Income Plan
    (SIP)
Sisters in Spirit, 132
skilled workers, immigration for,
    126
Smith, Adam, 25
social action, 13–15
    campaigns, 160
social assistance, 62–64, 87
    defined, 57
    nineteenth century, 24

social capital
    defined, 76
    model of social
        responsibility and, 77
    nonprofit organizations,
        151
    voluntary sector, 151
social citizenship, 113–116
    active, 116
    changing dynamics of, 119
    civil society linked to, 115
    reconceptualizing, 118
    social rights for, 114
    welfare state and, 115
social cohesion
    dimensions of, 118
    enhancing possibilities of,
        117
social Darwinism, 121
social democracy, 71–72
social democratic perspective, of
    welfare state, 77
social democrats, 71–72
social economy, 189–193
    defined, 189
    implication, 189
    social finance, 160,
        191–193
    third sector and, 190
social enterprise, 154, 190
Social Enterprise Canada, 154
social entrepreneurship, 153,
    158–161
    defined, 158
    rise of, 45
    social finance possibilities,
        192
social environment, 151
social exclusion
    implementing a process
        of, 117
    language of, 117
    poverty and, 117
    theories of, 117
    See also social inclusion
social finance, 160, 191–193
Social Gospel Movement, 28
Social Housing Reform Act, 15
Social Impact Bonds, 191
social inclusion, 116–119
    capability enhancement
        as, 118
    concept of, 116–117
    criticisms of, 118
    developmentally delayed
        adults, 147

    dimensions of, 118–119
    framework for analysis of,
        118
    language of, 117
    neo-liberal terminology,
        118
    notion of, 118
    social institutions and, 146
    See also social exclusion
social inequalities, 15–16, 138
social innovation, 45, 153,
    158–161
    collective model of, 160
    concept of, 158
    mutually beneficial
        partnerships, 164
    process-based, 158–159
    product-based, 159
    social finance possibilities,
        192
    socially transformative, 160
social institutions, 146
social insurance, 57
social investment, 191–192
Social Investment Funds,
    191–192
socialism, 72
Socialist Party of Canada, 71
social justice, 10–11
    local community initiatives
        and, 152
socially transformative social
    innovation, 160
social media, 160
social media activists, 45
social mobility, 188–189
social movements
    direct service
        nonprofits, 152
    nineteenth-century, 28
social policy, 1–2
    analysis. *See* policy analysis
    capitalism and, 19
    civic engagement and,
        193–194
    concept, 8–15, 18
    contradictory nature, 18
    cultural constructs, 18
    direct service nonprofits
        in, 151
    diversity and, 143–144
    erosion of tradional
        policies, 36–37
    evidence-based
        investigation, 163
    evolution, 18

social policy (*continued*)
    fundraising and, 20
    future directions in,
      185–194
    Gil's notion of, 176–177
    grand issues of, 177
    humanitarian aspects of, 18
    incrementalism, 11–12
    labour and, 143
    mirroring aspects of, 19
    models/functions of, 8–9
    operating principles, 175
    ordinary issues of, 177
    output/outcomes of, 176
    policy-making process. *See*
      policy-making process
    polycentric perspective,
      10–11
    roots of, 18
    to rural areas, 142–143
    social finance initiatives,
      192–193
    as social goals and
      objectives, 12–13
    social work and, 15–16,
      146–150
    structures, 44–67
    students and practitioners,
      148
    study of, 15–16
    values and, 9–10, 177
    varying impact of, 18
social rights, 186–187
    Charter of Rights and
      Freedoms and, 114
    of citizenship, 114
social scientists, 150
social security programs, 32
Social Service Council of
  Canada, 28
social services, privatization of,
  19
social solidarity agenda, 118
social statements, 10
social transformation, 11
Social Values Act, 190
Social Values Act, U.K., 190
social welfare
    anti-racist critique of, 78
    citizen participation for,
      119
    civic engagement and,
      193–194
    conceptualization of, 19
    cross-sector arrangements
      for, 154, 155

    deconstructive and
      re-constructive process
      of, 151
    defined, 2
    direct service nonprofits in,
      151–153
    Elizabethan period, 22–24
    empowerment and
      participation based
      model, 157
    empowerment perspective
      of, 78
    English Canadian history
      of, 18–43
    feminist perspective of, 78
    functionalists perspective,
      12
    governmental participation
      in, 160
    institutional perspective,
      19, 31–34
    manifestation, 2
    market state perspective of,
      35–43, 78, 109
    mezzo-level social work
      and, 150, 157
    neoliberal institutions and,
      109–110
    nonprofit organizations in,
      151–153
    patriarchy, 29
    under provincial
      legislation, 46
    public sector and, 150
    reduction in public
      resources for, 113
    residual stage of, 19–31
    as response to need, 79–90
    scholars, 150
    societal level well-being,
      6–8
    structural changes, 152
    theories of, 2–8, 76–79
    third/voluntary sector,
      78–79, 150, 151
    third way perspective of,
      78
    women as fundamental
      actors in, 78
social work
    in its early years, 30
    mezzo-level of, 150, 157
    nuclear skill of, 149
    oldest schools of, 30
    pioneers of, 149
    as profession, 149

    scientific approaches to, 20
    social policy and, 15–16,
      146–150
Social Work Code of Ethics, 136
Social Work Codes of Ethics, 16
social workers
    advocacy for social
      changes, 16
    collaborations/partnerships,
      157, 161
    commitment to social
      justice, 177
    direct service
      nonprofits, 151
    direct social service
      organizations and, 146
    efforts carried out by,
      156–157
    focus on individuals,
      149–150
    generalist approach for,
      142–143
    inner cities agencies and,
      149
    institutional arrangements,
      30
    in leadership positions,
      160, 166–167
    methods of engagement,
      160
    organizational
      practice, 161
    organizations and, 157
    social action campaigns, 160
    training programs and
      literature, 148
    understanding different life
      experiences, 16
    understanding
      interrelationship
      between societal
      sectors, 157
    women as, 130
    workplace environment, 19
societal level well-being, 6–8
socio-cultural well-being, 7, 162
socio-economic class, 20
socio-economic equality, 187–189
socio-economic well-being, 7, 162
socio-political exclusion, 117
socio-political well-being, 7
Soros, George, 111
soup kitchens, 44
Soviet Union
    Cold War and, 106–107
    communist regimes, 71

vertical imbalance, 48
Veterans' Pension, 59–60
Vikings, 25
visible minority, 123
  women, 131
voluntary/charitable programs, 44
voluntary sector. *See* third sector
volunteer activities, 152
volunteering/volunteerism, 3
  civic engagement and, 193–194
  school jurisdictions and, 194
Vosko, L. F., 81
vulnerable populations
  housing needs of, 163–164
  upward social mobility of, 188–189

W

War Veterans Allowances (WVA), 60
welfare diamond, 4
welfare liberalism, 74
welfare regime, 4, 185
welfare state
  anti-racist critique of, 78
  decline of, 44
  defined, 3, 44
  empowerment perspective of, 78
  feminist perspective of, 78
  green perspective of, 78
  as instrument of social control, 77
  market state perspective of, 78, 109
  post–World War II period and, 47–48, 77, 104, 107
  public sector and, 150
  social citizenship and, 115–116
  social cohesion dimensions and, 118
  social democratic perspective of, 77
  third way perspective of, 78, 150

welfare-to-work programs, 76
welfarism, 152
well-being, 6–8
  elements of, 162
  financial, 162
  HDI, 82
  measurements of, 81–83
  psycho-social, 162
  quality-of-life indicators, 6–7
  socio-cultural, 162
  socio-economic, 7, 162
  socio-spatial, 162
  subjective, 82–83
  unemployment and, 81–82
Western Economic Diversification (WD), 142
Westhues, Ann, 12–13
Wharf, B., 9, 16, 149, 173, 177–178, 179
Whitton, Charlotte, 32
Williams, Fiona, 136
Winnipeg City Council, 71
women, 130–133
  Aboriginal, 131, 132
  annual average income of, 131
  in Canadian population, 130
  charitable activities, 29
  child care allowance, 133
  with disabilities, 131, 132
  domestication of, 29
  Dominion Elections Act and, 130
  double discrimination, 132
  English Common Law and, 130
  equal pay legislation and policies, 132
  as mothers of dependent children, 132
  in paid labour force, 131, 133
  part-time work and, 131, 132
  Pay Equity Task Force and, 132
  pension benefits, 122, 132
  as persons, legal identity, 130

policy initiatives dealing with concerns of, 132
  poverty and, 131
  public policy and, 132–133
  in public sector, 131
  right to vote, 28, 29
  social advocacy, 29
  social policies and, 143
  social workers and, 130
  status of, 130–131
  as victims of domestic violence, 132
  visible minority, 131
Workers' Compensation (WC), 62, 98
  eligibility criteria, 62
workfare programs, 113, 114
workforce, 19
working class, 28
Workmen's Compensation Act of 1914, 30
World Health Organization, 34, 138
World War I, 60
  Ukrainian Canadians, 30
World War II, 106
  Japanese Canadians, 30
  universal programs, 57
Wright, R., 102
WVA. *See* War Veterans Allowances (WVA)

Y

Yelaja, Shankar, 12–13
young adult
  un- and under-employment, 166–171
Young Women's Christian Association, 28
Youth Employment Fund, 169
Youth Employment Strategy, 169
Yukon Territory, 46
  budget, 50

Z

Zapf, M. K., 141, 143
Zuberi, D., 187